KU-039-594

The Corporate Environment
A guide for human resource managers

Huw Morris and Brian Willey

Kingston Business School, Kingston University

PITMAN
PUBLISHING

London · Hong Kong · Johannesburg · Melbourne · Singapore · Washington DC

PITMAN PUBLISHING
128 Long Acre, London WC2E 9AN
Tel: +44 (0)171 447 2000
Fax: +44 (0)171 240 5771

A Division of Pearson Professional Limited

First published in Great Britain in 1996

© Huw Morris and Brian Willey 1996

The right of Huw Morris and Brian Willey to be identified
as Authors of this Work has been asserted by them in
accordance with the Copyright, Designs and Patents Act 1988.

ISBN 0–273–61604–8

British Library Cataloguing in Publication Data
A CIP catalogue record for this book can be obtained from the British Library

All rights reserved; no part of this publication may be reproduced, stored
in a retrieval system, or transmitted in any form or by any means, electronic,
mechanical, photocopying, recording, or otherwise without either the prior
written permission of the Publishers or a licence permitting restricted copying
in the United Kingdom issued by the Copyright Licensing Agency Ltd,
90 Tottenham Court Road, London W1P 9HE. This book may not be lent,
resold, hired out or otherwise disposed of by way of trade in any form
of binding or cover other than that in which it is published, without the
prior consent of the Publishers.

10 9 8 7 6 5 4 3 2

Typeset by Pantek Arts, Maidstone, Kent
Printed and bound in Great Britain by Clays Ltd, St Ives plc

The Publishers' policy is to use paper manufactured from sustainable forests.

£22.99

The Corporate Environment

A guide for human resource managers

BISHOP BURTON LRC
WITHDRAWN

Accession Number....TO27981

Class Number.........658.3

CONTENTS

PREFACE

It is now commonplace and somewhat clichéd to talk about the constancy of change in the business world. Management gurus and business pundits regularly suggest that the old certainties of stable markets, predictable sales and planned growth no longer exist, if they ever did. Foreign competition, rapid technological change and, above all, changing consumer tastes mean that customers can desert an organization overnight with consequent effects on business performance and jobs.

In addition to the immediate concerns for the economic well-being of organizations, wider changes in the pattern of social and political life have affected how people see their current position and future prospects. The collapse of communism, the growing role of women at work, increasing wealth and an ageing of the population in developed countries are just four of a myriad of changes which have challenged many people's views about how our social lives should be organized and regulated.

Faced with these rapid and significant changes in the world that surrounds us, it is now arguably more important than ever that current and prospective managers and employees are aware of and prepared for these developments. This book, therefore, aims to provide the intellectual tools they will need in order to analyse and evaluate the external pressures which currently confront their organizations.

The principal target market for this book is students studying the 'Corporate Environment' component of the Institute of Personnel and Development's (IPD) Qualification Scheme. Although the main focus is practising human resource managers, or those aspiring to perform this role, the book should also be of interest to lecturers and students involved in other related courses, e.g. Certificates and Diplomas in Management and MBA programmes.

To these ends this book sets out to:

- discuss different ways of conceiving of organizations and the external environments which confront them;
- outline important contemporary developments in the political, economic, legal, social and technological environments facing British-based organizations;
- spell out some of the implications for human resource managers of contemporary developments in labour, product and capital markets;
- indicate how further information can be gained about specific industrial sectors and named organizations;
- demonstrate how a number of analytical and evaluative tools can be used to examine recent developments in specific organizations' external environments; and
- specify how the results of any analysis can be discussed and communicated to other managers and employees.

Achieving these objectives presents a number of difficulties. Any informed analysis and evaluation of the environment surrounding contemporary organizations necessitates drawing together insights and observations from a range of academic disciplines, including economics, political theory, sociology, anthropology, psychology, organization theory and socio-legal studies. Within each of these disciplines there are a range of competing ideological and theoretical perspectives. Unfortunately, the similarities between these traditions are often obscured by differences in terminology and a wealth of academic jargon. As a consequence of this diversity of language there is a danger that any student of this area of study will become confused about the lessons to be drawn from different analyses and prescriptions.

In order to overcome these problems we have attempted to use a relatively standard set of terms throughout the book and to include a glossary to explain some of the more obscure terms. We have also attempted to draw connections between the different chapters and to develop and expand upon ideas as the book progresses.

The book begins by considering what is meant by the term 'corporate environment'. In Chapter 1 we explore how developments in the world surrounding an organization may impinge upon the decisions and actions of managers and employees. Here we focus on the variety of ways in which the staff of an organization can prepare for change and plan responses to external problems and opportunities.

Chapters 2, 3 and 4 move on to consider the immediate task environment within which most, if not all, organizations operate. More specifically we consider how an organization's demands for money, staff and customers affect the choices available to managers in general, and human resource professionals in particular. In these chapters we aim to demonstrate that organizations differ in terms of their ownership, organization and orientation as well as the ways in which they recruit and retain employees and deal with the consumers of their goods and services. By examining these differences we hope to shed some light on the range of alternatives that currently confront the people who devise, develop and implement personnel policies in organizations based in the United Kingdom.

Moving away from the day-to-day concerns of customers and internal resources, Chapters 5 to 11 of the book consider the wider political, economic, social, technological and legal environments within which organizations operate. The influence of these issues may seem distant from the pressing concerns of filling staff vacancies and meeting orders, but as we shall see, these wider changes can have profound effects. The issues considered in these chapters include:

- recent fluctuations in the economic fortunes of the United Kingdom;
- changes in the distribution of income, wealth, education and health;
- the effects of industrial activity and new technology on human welfare and the natural environment;
- the influence of the political system and party ideologies on the policies pursued by European institutions and recent United Kingdom governments; and

- the role of the individual and collective employment law in regulating the relationship between managers, employees and trade unions.

The final chapter of the book returns to the themes explored in the opening chapter. In this concluding section we draw together some of the issues discussed and speculate about possible future changes in the corporate environment of UK-based organizations.

AIDS TO LEARNING

This book has been designed to include the following pedagogical features to aid the learning process.

Introduction
Each chapter begins with a section which spells out the content, focus and scope of the chapter, to guide the reader through the material that follows.

Learning objectives
The reader is given a list of objectives that should be attained once the chapter and associated exercises have been completed.

Case study
The practical importance of the concepts and skills described in the book is illustrated by a short case study in most chapters, introducing the reader to a number of issues which will be discussed in that chapter.

Analysis and issues
This book aims to draw clear links between theory and practice, and so the main substantive component of each chapter consists of a discussion of competing ideological approaches and theoretical concepts which can be used either to analyse material contained within the case studies, or alternatively to examine developments within an organization known to the reader.

Figures and tables
Where possible, diagrams and illustrations have been included to help the reader visualize and quantify key elements of any theory or issue under discussion.

Exhibits
These give practical examples, supplementary information and summaries of recent debates on contentious issues.

Exercises
These invite readers to apply the concepts discussed to the operation of a case study organization or their own employers. Model answers are included, where appropriate, in an appendix at the end of the book.

Chapter summaries
A review of the main points of each chapter is included in the concluding section of each chapter.

Glossary
Key terms and definitions are explained in the glossary at the end of the book.

References
A comprehensive list of the materials cited in the text is included at the end of the book.

Index
The book includes an index designed to enable the reader to search quickly for relevant information when tackling problems in class, examinations or to use as the basis for assignments.

Huw Morris and Brian Willey
Kingston University

ACKNOWLEDGEMENTS

This book is the product of work undertaken by the authors at different times over a six-year period. Most of the material presented is drawn from teaching materials and lecture notes used on the Corporate Environment component of the Postgraduate Diploma and Masters Degree in Personnel Management at Kingston University. As such we owe a considerable debt to a number of people who in their various ways have provided us with intellectual stimulation, secretarial assistance, editorial guidance and financial support.

Past and present students on the personnel management teaching programmes at Kingston have contributed by being willing guinea pigs for many of the exercises contained within this book. They have helped us gain a better understanding of the subject area by asking difficult questions and making astute observations. Their experiences of the realities of people management in a rapidly changing business world have also provided the basis for many of the examples and case studies in this book.

Whatever its contents, this book would not have seen the light of day without the valuable assistance of Peter Haywood, Ian James, Dan Russell and Maureen Beard. With good humour and considerable patience they have corrected our grammar and sharpened the focus of our arguments. In addition, a number of anonymous reviewers and our publisher, Penelope Woolf, have provided insightful comments and useful editorial guidance on various drafts of the book.

We are also grateful for the financial support of the following organizations and individuals. The Academic Efficiency Fund at Kingston University provided funds to cover the initial research and writing of the learning materials which form the basis of this book. Converting this material into the final text was made possible by the generous support of colleagues in the School of Human Resource Management who provided cover to enable us to take sabbatical leave in order to complete the final manuscript.

Finally, we have benefited from the constant encouragement and patience of our families. Over the twelve months that it took to compile this book they have been prepared to let us put our domestic responsibilities to one side in order to meet the publisher's deadlines. We hope that the fruits of our labour will provide some consolation for the mountains of crockery and laundry which have been washed in our absence. Thank you Vicky, James, Ami, Ann, Ian, David and Helen.

CHAPTER 1

The corporate environment

INTRODUCTION

Every organization is confronted by external pressures which will have implications for the way it manages its internal operations and employees. Skill shortages, competition, recession, government regulation and new technology are just a few of the many problems which currently affect managers and employees within organizations based in the United Kingdom. While few managers and employees will welcome these developments, it is obviously essential that they are aware of these changes and are prepared to respond to them. By correctly identifying developments in the organization's external environment and evaluating their possible effects, managers and employees should be better placed to draw up and amend plans to ensure the long-term viability of the organization with which they are associated.

FOCUS AND SCOPE

This chapter begins the task of examining changes in the corporate environment of UK-based organizations, as well as developing the managerial skills necessary to respond to these pressures. It demonstrates that there are a variety of ways in which these tasks can be performed. Underpinning these various approaches are different assumptions which will have implications for the way in which the analysis is performed, the results of this evaluation, and any prescriptions for future action. This chapter explores these different approaches by reference to three sets of basic assumptions about the external environment: objective versus subjective interpretations; continuity versus turbulent change; and choice versus determinism. We believe that an awareness of these different assumptions and approaches will better enable readers to undertake their own environmental analyses, or comment upon the results of analyses undertaken by others.

LEARNING OBJECTIVES

Once you have read this chapter and completed the associated exercises, you should be able to:

- describe some of the external pressures and problems which may confront organizations based in the UK;
- outline the assumptions which underpin different approaches to the analysis of organizations' external environments;
- undertake environmental scanning activities using a variety of different methods;

● use the 'rational planning model' as a method for developing responses to the external pressures and problems; and summarize criticisms of the 'rational planning model'.

CASE STUDY

Hodsons

The following case study describes events within a real organization. The information contained within this case will be used as the basis for a number of skills exercises, as well as a general discussion of the problems associated with analysing the external environment confronting any organization. We will return to this case at various points throughout this chapter.

Hodsons is a builders' merchant with close to 100 outlets in the south of England. The company was founded in the early 1900s by the Hodson family and has subsequently grown through the acquisition of smaller competitor organizations. In the early stages of its operation the company specialized in supplying timber to house builders and other professional traders. As the organization has grown, its product range has expanded and it now sells builders' tools, a range of building materials and a variety of finished and semi-finished household improvement products. Despite the expansion of the business, the Board of Directors at Hodsons, which is still dominated by members of the Hodson family under the leadership of John Hodson (Managing Director), has consciously decided to limit its customer base to professional builders. This approach, together with the decision to allow acquired companies to trade under their former names and to rely upon word of mouth as a means of attracting new trade, has meant that the company's name is not well known outside the building industry.

Hodsons' operations are typically based on high streets in major towns and cities and are staffed by a small team of full-time male employees who have usually spent much of their working life with the company. These sales assistants pride themselves on their extensive knowledge of building techniques and their ability to advise customers as well as to deal with the more mundane tasks of manual stock ordering, storage and sales. The stores are open between 8 am and 5 pm, Monday to Saturday, with the exception of Wednesdays when they close at lunch time.

During the 1970s and early 1980s the company's sales and profitability grew steadily as the UK economy expanded and the housing market and associated building industry flourished. In the late 1980s and early 1990s, however, a number of external pressures have produced difficulties for the organization and have led directly to a decline in overall sales and profitability. Faced with these problems several senior managers within the company, who had been recruited for their retailing expertise, have been placing pressure on the Board of Directors to reappraise its business plans. One of the most vociferous of these critics is Michael Sellers, the company's Senior Operations Manager. He believes that Hodsons' traditional market base will continue to decline and that large out-of-town Do-It-Yourself centres will continue to take market share away from the company.

By comparison, John Hodson and many of the company's other directors believe that there is still a place for a high-street based chain of specialist builders' merchants. When the current recession in the housing market ends, they believe the long-term growth in the company's sales will resume. Furthermore, they do not have a very high opinion of the growing number of Do-It-Yourself centres which they believe fail to provide their customers with a high standard of service and advice. They have a pride in their company and do not really want their builders' yards to be transformed into a collection of large anonymous 'sheds'. They are prepared to pay the price of reduced

▶

sales and profits in the short term, in order to retain their skilled staff and ensure high levels of service in the long term.

In an attempt to overcome these differences of opinion, Michael Sellers has persuaded the Board of Directors to ask a team of business consultants to produce a report identifying the causes of the company's current predicament and outlining advice on the future development of the business. He believes this report will endorse his view by providing an objective view of the problems confronting the organization. He also hopes that, once this report has been accepted and agreed, it will also provide a basis for a radical restructuring of the company.

The consultancy team began its investigation by attempting to define the pressures facing the business. To facilitate this task, extensive research was undertaken before the preparation of the initial report. This research was based upon interviews with company employees at various levels within the organization, as well as discussions with senior managers from competitor organizations and representatives of various building trade associations. The results of this analysis were duly presented to the Board of Directors and a selection of senior and middle managers. It was hoped that, once agreement had been reached about the nature of the problems, some progress could be made in attempting to map out a plan for responding to these difficulties.

Exercise 1.1   The external pressures facing Hodsons

Assuming the role of one of the consultancy team and drawing upon your own general knowledge, list what you consider to be the five principal external pressures facing Hodsons.

ANALYSING ORGANIZATIONAL ENVIRONMENTS

The Hodsons case demonstrates how external business pressures and problems can affect a company. It also illustrates some of the problems which confront managers, employees and consultants when they attempt to analyse and evaluate these external pressures. Management writers and practitioners adopt different perspectives when they attempt to analyse organizations. Whether we say that these analyses are informed by ideology, theory, or just plain common sense, they all share some common features. They all implicitly say something about the essential nature of the concepts under observation and the relationship between these different concepts. The assumptions which underpin these different approaches can have a profound effect upon the results of any analysis, leading to very different diagnoses of current problems, predictions of possible future developments, and prescriptions for future action. In order to make sense of the immense variety of these approaches the following discussion focuses upon differences in terms of three dimensions:

- objective versus subjective interpretations;
- continuity versus turbulent change; and
- determinist versus free will views of human action.

Few writers and practitioners adopt an extreme position on any one of these dimensions, but there are significant differences of emphasis.

OBJECTIVE VERSUS SUBJECTIVE INTERPRETATIONS

A persistent trait in all human enquiry has been the search for universal facts – statements which can be considered true in all circumstances and at all times. In the physical sciences this has led to the statement of categories which precisely define the characteristics of, and relationships between, things. These definitions are considered by many to be objective truths because they remain true regardless of who is there to witness them. For example, awareness of the principles of chemistry or biology will enable us to categorize chemical elements or species regardless of time, place or the identity of the observer. To put this another way, it is believed that physical phenomena in the world that surrounds us have an independent existence and the act of observing does not change the nature of these things. As a consequence, it is assumed that it should be easy for researchers and practitioners to gather information in order to gain a better understanding of the world which surrounds them. This perspective is represented diagrammatically in Fig 1.1, where the person is merely an observer of events in the outside world. The person can gain more information about what is happening, and the act of perception may filter what is sensed, but the process of sensing does not alter this external reality.

The belief that the external world which confronts people is essentially objective is shared by social scientists from a range of disciplines. For example, many *free-market* economists believe in the primacy of markets and argue that the interplay of demand and supply determines, or should determine, what is produced, how it is made and the way in which it is distributed. They argue that markets are a natural phenomenon and that this reality confronts people in all economies regardless of social, cultural and historical setting.

By adopting this perspective it could be argued that Hodsons is experiencing a decline in business because of the combined forces of an overall decline in the level of demand for building products, and a change in the nature of demand away from building wholesalers towards 'Do-It-Yourself' centres. If we follow this logic, the Board of Directors has little choice but to scale back its operations and alter what it supplies in order to deal with the new competition.

A belief in a universal objective reality is not confined to free-market economists. Many Marxist and socialist writers from the opposite end of the political spectrum similarly argue that there are common truths confronting people in all situations. However, these writers focus upon what they term *capitalism* rather than the market in order to explain the position of people in different countries.

Fig 1.1 An objective view of the interaction between people and their physical environment

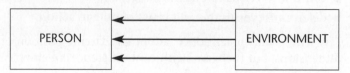

According to these Marxist critics, modern capitalism can be characterized as a system which promotes the exploitation of the economically weak by wealthy capitalists. Through the ownership of land, machinery and buildings, capitalists are able to force the working class to undertake work in exchange for wages. These wages do not reflect the true worth of what is produced and as a result profits can be made for the *capitalists* from the sale of these goods and services. Through the generation and accumulation of profits, the capitalists are then able to strengthen and improve their position at the expense of everyone else in society.

If we apply these insights to the Hodsons case then there is little that the current employees can do about their present predicament. The problems that they confront reflect the inequities of the capitalist system. According to this view, a solution to these problems can only be achieved when a more fundamental change in the structure of society and the attitudes of individuals is accomplished.

The preceding snapshots are not intended to provide a detailed examination of free-market and Marxist accounts of the working of modern societies – these approaches will be considered in more detail in subsequent chapters. However, these examples are intended to illustrate that at the heart of many analyses of organizations and societies is a belief in an objective and universal account of human behaviour. If we subscribe to this view, then – like Michael Sellers in the case study – we should believe that there is one best way of interpreting the case study at the beginning of this chapter. Our only task is to find out what this approach is and to implement it. The results of this analysis can then be used as a guide to future action by managers and employees.

Despite the seeming certainty of the objective approach many writers have questioned whether the world we live in is really understandable in these terms. Even within the physical sciences the view that external phenomena should be seen as independent objective entities has been questioned. For example, in the field of quantum mechanics (sub-atomic physics) scientists studying the behaviour of electrons have suggested that in some circumstances electrons behave like particles and in others like waves. Furthermore, when studying the behaviour of these electrons, the way in which events are observed may alter what is judged to have happened. Similarly in the study of the behaviour of stars and planets (cosmology) a number of physicists have suggested that the universe is not really understandable on a purely objective basis. At its most extreme this view is expressed in the 'anthropopic principle' which suggests that the universe is only there because we are here to observe it. In short, all physical phenomena depend upon observers generating and placing order over the world that surrounds them.

In the social sciences there are few if any areas where our theoretical understanding of the way people behave enables us to categorize things with the degree of certainty seemingly characteristic of the physical sciences. Much of what we believe about the world may depend upon shared understandings and attitudes expressed in a structured way by means of language. The words which we use to describe these beliefs may be useful in helping us to think about what is going on, but they may also influence the meaning of what is being described. For example, in the case study at the beginning of this chapter a distinction was drawn between Hodsons, the organization, and a number of external pressures. This seemingly straightforward separation relies upon common sense and legal definitions of organizations as groups of people, employed to work within specific buildings, to produce certain goods and services in pursuit of common objectives. By this measure the external environment consists of all the other people, objects and information which are not directly employed by the organization.

There are problems with this simple definition, however, as the case study itself demonstrates. When the consultancy team is called into Hodsons to advise the Board of Directors about possible future developments, are these visitors part of the organization or part of its environment? Similarly when the consultants visit competitor organizations to interview their managers, should these individuals be seen as adversaries or advisers – 'them' or 'us'?

Indeed some writers have even questioned whether it is appropriate to talk of organizations as distinct entities. According to David Silverman (1970) to consider an organization as having an identity which can be separated from the people of which it is composed is to be guilty of 'reification' – giving life to something which is abstract. Others have furthered these criticisms by arguing that individuals have to interpret the organizations within which they work and the surrounding environment; therefore, the act of seeing and thinking about the world involves the imposition of order. Here it is suggested that people subjectively create or enact much of the world in which they live. There is no external objective reality only a socially constructed reality which depends upon human beings interpreting, negotiating and reaching temporary agreements about an acceptable shared reading of the world that surrounds them.

By this measure the problems confronting Hodsons may be only one interpretation of the pressures confronting the company. The Do-It-Yourself centres may only be seen as a threat to the company because this is a generally acceptable and useful way of seeing the world. A number of other, as yet unrevealed, explanations of the perceived problems may be available and could emerge through discussion among the people with an interest in the future of Hodsons.

This alternative way of seeing the interplay between members of an organization and their environment can be illustrated by reversing the direction of the arrows in our earlier diagram (*see* Fig 1.2).

Figure 1.2 aims to demonstrate that people impose order on the world outside them. The environment which we experience is therefore a product of our perceptions, language, thought processes and dealings with other people.

Fig 1.2 A subjective view of the interaction between people and their physical environment

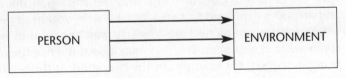

If we subscribe to this view of the external environment being subjectively constructed by people, it soon becomes apparent that there is considerable scope for disagreement about the form of external pressures and their effects. In recognition of this potential for disagreement a number of writers have laid stress on the role of cultural and political considerations in decision-making processes within organizations.

The powerful influence of national, industrial and organizational cultures in shaping attitudes, values and actions, has been recognized by a growing number of writers in recent years (Hofstede, 1980; Hampden-Turner and Fons Trompenaars, 1993; Pettigrew and Whipp, 1991; Schein, 1984; Pfeffer, 1992). According to these writers certain ways of seeing the world will tend to predominate in particular societies, industrial sectors or organizations. These ways of seeing the world will be communicated informally in all social settings via buzz words, stories, rituals and ceremonies, among other things. As a consequence of the messages received from these sources people become conditioned in their beliefs about how to find out more about their environment, what is deemed to be an acceptable interpretation of the problem, and what will be viewed as a satisfactory solution.

In some eastern cultures, for example, individual reflection and listening to the insights of older and more experienced workers may be seen as the most appropriate means of finding out more about the problem. By contrast, in Anglo-Saxon countries a premium may be placed on what are deemed to be more 'scientific' analyses of the situation based upon the systematic application of a programme of interviews or questionnaires. The extent to which the results of these analyses are accepted and acted upon may further be determined by the way in which the problems are described and analysed. The final report will need to be written using language and concepts with which the intended audience are familiar, as well as paying appropriate heed to dominant values and attitudes within the organization. However insightful the analyses, they will need to be culturally acceptable if they are to be agreed and acted upon.

If we apply these cultural insights to the Hodsons case, the problems which the company confronts can be seen to have deeper cultural roots. From this perspective Hodsons may be seen as typical of small and medium-sized firms operating in the UK. The company has grown under the direction of its original family owners and their beliefs about what is an acceptable form of business to undertake have conditioned decisions in the past. Their ability to lead in this way is dependent upon a national belief in 'managers' right to manage' and the importance of individual entrepreneurs. This has meant that decisions about the long-term future of the business are considered to be the preserve of the Board of Directors under the leadership of the Managing Director. In many other countries implicit cultural definitions of what constitutes an organization and who should be allowed to influence its operation may mean that a more participative view of how decisions should be taken would have been adopted. In these contexts employees, bankers and other representatives of groups with a stake in the organization may influence the definition of problems and the choice of appropriate solutions. At the level of the building industry, the form and function of building suppliers might similarly be seen as culturally determined. Traditionally, builders' yards have not been open to the general public and advertising has been seen to be an unprofessional activity. It could be argued that it has taken a challenge to these values, led by retailers who model their behaviour on retailing patterns in other cultures, to alter these views.

The way in which Hodsons will ultimately respond to the pressures it confronts might also be seen to be affected by established attitudes and behaviours within the organization. Under the direction of John Hodson the firm has adopted a relatively conservative and defensive approach to its operations. Against this background it is unlikely that he will wish to sponsor a radical solution to the current problems.

Aside from the influence of dominant patterns of values, attitudes and behaviours at the national and organizational level, there may also be considerable differences at the level of the group and the individual. Thus the beliefs of managers and employees, individually or in groups, can play an important part in determining how environmental threats and opportunities are interpreted. The members of an organization will not necessarily see their environment in similar ways and therefore they may wish to adopt different courses of action in response to the perceived threats. There is rarely one commonly agreed view on the causes of an organization's misfortunes, nor is there usually consensus on the means of solving these problems. Whatever the validity and merits of a particular diagnosis, prediction, or prescription, the ultimate decision to adopt or reject a particular proposal will invariably depend upon the interests and relative power of different groups within an organization. Where consensus is not forthcoming, these different groups will tend to resort to political tactics in order to achieve their desired ends. Whether this be through attempts to control or manipulate recalcitrant colleagues, to negotiate or collaborate with adversaries or to accommodate the interests of dissenting groups, the final form of any solution is unlikely to appear wholly rational to a dispassionate observer from outside the organization.

Once again by applying these insights to the Hodsons case we can see that there are fundamental differences of opinion between Mike Sellers and John Hodson. At the present time, John Hodson and the Board of Directors appear to have accommodated Mike Sellers' criticisms of the current approach by agreeing to appoint external consultants. Whether this compromise will produce a solution which is acceptable to all parties in the longer term remains to be seen. However, it is worth noting that John Hodson appears to have a stronger position within the organization. As a member of the founding family with many close friends on the Board of Directors he has a higher status and more resources at his disposal than Mike Sellers. If Mike wishes to change things he will be forced to rely on his expertise and charisma in any future negotiations or power struggle.

CONTINUITY VERSUS TURBULENT CHANGE

Another area of difference between analyses of the physical environment which confronts organizations is the extent to which writers portray things as dynamic and changing rapidly or alternatively relatively static and developing slowly.

If we subscribe to a relatively stable and static view of the external world then there is little need to anticipate, forecast or predict what will happen in the future. Things will continue to behave in the same way as they always have, and therefore managers and employees can afford to concentrate on ensuring that operations within the organization are undertaken in the most effective and cost efficient manner.

Approaches which emphasize stability have come under increasing attack in recent years. The rate of change is said to be increasing and there are few areas of organizational activity which are unaffected by this trend. Writers from a number of disciplines have suggested that this increase in the rate of change presents managers and employees with new problems when they attempt to analyse and make sense of the environment within which they operate (see Handy, 1991, 1994; Kanter, 1985, 1989; and Peters, 1989). Not only are there a myriad of variables, but all of these interact in ways which are often difficult to measure and to use as the basis for future predictions.

Chaos theory is one of the most recent examples of the recognition of the problems associated with complexity and change in the physical sciences (Gleick, 1987). According to advocates of this approach the behaviour of systems is often dependent upon small fluctuations in variables which are difficult to measure. These fluctuations may then become amplified with dramatic effects on the overall pattern of observed activity. For example, it has been suggested that the behaviour of weather systems is affected by a very large number of different factors including surface temperature, wind patterns and ocean currents. Furthermore, the way in which these variables interact means that small variations in humidity, wind speed or temperature in one area of the world can have dramatic effects upon the weather in other continents. To use one well worn cliché 'the beating of a butterfly's wings can produce a hurricane on the other side of the world'. This approach to understanding changes within particular systems has recently been extended to a number of areas of social scientific enquiry. For example, econometricians attempting to understand the workings of equity and commodity markets have suggested that a small variation in the price of one company's shares or a particular product in one exchange could have dramatic effects on other financial markets around the world.

A belief in the complex and dynamic view of the world implicit within chaos theory, and similar approaches to analysing the external world, presents us with two problems which could potentially limit the value of any analysis of current developments and future trends.

The first of these problems is overcoming the difficulties associated with getting accurate measurements of relevant variables and indicators. For example, the measures of the recession which have caused problems for Hodsons rely on calculations of consumer spending and building activity within the construction industry, as well as other measures of consumption and production. These figures are collected nationally by the government's Office for National Statistics and a range of trade and industry bodies. The resultant indices provide a snapshot of the overall level of activity within the sector, but this aggregate figure may mask significant variations. While the overall level of timber sales may have declined, some suppliers will have seen an increase in sales. Furthermore, the difficulties associated with compiling this data will often mean that figures are not available for many months. Even when these measures have been collected and published, errors in their compilation may mean that the original figures are subject to significant revision at a future date.

A number of critics have drawn attention to these physical and mental limitations on our ability to gain accurate measurements of changes in the world that surrounds us (Simon, 1976; Cyert and March, 1963). According to these writers all human decision making takes place within the context of 'imperfect knowledge', 'bounded rationality' and 'uncertainty'. Even the most complex computerized models of the world are limited by the quality of the raw data which is fed into them. Computing engineers use the acronym 'GIGO' to refer to this phenomenon – 'garbage in, garbage out'. In short, this slogan means that if you put the wrong data into a computer you will get the wrong information out. Because all organizations face limitations in terms of the money and time they can invest in collecting information, the data they collect is often incomplete or inaccurate. As a consequence the managers and employees that have to interpret the results of any analysis, whether computerized or otherwise, will usually find that many of the questions they would like to ask are not answerable with the information provided. Even if these decision makers have a perfect and complete set of data with which to perform their analyses, the interpretation placed upon this information will still be constrained by the physical limitations of individual managers' memories and powers of thought. Most of us can only remember between seven and eight things at any one time. Furthermore, our ability to manipulate this information is very limited. Awareness of these problems has led a number of writers to draw attention to the messiness of most management decision making and action. In the words of one writer, strategy formulation and implementation is best seen as the 'science of muddling through' (Lindbloom, 1959).

The second problem associated with any analysis of complex and changing systems concerns what is done with the raw data and information. Any prediction or forecast of future trends will be based upon assumptions about the relationship between different indicators. For example, in the Hodsons case study it may be assumed that a general rise in the level of consumer confidence and an increase in the number of new house sales will lead to an upturn in the construction industry with consequent improvements in the company's sales position. This relationship is illustrated in Fig 1.3.

However, this simple model with its in-built assumptions about cause and effect relationships between different variables may oversimplify what is really happening within the building industry. The variables may be difficult to disentangle from one another; the nature of cause and effect may be more

Fig 1.3 Cause and effect: the implied relationship between consumer confidence and Hodsons' sales

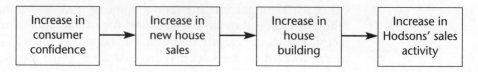

complex than this simple chain implies; and there may be other variables at work. For example, the number of new house sales will have an effect upon the level of consumer confidence and the amount of building activity will influence the volume of house sales. Furthermore, the availability of mortgages, older housing stock, and rented accommodation, among other things, could all affect one or more of the variables. These complexities and interrelationships between the phenomena we observe will inevitably affect our ability to produce effective analyses of current activity and future trends.

Other accounts have challenged the view that events that surround us can be isolated as specific variables which relate to one another in a manner which can be determined. For some writers it is more appropriate to think of the things which we see around us as elements of a complex web, or threads of a woven fabric. Each component of the web or fabric is thus seen as part of an interrelated whole which can only be understood in terms of its relationship to other parts (Collins, 1994).

One form of this analysis is generally referred to as systems theory. Drawing upon models developed in the biological and engineering sciences, this approach encourages us to see organizations as dynamic structures characterized by the flow of information and materials. In order for these organizations to transform raw materials into goods and services, while satisfying the objectives of the organization's members, all parts of the system must be in balance with one another, and with the environment that surrounds them (see Von Bertalanffy, 1967; Katz and Kahn, 1966; Lovelock, 1979).

More radical forms of this analysis suggest that our attempts to fragment and name parts of the world that surrounds us are at best misguided. By defining the world in terms of basic units and then seeking to determine how these elements relate to one another, we can only gain a partial understanding of the nature of reality. According to this view it is not appropriate to isolate and pick out one aspect of an organization's environment. All aspects of the organization and its environment have to be considered together as a whole because they are all interrelated. Furthermore the nature of the whole is constantly changing. The future is not a continuation of established patterns or cause and effect, but a gradual unfolding of a complex and indivisible whole (Bohm, 1980).

Exercise 1.2 ## Representing the external environment

Refer back to the list of pressures confronting Hodsons and set out this information as creatively and imaginatively as you can on an overhead projector slide or a plain A4 sheet of paper. You may find it helpful to refer to the suggestions in Exhibit 1.1 when undertaking this analysis.

Exhibit 1.1

Representing the external environment

There are a range of ways in which the pressures confronting the members of an organization can be represented and communicated. A brief description of the most common forms of analysis follows.

▶

LIBRARY
BISHOP BURTON COLLEGE
BEVERLEY HU17 8QG

Lists

The easiest and perhaps least demanding form of analysis involves merely listing the pressures, either in the order they occurred to you, or on the basis of their perceived level of importance.

Categories

If your list of external pressures becomes very long, or you are anxious to ensure that equal attention is focused on all forms of possible external change, it may be appropriate to order the information on the basis of a series of categories. One of the most common approaches is a *PEST analysis*.

PEST analyses draw our attention to the Political, Economic, Social and Technological (PEST) changes which confront the organization. The use of these headings is designed to ensure that equal attention is focused upon all these areas of possible external change. A number of writers have amended the PEST acronym to include legal, cultural and ecological pressures (PLESCET).

There are two problems commonly associated with conducting a PEST analysis. First, there is a possibility that a particular pressure may be listed under only one heading when it should occur under several. This reflects the somewhat arbitrary nature of the categories being used in this form of analysis. Second, there is a danger that by merely listing the pressures the relative importance of different trends may be overlooked. This problem can be overcome by ranking the pressures in order of importance and allocating a number from 1 to 100 to each external pressure.

Maps and rich pictures

This is a more elaborate form of analysis which can be undertaken by carrying out the following five steps.

1 Draw up a long list of external pressures and problems confronting the organization. It may be helpful to write these down on individual small pieces of card.

2 Edit the list to ensure that there are no exact duplications of information or imprecise statements.

3 Group the list or cards into related categories. By rearranging the list or cards on a large sheet of paper or board it should be possible to iso-late a number of groups of issues. If one issue within these groups appears to subsume a number of others, cluster these constituent issues around the main heading. For example, the following issues might be clustered under the heading 'economic recession': a collapse in house prices, a decline in consumer confidence and rising unemployment.

4 If issues are difficult to group but are clearly interrelated, arrows can be drawn to indicate the nature of the relationship between these factors. The strength and nature of the connection between particular issues can then be indicated by the width of the line which is drawn and the direction of the arrows entered on that line.

5 The relative importance of particular developments can be indicated by assigning numbers to particular issues to indicate their relative ranking. It should also be possible to indicate whether a particular factor is stable and predictable or subject to rapid and turbulent change by assigning a colour to that issue. For example, yellow and red could be used to indicate 'hot issues' which are likely to change their form rapidly, while blue and purple indicate issues which are 'cold' and unlikely to alter in the foreseeable future.

Images and metaphors

According to Gareth Morgan, pictures, images and the use of appropriate metaphors can provide a powerful basis for analysis of the interplay between an organization and its environment (Morgan, 1986; 1993). For example, by drawing an image of the organization as an iceberg or termite hill and extending this image through annotating the diagram, important aspects of the organization's current position may be revealed. Morgan suggests that this approach works because it encourages members of the organization to think creatively and outside of the confines of accepted categories and definitions.

Models

This approach attempts to specify the exact nature of, and the relationship between, things. The most sophisticated forms rely upon the statement of equations which define specific measurable variables and indicate the precise interplay between these ele-

►

LIBRARY
BISHOP BURTON COLLEGE
BEVERLEY HU17 8QG

ments. Where these models and theories have been appropriately constructed and expressed, it should then be possible to draw up a number of propositions or hypotheses which specify exactly what will happen if one or more variables within the equation is altered. If a model or theory is to be tested in this manner it is essential that hypotheses drawn from it can be expressed in a form which allows them to be verified or refuted by reference to information drawn from laboratory experiments or observations in the field. In short, it must be possible to prove that the model is incorrect – it must be falsifiable. Once these tests have been conducted and the component hypotheses and propositions have been demonstrated to provide a reliable explanation of observed phenomena in a range of settings, it should then be possible to use the model as the basis for forecasts and predictions.

In the social sciences a number of models have been developed to explain the behaviour of the UK economy, social classes and product and market development by companies. Unfortunately the difficulties associated with collecting reliable information and manipulating this data have meant that, at present, few of these models provide a reliable basis for accurate forecasts of the future. Nevertheless, companies, institutions and other organizations still frequently use these models as the basis for anticipating and planning responses to possible future developments.

Scenario building

Another approach to analysing external pressures is to develop a series of scenarios outlining what could possibly happen in the future. In a rapidly changing world it may not be possible to produce an accurate prediction of the future, but by producing several different predictions it may be possible to challenge managers' existing assumptions and get closer to what will really happen. For example, managers might wish to consider what they would do in the event of a recession, steady growth or an economic boom. By outlining these various scenarios managers will have an opportunity to rehearse the reasons for particular decisions before they are forced to confront them directly.

CHOICE AND DETERMINISM

So far in this chapter we have considered how different views about the nature of the physical environment that surrounds us can affect how we analyse our own current position, or the position of a particular organization, and predict possible future developments. In this next section we move on to consider how much discretion managers and employees have in responding to these external pressures. To what extent do managers individually, and employees collectively, have a choice about what they do in the future? Can they alter the position of their organization and respond to, or master, the pressures which confront them? Or, are they forced to remain where they are – buffeted and pulled along by external developments over which they have no control? In short, how much choice do managers and employees have when making and implementing decisions?

As we shall see, writers differ in their views on these questions. For some, senior managers and directors can choose from a wide range of possible courses of action and will have few problems in implementing their preferred solutions. For others, perceptions of choice are often illusory as managers are frequently servants rather than masters of their environment. Thus, in practice, it may appear as if managers and employees consciously choose certain courses of action, but in reality what they do is determined by wider forces over which they have no control.

Choice

Those writers who emphasize choice suggest that managers are always confronted with different possible courses of action; therefore they are able to decide for themselves what they wish to do and how they wish to do it. There may be external pressures and influences, but people are always free to ignore, avoid, or meet these challenges as they see fit. This approach is particularly influential within the field of management theory and practice. Indeed the belief that managers and employees are masters of their own destiny and the future of their organizations has become so pervasive in the UK and USA in recent years that it is often treated as basic common sense.

An important example of this view is provided by the *rational planning* approaches to decision making within organizations. The assumptions implicit in this approach underpin many contemporary accounts of how decisions should be taken at all levels, and within all areas, of an organization's activities. For example, this approach might be used to determine the content and form of the organization's investment decisions, marketing campaigns, information systems, and human resource management policies. Although the details as put forward by different authors vary, there are a number of common features. Thus in general it is suggested that almost any organizational problem or external pressure can be addressed by going through a series of logical and sequential steps (*see* Fig 1.4).

Fig 1.4 Choice: the strength planning approach

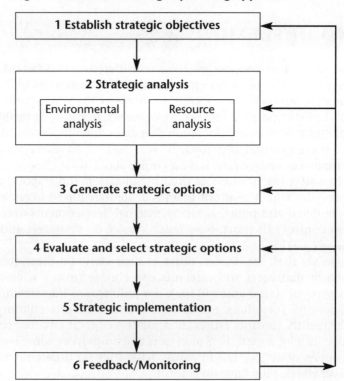

1 Establish strategic objectives

According to the proponents of this rational planning approach, when managers and employees are faced with an external pressure the first step they should take is to determine or reaffirm their basic aims. In practice this often involves the Board of Directors or senior executives overseeing the formulation and agreement of a statement of the organization's mission and objectives. Mission statements consist of a general declaration of the aims of the organization and are usually fairly vague. For example, the mission statement at Hodsons may say that it intends to be the best builders' supplier in the country. Such a broad expression of intent is usually worthless unless it is accompanied by some more specific statement of objectives which can be measured at a later date in order to evaluate whether the organization is progressing in the right direction. If we return to the example of Hodsons, the specific objectives associated with the company's mission statement might include a 2 per cent reduction in operating costs, a 5 per cent increase in sales, a 5 per cent increase in profits, a lengthening of opening hours and the maintenance of high levels of employee and customer satisfaction.

2 Strategic analysis

The second stage in the rational planning approach involves an analysis of the strengths and weaknesses of an organization's internal resources and the threats and opportunities presented by the external environment. This form of analysis is usually referred to by its acronym SWOT – Strengths, Weaknesses, Opportunities and Threats.

In the case of Hodsons, internal strengths include well trained staff, an established company, a good reputation in the south of England and funds available for investment. By contrast, the weaknesses consist of declining sales, a customer base limited to professional builders, and poor stock ordering and monitoring procedures. Among the opportunities are a possible recovery in the building industry, a growth in general consumer interest in Do-It-Yourself materials and a lengthening of the shopping week – including late night and Sunday opening. The threats facing the company might include ruthless competition from Do-It-Yourself centres, and growing customer concern about the environmental consequences of the timber trade.

3 Generate strategic options

The third stage of the rational planning approach involves establishing what are the available strategic options for achieving the organization's objectives, given the constraints imposed by external pressures and internal resources. Here it is assumed that in all situations decision-makers will be confronted by more than one possible course of action. For example, in the case of Hodsons an increase in opening hours could be achieved by adopting one of the following five options.

- The staff could be offered overtime work.
- A shift system could be introduced by negotiating a change to the contracts of existing staff.

- Current staff could be allowed to retain their existing terms and conditions, but new staff would be required to sign more flexible contracts which stipulate that they will be expected to work in the evenings and at weekends.
- Additional part-time staff could be hired to cover the evening and weekend opening hours.
- There could be no changes to the total number of hours worked by staff but some changes to the days on which the stores opened. For example, by analysing sales trends within different branches, peaks and troughs in demand could be determined. Once the busiest days of the week have been identified the days on which the stores open could be adjusted. By adopting this approach, the company's managers may find that by closing on Tuesdays and opening on Sundays, the sales increase without any need to increase the amount of time staff spend at work.

4 Evaluate and select strategic options

The fourth stage consists of choosing which of these possible courses of action should be selected and implemented. This process of selection will involve some form of evaluation in which alternative courses of action are assessed by reference to a range of criteria. The choice of these criteria may be influenced by a number of factors, but if the company's longer term objectives are to be achieved it would seem sensible to use these as the criteria for the evaluation exercise. For example, if we return to the Hodsons case, the criteria could include financial costs, the effects on sales and profits, as well as the consequences for customer service and staff morale. Once the criteria have been chosen the next stage is to assess the different options by reference to these criteria. One way of undertaking this evaluation is to compile a matrix with the options listed along one side of the grid and the evaluative criteria listed along the other side (*see* Table 1.1). Once this matrix has been drawn up it should be possible to rank the various options against the criteria on a scale from one to five – one being the most preferable course of action and five

Table 1.1 A pay-off matrix evalutating the options at Hodsons

	Anticipated effect on organizational performance				
	Costs	Sales	Profits	Employee morale	Customer service
Overtime payments	4	2	2	1	2
Shift system	2	1	1	5	1
Part-time staff	5	3	2	2	4
New staff on new contracts	1	5	4	4	3
Change days of opening	2	4	5	3	5

Note: This technique can be improved by weighting the various evaluation criteria. For example, in most organizations the effects of a specific initiative on the costs and sales are more important than the consequences for staff morale. To reflect this reality, the weighting of the various criteria can be changed by awarding ranks of 0, 2, 4, 6 and 8 for cost and 1, 2, 3, 4 and 5 for employee morale.

being the least attractive. When it comes to choosing which of the various options should be adopted, the rankings of each alternative are added together and the one with the lowest score is chosen. Corporate strategists have christened this technique a *Multiple Attribute Utility Test* (MAUT) or a *pay-off matrix*.

In the case of Hodsons' response to longer trading hours, the various options get the following scores: overtime payments for existing staff = 11, introduction of a shift system = 10, employment of part-time staff = 16, flexible contracts for new staff = 17, and changing the days of opening = 19. With these results the organization might wish to consider introducing a shift system and giving their staff some form of bonus payment for accepting this change in their terms and conditions of employment.

5 Strategy implementation

The fifth stage in the planning process is the implementation of the proposed changes. For most writers adopting the rational planning approach this stage is not a problem because it is assumed that paid employees will inevitably comply with the decisions of their managers and, furthermore, that they will change their working practices as directed quickly and without fuss. According to this view organizations can be restructured and internal control systems amended without significant disruption to the organization. For example, at Hodsons changes in the shift pattern might involve analysing when staff are needed and drawing up a rota on this basis. It is assumed that the introduction of these new rotas will meet with automatic agreement and support from the affected staff. Whether or not this provides an accurate reflection of what happens in practice, or a sensible comment on what should happen, will be returned to later in this chapter.

6 Feedback/Monitoring

The final stage in the rational planning model involves measuring the success of specific initiatives and using this information to decide whether to continue with, or amend, past decisions. The success of the programme to increase store opening hours at Hodsons could be monitored by charting trends in costs, sales, profit, employee morale and customer complaints, etc.

Determinism

For writers adopting a determinist perspective, various environmental factors (market conditions, technology, culture, organization structure and internal organizational politics, etc.) either significantly constrain or determine the strategies available to an organization. As a consequence managers and employees within companies have few real choices. For example, the theory of the firm which lies at the heart of mainstream economic analysis adopts a deterministic view of how organizations operate. Other things being equal, the amount of goods supplied by individual firms or the economy in general is determined by the interplay of the level of demand and supply. If firms wish to exploit this demand and make a profit they need to ensure that the most efficient balance is achieved between their sales and costs. If they fail to follow this logic then they can be sure that their competitors will, and in the long run they will be driven out of business.

This deterministic approach is not confined to the field of economics; indeed similar models have been presented by management theorists and sociologists. In one famous study of the Scottish electronics industry in the early 1960s it was suggested that organizational structure and operating style are strongly influenced, if not determined, by the market pressures facing the company (Burns and Stalker, 1961). The results of this study indicate that in stable market conditions with relatively low levels of product and process innovation, bureaucratic forms of organization are most appropriate. A key feature of this form of organization is a clear hierarchy of managerial control and a strict division of labour. By contrast, in more volatile market conditions where there is rapid technological change, flexible and organic forms of organization are more appropriate. The main elements of this form of organization are blurred reporting lines and employer reliance upon worker loyalty and a general willingness to undertake a wide variety of tasks in order to get the job done. According to Burns and Stalker, although it is relatively easy to specify the best match between an organization and its environment, there are problems associated with changing from one form to another. Changes to the formal organizational structure will not radically change the career aspirations of staff or their internal political loyalties. Indeed, these aspirations and ties may act as a major, if not insurmountable, barrier to internal organizational change initiatives.

Later elaborations of this approach have suggested that organizational success is contingent upon achieving the best match between an organization and its environment. Referred to as *contingency theory*, this approach has led to a number of different lists of external and internal pressures and recipes for dealing with these constraints (*see* Lawrence and Lorsch, 1967; Miles and Snow, 1978; Morgan, 1986). Thus decision makers within any organization are not completely free to make choices. If they ignore the lessons to be learnt about the best match between market conditions and the activities of their organization they will perform poorly or go out of business. Thus the aim in these circumstances should be to gain a congruent match between environmental conditions and internal business operations. An example of this approach is provided in Fig 1.5.

Applying this form of analysis to the Hodsons case study it would appear that the organization is poorly adapted to its environment. The environment has become turbulent and unpredictable, but the Board of Directors has retained a defensive attitude to goal setting and continues to rely upon bureaucratic and authoritarian management methods. Meanwhile the staff in the branch operations remain committed to their jobs primarily because of the discretion and expertise that they are encouraged to develop and demonstrate at work. If the members of the organization wish to remain in business and assure their longer term future they will have to find a higher degree of congruence between their internal operations and the external environment. They have choices available to them, but these are severely constrained by the natural logic of acceptable matches between environmental conditions and organizational structure and operations.

Fig 1.5 Congruence and incongruence between organizational sub-systems

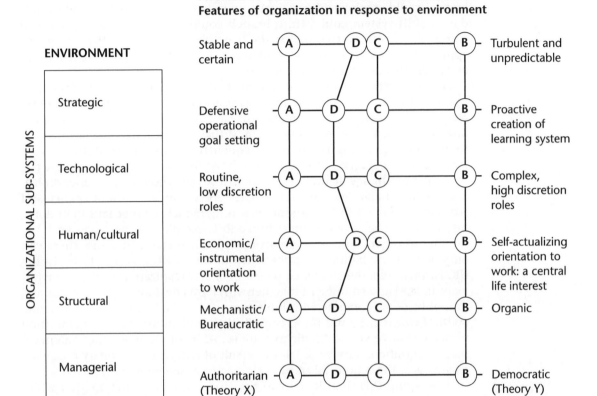

Source: Morgan (1986:63). *Imaginisation: The Art of Creative Management,* Copyright © 1986 by Sage Publications, Inc. Reprinted by permission of Sage Publications.

Many other forms of determinist analysis draw upon the biological sciences in general, and evolutionary theory in particular to analyse organizational behaviour. Using models of product and organizational life cycles they suggest that like human beings products and organizations are born, they grow, mature, decline and then die. Steps may be taken to extend the life of a particular product or organization, but in the end its demise is inevitable (Levitt, 1965; Greiner, 1972).

In response to these insights, and a belief that the world is increasingly characterized by rapid change and uncertainty, a number of writers have suggested that managers and employees should abandon attempts to rationally plan a response to external pressures. Instead it is suggested they should become more flexible in their approach to planning. This may be achieved by building some variety into the way in which the organization operates, perhaps by allowing junior managers and employees more discretion and decision-making authority in an attempt to get them to find their own local solutions to wider problems. Alternatively, senior managers and directors may wish to sponsor several different solutions simultaneously in order to reduce the chances of failure.

If we return to the Hodsons case, a flexible approach to increasing opening hours might involve experimenting with the different options outlined in Table 1.1 (*see* p 16) in several of the company's branches. For example, one branch would employ additional part-time staff; another branch might introduce a shift system; and a third branch could introduce new contracts of employment. After a trial period the benefits and pitfalls of these different approaches could then be assessed and a decision could be reached about extending this experiment to other stores.

The most extreme forms of determinist analysis adopt a fatalist perspective by suggesting that people and the organizations of which they are members are prisoners of their environment and have little choice but to go with the flow of the events that surround them. If they do not move in this direction then their organizations will die. Frequently labelled as 'evolutionists' or 'population ecologists', these writers have focused their analysis on the dynamics of change at the level of industries or whole groups of organizations (Hannan and Freeman, 1988). They argue that the form of change and adaptation implicit in the rational planning model is easier said than done. Instead they suggest that competition and scarce physical resources limit the number of organizations an environment can sustain. In short, there can only be so many building suppliers within the construction industry in the UK. Furthermore, the combined pressures of an organization's existing investment in land and equipment together with legal constraints on what can and cannot be done, combine with limitations on available information, internal political constraints, and the existing history and culture of the organization to make change very difficult to achieve. As a consequence they maintain that organizations survive or fail as a result of natural evolutionary processes, regardless of the actions taken by their managers and employees.

If we apply this final insight to the Hodsons case it may be that wider changes in the business environment confronting the organization are so profound and the internal capacity to respond is so limited that senior managers have no choice. Their only option is to plan the sale of all or part of the company assets and concentrate their efforts on finding alternative employment for themselves and the other employees.

Exercise 1.3 — Choosing an appropriate response to declining sales at Hodsons

Using the information contained in the Hodsons case study and your own general knowledge produce a list of possible responses to the decline in sales produced by the recession. When you have completed this list decide which if any of these options is feasible and then determine which is the most appropriate or suitable. You may find it useful to consider some of the suggestions outlined in the preceding section.

SUMMARY AND CONCLUSION

This chapter has considered three sets of differences in the basic assumptions which underpin many contemporary accounts of the way in which organizations and their members deal with external pressures and developments. These distinctions between objective versus subjective interpretations, continuity versus turbulent change, and choice versus determinism have been described and illustrated with reference to the Hodsons case study at the beginning of the chapter.

Although few writers and practitioners adopt an extreme position on any one of these dimensions there are significant differences of emphasis in their accounts. These differences have a profound effect upon suggestions about the most appropriate means to:

- investigate and analyse external pressures;
- diagnose the problems confronting an organization;
- predict future trends and developments; and
- propose prescriptions for future remedial action.

Different assumptions lead to different approaches, analyses, predictions and proposals and so it has been suggested that before attempting any reading of environmental pressures, managers and employees should consider the assumptions that they are making and ensure that alternative ways of seeing the situation are considered. We may favour one particular approach, but it is important to consider other perspectives. A full analysis of the problems confronting any organization can best be achieved when all facets have been considered.

As a general rule, before beginning any analysis of a problem confronting an organization it is important to consider:

- a variety of methods of gathering data and information;
- different interpretations of the problem;
- the extent to which it is possible to define and predict future trends and changes; and
- whether managers and employees within the organization will be able to take the necessary remedial action.

Exercise 1.4 ## Analysis of pressures and problems

Compile an analysis of the pressures and problems confronting either your employing organization or a company with which you are familiar. There are a range of library and other resources which should enable you to complete this task quickly.

- *CD ROM. A number of national newspapers, business magazines and academic journals are available on CD ROM disks either in full text or abstract form. By using a CD ROM machine it should be possible to locate recent relevant articles and then download them onto a computer disk for subsequent editing.*

- *Indexes. If your library does not have a CD ROM machine it should have a number of indexes which list relevant publications under subject headings. The Research*

Index provides a list of articles which have appeared on specific topics or companies on a fortnightly basis.

● *__Organizational sources__. You may wish to contact the organization directly. Most large companies will have a press or public relations office and many have a separate education department which can provide you with copies of the annual report and other literature about the organization. Obviously these materials will have been drawn up to show the company in the best possible light and therefore you should always read these materials in a critical manner, and compare this information with analyses in the business, trade or professional press.*

When you have collected the material, analyse the current position of the organization and possible future directions using one or more of the techniques covered in this chapter.

CHAPTER 2

Ownership, control, objectives and organization

INTRODUCTION

Organizations operating in the UK are very varied. Small corner shops financed and operated by their owners exist next door to large multinational companies with thousands of employees and finance drawn from stock markets around the world. In addition to these different forms of private enterprise, agencies supported by central or local government, together with charities and voluntary bodies, provide a range of goods and services to people across the country. These different types of organization share a number of features and yet remain very different in other ways.

FOCUS AND SCOPE

This chapter aims to outline some of the major differences which exist between organizations in terms of their ownership, organization and objectives. By undertaking this analysis we hope to demonstrate that these factors have a significant impact upon the nature and form of the pressures affecting organizations in different sectors of the UK economy. In addition, the way in which particular organizations deal with specific external pressures will be, at least in part, conditioned by their owners and other individuals with an interest in their operations. Thus, private sector companies which aim to gain a profit from their activities will behave in a very different manner by comparison with large public sector services which seek to provide a service to members of the community.

The chapter begins with an outline of the main differences between private and public sector organizations. We then move on to consider recent changes to the ownership, organization and objectives of various public and private sector bodies. Here we aim to demonstrate that in the public sector government-sponsored reforms including privatization have had a significant effect on the operation of current and former public sector agencies. Similar attention is paid to the private sector where we discuss the effects of recent waves of merger and acquisition activity and the gradual expansion of multinational company operations.

Moving away from a focus on general trends, the chapter concludes with an outline of some of the varied methods of operation in specific organizations. While we may be able to discern general trends at the level of the international and national economy, a fuller appreciation of the operation of specific organizations requires more refined forms of analysis. At this level, therefore, we aim to demonstrate the importance of analysing the different interests of key groups inside and outside the organization. By identifying these groups we hope to demonstrate their influence on the stated objectives of specific organizations. In undertaking this analysis we also seek to outline ways in which the stated and unstated goals of an organization may be examined in order to measure progress and expose gaps between the goals as laid down by its senior managers and the actual day-to-day behaviour of employees within that organization.

LEARNING OBJECTIVES

Once you have read this chapter and completed the associated exercises, you should be able to:

- define different forms of organization and comment upon the implications of these differences for the goals pursued by managers and employees;
- describe trends in the ownership and orientation of UK organizations;
- discuss the factors influencing a specific organization's goals; and
- outline the goals being pursued by an organization known to you.

CASE STUDY

Flexington University

The following case study examines the ownership, organization and objectives of Flexington – a medium-sized university based in the southeast of England. The material presented in this case is drawn directly from the experiences of employees at a number of institutions of higher education. As such it is not based on people and events within any one university, but represents a stylized account of developments within the sector as a whole over the last 90 years. The information presented in this case study will form the basis of later discussion in this chapter.

The changing status of Flexington University
The history of Flexington University can be traced back to the late nineteenth century when members of the local Mechanical Institute founded Stanmead Technical College. This college was set up in response to concerns about the failures of British industry and commerce in overseas markets. Leading members of the Institute believed that these failings were caused by the poor training and education of British workers. Taking a lead from the experiences of German industrialists and trainers, they were determined to establish an institution which would provide high standards of instruction in technical and vocational subjects.

Financed through voluntary subscriptions from the Institute's membership, the college began its operations by renting space in local schools and charging students a nominal fee for evening classes in subjects as diverse as geometry, technical drawing, building construction and electricity. Because of Stanmead College's reliance on private funding, classes were available only when a sufficient number of students enrolled on these courses. Furthermore, students who attended these courses were not awarded nationally recognized qualifications; instead they had to rely upon local employers accepting certificates of attendance from the college as proof of their skills and abilities.

As the college expanded its operations, it became more dependent upon local government for its funding and in the early 1900s Flexington County Council assumed responsibility for the day-to-day operation of the college. For the next 45 years, the college remained relatively small, although the range of courses on offer changed in response to changes in the skills demanded by local industry.

In the 1940s, the onset of the Second World War placed new demands on the college as a growing number of male and female armaments workers needed training in modern production techniques. At the end of the war, the government introduced an Education Act which committed the country to providing secondary education for all and introduced a requirement for local authorities to provide further education in technical and design subjects. In the period immediately following the Second World War, the college also began to hasten the process of linking courses to nationally recognized qualifications. This initiative gained extra momentum when the college was allowed to register its students as external candidates for University of London degree courses.

As the college continued to expand, an increasing proportion of the teaching was at the undergraduate level and in 1962 the college split into two. Stanmead College of Further Education focused its work on vocational further education for school leavers, while Stanmead Institute of Technology concentrated on providing academic study for more mature students. Despite these changes, both colleges remained committed to providing training and education in technical subjects.

In 1970, Stanmead Institute of Technology merged with the Roseberry College of Art and Design and the Peabody Teachers' Training Academy to form Flexington Polytechnic. The new organization was set up in response to a government initiative designed to increase the number of graduates with vocational skills in a range of subjects. At the same time a new body – the Council for National Academic Awards (CNAA) – was set up to oversee the quality of the wider range of courses provided by Flexington and other polytechnics.

Over the next 18 years the polytechnic, although still formally owned and controlled by the local authority, reorganized its operations and concentrated its work within six faculties – Business, Education and Social Work, Science, Art and Design, Technology and Social Sciences. Accompanying this broadening of the work of the organization there was a gradual change in the balance of work undertaken by these sections of the polytechnic. These changes took place for four reasons.

1 The Faculties of Science and Technology became less significant in the overall work of the institution as manufacturing industry declined in importance within the local economy.

2 The Business and Social Science Faculties became more important as local residents sought qualifications which would help them advance their careers in the growing number of local service-sector industries.

3 Staff increasingly undertook research and consultancy work in addition to their teaching duties.

4 Various departments within the Polytechnic gained approval from the CNAA to offer higher level degrees in various disciplines.

In combination these changes began to blur the differences between Flexington and the older, established universities.

In the early 1980s the government relaxed the rules governing the establishment of universities. In response to these changes, Britain's first private university was established at Buckingham.

Later in the same decade Flexington, like other polytechnics, was encouraged by further government action to increase rapidly the number of students taught on its courses. The older, more established universities were much slower in their response. In recognition of the increases in student numbers within polytechnics, and in an attempt to encourage the older universities to compete, the government decided in 1991 to allow the polytechnics to adopt the title of university. Thus in 1991 Flexington became an independent university with the ability to award degrees and manage its own financial affairs.

During the mid-1990s the level of government financing for undergraduate students diminished as existing funds from the Higher Education Funding Council were spread among an increasing number of students. In response to these financial pressures the governors and managers of the new university launched three initiatives.

▶

- Steps were taken to increase the number of overseas and commercially-sponsored students at the university. These students would pay higher fees than those individuals who could claim government grants.
- Plans were developed to improve the research profile of the organization in order to attract additional funds from government research councils and private sector sponsors.
- The University set up a private company – Flexington University Enterprises Limited (FUEL) – to register patents and copyrights, as well as sell consultancy services and merchandise.

Although these steps led to a doubling of undergraduate student numbers in the early 1990s, this growth was not welcomed by everybody. The parents of many students and the various trade unions representing staff and student interests criticized the government directly for reducing the level of student grants. Meanwhile several academics used the media to question the effectiveness of cheap mass higher education and a number of employers restricted their graduate recruitment to those universities which had not engaged in rapid expansion.

THE DEVELOPMENT OF PRIVATE SECTOR COMPANIES AND PUBLIC SECTOR BODIES

In order to make sense of the immense variety of business operations in the UK it is useful to consider some of the ways in which they differ. This section draws upon the work of economic historians, industrial sociologists and business commentators to consider one of the more significant forms of difference.

A common way of distinguishing between organizations is to consider their ownership – who owns the assets or capital of the business (property, premises and equipment). Are they owned publicly with the organization's assets held by all the citizens of a state, but controlled by government nominees? Alternatively, are the physical resources of the organization privately owned by individuals, groups or other organizations, with the responsibility for day-to-day operations vested in the hands of a board of directors, trustees, or governors?

Private companies, as we currently understand them, are a relatively recent phenomenon and their historical roots can be traced back to the end of the sixteenth and seventeenth centuries. At this time the UK was beginning to emerge from a feudal agricultural system in which the Crown, Lords and Guilds of skilled workmen owned most of the land, property and tools with which ordinary people worked.

The expansion of international trade in the Tudor and Stuart periods meant that merchants needed the backing of a large number of financiers in order to fund their trading operations. Individually funded businesses and partnerships were unable to provide sufficient investment and faced legal difficulties. If the owners of the business wished to sue one of their customers or suppliers, all of the partners had to be involved in the legal action. Similarly any legal action by another party against the partnership could be taken only if all the members of the partnership were named in the writ.

The restrictions outlined above did not apply to organizations which had received a Royal Charter from the monarch, giving them a legal status which was independent of their owners. In these circumstances any legal action against the organization could be limited to naming the company and not its individual owners. The first such company was the Muscovy Company of Merchant Adventurers which received a Royal Charter in 1553 from King Edward VI. Over the next three hundred years many more organizations sought corporate status, either through an application for a Royal Charter or from the mid-eighteenth century onwards through the passage of a Private Act of Parliament.

The beginning of the Industrial Revolution at the end of the eighteenth century unleashed a spate of technological innovations. The emergence of steam power, deep-seam coal mining, iron foundries, cotton spinning machines, canals, turnpikes (private roads) and railways produced fundamental changes. In order to exploit these developments a new breed of industrialists required substantial material and financial resources to make their new inventions work. It was against this background that laws were passed in the first half of the nineteenth century which enabled businessmen to establish companies with limited liability. Under these regulations the risk attached to any investment in a company was limited to the value of the investors' shares in the company. If the organization went bankrupt shareholders would lose their initial stake in the company, but they were immune from further legal action by other parties.

Accompanying the changes in the country's industrial base were improvements in agricultural techniques (the Agrarian Revolution). The systematic adoption of new planting and harvesting methods, the enclosure of common land and crop rotation produced substantial improvements in the productivity of many farms. As the adoption of these new methods gathered pace and combined with rapid industrialization, people were attracted to the growing number of towns and cities which provided a home for the new manufacturing companies. Within these new and expanding urban centres, the need to provide effective sanitation, health care, transportation, education and housing provided a basis for the development of social welfare provided by central and local government. Early attempts to cope with these problems led to the passing of a number of laws designed to regulate industrial activity and working conditions. At the same time there was a steady expansion in the role of local and central government.

During the twentieth century the role of the public sector was further extended. At this time a combination of economic crises and a poor record of investment and management by particular companies, as well as a desire to promote a more equal society, provided the impetus for the nationalization of many previously privately owned organizations. This process of nationalization was also accompanied by the establishment of new public sector bodies or an extension in the role of existing bodies. For example, the BBC was set up to provide radio entertainment, the National Health Service was established to provide a comprehensive system of medical care, and social work and probation services were added to the list of services provided by many local authorities.

Today the British economy contains a variety of organizations with different forms of ownership. These differences are recognized legally and it is therefore possible to distinguish between a number of distinct types of private and public sector organizations. As we aim to demonstrate in the following section, variations in the ownership of these organizations will affect who controls these organizations and the objectives they choose to pursue.

Private sector organizations

Private sector businesses provide the backbone of British industry and commerce. This form of organization accounts for approximately three-quarters of economic output and over two-thirds of employment within the national economy (Sawyer, 1992: 238). In addition to profit-making businesses, there are a smaller number of private sector charities, trusts and associations which provide a variety of valuable services. Taken together it is possible to distinguish the following forms of private sector organization.

Sole traders

These are individuals who have set up a business with a view to making profit. There are few specific legal formalities associated with this form of organization, excluding notification to the Inland Revenue and, if their sales exceed a specified level, registration with HM Customs and Excise for VAT payments. These businesses have unlimited liability. This means that if the business incurs debts or becomes bankrupt, any part of the owner's property or assets may be sold to raise funds to repay these bills.

In some sectors of the economy this form of organization dominates business activity, especially within industries where only relatively low levels of capital investment are required, e.g. retailing, building and catering services. Although definitive figures are hard to come by due to the lack of legal formalities associated with this form of organization, the Customs and Excise records suggest that sole trader status is the most common form of business operation in the UK.

Partnerships

This form of business organization generally consists of two to twenty people who come together to form a business with a view to making a profit. In the case of large professional practices, limitations on the number of partners may not apply.

Under the terms of the Partnership Act 1890, the name of the partnership has to be registered, unless it only consists of the names of the partners. Like sole traders, partnerships do not have a separate legal identity from their owners and therefore the financial liability of a partnership is usually unlimited. In other words each partner is eligible to share in the profits of the enterprise, and is also responsible for the debts of other partners. The exact division of these profits and debts is usually specified in a formal written agreement referred to as a Deed of Partnership. This document will usually specify the names of the partners, the trading name and address of the business, the aims of their partnership, the amount of any initial investment, and the principles which will govern the division of profits and liabilities.

In certain circumstances, under the terms of the Limited Partnership Act 1907, the business partners may elect to form a limited partnership with the amount of an individual partner's liability limited to the sum he or she originally invested. However, this form of organization is relatively rare.

Like sole traders, partnerships are required to register with the Inland Revenue and, where appropriate, HM Customs and Excise.

This form of organization has a number of advantages in comparison with sole trader status. First and foremost, it enables the business to draw upon finance from a larger number of people. It also enables small businesses to set up operations without having to comply with the financial and other reporting requirements which apply to private and public limited companies. On the downside, partnerships rely upon sustained co-operation between the individuals involved within the business. This may present difficulties when the partners disagree about business priorities.

Despite these difficulties, partnerships remain the second most popular form of business organization within the UK. This form of organization is commonly adopted by small family-owned businesses and professional practices including accountants, architects, doctors and lawyers.

Private limited companies

The majority of large private businesses operating in the UK are registered as private limited companies. This process involves the drawing up of Memoranda and Articles of Association and a formal application to the Registrar of Companies.

Private limited companies, unlike sole traders and partnerships, have a legal identity which is distinct and separate from that of their owners, directors and employees. As a consequence these organizations have limited liability which, as previously mentioned, means that the shareholders who own the company only risk losing their investment in shares should the company go into liquidation. In return for their investment, shareholders may share in the success of a company through the payment of annual dividends (a proportion of the company's annual profits).

Shareholders are also entitled to have a say in the way the company is run. This right is exercised at the company's annual general meeting where the company's Board of Directors is appointed, the previous year's performance is reported, questions are answered and resolutions proposed. The Board of Directors is also required to submit audited accounts and other information to the Registrar of Companies.

Public limited companies (PLCs)

These organizations share the same basic characteristics as private limited companies but differ in two important respects. First, these organizations are required to publish an annual report and statement of accounts which should be available for public inspection. Second, shares in these companies are traded on the Stock Exchange which means that they invariably have a greater number of shareholders and are therefore able to gain access to larger financial resources. As a consequence, public limited companies tend to be larger than their private counterparts.

The *Financial Times* and a number of other business publications provide a detailed breakdown of movements in the share prices of these companies. These printed figures appear daunting at first sight. However, the information contained on these pages is useful for gauging the relative performance of specific companies.

Exhibit 2.1

Reading the financial pages

The information contained in Table 2.1 is printed in a number of quality newspapers on a daily or weekly basis. This information is broken down into a number of columns of figures to give investors an indication of the current worth of particular companies' shares. The meaning of the figures entered under each of these column headings is generally defined as follows:

- **Price** refers to the cost of a single share and is expressed in pence. However, the figure does not include the cost of brokers' fees which any shareholders will incur when they decide to buy or sell shares.

- **+ or – signs** specify the change in the price of the share on the most recent day of stock market trading.

- **High and low**. These figures give an indication of the highest and lowest prices quoted for the company's shares in the previous year of trading.

- **Mkt Cap £m** refers to market capitalization in sterling – the value of the company on the stock market. This figure is usually expressed in millions and calculated on the basis of the total

number of shares multiplied by their quoted price.

- **Yld Gr's** is shorthand for the gross yield of shares. This figure refers to the dividend paid to shareholders as a percentage of the share price. In other words, it provides a measure of the rate of return on an investment in these shares. The figure is quoted as gross because no account has been taken of the effects of tax.

- **P/E**. The price/earnings ratio gives an indication of the level of investors' confidence in the company. It is calculated by dividing the current share price by the latest available figure for that company's net earnings per share. A P/E ratio of 5.7 would mean, therefore, that the share price is currently 5.7 times the company's earnings per share. In general, the higher the P/E ratio the greater the confidence investors have in the firm's future profits. However, a high P/E ratio can also reflect special factors such as expectations of a takeover by another company. It is worth noting that P/E ratios can be sensibly compared only between companies engaged in similar businesses.

Table 2.1: Share price information for selected food retailing PLCs

Food retailing	1995				Mkt Cap. (£m)	Yld Gr's	P/E
	Price	+ or –	High	Low			
ASDA	$39\frac{1}{2}$	$+1\frac{1}{2}$	102	$39\frac{1}{2}$	2993	2.7	17.2
Argyll	348	+4	369	$254\frac{1}{2}$	3942	4.3	14.9
Sainsbury	466	+2	479	$403\frac{1}{2}$	8453	3.1	15.7
Tesco	316	$-\frac{1}{2}$	324	236	6531	3.4	15.5

Source: Financial Times, 8 August 1995

The *Financial Times* Stock Exchange 100 Index – known as the *FTSE Index* (pronounced *footsie*) – is an index which provides a measure of the stock market value of shares in the hundred largest registered companies, as measured by the their market capitalization. The index was established in 1984 at a base value of 1000. Within this index the share price movements of larger companies carry more weight than those of smaller companies.

| Exercise 2.1 | Reading the financial pages |

Which of the companies listed in Table 2.1 has:

(a) the most expensive shares?

(b) experienced the widest fluctuations in share price in the preceding year?

(c) has the greatest number of issued shares?

(d) the appearance of high shareholder confidence in its future performance?

Voluntary organizations

This category includes charities, political parties, religious organizations, professional institutes, trade unions, employers' associations and voluntary bodies (e.g. Womens' Institute, St John's Ambulance, Rotary Club, etc.). These organizations are unlike private sector businesses in a number of respects.

1 Their affairs are often overseen by representatives elected by the members of the organization on the basis of one member one vote. By contrast, the election of directors of private companies is carried out on the basis of one vote per share; thus larger shareholders have a greater number of votes. Once elected, voluntary body representatives are responsible for managing these organizations according to policy decisions democratically taken by the wider membership at annual conferences or similar meetings.

2 The primary objective of almost all voluntary bodies is to further the well-being and interests of a specified group within society. In the case of charities, these organizations provide a means for channelling resources between those who donate funds to those that need this money. As a consequence they are unlike businesses because they rarely sell a product or a service and it is not their intention to generate a profit.

3 Voluntary bodies often rely on the work of large numbers of unpaid volunteers.

The scale of activity undertaken by these organizations is partly revealed by the following figures:

- Twenty-five charities in the UK had incomes in excess of £15 million in 1994.

- Membership of mainstream Catholic and Protestant churches declined to 6.7 million in 1990 – a fall of approximately 1.5 million over the preceding 15 years. Meanwhile, membership of other faiths grew substantially; for example, the number of Sikhs, Muslims, Jews and Hindus doubled over the same period and now stands at 1.86 million.

- Membership of many professional institutions within the UK grew during the 1980s. Today, the Institute of Chartered Accountants in England and Wales, the British Medical Association and the Institute of Personnel and Development have registered memberships of 110 000, 106 000 and 70 000 respectively.

- Trade union membership in the UK stood at approximately 7.5 million in 1994.

Those voluntary bodies which are able to register as charities enjoy considerable tax advantages as they are generally not required to pay VAT on sales, or corporation tax on retained surpluses. Because of these financial advantages there are strict controls governing which types of organization may register as a charity and the means by which they can organize their activities and raise funds.

Public sector organizations

At its broadest the term public sector is used to refer to government and state-sponsored organizations. Within this general category, three distinct groups can be isolated: central government, local authorities and public corporations.

Central government

Central government bodies include all those ministries and departments which are the direct responsibility of a Minister of State, as well as the Quasi Autonomous Non-Governmental Organizations (Quangos) which are free from direct parliamentary control. At present, there are approximately 20 central government ministries, e.g. Agriculture, Defence, Social Security, Health, Treasury, Environment, Trade and Industry, Education and Employment as well as the Home and Foreign Offices. Each government ministry and department is overseen by a ministerial team; the most important of these teams include a Secretary of State who has a seat in Cabinet. Many central government departments consist of a number of divisions; for example, the Department for Education and Employment oversees the work of the Further and Higher Education Funding Councils, the Employment and Training Agencies.

The funding of the various government departments is determined in the annual public expenditure survey (PES), when ministers from the various spending ministries submit their claims for the following year to the Treasury. The functioning and efficiency of each of these ministries is open to written and verbal questioning on the floor of the Houses of Parliament. More detailed scrutiny is undertaken by Parliamentary Select Committees comprised of ordinary Members of Parliament drawn proportionately from each political party.

Local government

Local government in the UK operates according to a patchy system of one-, two- and three-tiered arrangements. In some areas of the country, therefore, there is one level of local government, in others two, and in a few regions three. These levels of operations go under a variety of names including metropolitan, county, district and parish councils. The first three of these bodies are responsible for the local provision of roads, environmental health, controls on development, education and housing, etc.

The management of local authorities mirrors the organization of central government with a split between the roles of elected councillors and council officers. Councillors are responsible for the formulation of overall policy. Council officers are charged with the execution of this policy and the day-to-day management of the council's services.

Since 1979 there has been a considerable reorganization of local government within the UK. In 1986 the seven metropolitan county councils of London, the West Midlands, Greater Manchester, Merseyside, Sheffield, Leeds and Tyneside were abolished. Eight years later local government in Wales and Scotland was reorganized following the report of the Local Government Commissions for Wales and Scotland. A similar reorganization is scheduled to take place in England in 1996–7 when the Local Government Commission for England will produce its proposals for the reorganization of district and county councils.

Public corporations

There are over 50 public corporations and nationalized industries which engage in a range of activities (e.g. Bank of England, Royal Mint, hospital trusts, the BBC and the Post Office). These bodies have been created by statute or Royal Charter and this legal identity enables them to operate like businesses within the private sector with one important exception – their debts and liabilities are effectively underwritten by the State.

Public corporations gain their revenue through sales of their products/services or through central government grants or loans. The managing boards of these bodies are appointed by ministers who have the power to give general directions, but are not supposed to be involved in day-to-day management decisions. These bodies are also subject to public scrutiny through House of Commons Select Committees (e.g. the Treasury and Public Accounts Committees), the National Audit Office and special reports commissioned from management consultants or the Monopolies and Mergers Commission.

Public and private sector ownership and control

In the preceding section we have seen that organizations currently operating in the UK may be divided into two broad categories of private and public sector ownership. The first of these categories includes companies and voluntary bodies which, according to their legal status and size, will be managed and controlled either directly by their owners or indirectly by appointed or elected directors. For example, voluntary bodies will generally be owned by their members and managed by elected officials who are charged with ensuring that the organizations achieve their stated welfare and charitable aims. By contrast, within the commercial world, sole traders with small businesses will generally oversee the day-to-day management of their business according to objectives they have set for themselves. Meanwhile, within larger private sector enterprises which have adopted private or public limited company status there is likely to be a split between ownership and control so that the people who own the business are not necessarily involved in managing its operations. Indeed, the individual shareholders of many large British companies may have little or no direct say over who represents their interests in the boardroom. In these situations the management of the organization is often left to a group of professionally trained directors who are appointed by the largest shareholders and charged with maximizing the company's financial performance.

Within the public sector the position is somewhat different. Here, the assets of the organization are held in trust by central or local government on behalf of their electors. However, the day-to-day management and control of these bodies is overseen by government ministers and local councillors directly, or indirectly through their appointed managers, civil servants or local government officers. As a consequence the objectives of these organizations are often fashioned by the political priorities and policies of politicians and their parties.

Exercise 2.2 ## Public or private?

The ownership and control of Flexington University, and its forerunner colleges, underwent a number of changes during its development. By reference to the list of different forms of public and private sector organization, construct a grid similar to Table 2.2 and fill in the boxes to indicate the ownership, control and objectives of the organization at different points in its history.

Table 2.2

	Ownership	*Control*	*Objectives*
Stanmead Technical College			
Stanmead Institute of Technology			
Flexington Polytechnic			
Flexington University			
Flexington University Enterprises Limited			

ORGANIZATIONAL AND OPERATIONAL CHANGES IN THE PUBLIC, PRIVATE AND VOLUNTARY SECTORS

Having examined current legal definitions of organizations operating in the UK, we now move on to examine recent changes in the organization and operation of public sector bodies and private sector businesses. As we noted in the introduction to the preceding section, the legal regulation of organizations and their operations has changed gradually over time. This process of change continues today. Our intention in this section is to demonstrate that these changes have altered the way in which private and public sector organizations define and deal with their external environments. Thus privatization and other reforms have exposed many former public sector bodies to competition with the private sector for funds from investors and business from customers. Similarly, in the private sector, internationalization has led the directors and managers of many businesses to redefine their operations on a global scale. In this new environment they no longer see the UK as the sole source of sales, capital or staff. As we hope to demonstrate, these and other changes have had profound implications for our understanding of how these organizations currently work, and how they might operate in the future.

Changes in the public sector

Under the Thatcher and Major administrations changes in government policy fundamentally altered the operation of public sector services and public corporations in the UK. In this section we consider three of the most important changes under the following headings: privatization; deregulation, liberalization and marketization; and financial constraints, commercialization and managerialism.

Privatization

Privatization is a widely used term which has come to be associated with steps to increase private forms of capital ownership, raise public revenue and increase efficiency. The measures introduced in this area have included:

- the sale of public corporations or parts thereof to private sector businesses or investors (e.g. Rover Group to British Aerospace);
- the transfer of public corporations to the private sector through the sale of shares (e.g. British Telecom and British Gas); and
- management or employee buyouts (e.g. National Freight Consortium). (*See* Table 2.3.)

Table 2.3 Major privatizations since 1979

Company	Date	Company	Date
British Petroleum (1)	1979, 1983 and 1987	BAA	1987
British Aerospace	1981	Rover Group (3)	1988
Cable and Wireless	1981	British Steel	1988
Amersham International	1982	National Bus Company (4)	1988
National Freight (2)	1982	General Practice Finance Corp	1989
Britoil	1982	Regional Water Authorities	1989
Associated British Ports	1983	Girobank (5)	1990
Enterprise Oil	1984	Area Electricity Boards and National Grid	1990
Jaguar	1984	National Power and PowerGen	1991
British Telecom	1984	Scottish Hydroelectric	1991
British Shipbuilders (1)	1984 and various other dates	Scottish Power	1991
British Gas	1986	East Midlands Airport	1993
British Airways	1987	National Coal Board	1994
Royal Ordnance (3)	1987	Nuclear Power	Planned
Rolls-Royce	1987	British Nuclear Fuels Ltd	Planned

Notes: (1) Shares in British Petroleum and British Shipbuilders were sold in a number of tranches to different investors at various dates during the 1980s. (2) National Freight shares were sold to a consortium of managers and employees. (3) Royal Ordnance and Rover Group were sold to British Aerospace. (4) The National Bus Company was sold as 72 separate local bus companies. (5) Girobank was sold to the Alliance and Leicester Building Society. (6) The government also divested itself of minority shareholdings in British Sugar, ICL, Ferranti and British Technology Group.

Although in excess of £30 billion has been raised through the sale of these companies, significant costs were incurred preparing these organizations for flotation. In the period preceding each new sale of shares in a former public sector body money was spent on cutbacks and restructuring within these organizations, as well as writing off debt and on occasion financing lengthy industrial disputes with unions (e.g. the miners' strike of 1984–5 and railway disputes in 1994).

Despite the sale of shares to the private sector, the Thatcher and Major governments retained a 'golden share' in many of these companies for the first few years of their operation. This special share gave the government ultimate control over the future direction of a company and could be used to block any takeover attempt which it judged to be against the national interest.

Accompanying transfers of ownership from the public sector to the private sector were other measures involving the transfer or quasi-privatization of public sector services – for example, direct service organizations in local authorities, agencies within the Civil Service, and incorporation status in the higher and further education sectors. These new organizations were formally listed as privately owned, or treated as if they were, even though the assets of these organizations could not be sold without the permission of the appropriate government agency. Ministers within the Thatcher and Major governments believed that by changing the ownership of these organizations in this way managers would be encouraged to adopt a more entrepreneurial, innovative and cost-effective approach to delivering services.

Among public sector services, the most significant form of privatization was the sale of council houses. As a result of legislation introduced in the early 1980s, almost 1.5 million council tenants exercised the right to buy their homes. Annual sales peaked at 226 000 in 1982, but fell to less than half of this level in 1985 and 1986. Between 1986 and 1989, sales increased in each year before falling throughout the late 1980s and early and mid-1990s.

Deregulation, liberalization and marketization

Accompanying changes in the ownership of organizations were measures designed to:

- remove direct governmental control of public corporations and services (*deregulation*);
- promote competition between private and public sector organizations (*liberalization*);
- introduce the discipline of the market place within public sector monopolies (*marketization*).

The intention behind all of these moves was that through competition the quality of service provided would be increased while costs decreased. It was assumed that under these conditions public sector managers would improve their expertise and ensure that resources were directed to improve the services and products demanded by customers. Furthermore, that customer choice would be improved by breaking up public sector monopolies and promoting competition.

Under *deregulation*, the direct influence of government ministers on the definition and direction of public sector corporations was either relaxed, replaced by other systems of control, or became less visible. Under the slogan of 'rolling back the frontier of the state', the traditional model of central government control of management decisions within public sector enterprises was relaxed in many areas. For example, the centralized planning of energy provision by ministers and civil servants within the Department of Energy was gradually replaced by business plans determined by managers within the industries concerned. Similar initiatives are apparent within public sector services where agency status removed many bodies from direct governmental control. Despite these changes, regulation has not been completely removed. In many instances direct control of an industry or service has merely been replaced by other indirect methods of regulation. This trend has been referred to by some commentators as a gradual process of deregulation and re-regulation.

During the 1980s and early 1990s, therefore, the privatization of many public sector utilities was accompanied by the creation of statutory bodies charged with the regulation and policing of these new private sector companies – for example, Ofwat, Ofgas, Oftel and Offer to oversee the operations of the 12 regional water companies, British Gas, British Telecom and the electricity industry respectively. Similarly within the public services, direct governmental control was replaced by a system of financial control. Finally, it is worth noting that, although government ministers in the Thatcher and Major administrations were apt to talk of their success in 'removing the dead hand of government' from the operation of newly privatized companies and public sector services, government influence still affected the decisions of managers and officials within these organizations.

A number of other measures, which we refer to here as *liberalization*, allowed private sector companies into markets traditionally reserved for public sector bodies. Examples of these initiatives included licensing Mercury, British Rail and a number of private cable television companies to provide telecommunication services, the promotion of independent production services in the television and radio broadcasting industries, and the removal of competition controls in the bus industry. The momentum behind these initiatives was increased in the early 1990s by the more active application of competition policy by the European Union. This policy was designed to break up monopolies in any sector of industry, whether public or private.

The most radical of *liberalization* policies was the compulsory competitive tendering (CCT) of functions in many areas of the public sector. As a consequence, the National Health Service, Civil Service and local authorities were required to seek competing tenders (bids from private sector companies as well as estimates from their own workforce) for refuse collection, street and building cleaning, laundry services, vehicle and ground maintenance, the management of leisure facilities and various personnel management functions.

The final set of policy initiatives – *marketization* – attempted to introduce the discipline of the market place in a number of public sector services that for political reasons remained virtual monopolies. Examples of this included the break up of the water, electricity and rail industries prior to privatization, as well as the introduction of an internal market within the NHS. District

Health Authorities and some general practitioners are now allocated funds and are able to shop around to get the most cost-effective service from local and general hospitals.

Another example of attempts to get the public sector organizations to behave like private sector businesses in a competitive market was provided by voucher schemes. Here the customers of public sector bodies were given cash vouchers which could be used to pay for sight tests by opticians and nursery school places.

Financial constraints, commercialization and managerialism

The Thatcher and Major governments believed that public sector services should be encouraged to behave more like their private sector counterparts. In order to achieve this objective, a number of policies were developed and implemented to promote financial prudence, a commercial orientation and so-called professional management practices.

Financial prudence was promoted by the establishment of principles to govern investment decisions and the establishment of financial targets. Examples of particular initiatives in this area included the following.

- The imposition of investment appraisal formula within public sector corporations. For example, prior to privatization British Rail was encouraged to use strict pay-back criteria when planning future capital expenditure. This meant that any investment funds had to be repaid within a short period of time.
- The use of cash limits within the Civil Service and armed forces, together with council tax capping for local authorities.
- The reduction of public sector subsidies covering drug prescription charges, museum and art gallery maintenance and school meals services.

Accompanying these measures to promote financial stringency were other steps designed to foster commercial attitudes and practices (*commercialization*). Thus, a number of public sector services introduced new services which were funded by direct charges to their clients – for example, rapid land searches by local government officers, company information provided by central government agencies, video and books produced by the BBC, and conference facilities within publicly owned buildings. Other public sector bodies went even further and set up separate enterprise companies/trusts which seek to attract external funds either through external sponsorship or joint investment projects involving private and public sector capital.

The final set of initiatives, which we have labelled *managerialism,* aimed to develop the management skills of civil servants and other public sector workers. Examples of these changes included the following.

- Business representatives appointed to the boards of almost all public sector bodies including school governing bodies and the appointment or secondment of professionally qualified managers to run public sector services like NHS hospitals.
- The devolution of management decision making and budgetary controls to cost and profit centres. Under this system each component part of the

organization was required to generate a pre-specified level of profit or operate within centrally determined cost limits. This system replaced a more centralized system of cost and profit controls in which surpluses in one area could be used to subsidize other less economic but socially worthwhile objectives pursued by other departments within the organization.

- A requirement for public sector bodies to produce regular corporate plans specifying objectives and monitoring their achievements against these objectives. In addition, reviews of the performance of these bodies were strengthened by an extension of the role of government-appointed inspectors including the Audit Commission and the National Audit Office.

- A gradual withdrawal from an established series of national systems for determining the pay and conditions of public sector workers through negotiation with trade unions. These national systems were replaced by a more fragmented and less uniform system in which the pay and conditions of public servants were determined through local negotiations with trade unions and unilaterally by local managers.

As previously mentioned a consistent theme running through all of these changes was the apparent desire to emulate the behaviour of private sector organizations. One of the most recent examples of this approach is the introduction of the Citizens' Charter Programme and Charter Mark award scheme.

Exhibit 2.2

The Citizens' Charter

The Citizens' Charter White Paper was published in July 1991. This policy document underlined the themes of quality, choice, standards and value in government policy as applied to all areas of the public sector. The Charter specified six clear principles which it suggested should guide the provision of public services as well as services like gas and electricity that are now in the private sector. The White Paper also set out to encourage public services to develop their own follow-up charters. In order to encourage public sector services to adopt these principles, the government announced its intention to introduce new forms of redress for aggrieved customers of public services. The White Paper also announced the government's intention to establish a Charter Mark which would be awarded to organizations which could demonstrate that they had delivered service to the highest standard in keeping with the Citizens' Charter's six key principles as set out below.

1 Publication of standards of service that the customer can reasonably expect, and of performance against those standards.

2 Evidence that the views of those who use the service have been taken into account when setting standards.

3 Clear information about the range of services provided in clear language.

4 Courteous and efficient customer service, from staff who are normally prepared to identify themselves by name.

5 Well signposted avenues for complaint if the customer is not satisfied, with some means of independent review, wherever possible.

6 Independent validation of performance against standards and a clear commitment to improving value for money.

Organizations which were awarded the Charter Mark were allowed to use the Citizens' Charter logo for up to three years on their stationery, vehicles and promotional material.

Exercise 2.3	Changes in the public sector

By reference to the case study at the beginning of the chapter, list examples of changes in the public sector that have affected Flexington University and those that have not. From the examples of experiences in other areas of the public sector, what changes might the senior managers at Flexington expect to see in years to come?

Changes in the voluntary sector

The voluntary sector was also affected by many of the initiatives outlined above. During the 1980s and early 1990s an increasing range of services tradi- tionally provided by the State were transferred to the voluntary sector. Furthermore, legislation and other policy measures were used to encourage these organizations to embrace the new spirit of commercialism and manage- rialism. Examples of these moves included the flotation of the Abbey National and Halifax Building Societies, the introduction of charity credit cards and the changed approach of many trade unions.

Changes in the private sector

The private sector in the UK, like the public sector, witnessed changes in the ownership and orientation of companies over the last 16 years. Many of these changes were a continuation of established trends – for example, a decline in the size of the agriculture, extraction and manufacturing sectors and an expansion in the size of the service sector, an increase in the number of small firms, and a continuation of growth in the size and importance of large com- panies. Within large businesses these changes were accompanied by a gradual concentration of share ownership within the hands of pension funds and insurance companies.

Other changes had more recent origins. The growing interest in quality and customer service, as well as concerns about business ethics, arguably demon- strated a shift in the orientation and focus of business leaders and their employees. In this section we explore these developments in more detail under the following headings: composition and size; mergers and acquisi- tions; ownership; quality and customer service; and business ethics. It is worth noting that the last of these two changes were not confined to the pri- vate sector and similar changes were observed in the public sector.

Composition and size

Economists traditionally divide the work performed within an economy into three sectors which they refer to as the primary, secondary and tertiary sectors.

- *The primary sector* consists of organizations which extract basic raw mat- erials from the earth and includes agriculture, forestry, mining and fishing.
- *The secondary sector* is comprised of firms which process raw materials into finished products. This category includes manufacturing, construction and energy-producing companies.

● *The tertiary sector* covers the distribution of goods and provision of attendant services. Examples of the types of organization in this sector include hotel and catering, security, financial and banking services.

Since the beginnings of the Industrial Revolution the importance of the primary sector to the British economy has been in relative decline. Although Britain remains self-sufficient in the production of oil and a range of agricultural products, advances in technology and cheaper imports from overseas have combined so that agriculture is now responsible for less than 2 per cent of the total domestic economic output and 5 per cent of employment.

The secondary sector has also been of declining importance within the UK over the last 30 years. Output and employment in this sector peaked in the late 1960s and declined constantly, although at varying rates, thereafter. Meanwhile, the level of employment and output within the service sector expanded throughout the post-war period with the exception of the recession in the early 1990s.

Accompanying changes in the distribution of economic activity within the UK have been changes in the size and organization of private sector companies.

Over the past fifteen years there has been a substantial growth in the number of small firms in the UK. For example, within the industrial sector the proportion of employees employed by companies with less than 100 employees rose from 17 per cent in 1978 to over 24 per cent in 1989. Despite this rapid increase in employment these small firms were less important in terms of their contribution to overall output. Over the same period, their share of overall output within the sector rose from 15 per cent to 19 per cent (Sawyer, 1992). The seeming mismatch between employment and output is largely explained by the economies of scale available to larger companies. Put simply, this means that large companies are able to acquire raw materials more cheaply and arrange their production processes more effectively than their smaller competitors. Thus, although the share of overall employment within the manufacturing sector accounted for by companies with over 5000 employees decreased during the 1980s from 45 per cent to 9 per cent, the proportion of overall output attributable to these firms remained relatively constant. The largest 100 firms in the industrial sector remained responsible for over a third of all production from 1968 to 1989 (Sawyer, 1992).

Exhibit 2.3

Is the decline of the secondary sector a cause for concern?

Economists and politicians have not generally worried about the decline in the importance of the primary sector. Although some have expressed concern about an overreliance on imports in times of international conflict, and others have fears about the future of the countryside if farming is no longer viable, steps to prevent the further decline of the primary sector have not been seen as a political priority.

A more general source of concern and debate has been the continued decline of the secondary or industrial sector. Here economists and politicians differ in their assessment of the present situation and future developments. Those that express concern about the decline in the industrial sector usually raise one or more of the following arguments.

▶

- The decline in the industrial sector within the UK has been more rapid than in other advanced western economies.

- The industrial sector is the main source of wealth generation within the economy. It is here that productivity increases most rapidly.

- It is through the sale of manufactured goods overseas that we are able to raise the money to pay for the import of primary goods and the supply of tertiary services at home.

- The industrial sector provides highly skilled and highly paid jobs which are not available in the hotel, catering, security industries and other elements of the tertiary sector.

- Most research and development activity is undertaken by industrial firms. If the UK loses its own manufacturing base we cannot rely on foreign firms bringing their know-how and new techniques to this country.

In response, those less concerned about the decline of Britain's manufacturing industry raise the following counter-arguments.

- All developed economies have experienced a change in the role and relative importance of their industrial sectors.

- The decline in this sector was more rapid within the UK during the 1980s and 1990s because exports in this sector declined as exports from the North Sea Oil increased. As the overall value of all exports should be equal to the value of imports, an increase in the primary sector will be matched by a decline in another area, in this case manufacturing.

- The tertiary sector, like the industrial sector, includes a wide range of different business activities. While hotel and catering and security services may not produce highly skilled, well paid jobs within profitable businesses, finance, banking, music, video and information technology services do require high skill levels, highly paid staff and considerable investment in research and development if they are to generate high levels of sales and revenue for the country.

- The UK cannot and should not wish to compete with countries which are developing or maintaining their industrial sector through an overreliance on cheap labour and cheap land.

Multinational enterprises

Another element of the changing size and structure of UK businesses has been the rise of the multinational enterprise. The UK economy is more dependent upon the activities of multinational enterprises (MNEs) than almost any other nation in the world. As a proportion of total activity within the domestic economy, the production and sales of British MNEs exceed that of MNEs based in any other country with the exception of the Netherlands. In recent years, this *internationalization* or *globalization* of UK companies has accelerated in response to steps taken to form a single European market and as a reaction to increased international competition from companies in the Far East and America. The first of these pressures has fuelled an increase in cross-border mergers and acquisitions within the European Union as companies have sought to establish a wider operating base with outlets in many of the member states. The second set of influences has prompted a number of companies to relocate their operations to areas with greater sales opportunities or lower operating costs. According to Reich (1991), these pressures may lead to the gradual rundown of UK MNE operations in their home country. In other countries this phenomenon has been referred to as the *doughnut effect* – MNEs with small or nominal head office facilities in their home country while the bulk of their investment, operations and employment are located overseas.

Among the foreign-owned MNEs operating in the UK, the largest number have their origins in the USA although this position may be challenged in the future as an increasing number of Japanese companies have decided to locate their European operations in the UK. The influx of these organizations has had a profound effect upon the managerial policies adopted by UK-based organizations. Indeed in the 1980s, it was common to hear talk of the *japanization* of British industry.

The arrival of an MNE is often welcomed by the government of the host country as it will generally involve new investment and the creation of employment. Furthermore, MNEs may bring new technology and management expertise. In order to attract MNEs, however, governments – both national and local – often offer substantial investment subsidies and tax exemptions; indeed, the incentives offered to Nissan, Toyota and other Japanese companies have often approached a third of their set-up costs. Once the new facilities have been established future decisions about investment and employment at that site tend to be taken by people outside the country concerned. For this reason MNEs have been criticized for four reasons. First, it is argued that MNEs limit their overseas operations to low-technology and low-skill tasks. Second, it is claimed that MNEs will price their products and move money between countries in order to avoid taxation which may disadvantage the host country. Third, it has been suggested that these organizations are like seagulls. They land in a new area, gain sustenance from local grants and subsidies and then take flight the moment trading conditions worsen or larger grants become available elsewhere. Finally, it has been argued that the large size of these companies and their spread of operations make it impossible for national governments to regulate business behaviour effectively.

Mergers and acquisitions

An important cause of changes in the structure of private sector industry and the size of firms has been merger and acquisition activity. There is a technical difference between a merger (when two companies fuse together to form a new company) and acquisitions (where one firm takes over another); in keeping with the common use of these words, however, the following section makes no distinction between these terms.

The number and value of acquisitions have fluctuated substantially from year to year. Over the last 90 years, the UK has experienced five waves of acquisition activity – the 1920s, 1967–69, 1972–73, 1984–89 and 1993–96. Each of these waves of activity has corresponded with an upturn in the general fortunes of the UK economy, but the magnitude of each successive wave has grown larger. Even accounting for inflation, the value of merger transactions has increased with each surge of acquisition activity, with companies often prepared to take on substantial debts to finance takeovers.

Mergers and acquisitions are usually classified under one of three headings according to the form of the takeover. *Horizontal mergers* involve companies acquiring other firms engaged in similar activities, e.g. a high street grocery chain purchasing another chain of stores. *Vertical mergers* refer to situations in which an organization buys a controlling interest in its suppliers or customers, e.g. a car manufacturer buys a car dealership or steel producer. The third category is known as a *diversified merger* and involves the purchase of a company engaged in a seemingly unrelated business, e.g. a cigarette company buys shares in an insurance company. Between 1970 and 1990, approximately 65 per cent of mergers in the UK were horizontal, 30 per cent were diversified and 5 per cent were vertical (Hunt and Downing, 1991).

In addition to differences in the form of merger activity there are also differences in the approach adopted by the bidding company. Thus takeovers may be hostile, friendly or contested bids. Similarly the company formed by the merger of two organizations may result in complete integration, the slotting in of a new division or loose inclusion within a holding company.

Accompanying the merger waves of the late 1980s and mid-1990s there was also an increased interest in forms of collaboration between companies that did not necessarily involve one company purchasing another. The development of franchising, licensing and joint venture arrangements often provided a formal basis for collaborative arrangements between a large number of organizations. Indeed a number of companies developed the technique to such an extent that they were able to build large business empires on the basis of these arrangements, e.g. McDonald's, the Body Shop.

Under a licensing or franchising arrangement the right to use various patented techniques, trademarks or copyright-protected materials is sold to another organization for a specified period of time. For example, many Benetton shops are operated under franchise arrangements under which the owner of a particular shop is required to purchase goods from Benetton and to sell these items in a specified manner.

By contrast, joint venture arrangements tend to be reserved for specified short-term projects in which two or more partners agree to share resources and expertise in order to develop or sell a particular product or service. Airbus Industries provides a good example of this phenomenon; in this case four European aerospace companies agreed to share the costs of developing a range of European civilian aircraft.

Ownership

The ownership of British companies has gradually changed over the past one hundred years or more as owner-managed companies have developed to become large PLCs whose shares and financial resources are provided by other institutions. Today, the pattern of corporate ownership in the UK can now be characterized as a complex web of interlinked share holdings and finance arrangements. Companies no longer just buy each other's products and services; they also often provide finance for each other through shareholdings, joint ventures and other co-operative arrangements. This gradual trend towards the institutional ownership of UK industry continued throughout the 1980s, despite the much publicized desire of the UK government to promote share ownership among the general population. While the number of individual shareholders increased dramatically from 7 per cent of the population in 1979 to 25 per cent in 1991, the value of these shares as a proportion of all shareholdings decreased (*see* Table 2.4).

Table 2.4 Percentage distribution of shareholdings in British PLCs by value

	1963	1975	1981	1992
Individuals	54.0	37.5	28.2	20.0
Non-profit making bodies	2.1	2.3	2.2	2.2
Public sector	1.5	3.6	3.0	1.2
Banks	1.3	0.7	0.3	0.2
Insurance companies	10.0	15.9	20.5	20.7
Pension funds	6.4	16.8	26.7	31.1
Unit trusts	1.3	4.1	3.6	5.7
Other financial institutions	11.3	10.5	6.8	2.8
Companies	5.1	3.0	5.1	3.3
Overseas	7.0	5.6	3.6	12.8

Source: 'The 1992 Share Register Survey' in *Economic Trends*, No 446, August 1992, pp 90–8, Office for National Statistics. Crown Copyright 1992. Reproduced by permission of the Controller of HMSO and the Office for National Statistics.

A recent survey by the government's Office for National Statistics revealed that 54 per cent of individual shareholders have a small number of shares in only one company, usually one which has been recently privatized (HMSO, 1992). Furthermore, many of these investors sell their shares within the first year of acquisition in order to make a quick profit.

Despite the increased value of shareholdings by institutional investors, John Scott has shown on the basis of data from the UK and USA that share owners rarely control a sufficient percentage of the company's shares to influence the decisions of the board of directors (Scott, 1985). In his studies he has demonstrated that, as the role of institutional investors has increased, these organizations have not sought to gain a controlling influence over the management of companies. Thus few companies are directly controlled by their owners. This research supports the findings of an earlier study by Berle and Means (1932) which suggested that as companies have grown in size over the last one hundred years a split has occurred between those that own the organization and those who manage its day-to-day operations – *the divorce of ownership and control*. On the basis of this research it has been suggested that large companies are apt to act in the interests of their managers rather than their shareholders. Other research has indicated that one consequence is that managers are likely to concentrate on increasing sales, the size of their companies, or more sceptically their own salaries including money derived from short-term share options, rather than focus on the long-term viability of the company.

Other writers have suggested that, despite the divorce of ownership and control, there are still powerful pressures on company directors to ensure that they manage their firms in the interests of shareholders. These pressures arise from the threat of a hostile takeover by another company or the withdrawal of financial support by institutional investors. In the UK, there is also said to be a culture of *financial short termism* which exerts considerable pressure on company directors to ensure that their company's shares are performing well even if investment in research, development and training has to be sacrificed as a consequence (Hutton, 1995). This culture is further supported by the practice of allowing key individuals, usually with the same cultural and educational background, to hold board-level positions in several companies. This means that similar approaches are adopted in seemingly very different companies.

Customer culture

During the 1950s, 1960s and 1970s, a number of writers commented on the emergence of very large, private sector companies which had been able to grow through selling standardized products which were assembled by unskilled and semi-skilled labour. These products were then sold to the emerging mass markets of the developed world through the use of advertising and other mass marketing techniques. This approach to the organization of business operations was referred to as *Fordism* in recognition of the influence of the Ford Motor company in the development of this approach. Although this approach to the organization of companies and industries offered the prospect of cheaper goods and services for customers in the western world, it was not without its critics. Indeed, a number of writers in the 1960s and 1970s suggested that these large companies failed to serve the interests of their customers (Packard, 1957; Galbraith, 1967). In particular, it was alleged that these companies manufactured products which would not last very long in order to ensure that their customers came back to buy replacements at regular intervals. Furthermore, it was suggested that these organizations used mass advertising to promote changes in fashion and to encourage customers to buy products they did not really need. This, it was argued, contributed to the development of an increasingly *consumerist* society. Finally, it was argued that the senior managers of these organizations decided what customers would want and used the dominant position of their companies within specific industries to ensure that customers were forced to buy their products.

In more recent times, other commentators have claimed that this traditional Fordist approach to production is becoming less widespread as western companies have been forced to respond to increased international business competition, changes in technology and more sophisticated customer tastes. They maintain that in place of the traditional Fordist model a new *post-Fordist* model of industrial organization has emerged (*see* Table 2.5). Here companies, individually or through close links with other organizations, concentrate their efforts on supplying the needs of specific groups of customers by using highly skilled workers to produce specialized products using adaptable machines. These organizations make extensive use of new technology to identify changing consumer tastes and to contact potential customers through targeted advertising or direct marketing via mailshot or telephone. This highly focused approach means that these organizations are highly reliant on accurate information and marketing analyses to ensure that they do not waste materials producing goods that nobody wants. This information is constantly fed back to employees so that they can adapt products to meet each new change in customer fashion.

Table 2.5 A comparison of Fordism and post-Fordism

	Fordism	*Post-Fordism*
Market	Mass markets of largely similar consumers	Niche markets of customers with specific needs
	Manufacturers dictate to retailers and consumers	Consumers and retailers dictate to manufacturers
Product	Limited range of standardized products	Large variety of specialized products
Production method	Large-scale assembly line operations using machines dedicated to specific tasks	Small-scale batch operations using machines which can be adapted for a number of tasks
Research & development	Separated from production and concentrates on developing new products	Linked to production and concentrates on constantly developing and improving products
Inputs	Material intensive	Material saving, information intensive
Work	Strict division of labour between semi-skilled and unskilled employees who complete manual work and managers who undertake mental work	Highly skilled workers with an integration of mental and manual work More routine work performed by sub-contractors and suppliers
Management	Extensive managerial hierarchies	Limited managerial hierarchies
Competitive strategy	Compete by working at full capacity	Compete through selling high-quality, innovative products

Whether this post-Fordist approach is as widespread as some commentators would suggest remains in doubt; however, there is some evidence that elements of this new approach have been adopted by many large and medium-sized companies. In particular it has been noted that many British companies implemented total quality management programmes during the 1980s and 1990s. These initiatives were designed to promote a greater understanding of a customer-orientated culture among the staff of their organizations.

Business ethics

Interest in business ethics re-emerged in the late 1980s and early 1990s, after a decade or more of neglect, in response to a number of scandals, scares and disasters which rocked many organizations and industries. Among the most publicized of these pressures were the following:

- Corruption was exposed in a number of well publicized incidents involving the fraudulent behaviour of senior company executives (e.g. the collapse of Barlow Clowes, BCCI, Maxwell Communications, Barings Bank, as well as *insider dealing* in the Blue Arrow and Guinness Affairs).

- Environmental concerns confronted many managers for the first time as evidence grew of climatic change as a consequence of the *greenhouse effect* and *ozone depletion*. Similarly, many powerful campaigning groups developed to voice their concern about the squandering of natural resources and importance of conservation (e.g. Friends of the Earth, Greenpeace and the Campaign for the Conservation of Rural England).

- Safety standards and enforcement were questioned after a catalogue of disasters revealed the often lamentable state of safety procedures within British industry (e.g. Piper Alpha disaster in the North Sea, the Kings Cross Underground fire, the sinking of the *Herald of Free Enterprise* and *the Marchioness*, as well as the Clapham and Purley railway crashes).

- Low levels of job security, long hours of work, low pay and a lack of formal mechanisms for employees to voice their concerns about the way in which they are managed were exposed in a number of surveys of working conditions in the UK (NACAB, 1993).

- Health scares forced many organizations to review their practices (e.g. salmonella in eggs, BSE in beef, listeria in cheese, repetitive strain injury (RSI), stress-related illnesses, passive smoking and the effects of VDU usage).

- Evidence was revealed about the prejudice and discrimination faced by older workers, homosexuals, disabled persons and other disadvantaged minority groups within the UK.

In response to these scandals and scares a number of bodies have developed codes of conduct to guide the behaviour of managers and employees in public and private sector organizations. In certain circumstances these codes may be used as the basis for bringing disciplinary proceedings against employees. On occasions they may also be used as evidence in court proceedings.

Exercise 2.4   ## Changes in the private sector

How have the changes outlined above affected the behaviour of a private sector organization known to you? Try to be specific about the measures and their effects.

ANALYSING THE OBJECTIVES OF SPECIFIC ORGANIZATIONS

In this chapter we have outlined a number of general trends which have affected specific private and public sector organizations to varying degrees in recent years. Although we may recognize some of these trends we need to adopt a more refined form of analysis if we wish to gain a better understanding of the current and future operation of our own organizations.

In order to facilitate this task the following section describes two analytical techniques. The first – *stakeholder analysis* – concentrates on defining those key groups who have an influence on the determination of an organization's objectives. The second model – *the wheel of objectives* – is designed to enable members of an organization to define the objectives which have been adopted.

Stakeholders

The objectives of most organizations are rarely determined by their senior managers alone. In practice, the details of what is planned and what is actually done are decided through a process of acceptance, compromise, negotiation and accommodation between a number of key groups with a vested interest in the organization (*stakeholders*). One way of gaining a better understanding of this process of objective formulation is to identify the stakeholders. Within political parties it is often easy to spot these groups; however, within other organizations the composition of stakeholder groups is more fluid and apt to change according to events.

Most, if not all, stakeholder groups in the private sector have a common interest in the profitable operation of the business. In the public sector the situation is more complex, with the expectations of some groups in direct conflict. Examples of typical stakeholder groups in the public and private sector are listed in Table 2.6 on p 50.

Each of the groups listed in Table 2.6 may have different priorities; for example, within a local council increases in the pay of manual workers may be promoted by the unions, but resisted by the taxpayers, managers and elected representatives. Similar divisions may be apparent among stakeholders in the private sector. The decision to grant company directors special share options may be supported by large institutional shareholders and the directors themselves, but criticized by customers, small shareholders and government officials.

| Exercise 2.5 | **Identifying the stakeholders** |

Identify the stakeholders either in an organization known to you or in Flexington University.

Using any form of diagram, map out the groups that influence the organization's objectives. Try to give examples of the different priorities of these groups.

Defining objectives

A number of management texts suggest that senior managers should begin the process of planning to meet future objectives by defining what is important to

Table 2.6 Stakeholder groups

Public sector	Private sector
• Elected representatives	• Shareholders and other financial investors
• Public servants	• Directors
• Senior managers	• Senior managers
• Employees	• Employees
• Trade unions	• Trade unions
• Taxpayers	• Competitors
• Consumers	• Customers
• Lobby groups	• Pressure groups
• Political parties	• Suppliers
• Government inspectors	• Industry regulators
• National and European government ministers	• National and European government ministers

their organization in terms of the standards, behaviour and attitudes of staff. When agreed, this generalized statement of priorities is often set out in a formal written document and referred to as a statement of shared values or aspirations. Having determined what senior managers believe members of the organization value, the next stage involves the more detailed definition of the future aims of the organization. Once again the results of this exercise are often written down and circulated to staff in the form of a vision or mission statement. In order to ensure that the message contained within this document is effectively conveyed to the staff concerned, management consultants frequently advise that this statement should be short, ideally less than four sentences long, and written in clear and comprehensible language.

The next stage in this process of formal planning is the detailed specification of medium-term (three to five years) objectives for the different units, departments and groups within the organization. In many organizations this activity results in the annual production or revision of a corporate plan specifying what has to be achieved, by which date and by whom. In other organizations, resource limitations and the rapid pace of change may mean that it is inappropriate to set out objectives in such a formal manner. Instead it may be considered more appropriate to allow objectives to evolve through a process of more or less formal understandings or agreements between managers and their subordinates.

Whichever method is used to specify medium-term objectives, if they are to be meaningful, it is important that they should be SMARTA – an acronym used to refer to the following six features of effectively drafted objectives.

- *Specific* – clearly and unambiguously stated so that there is no confusion on the part of the individuals and groups required to achieve these objectives.

- *Measurable* – capable of objective quantification so that managers will know when the target has been met.

- *Achievable* – the goal can be accomplished by members of the organization.

- *Realistic* – the objectives take account of the circumstances and competing priorities facing the organization.

- *Timely* – the objective can be achieved within the specified time frame.

- *Agreed* – understood and accepted by everyone with direct responsibility for achieving the stated goal.

Once the process of defining objectives has been completed, the next stage is to ensure that an appropriate course of action has been devised to make sure that these goals are realized. Formal statements setting out how these steps will be taken are often referred to as strategy documents or action plans. Finally, it is often suggested that an annual review of progress be undertaken to check whether the objectives have been achieved or revised in the light of changes in the business environment.

Despite the obvious logic of the process outlined above, research evidence suggests that in practice the objectives of most organizations are rarely committed to paper or widely communicated. It is quite common for objectives to be poorly defined, unstated or only discernable in retrospect. Perhaps most importantly, there may be a considerable difference between senior managers' stated objectives for the organization, and the goals other employees appear to be pursuing. With these problems in mind, *the wheel of objectives* has been developed to make sense of the goals of an organization.

In order to define the objectives of an organization, division or department with no formally stated objectives or a poorly defined values or mission statement, it may be useful to plot the assumed goals on the chart set out in Fig 2.1. Using this chart it should be possible to undertake one or more of the following forms of analysis.

- Define the current priorities of senior managers, employees and other stakeholders inside and outside the organization.

- By combining the current priorities, provide an overall assessment of the objectives actually pursued over recent years by the organization as a whole or constituent divisions, departments and groups.

- Measure the differences between objectives as formally stated by senior managers and the informal or unstated objectives as determined by individuals in constituent divisions, departments or groups of the organization.

- Evaluate the organization's recent success in achieving its stated or unstated objectives.

Fig 2.1 A wheel of objectives

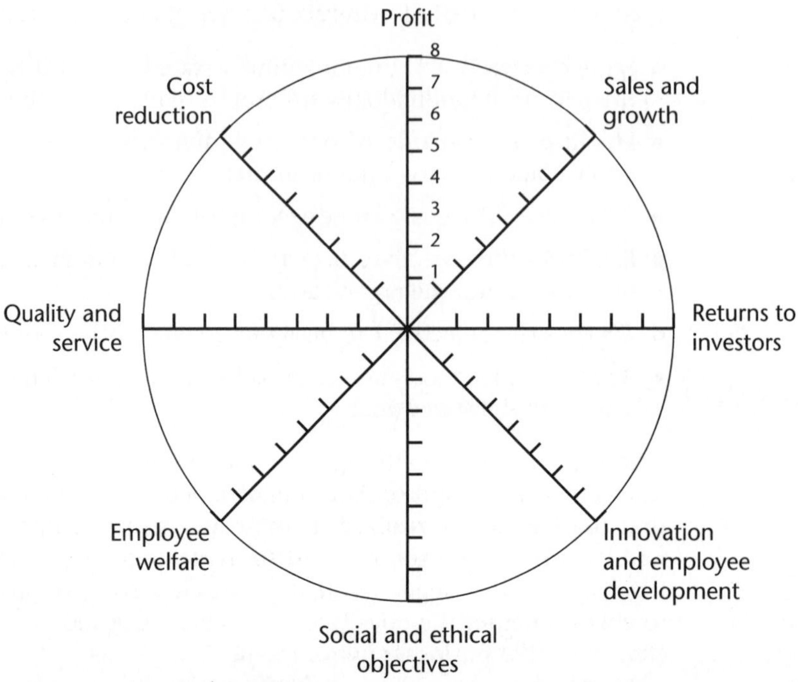

These last two forms of analysis may help managers and employees to draw up action plans to bridge the gap, maintain the close fit, or deal with the difference in other ways.

| Exercise 2.6 | ## Defining an organization's objectives |

Obtain a copy of an organization's mission statement, or any other declaration of overall corporate objectives (i.e. an interview with a senior manager). Drawing on the information obtained from one of these sources, rank from 1 to 8 the profit, growth and social objectives of the organization. A score of 8 should be attached to the most important objectives and a score of 0 or 1 to the least important. If two or more objectives are given equal weight then give them an equal ranking score.

Once you have a rank for each objective, transfer these scores to a blank wheel of objectives and draw a line between the appropriate points on each strut. When you have completed this task, repeat the exercise basing your scores upon your own current personal experience of the organization. When you draw the line connecting the points for the second part of this exercise be sure to use a different coloured pen.

Next, consider what you feel should be the overall objectives of the organization and rank these objectives using the same procedure.

Finally, by reference to the completed diagram, list the main areas of difference between the stated objectives and your own view of what is happening and what should be happening. What could be done to bridge the gaps revealed by your diagram?

SUMMARY AND CONCLUSION

In this chapter we have described and analysed some of the principal differences between organizations in terms of their ownership, organization and objectives. More specifically we have sought to demonstrate that private companies, voluntary bodies and public services adopt different forms of organization and pursue distinctive objectives. Thus the directors and managers of large multinationals are apt to show more concern for the interests of their shareholders and other financial investors than people in positions of power within charities, trade unions and other voluntary bodies. Similarly, officials within public sector organizations are more likely than the managers of small businesses to place an emphasis on the concerns of political parties and pressure groups.

Meanwhile, few of the shareholders in large UK-based companies own sufficient shares to directly influence the policies pursued by the company's senior managers, in the public sector politicians and their appointees continue to exert considerable influence over state-owned agencies and other services. Even newly privatized companies and deregulated services continue to be subject to some direct government control, albeit in a less direct and effective form.

As this discussion has shown, the nature of the external environment confronting specific organizations in the public, private and voluntary sectors is likely to vary significantly. Thus, the range of options open to the managers and employees planning a response in these organizations to external changes is likely to be constrained in different ways. For example, the managers of private sector multinationals may choose to react to poor trading conditions, increasing labour costs, or interventionist legislation by moving their business operations to another country. By contrast managers in the public and voluntary sectors do not generally enjoy the same freedoms.

In addition, the decisions of managers within a large private company are frequently influenced by concerns about their organization's share price and financial performance. While public sector managers also have to retain the confidence and support of their backers if they experience difficulties, they are rarely faced with the same threats of an aggressive takeover or the withdrawal of funds.

For these reasons it is important to have a fuller understanding of the ownership and objectives of an organization before beginning the task of reviewing the possible problems and pressures in its external environment. To ensure that this understanding is based on an analysis of the unique influences and particular objectives of a specific organization, this chapter ended by outlining how to identify the stakeholders in an organization and their influence on the range of objectives it pursues.

LIBRARY
BISHOP BURTON COLLEGE
BEVERLEY HU17 8QG

CHAPTER 3

The product market

INTRODUCTION

As we saw in the opening chapter of this book, organizations exist to produce goods and services. The way in which they produce these, and their ability to find customers will in the longer term determine the success of the organization. It is through the matching of the capabilities of an organization with the demands of its customers, therefore, that employees within the organization can ensure not only their own economic survival, but also the satisfaction of the demands of other key stakeholders.

Over recent years a number of writers and commentators have argued that this key interaction between the organization and the market it serves has become more problematic. It has been suggested that customers have become more demanding and that competition between organizations has increased, forcing managers and their employees to place a greater emphasis on the development of capabilities which more closely meet the needs of their customers. In addition, new markets have emerged, whether defined in terms of geography or consumer taste, which place different demands upon the organization's members.

FOCUS AND SCOPE

The aim of this chapter is to examine the operation of organizations' product markets in more detail. To this end we begin by outlining what is meant by the terms 'goods' and 'services'. We then move on to consider the key features of different types of market and the industries which serve them. The chapter concludes with an outline of some of the choices and constraints facing managers confronted with the need to develop the goods and services they offer.

LEARNING OBJECTIVES

Once you have read this chapter and completed the associated exercises, you should be able to:

- define the key features of goods and services;
- describe different market environments;
- outline the industrial position of an organization; and
- comment on some of the options available to an organization when responding to changing market conditions.

CASE STUDY

Fine Fragrances Ltd

Fine Fragrances Ltd is an established toiletries company which produces a range of specialist soaps, talcum powders, bath oils and salts. The company was formed by Richard and Amanda Herbert (a husband and wife team) in the mid-1950s and grew slowly but steadily during its first 40 years of operations. This growth was fuelled by increasing demand from a customer base of newly affluent consumers who sought out the company's products to give to friends and relatives as presents. Over this period the company developed a reputation for selling at a premium price high quality soaps and related products which appealed to middle-aged and older women. Today, typical products include the 'Heritage Line' of gift soap sets, scented with Lily of the Valley and Evening Primrose Oil wrapped in lace and sold in highly decorated enamel tins.

Fine Fragrances Ltd currently employs a total of 120 staff of whom 100 work at a large head office and factory site in Solihull, West Midlands. The remaining 20 staff are employed as travelling sales and marketing staff and it is their job to ensure that chemists, supermarkets and corner shops across the United Kingdom stock and promote the company's products.

The company's reliance on the domestic gifts market has meant that much of the year is dedicated to building up stock for the peak periods of demand in the run-up to Christmas and Mothers' Day. Furthermore, the small scale of operations has meant that the firm cannot afford a large advertising budget and therefore limits its promotional activity to occasional adverts in women's magazines and specialist trade journals for grocers and pharmacists.

In the early 1990s concern about the company's declining level of sales and increased competition from a number of continental companies led the now elderly Richard and Amanda Herbert to hire David Blackburn to take over as Managing Director.

David was recruited from Supersoap, a large multinational toiletries manufacturer, where he had been employed as a marketing executive and product manager. In his previous job, David had overseen the development and promotion of a range of specialist soaps, shower gels and shampoos targeted at the growing sports and leisure markets. In addition to taking a role in defining the image of these products, David was also responsible for their initial advertising for which he had a budget of £1 million.

On his arrival at Fine Fragrances, David was anxious to make an impression and to begin work on redefining the goods and services the company offered. One of his first actions was to hire two of his former colleagues from the marketing department at Supersoap. Their job was to undertake a programme of market research to determine the company's current market and industry position, as well as producing recommendations for new product and market developments.

GOODS AND SERVICES

So far in this chapter we have used the term product to refer to any item which is made by an organization and sold to a consumer. Within this general category, however, there is a wide range of variation. The demands facing the managers and employees of an organization producing cars or televisions are unlike those facing similar individuals involved in the delivery of financial and professional services. In order to analyse some of these differences in more detail the following section focuses on the important distinction between goods and services.

The distinction between goods and services is common in many strategy and marketing texts and is used to draw attention to aspects of these different types of product which will affect the way in which members of an organization deal with their customers (see Table 3.1). Put simply, goods are physical products which exist independently of the people who make them. By contrast, services tend to be rather ephemeral and difficult to separate from their producers.

Table 3.1 The key features of goods and services

Goods	Services
Tangibility. The good has a physical presence and may be examined directly by potential customers before deciding to buy.	*Intangibility*. The service is ephemeral and therefore potential customers cannot normally gain direct experience.
Separability. It is possible to separate the good from the people that make it; therefore the product can be consumed in any location at any time.	*Inseparability*. It is only possible to experience the service in the presence of the provider.
Non-perishable. Goods can normally be produced in advance of consumption and stored until needed.	*Perishable*. Services cannot be produced in advance and stored until needed.
Homogeneous. The quality of a good can be standardized so that within reasonable limits all the items produced are the same (homogeneous).	*Heterogeneous*. Because the customer and provider are both part of the product, it is difficult to standardize services and as a consequence there will tend to be greater variation (heterogeneity).

As Table 3.1 shows, managing service delivery will place special demands on the employees and managers of an organization.

The *intangible* nature of services means that the reputation of the organization and the products it provides are very important in attracting new customers. Customers can normally only build up their own independent view of the relative quality of a service provider when they have tried a number of alternative suppliers. In the case of a hairdresser this may happen relatively quickly; however, with medical and educational services it is rare for patients or students to submit themselves to two operations or two degree courses in order to evaluate quality. Because of these constraints reputation is an important criterion which customers can use when choosing between service providers.

The level of *product separability* also has implications for the management of employees. A company which makes cars does not necessarily need to locate its manufacturing activities in the same geographical area as its customers. However, many service organizations will need to ensure that their staff can have direct contact with their customers. For example, it would be impossible to have a haircut without the barber or hairstylist being present in the same room and at the same time as his or her client. This geographical imperative has been overcome by the providers of some services who use telecommunications technology to remove the need for the customer and provider to be in the same area or country. For example, a number of banks have established telephone-based financial services which allow account clerks to be based many miles from their customers. However, these arrangements do not remove the requirement for the staff and customers to be in contact with one another at the same point in time.

The varying degree of *perishability* between goods and services has further implications for the management of staff. The makers of goods can continue to make their products even when there are no immediate customers. In the case of Fine Fragrances Ltd the soaps it produces can be placed in stock in preparation for short-term peaks or longer term increases in consumer demand. However, for service providers fluctuations in demand cannot be accommodated in this way and producers will therefore be forced to find ways of varying the number and types of staff they employ to accommodate shifts in the demand for their products.

Differences in the way in which services and goods are produced also have implications for the maintenance and enhancement of an organization's product quality. With goods, unlike many services, it is possible to carry out inspections during and after production to ensure that the final customer is satisfied with what they have bought. As a consequence if an employee lacks the skills required to produce a particular item, makes a mistake, or is disruptive, the problem can often be rectified without the customer's knowledge. With the provision of services not only is this not possible, but it is also worth noting that the way in which the service is provided will have a bearing on the customer's overall satisfaction. In these situations customers will usually expect staff to provide reliable, prompt, knowledgeable and courteous service. This emphasis on staff attitudes and behaviour means that managers will need to ensure that their employees are not only skilled, but are also dedicated to providing a high standard of service.

Finally, because service delivery can rarely be monitored constantly, managers in these organizations will tend to be more reliant than goods manufacturers on building and sustaining a culture of high trust with their employees. In practice this means developing a climate of opinion in which managers, employees and customers feel that they can trust one another. Without this trust it will be difficult for managers to predict what their employees will do when supplying customers. This uncertainty will add to the problems and costs associated with the maintenance and enhancement of any image customers may hold of the organization as a high quality provider.

The goods/service mix

Very few organizations produce only goods or services. Most organizations produce a mixture of these two forms of product. For example, Fine Fragrances Ltd produces a good in the form of its soaps and toiletries, but also provides a service through the promotional and marketing work of its sales force.

To reflect the balance between services and goods a spectrum may be used to illustrate different mixes in the provision of a wide range of products. As Fig 3.1 demonstrates it is not just service organizations that have to deal with the special demands imposed by managing service delivery. At one end of the spectrum are a number of manufacturing organizations which, despite their focus on producing goods, will also employ service staff to deliver and when necessary repair faulty items. At the other end of the spectrum are organizations which, although dedicated to providing a service, will also provide their customers with some form of product, even if it is merely to verify that the service has been received. Between these two extremes are a range of organizations where the enjoyment of a particular product or service is dependent upon the service which accompanies it.

Figure 3.1 should not be seen as inferring that the split between goods and service provision is static and unchanging. For particular consumer demands there will often be a choice between different combinations of goods and services. For example, undergraduate education may be provided as a service – in the form of lectures, tutorials and individually marked assignments – or as a good – through correspondence courses and computer-assessed multiple-choice examinations.

Market definition

Having discussed the different features of goods and services we now turn to consider how the market for these products can be defined and analysed. Here we hope to demonstrate that in the short term the way in which managers and employees define the markets for their products will have a significant impact on the way in which these items are packaged, marketed and distributed. In the longer term, definitions of the organization's principal product markets will affect the products it chooses to develop and ultimately the success or otherwise of the enterprise.

Traditional approaches to market definition focus on the concept of substitution. Here goods and services are treated as belonging to the same market if either customers or industry experts believe that they can be substituted for one another. Following this line of reasoning and returning to the case study example, we can see that the 'Heritage Line' belongs to the soaps market because most customers will readily buy another brand of soap if they cannot buy the Fine Fragrances brand.

However, the 'Heritage Line' could also be said to belong to the gifts market. The company's heavy reliance on sales at Christmas and on Mothers' Day may mean that many of the company's potential customers would readily buy gift-wrapped chocolates, jewellery or other trinkets as a substitute for the soap.

Fig 3.1 The goods/services spectrum. The proportion of goods and services in a range of typical purchases

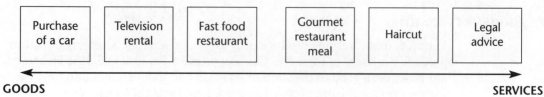

| Purchase of a car | Television rental | Fast food restaurant | Gourmet restaurant meal | Haircut | Legal advice |

GOODS   SERVICES

The choice of market, whether soaps or gifts, will have implications for the way in which Fine Fragrances prices, places and promotes its products. If the company chooses to define the product as part of the soaps market, then the price will have to be fixed at a level which is competitive with other brands. Adopting this approach, it would also seem sensible to continue distributing the product via supermarkets and pharmacies, while promoting and advertising the product in women's magazines, etc.

If, on the other hand, the company decides to place a greater emphasis on the gifts market, price may become less critical and other distribution channels may appear more appropriate. For example, the company might decide to promote the product via gift catalogues and the gift sections of large department stores, museums and country houses.

In the case of the 'Heritage Line' of soaps it is fairly clear that Fine Fragrances is offering this product to two markets simultaneously. However, this case also illustrates the problems associated with market definition. These problems may be even more pronounced in other product and service markets. In a famous *Harvard Business Review* article, Leavitt argued that the decline of the railroad industry in the United States stemmed directly from poor market definition by senior managers within the industry.

> They let others take customers away from them because they assumed themselves to be in the railroad business rather than the transportation business. The reason they defined their industry wrong was because ... they were product orientated instead of customer orientated. (Leavitt, 1975:1)

Following Leavitt's warning, a number of marketing specialists have suggested that it is useful to think of markets in terms of the characteristics of the potential purchaser as well as the nature of the product or service which is on offer. By defining markets in this way it is possible not only to gain a more accurate picture of the target customers, but also to consider the particular needs of constituent groups or segments (*see* Table 3.2 on p 60).

Answers to the questions posed by the list of criteria in Table 3.2 can be gained from group discussions with current and potential customers, surveys of the organization's existing customer base, independent research by marketing companies, or by canvassing the opinions of staff within the organization.

Although this activity will not necessarily lead to robust and enduring definitions, the act of engaging in this type of review should enable staff to appreciate better the present and potential market position of the organization.

Exercise 3.1   Defining markets and market segments

With reference to one of the goods or services offered by an organization known to you, use the list in Table 3.2 to define the market within which it operates.

Table 3.2 Some criteria for market definition and segmentation

Criteria for market definition	Examples of consumer markets	Examples of questions to be addressed
Characteristics of people and organizations currently in the market and potential customers	Age, sex, race, income, family size, lifecycle stage, location, lifestyle	• What is the sex, age, race, etc. of people?
Where the product is bought and how it is used	Location of purchase, purpose of use, importance of purchase	• Is the product sold in supermarkets, small shops or via mail order? • Is the product used on its own or with other items?
Users' needs and preferences for product characteristics	Product similarity, price preferences, brand preferences, characteristics and quality	• Are customers loyal to brands or price sensitive? • What desired features criteria are used when choosing a product?

Source: adapted from Johnson, G and Scholes, K (1993:102) *Exploring Corporate Strategy: Text and Cases*, Prentice-Hall, Hemel Hempstead. Reprinted by permission of Prentice-Hall.

MARKET ENVIRONMENTS

Once managers and employees within the organization have defined the nature of the product they wish to make, and determined the boundaries of the market they intend to serve, the next stage is to review the level of competition which exists within this market. By gaining a fuller understanding of the dynamics of this market environment, they should be better placed to appreciate the choices and constraints they will face when attempting to sell this product.

Traditionally, neo-classical economists have explained the behaviour of companies by reference to the market environments they face. They suggest that the ability of the company's owners and managers to set prices and determine the quantity of the goods and services they supply is usually limited by the level of competition they face within their chosen markets. In highly competitive markets the company will have little choice but to match the standards and prices offered by other firms. Where there is little competition, however, the company's owners and managers will have more latitude. Put simply they will be in a better position to set their prices above their costs and make substantial profits.

To reflect the importance of the level of competition in explaining the behaviour of companies, economists have developed a number of terms to describe different market environments.

Monopoly

Monopoly is used to refer to situations where one firm controls the total supply of a good or service to a number of buyers. Here the supplying firm is free to set the price for its products at whatever level the market can bear. Monopoly positions develop when one company owns the physical or intellectual resources needed to produce a particular good or service. Because of the enormous power wielded by monopoly suppliers, governments in almost all western economies have developed statutory controls or regulatory mechanisms to limit the damaging effects of these arrangements.

Although it is commonly assumed that monopoly arrangements are a bad thing this is not necessarily always the case. As the Austrian economist Schumpeter (1987) has argued it is only large organizations in monopoly positions who have sufficiently stable market positions and the necessary reserves to invest in long-term research and development. Furthermore, the extra revenues available to these companies provide an incentive for new competitors to enter the market and challenge established firms. Without this incentive many economies would lack the rewards to promote innovative and entrepreneurial activity.

There are few pure monopolies in the UK although a number of former and current public corporations, including the regional water and electricity companies, operate virtual monopolies. On an international scale De Beers controls a sizeable portion of the world diamond market and Microsoft supplies MS-DOS which until recently was treated as an 'industry standard' operating system for personal computers.

Oligopolies

In the case of oligopolies a small number of producers act in concert to maintain their preferred prices and level of supply. Where these agreements are formalized they are referred to as cartels in Europe, and trusts in the United States. Over the last hundred years or more, UK domestic and international company law has developed to severely limit this type of behaviour. Under these controls companies that are found to have concluded formal anti-competition agreements are usually subject to heavy penalties by the courts. However, although formal agreements are unlawful, in a number of industries informal arrangements between companies mean that they appear to act together to limit the degree of direct competition. In these situations there is often an implicit understanding that unlimited competition would be damaging to the long-term health of all the companies in the industry. Therefore a culture emerges within which the major players agree to maintain certain price levels and limit competition to various forms of marketing. Examples of these unwritten rules have been found in the soft drinks, detergents, banking and oil businesses.

Monopsony

Under monopsony many producers compete with each other to supply one customer. The ability of the customer to choose between suppliers means that there is considerable pressure on the suppliers to offer the lowest price and highest quality of service.

Examples of monopsonistic competition include the award of construction contracts to build the Channel Tunnel. In the run-up to the agreement of these contracts, the potential suppliers were required to compile a secret bid or tender outlining the services they would provide and the fees expected in return.

Just as monopoly positions enhance the power of suppliers, monopsony positions increase the power of purchasers. Indeed research suggests that the tender bidding process invariably leads to results which are detrimental to both producers and customers. This is because the bid which is finally accepted is likely to be awarded to the company which overestimates the revenues and underestimates the costs of a particular project (Kay, 1993). Companies who make accurate predictions of costs and revenues will not win contracts and will go out of business, while companies who produce poor forecasts will gain contracts, but may not be able to make any money. If the initial forecasts are very wrong the company which initially won the bid may be forced out of business and their services will either be suspended, or taken over by another company.

Perfect competition

Perfect competition is used to refer to market situations where a number of similar sized producers vie with each other to supply a large number of consumers. In these circumstances, it is assumed that producers and customers will be aware of the price and quality of similar goods being supplied by other organizations in the market. As a consequence customers will seek out those goods and services which offer the best value for money. In other words they will continue to search for goods until they can find those items which offer them the highest standards of quality at a price they are prepared to pay. At the same time producers will be anxious to ensure that they are not forced out of business by offering goods and services on terms which are less favourable than their competitors. They will therefore also seek to ensure that the quality and price of the products they have on sale matches the 'going rate'.

This short description of the features of perfectly competitive markets demonstrates that a number of key assumptions are being made about how markets can and should operate. First, it is assumed that producers and customers will have perfect knowledge of the prices being charged for similar products in the market place. Second, it is assumed that customers are aware of the relative advantages and disadvantages of products with apparently similar properties. Third, it is assumed that customers are sufficiently mobile to take advantage of any discounts being offered by other producers.

In practice it is rare to find market conditions where these ideal assumptions are realized. Imperfect knowledge and limited mobility often constrain the level of competition. The nearest approximations to the ideal of perfect competition, therefore, are provided by street trading and financial markets, where producers and customers operate in close proximity, or can use technology to bridge the gaps, and the costs of gaining information about rival products are relatively low.

Exercise 3.2   ## Market environments

With reference to recent newspaper and magazine articles, produce a list of four companies, one of which operates in each of the following types of market environment: monopolistic, oligopolistic, monopsonistic, near perfect competition.

ANALYSING INDUSTRY POSITIONS

Michael Porter, an influential academic and consultant based at Harvard Business School in the USA, has developed and elaborated upon the traditional economic and marketing analysis of product markets (1980 and 1985). Thanks to the popularity of his writings, the models he advocates have had a powerful influence on the thoughts and actions of business people and other management consultants across the western world.

According to Michael Porter, the key objective for any organization should be to gain advantage over its competitors by occupying a market position in which it is able to use its strengths to generate the highest level of added value. He defines added value as the difference between the costs of the raw materials and capital required by an organization and the price of the final goods and services it sells. For managers and employees who wish to increase the added value generated by their organization, therefore, the first step is to undertake a thorough analysis of their organization's position within existing markets and industries. By assessing the level of competition and gaining a better understanding of industry dynamics, the firm's managers and employees will then be in a better position to judge the long-term attractiveness of the industry. This should help key decision makers to determine whether the organization has a viable long-term future in these markets.

The level of competition and attractiveness of a particular industry or market is determined by the interaction of five competitive forces. Porter labels these forces as:

- the entry of new competitors;
- the threat of substitutes;
- the bargaining power of buyers;
- the bargaining power of suppliers; and
- the level of rivalry among existing competitors. (*See* Fig 3.2.)

The strength of these five competitive forces reflects the strength of a number of factors which Porter refers to as structural determinants. The form and power of these structural determinants vary between industries and over time, and so no two markets are likely to be equally attractive in terms of their potential for yielding added value. The key features of these structural determinants are outlined below.

Threat of potential entrants

The following five structural determinants affect a company's ability to enter new markets.

Fig 3.2 Elements of industry structure

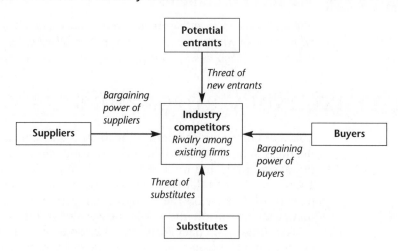

Source: Porter (1985:5). Reprinted with the permission of The Free Press, a division of Simon & Schuster, from *Competitive Advantage: Creating and Sustaining Superior Performance* by Michael E Porter. Copyright © 1985 by Michael E Porter.

1 *Economies of scale* In most industries the cost of producing goods and services declines with size. The larger you are, the cheaper it is to produce each unit of output. This may present a substantial barrier to new entrants who would have to invest considerable amounts of money in order to build up the productive capacity necessary to compete. For example, the economies of scale in the computer industry present formidable barriers to new entrants considering launching a range of computer hardware. By contrast, the economies of scale in the restaurant industry are relatively small.

2 *Access to distribution channels* In a number of industries, while the required level of initial investment is small and the economies of scale are negligible, access to distribution channels is limited and this may dissuade new entrants. For example, in the brewing industry individual pubs are frequently tied to a brewer; this effectively prevents small independent brewers from gaining access to many retail outlets.

3 *Experience curve* Regardless of company size, early entrants to a market will have gained experience, established useful contacts, and learnt how to exploit market opportunities at low cost. These benefits can present a powerful barrier to potential entrants.

4 *Legislation and regulation* The provision of some goods and services is tightly regulated by legislation which may prevent new competitors from entering the market. These forms of regulation include copyrights, patents and licences governing intellectual property rights, laws specifying the level of qualification required by employees, and regulations which limit the provision of certain services to approved organizations.

5 *Differentiation* This term refers to the provision of goods or services which are regarded by the consumer as different from the competition. This difference may manifest itself in the form of brand loyalty, so that certain products are associated with a particular company – for example, jeans (Levi's), beans (Heinz), vacuum cleaners (Hoover) and computers (IBM).

The power of buyers and suppliers

The following two structural determinants influence the level of both buyer and supplier power within an industry.

1 The concentration and the availability of alternatives

This will greatly influence the bargaining power of firms vis-à-vis their customers and suppliers. For example, in the food retail industry there have traditionally been a large number of small retail outlets which had relatively little bargaining power in their dealings with grocery wholesalers and producers. In more recent years, the growth of several large supermarket chains has changed this balance of power. Today, companies like Marks & Spencer and Sainsbury's are able to use their substantial buying power, and the knowledge that there are equally good alternative sources of supply, to control the price and quality of goods supplied by their smaller suppliers. For smaller retailers the problems associated with this lack of power may be overcome by cooperative buying arrangements through which they pool their demands in order to gain discounts from suppliers.

2 Threat of backward or forward integration

The power of a buyer or supplier will be undermined if the organization with which they deal can take over the functions they perform. For example, a company that bottles fizzy drinks could threaten suppliers by building its own bottle manufacturing plant (*backward integration*). Similarly, the role of buyers could be threatened if the organization decided to operate its own distribution network and retail outlets (*forward integration*).

As a counterpoint to Porter's analysis of buyer and supplier power it is worth noting that modern total quality management philosophies place their emphasis on developing long-term non-adversarial relationships with buyers and suppliers. Advocates of this approach suggest that there can be significant long-term returns to those companies which can resist the temptation of exploiting their bargaining power. Instead they suggest that managers and employees should foster partnerships and alliances with their customers and suppliers to ensure that they learn from one another and therefore improve the efficiency and effectiveness of their operations.

The threat of substitutes

The threat of substitutes is an important pressure on the competitive position of any organization. If consumers can substitute the goods and services supplied by one organization with those from another, managers and employees should consider the steps they can take to alter this position. For example, the completion of the Channel Tunnel has enabled business passengers, travellers and freight transporters to mainland Europe to opt for rail, rather than air or ferry travel.

Extent of competitive rivalry

The fifth of the competitive forces facing companies is the level of rivalry within an industry. The most important are:

Relative size of organizations

If there are a number of similarly sized organizations within an industry the competition is likely to be fierce as one or more of these bodies attempts to gain dominance over the others.

Rate of market growth

If the overall rate of sales growth within the markets served by companies in a specific industry begins to decline, or overall demand within the economy contracts, there is likely to be strong competition between organizations to ensure that their overall revenue is not affected by this change. This rivalry may manifest itself in the form of price wars, aggressive advertising or other marketing campaigns. By contrast, if there is a high level of sustained growth, companies are likely to be able to increase their sales and profitability without impinging on another organization's market share. In these situations there may be no need to reduce the price of products or improve the organization's marketing in order to ensure that sales increase.

Exit barriers

The costs of leaving an industry may encourage companies to continue to compete while making a loss rather than suffer even greater financial losses if they withdraw from the market. In these circumstances, firms are likely to fight to the bitter end because the costs of leaving the industry would be too high.

Exercise 3.3 ## Industry structure

1 *Use Porter's model to describe the effect of the five competitive forces on the operation of a private sector industry known to you.*

2 *Can Porter's model be usefully applied to public sector organizations and services?*

COMPETITIVE STRATEGIES

Having analysed the nature of the market and industry, the next step for the managers and employees of any organization facing product market pressures is to consider what actions can be taken to maintain or improve their position. Tackling this issue in a logical and systematic way will involve a detailed consideration of the following questions.

- What is the current basis of the organization's competitive advantage over rivals in the industry?

- What options are available for developing the products and markets the organization serves?

- Which of the available options should be adopted in the light of the organization's current strengths and future objectives?

What is the current basis of the organization's competitive advantage over rivals in the industry?

In answer to this question Michael Porter suggests that organizations can gain a competitive advantage over their rivals either by offering lower prices than competitors for equivalent products or providing unique benefits that more than offset a higher price (1985:3). He refers to these two different approaches as *cost leadership* and *differentiation*. When these two types of competitive advantage are combined with the scope of competitive activities, three distinctive *generic strategies* are revealed: *cost leadership*, *differentiation* and *focus*. The adoption of one of these approaches will provide the context for actions taken in each of the organization's functional areas, e.g. production, marketing and personnel, etc. The three generic strategies are mapped out in Fig 3.3.

Fig 3.3 Three generic strategies

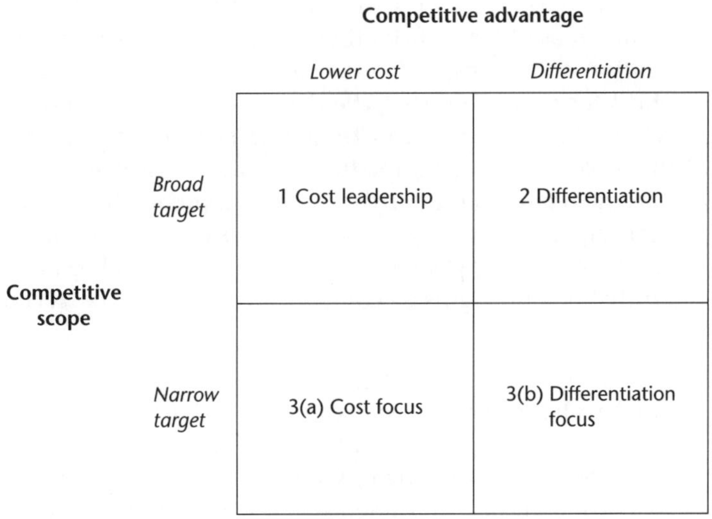

Source: Porter (1985:12). Reprinted with the permission of The Free Press, a division of Simon & Schuster from *Competitive Advantage: Creating and Sustaining Superior Performance* by Michael E Porter. Copyright © 1985 by Michael E Porter.

Cost leadership

Firms adopting a generic strategy of cost leadership set out to be the lowest cost producer in their industry. Among the more common sources of cost advantage are economies of scale, specialist technologies which are owned by the company and preferential access to raw materials. For example, manufacturers of low priced cars require large manufacturing facilities, low cost designs, a ready supply of components and semi-skilled labour and a large number of sales outlets in order to ensure that their products are sold. Companies like the car manufacturer Lada are able to exploit this market effectively by buying old designs from established manufacturers and using the ready supply of local low priced steel and labour.

Within the UK retail food industry, examples of cost leaders include Somerfield and Kwik Save who have successfully marketed a range of low-price, plain-labelled products in a no-frills environment. By adopting this approach these companies have been able to attract customers whose prime motivation is minimizing the cost of their weekly groceries.

Differentiation

Firms adopting a generic strategy of differentiation seek to be unique within their industries along some line which is widely valued by buyers. A company which adopts a differentiation strategy is rewarded for its uniqueness by being able to charge a high price for its goods or services. This will lead to higher profits if the price premium is greater than the cost of differentiation.

Returning to the car industry, BMW, Volkswagen and Mercedes have all been able to establish quality reputations for their cars which clearly mark them out as different from their competitors. Because of this reputation many quality- and status-conscious customers are prepared to pay above average prices for these products. The design specification and engineering standards achieved by the makers of these cars may not be significantly different from that of lower priced competitors, but their customers do not see it this way.

In the retail food industry, a similar approach has been adopted by Marks & Spencer. This company pioneered the sale of high quality cook-chilled foods and speciality recipes and as a consequence has been able to achieve significantly higher margins by comparison with many of its competitors.

Focus

The third generic strategy rests on the choice of a narrow segment of the market. Organizations adopting this approach aim to obtain a competitive advantage by specializing in serving the needs of a small group of buyers. *Cost focus* strategies are designed to meet the price concerns of small specialist markets, while *differentiation focus* strategies aim to meet the specialist design and status needs of customers.

A good example of a company pursuing a cost focus strategy in the retail food market is provided by Costco, an American supermarket which has opened up a number of food warehouses in the UK over recent years. In order to gain access to these facilities, customers must first join a company-organized club and agree to buy items in bulk. To ensure that customers will buy in quantity the earnings and lifestyle patterns of potential club members are screened by the company. Inside the company's warehouses, goods are loaded on to shelves with fork lift trucks and very little money has been spent on decorating the store. For customers whose sole concern is the cost of the items they buy, Costco offers extremely good value for money.

There are few car companies which adopt precisely the same approach although the Korean cars, Protons, are largely promoted on the basis of their low cost.

At the other end of the market, there are a number of food retail and automobile companies who focus on producing prestige goods which attract customers because of the status associated with shopping in their stores or owning a particular model of car. Economists refer to these products as 'giffen goods' because the demand for these items may actually increase with the prices that are charged. Examples of companies adopting this approach include Fortnum and Mason in the groceries market and Ferrari and Aston Martin in the car industry.

Porter suggests that firms that do not pursue a generic strategy will tend to lose out to competitors that do. He is particularly damning of companies which get stuck in the middle and neither pursue a low cost nor a differentiation strategy. He suggests that it is better to concentrate on one of the three generic approaches listed above than to attempt to please all sections of a particular market. This may mean of course that the company has deliberately to limit its sales to particular groups of customers and thereby pass up opportunities to extend its operations to other market segments. The rise and decline of the Next and Laura Ashley groups in the UK has often been blamed on the failure of these companies' senior managements, who, it is argued, did not realize the long-term importance of sticking to a core customer base. According to this diagnosis the ill-fortunes which beset these two companies can be traced directly to the decision to extend the number of products they sold and range of markets they served. As these companies expanded, their market image became blurred and their profitability suffered.

One way of overcoming the dangers associated with becoming stuck in the middle is to restructure the organization in recognition of these pressures. During the 1980s a number of companies reorganized their operations along divisional lines in order to allow different groups of employees to develop goods and services which met the specific needs of different customer groups. Examples of this approach within the car industry include Ford who in addition to maintaining its commitment to the low-cost high-volume car market, also bought a number of specialist car manufacturers including Aston Martin and Jaguar in order to develop a presence in the differentiation focus segments of the market.

Within the UK retail optical industry, Dollond and Aitchison reorganized its branch operations during the 1980s into four divisions: *First Sight* which adopted a cost focus strategy; *Theodore Hamblin* which offered higher priced lenses and designer frames to status-conscious customers; *Dollond and Aitchison* branches which concentrated on a differentiation strategy of providing above average quality and value for money; and *Vision Express* a large out-of-town supermarket which specialized in selling a wide range of spectacles at discounted prices.

Exercise 3.4   Generic strategies

What generic strategy has Fine Fragrances Ltd traditionally adopted? Is this approach appropriate for the future development of the company? Give reasons for your answer.

The human resource implications of different generic strategies

Schuler and Jackson have adapted and re-labelled Porter's generic strategies and identified the different demands made upon employees by quality enhancement, cost reduction and innovation strategies (1987). They argue that companies pursuing an innovative approach will generally require their staff to be more creative, cooperate in teams and to accept longer term goals, than corresponding staff in organizations pursuing a cost reduction or quality enhancement approach. In recognition of these differences they suggest that the human resource policies of these organizations will be different in the key areas of recruitment, job design, development and reward. Therefore, in organizations which focus on cost reduction there are likely to be detailed individual job descriptions, a low emphasis on training and development and reward systems which recognize the achievement of short-term goals. By contrast, in organizations which concentrate on the enhancement of quality there will tend to be more training and development opportunities, developed systems of employee participation, and reward systems which recognize team contributions, as well as the efforts of individuals (*see* Table 3.3 for further details).

Table 3.3 The human resource management (HRM) policy implications of different generic strategies

Generic strategy	Employee role behaviour	HRM policies
Quality enhancement	Relatively repetitive and predictable behaviour	Relatively fixed and explicit job descriptions
	A long-term or intermediate focus	High levels of employee participation in decisions relevant to immediate work and job
	A moderate amount of cooperative, interdependent behaviour	A mix of individual and group criteria for performance appraisal that is mostly short term and results orientated
	High concern for quality	A relatively egalitarian treatment of employees and some guarantees of job security
	Modest concern for quantity of output	Extensive and continuous training and development of employees
	High concern for process	
	Low risk-taking activity	

Table 3.3 (continued)

Generic strategy	Employee role behaviour	HRM policies
Cost reduction	Relatively repetitive and predictable behaviour	Relatively fixed and explicit job descriptions
	A rather short-term focus	Narrowly defined jobs and careers
	Primarily autonomous or individual activity	Short-term results-orientated performance appraisal
	Moderate concern for quality	Close monitoring and matching of market pay rates
	High concern for quality of output	Minimal level of training and development for employees
	Primary concern for results	
	Low risk-taking activity	
	Relatively high degree of comfort with stability	
Innovation	A high degree of creative behaviour	Jobs that require interaction between individuals and groups
	Longer term focus	Performance appraisals that reflect group achievements and long-term goals
	High degree of cooperative behaviour	Jobs that allow employees to develop skills
	A moderate degree of concern for quality	Reward systems that emphasize internal equity
	A moderate degree of concern for quantity	Pay rates that tend to be low but that allow employees to become shareholders
	An equal degree of concern for process	Broad career path to reinforce the development and results of a wide range of skills
	A high tolerance of ambiguity and unpredictability	

Source: Storey and Sisson (1993:66), adapted from Schuler and Jackson (1987:209–13)

What options are available for developing the products and markets the organization serves?

Having determined the organization's overall approach to the goods and services it produces and the markets it serves – its generic strategy – the next step involves a review of current operations in these areas.

Igor Ansoff (1968) has developed an influential model which can help managers and employees undertake this review. The key elements of this model are illustrated in Fig 3.4.

Fig 3.4 Ansoff's model for undertaking a review of alternative directions for development

Product

	Present	New
Present	• Do nothing • Withdrawal • Consolidation • Market penetration	• Product development
New	• Market development	• Related diversification • Unrelated diversification

Market

Ansoff's model enables us to identify a range of product development and marketing initiatives which may be taken in the short, medium or longer term. The following section provides a more detailed outline of each of these options and describes some of the benefits and limitations of these different courses of action.

Do nothing, withdrawal, consolidation or market penetration

The top left-hand quadrant of the box lists those actions or inactions which may be considered in the here and now. The first of these options – *do nothing* – is frequently dismissed by students of business, but regularly adopted by practising managers. For a small group of managers this is a conscious decision which they justify with the statement 'if it ain't broke, don't fix it'. Instead they suggest it is better to concentrate the organization's efforts on more pressing problems and difficulties.

For a larger group of managers the 'do nothing' option is not a conscious decision, but reflects the lack of time and resources available to undertake systematic reviews of the organization's current position and future prospects. As a number of commentators have pointed out, it is one of the ironies of business that it is difficult to gain sufficient commitment from staff to review operations when the organization appears to be operating effectively. It is only when difficulties emerge that reviews of this nature are possible. Unfortunately for the employees of these organizations, when problems become apparent it is often too late to do anything to save the situation.

The second of the list of short-term options is *withdrawal*. For organizations which treat subsidiary divisions or product lines as assets to be managed, the decision to withdraw may be taken when senior managers believe that either the business as a whole or component parts have reached their maximum market value. At one extreme this might involve an entrepreneur selling the small business he or she has built up over the course of a working life in order to release funds for retirement. At the other extreme, the directors of a large conglomerate may sell one or more of their subsidiary businesses or product lines in order to finance developments in another area. Obviously withdrawal from a market does not only occur when businesses are doing well. It is far more common for this type of behaviour to take place when things are going badly. In these circumstances it may not be possible to withdraw by divesting elements of the business and members of the organization may have to reconcile themselves to large-scale redundancies and the writing-off of substantial investments.

Consolidation and *market penetration* are the last of the short-term options. Both of these courses of action aim to improve operating margins – the difference between costs and revenues. The ways in which this may be achieved vary.

Consolidation measures are designed to improve the internal operating effectiveness and efficiency of the organization. By rationalizing the range of goods and services on offer and developing economies of scale and scope, these initiatives aim to ensure that employees within the organization are doing the right things, at the right time, at a minimum of cost. By contrast, market penetration measures are designed to increase the organization's share of the markets it serves. This increase in sales may be achieved by the use of advertising, promotional campaigns, public relations initiatives or direct marketing to potential customers. The final choice of marketing tactics should be based upon a thorough review of the nature of the existing and potential markets.

Product development

When marketing specialists and corporate strategists discuss the current health and future prospects of a particular good or service, they frequently refer to its 'product life cycle'. The notion that products, like people, pass through a number of developmental stages has a long and established pedigree in business circles. According to this reasoning, products are born and over time their sales grow, mature, decline and then die. This view of the behaviour of products is often represented diagrammatically as in Fig 3.5.

Fig 3.5 The product life cycle

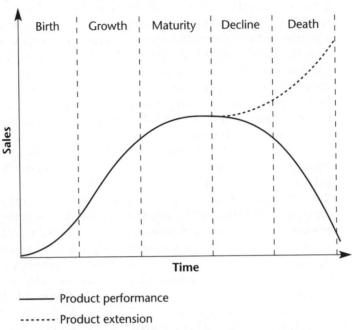

— Product performance

------ Product extension

Unfortunately, despite the appeal of comparing products to people, there is little evidence that in practice the sales of products and services pass through the stages indicated by the product life cycle model in a neat and orderly manner. Product sales are apt to fluctuate in the short and medium term as a consequence of seasonal and cyclical fluctuations in customer demand. It is therefore difficult for managers and employees to know whether their products are suffering from a short-term setback or have succumbed to terminal decline. Despite the difficulties associated with plotting the exact position of a product on the life-cycle model, managers frequently use this approach to justify actions designed to maintain or enhance the sales of their products.

A more elaborate form of product life cycle analysis is provided by the Boston Consulting Group's Matrix (*see* Fig 3.6). Commonly referred to as the BCG matrix, this model combines an analysis of the present sales position of a product (*market share*) with its future potential (*market growth*). The bringing together of these two dimensions enables organizations to place individual elements of the portfolio of products they provide into one of the following four categories: dogs, stars, cash cows and question marks. The relative position of products within this matrix can then be used as a guide to future actions by managers and employees.

Cash cows are a valuable asset to any organization because they generally require little further investment, but promise a stable flow of income which can be used to finance existing activities and future market and product development. By contrast, *stars* will require considerable management attention and financial investment if they are to increase their share of a growing

Fig 3.6 The Boston Consulting Group Matrix

Market share

		Low	High
	High	Question marks	Stars
Market growth	Low	Dogs	Cash cows

market. Here the long-term aim for managers should be to increase sales until the market matures when with luck this product may become a cash cow. *Dogs* and *question marks*, as the names imply, are more problematic for managers. Both of these categories of products have a low market share, but in the case of question marks overall market growth may mean that this position can be improved upon. For organizations with limited funds and management time, therefore, it may be appropriate to discontinue making products in the dogs category, while carefully appraising any further investment in goods or services in the question mark category.

The BCG matrix, like the product life cycle model, has been subject to criticism. In addition to the problems associated with determining the potential sales of current products, critics argue that it is impossible accurately to predict potential future growth within a particular market. Despite these criticisms the model is still widely used as a means of appraising the current position of products and the potential for future development.

Two of the most commonly adopted strategies for product development are product extension and product diversification.

Product extension

Product extension involves attempts to prolong the life of a product by redesigning or relabelling. Within the automobile industry, car manufacturers typically produce a new model every seven to fifteen years. This product will have a new frame, engine, chassis and interior fittings. However, the development costs associated with these different elements of the car will vary.

Designing a new engine requires considerable research and investment, while restyling a chassis and adding 'extras' to the interior is less expensive and time consuming. In recognition of these different costs, car manufacturers attempt to offset the decline in sales which accompany a new model as it grows older by regularly restyling its chassis and adding new extras. In this way the sales may be maintained in the period running up to the launch of entirely new models.

Product diversification

This involves extending the organization's range of products which share a common feature. This technique can be used to exploit the existing reputation and market position of established products. For example, Mars has been able to expand its product range and increase its overall sales by releasing 'bite-size' and 'king-size' bars, as well as Mars ice-creams and soft drinks. A similar approach has been adopted by the manufacturers of Ribena who have supplemented their traditional product range with 'ready-to-drink packages' and a range of new flavours including apple, apricot, orange, carbonated and sugar-free varieties.

At its most extreme product diversification may involve the production of complementary goods and services which exploit the image and position of established brands. The term 'complementary' is used by economists and marketing specialists to refer to products whose consumption is commonly associated with other goods and services. For example, shoes, and socks or tights, are often seen as complementary goods, because in order to wear shoes we also need to buy socks or tights to wear with them.

Market development

Market development involves attempts to find new customers for an organization's existing goods and services. This may include targeting new market segments, expanding into new geographical areas, or exploiting new uses for existing products.

Targeting new market segments will involve focusing the organization's marketing efforts on customers of a different age, race, sex, life-cycle stage or lifestyle. For example, Kelloggs, a large manufacturer of breakfast cereals, has increased the sales of its cornflakes and frosted cereals by targeting its advertising at young adults and the middle aged. The slogan 'have you forgotten how good they taste' was used to encourage this group of consumers to buy its products in preference to newer brands targeted at young children.

Expanding into new geographical areas is another facet of market development which may be attempted on a regional or international basis. Within the UK a recent example of the first of these types of activity is provided by Irn Bru. With this established and traditional soft drink which is already sold in large volume in Scotland and the north of England, the marketing managers sought to focus on young consumers in the south of England in order to increase the sale of the product. This was achieved by using television advertising which poked fun at images from adverts for Coca-Cola and Pepsi – the industry leaders in this market.

On an international scale market development might involve exporting products to overseas markets, or alternatively establishing subsidiary operations in the target countries. This is often a risky exercise as managers from the host country may be unaware of consumer demands and expectations, as well as the laws, regulations and local customs governing the distribution and sale of their products in the new market. To overcome these difficulties many organizations prefer to begin the marketing of their products in foreign markets by appointing local sales managers who are aware of these differences. As the scale of operations in these markets increases and it is decided to locate production facilities in the new market, it may then be appropriate to employ expatriate managers to oversee these foreign operations.

Market development often occurs in tandem with some forms of product development. If new markets are to be successfully developed by finding new uses for existing products, the current image of this item may need to be changed through relabelling or repackaging. For example, Lucozade was able to expand the sale of its products by redefining and expanding its customer base. Lucozade, a fizzy glucose-based soft drink, was traditionally marketed as a tonic for people recovering from common illnesses. As medical and scientific advances began to question the benefit of this drink, the company's marketing managers sought to reverse the decline in sales by targeting the growing leisure and sports markets. Through the combination of an effective marketing campaign and the creation of a wide range of new products, the image of this product changed. Customers are now more inclined to see Lucozade as an energy-enhancing drink for sportsmen and women, rather than as an aid to recovery from illness.

Related and unrelated diversification

In the longer term senior decision makers within the organization may prefer to avoid current competitive threats or exploit future market opportunities by related or unrelated diversification.

As mentioned in the section on industry position, an organization may improve its fortunes through either backward, forward, or horizontal integration. These different forms of activity are all commonly referred to as related diversification because they imply the development of related skills and abilities in order to improve the production or distribution of the organization's core products.

Backward integration involves either the purchase of suppliers or the development of the capacity to produce some of the organization's raw materials. Similarly, *forward integration* typically involves the extension of the organization's activities into the sale or distribution of its products. *Horizontal integration*, by contrast, consists of an expansion of the scope of the organization's activities through the production of related products. In practice, these products will usually be viewed as 'substitute' or 'complementary' goods and services. The recent extension of the range of goods and services sold by high street supermarkets provides one example of this type of activity. In these cases the organizations' senior managers have sought to increase their sales by offering customers the opportunity to buy petrol, home furnishings and even financial services. Another example is provided by the tobacco industry where Dunhill and Camel both produce lighters and smokers' accessories to accompany their established brands of cigarettes.

The boundaries between related and unrelated diversification are difficult to draw. However, in general it is assumed that *unrelated diversification* involves the development of goods and services which fall outside the established borders of the organization's current industry or market bases. Unrelated diversification may be undertaken in order to exploit particular technologies or skills within the organization. For example, SAAB, a Swedish company, manufactures both cars and military aircraft.

In other instances unrelated diversification may mean that there is little if any exchange between staff involved in the organization's established and new activities. In these circumstances the combination is usually justified by reference to the financial skills of the organization's most senior managers and directors. It is suggested that by combining these different activities, the organization will be larger and therefore able to gain cheaper finance and access to more professionally competent managers.

Exercise 3.5 Product and market development

Outline four options for the future development of the toiletry goods supplied by Fine Fragrances Ltd.

Which of the available options should be adopted in the light of the organization's current strengths and future objectives?

The choice of an appropriate development or survival strategy will ultimately depend on an evaluation of the options which takes into account the organization's goals, as well as the internal and external constraints facing any future initiative. This evaluation may be undertaken using the pay-off matrix approach outlined in Chapter 1 of this book. This approach involves ranking various options against the long-term objectives of the organization.

According to Johnson and Scholes another method for determining which option or options to pursue involves assessing each course of action against the following three criteria (1993:244–6).

- *Suitability* Will the proposed initiatives deal with the threats and opportunities identified in the organization's product market?

- *Feasibility* Does the organization have sufficient funds to finance the proposal? What are the implications for the training and development of staff, investment in new technology and the acquisition of supplies and raw materials if the new arrangements are to work effectively?

- *Acceptability* How will the new arrangements alter the financial risks faced by the organization? Is the proposed course of action supported by stakeholders inside and outside the organization?

SUMMARY AND CONCLUSION

This chapter has concentrated on the characteristics of the product markets facing modern UK-based organizations, and the choices available to managers who have to deal with the pressures imposed by these markets.

We began by considering the differences between goods and services, and while noting that few organizations produce solely goods or services, it was suggested that the intangible, inseparable, perishable and heterogeneous nature of services places particular demands on the management of staff within service providing organizations.

Having examined the nature of the products provided by organizations, we then moved on to consider market definition, market environments and industry position. In these sections we considered the difficulties associated with the accurate definition of markets and the factors influencing the level of competition within different industries. Here it was suggested that managers will have more choice and greater influence in situations where there is little competition and where their organization's position is protected by economies of scale, experience and legal regulation. These higher levels of managerial choice and influence mean that employers will have greater discretion in determining the terms and conditions of their employees.

The penultimate section of this chapter was devoted to considering some of the choices available to organizations which wish to change their current market and industry position. Of primary importance in this context is the organization's generic strategy – whether competitive advantage over other organizations is sought on the basis of cost or differentiation. As we noted, the personnel implications of these different approaches may have profound consequences for the way in which managers deal with their staff. In order to pursue a generic strategy based on building innovative products, therefore, managers may wish to consider personnel policies which foster collaborative team work and long-term creative thinking, rather than the individual execution of repetitive tasks in order to meet short-term targets.

The chapter concluded with an outline of some of the options available for developing an organization's products and markets. Here again we attempted to demonstrate the different personnel implications of strategies based upon consolidation, product extension, the exploitation of foreign markets, or unrelated diversification.

CHAPTER 4

The labour market

INTRODUCTION

Over the last 50 years technological, economic, social and legal changes have combined to produce a number of fundamental changes to both the composition of the UK labour market and management approaches to the organization of staff. Today, the UK labour market is no longer characterized by the near full employment of male manufacturing employees, working from 9 to 5, five days a week, until they reach the statutory retirement age. Instead, unemployment has grown and remained high; nearly half the workforce is female; and most employees work in the service sector where their hours of work and length of continuous employment are very variable.

These national trends reflect changes in the way in which employers organize their workforces and employees arrange their personal, family and social lives. As a consequence there is now considerably more variety in the forms and types of employment being offered by UK-based organizations. Many large and hierarchical companies have reorganized into divisions or business units, cut out layers of management and reduced the overall size of their domestic workforces. Meanwhile, the number of small firms has increased and employers appear to be more willing to use the services of temporary staff, consultants, sub-contractors and suppliers, rather than direct employees, to meet their production and general business needs.

Against this background of national- and local-level change, this chapter attempts to provide an overview of the relationship between organizations and the labour markets which provide their employees. We aim to demonstrate that the exact form of this relationship will be affected by the following three factors:

1 The composition of the current workforce and pool of potential recruits – including the age, sex, race and skills of employees.

2 Strategic decisions taken by employers about the division of work between their own operations and those of suppliers, and the structure of jobs within their own organizations.

3 Tactical and strategic decisions taken by employers in response to shortages or surpluses of appropriate staff.

FOCUS AND SCOPE

We begin by describing recent trends in the UK labour market before moving on to consider a number of different theoretical models of employer behaviour. These conceptual frameworks have been developed in order to explain the variety of approaches available to employers anxious to manage their organization's relationship with the labour market more effectively and efficiently.

LEARNING
OBJECTIVES

Once you have read through this chapter and completed the associated exercises, you should be able to:

- comment on recent trends in the UK labour market;
- collect labour market information from a range of sources;
- outline the causes and consequences of status differences between groups within the labour market;
- describe a range of theoretical models which attempt to explain employers' approaches to the labour market; and
- suggest ways in which the managers and staff within a named organization could respond to a shortage or surplus of staff.

CASE STUDY

Grimbles and Timpanies

This case study describes two retail companies – Grimbles and Timpanies – who have adopted very different approaches to staffing their stores. Like previous case studies, the information presented in this section draws on material from a number of different organizations.

Grimbles is a large department store operating in London's West End. The store was founded in the late nineteenth century by Charles Grimble, a wealthy shoe manufacturer who was eager to bring North American methods to the British high street. He believed that by building a large store in an area of London where land was inexpensive and taking advantage of the buying power of a large company, he could sell goods more cheaply than the competition. Charles Grimble also believed that, if he looked after his staff, paid them well and offered opportunities for promotion and progression within the company, he would be able to build up a team of loyal, diligent and expert staff. He hoped that by investing in his staff in this way they would return his commitment and provide the store's customers with high standards of customer service.

In order to put Mr Grimble's vision into practice staff at the store were organized into four categories: directors and controllers; buyers and department heads; supervisors; and sales assistants. This approach to staff grading is still used today although the number of people in each category has grown substantially over the years.

Today there are 12 directors and controllers who oversee the development of general policy in sales and non-sales areas. The senior staff are supported by a group of 36 buyers and department heads who look after day-to-day business within the store. These departments include areas as diverse as women's fashion, men's tailoring, perfumery and toiletries, furniture, leisure and sport, personnel and management services, distribution, marketing, finance and credit control. Within each of these departments there are up to 6 supervisors and 40 staff.

Recruitment and selection for the various categories of staff have changed gradually over the years. During the first 60 years of the store's growth most of the staff joined straight from school. For male members of staff, their early years in the store were a form of apprenticeship and they knew that if they worked hard they would ultimately be rewarded with promotion to the level of supervisor, department manager, buyer or even director. Female members of staff did not enjoy the same prospects. Joining in their teenage years and early twenties they could usually expect to stay with the company until they married and left work to concentrate on domestic responsibilities. Over the last 40 years this pattern has begun to change as potential recruits have become more plentiful and an increasing number of women have decided to return to work after having children. One consequence of this change has been a

▶

LIBRARY
BISHOP BURTON COLLEGE
BEVERLEY HU17 8QG

slow but significant increase in the number of women in middle and senior management positions – helped in part by the company's greater willingness to employ staff on a part-time basis. Today, 7 per cent of middle managers are women.

Despite these changes women have remained confined to the women's fashion, personnel, perfumery and toiletries departments, while men retain the senior positions in the distribution, finance and credit, marketing and leisure and sport departments.

During the 1960s and 1970s Grimbles' traditional approach to recruitment and selection began to change. Increases in the school-leaving age and a steady expansion in the number of people who went on to study for A levels and degrees led the store's personnel department to introduce a Graduate Training Scheme in 1974. In future the majority of department managers would be recruited from employees who had successfully completed this course. Potential graduate recruits were encouraged to apply to the store through glossy brochures sent to university career offices, the availability of temporary vacation jobs and visits to graduate recruitment fairs by the company's personnel staff.

In addition to these changes in initial recruitment, the personnel department became more willing to use press advertisements and recruitment consultants to help them find suitable staff to fill senior management vacancies and to target older workers to work as sales assistants. The success of this new approach, like the graduate recruitment scheme, was regularly evaluated in the personnel department's annual report to the Board of Directors.

Timpanies by contrast is a relatively new firm. Formed in the early 1980s as the UK retailing arm of the Italian Timpania Clothing company, this organization concentrates on selling retailing franchises. The owners of these franchises are required to set up their shop according to guidelines laid down by Timpanies. They are also allowed to sell only stock produced by the Timpania Clothing Company. In exchange for following these regulations, the franchise holders are able to take advantage of Timpanies' substantial investment in marketing and advertising.

In Italy, the parent company – Timpania Clothing – employs a total staff of 1000 designers, marketing and finance staff. All of the company's production work is sub-contracted to other firms in the Far East who are able to produce garments at a fraction of the cost of textile companies in Europe.

Fourteen years after the first store opened, there are now over 100 Timpanies stores in the UK. These shops can be found in the high streets of most major towns and within an increasing number of large department stores. Excluding the owner managers, staff within the company's stores are divided into three categories: deputy and assistant managers, supervisors and sales assistants. Recruitment to these posts is conducted in an informal manner, with most new recruits responding to advertisements placed in the shop window or on occasion in the local job centre. Most of the shop staff are women and employee turnover is high. As a consequence those employees who stay for two or more years can normally expect to be promoted to the post of supervisor or assistant manager. In the longer term, however, there are few if any prospects for further progression unless these members of staff are prepared to take on the financial risks associated with starting their own franchise.

At the end of the 1980s the senior management team at Grimbles became concerned about the falling level of sales within their store and their seeming inability to compete with other department stores in London's West End. In response to these concerns a team of management consultants was hired to examine ways in which the company could change its approach. One of the main recommendations of the consultants' final report was that the store should offer to rent sales floor space to other retail companies.

In 1990 this recommendation was put into effect when Grimbles concluded its first deal with one of Timpanies' franchise holders.

RECENT TRENDS IN THE UK LABOUR MARKET

The term labour force is used to refer to all those individuals who are available for work, whether or not they are actually in paid employment. Most government statistics refer to the *civilian labour force* and as the name implies this figure excludes those employed in the armed services. During the economic boom years of the mid-1970s, the UK civilian labour force grew at an average rate of 130 000 a year to reach 26.2 million in 1981, before falling by over 300 000 during the recession of the early 1980s. The upward trend then resumed and in 1990 the civilian labour force had reached 28.2 million. The influence of economic pressures on the size of the overall labour force was demonstrated again in the early 1990s when another recession led to a reduction of 200 000 in the size of the civilian labour force. According to a number of commentators, this reduction reflected:

- an increase in the number of people registering for further and higher education;
- women temporarily delaying their return to the labour market after having children; and
- stricter social security and unemployment benefit regulations.

This section describes six recent trends within the UK labour market. Among the developments singled out for detailed attention are the feminization of the labour force; unemployment; occupational change; sectoral change; hours of employment; and 'the demographic time bomb'.

Feminization of the labour force

Although the size of the labour force fluctuates in line with general fortunes within the economy, it is also influenced by the size of the population and individuals' willingness and ability to work. An important source of the post-war growth in the size of the UK labour force, therefore, has been the high birth rates of the late 1940s and early 1960s. A more important development, however, has been the growing number of women who are in employment or are looking for a job. Approximately 90 per cent of the overall increase of 3 million in the labour force between 1971 and 1992 was attributable to an increase in the number of women in the labour force.

Many economists and sociologists have referred to this trend as the *feminization* of the labour force and this trend is expected to continue between now and the end of the century. The number of males in the labour force is projected to stay relatively static or decline slightly as the chances of men being out of work once they are over the age of 55 increases. By contrast, the number of women in the labour force is forecast to continue its upward trend and by 2006 women are expected to make up 46 per cent of the UK's workforce (Ellison, 1994). Like all forecasts these figures are subject to substantial margins of error, reflecting inaccurate data collection, inappropriate assumptions about future rates of growth and technological developments, as well as mistaken beliefs about people's willingness and ability to work in certain occupations.

The growth in the number of women workers reflects their increased desire to participate in the labour force. Economists use the term *participation rate* to refer to the proportion of people who are in paid employment as a percentage of all the people eligible to seek this form of work. This figure is calculated by using the following formula:

$$\text{Participation rate (\%)} = \frac{\substack{\text{Number of people from a specific} \\ \text{category in work,} \\ \text{e.g. women, men or young workers}}}{\text{Total number of people in this category}} \times 100$$

The increase in female participation rates reflects a general increase in the availability of part-time jobs, lower birth rates, a rise in the average age at which women have children, and other changes which have made women returning to work more socially acceptable. Indeed, of those that worked part-time in 1993, 85 per cent were women. Although, some commentators have questioned whether this is a desirable trend because of the low wages and poor conditions that part-time work typically attracts, a recent survey suggests that 81 per cent of women part-time workers have voluntarily chosen to take this form of work. Meanwhile, less than 5 per cent chose part-time work because full-time jobs were not available (Ellison, 1994).

At the present time it is difficult to anticipate whether increases in the numbers of female part-time workers will continue. A recent report by the Policy Studies Institute showed that mothers are now more likely to return to full-time employment, and to the same job, working for the same employer, than they were in 1981. In the early 1980s mothers returning to work mostly sought part-time work, or less challenging positions. This often resulted in a waste of their skills and a reduction in their hourly rates of pay. In the 1990s, however, women who leave full-time employment when they become pregnant are now just as likely to return to full-time employment as part-time work following the birth of their child. This trend is most pronounced within

Table 4.1 Allocation of household tasks (%)

	1983			1991		
	Man	Women	Shared	Man	Women	Shared
Household shopping	5	51	44	8	45	47
Makes evening meal	5	77	17	9	70	20
Does evening dishes	17	40	40	28	33	37
Does household cleaning	3	72	24	4	68	27
Washing and ironing	1	89	10	3	84	12
Repairs household equipment	82	6	10	82	6	10
Organizes household money and bills	29	39	32	31	40	28
Looks after sick children	1	63	35	1	60	39

Source: Social Trends 1991, No 21, Office for National Statistics. Crown Copyright 1991. Reproduced by permission of the Controller of HMSO and the Office for National Statistics.

the public sector and among female professional and managerial workers.

Changes in the domestic division of labour may help to explain some of this shift in the form of employment chosen by women. Recent surveys of how work is divided within the home by married and co-habiting couples seem to suggest that family roles are beginning to change, albeit slowly. Although women continue to undertake the vast majority of housework, therefore, the amount undertaken solely by men, or on a shared basis, has increased (*see* Table 4.1). Whether these increases reflect a genuine change in social attitudes and the final arrival of the much trumpeted 'new man' remains a moot point. It may be that these changes simply reflect declining birth rates and increasing male unemployment.

Unemployment

The unemployment rate within the UK is a measure of the mismatch between the number of people who are available for work (*the civilian labour force*) and the number of people who are actually in paid jobs (*employees in employment*).

Before considering different forms of unemployment, it is important to note, as previously mentioned, that neither the size of the civilian labour force nor the number of employees in employment are static figures. Over the last 50 years the number of people who wish to work and the number of people who actually have jobs have increased at a faster rate than the general increase in employment. Thus, although the level of unemployment has tended to increase there has also been an increase in the number of people with jobs (*see* Fig 4.1).

Fig 4.1 UK civilian labour force and employees in employment (1971–93)

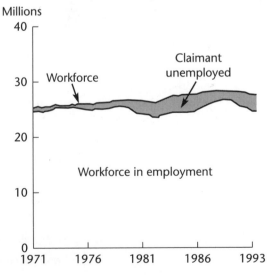

Note: Figures are seasonally adjusted
Source: *Social Trends 1994*, No 24, Office for National Statistics. Crown Copyright 1995. Reproduced by permission of the Controller of HMSO and the Office for National Statistics.

When considering the level of unemployment within an economy, economists often differentiate between three different types, which they refer to as *seasonal*, *cyclical* and *structural* unemployment.

Seasonal unemployment refers to changes in the level of employment as a consequence of the weather, festivals and other specific events during the year. For example, the level of unemployment will normally rise in September each year as pupils leave school in search of work. Similarly, the level of unemployment often falls in late autumn as retailers take on extra staff in preparation for Christmas and the New Year sales. Similar trends may be observed in the summer months when the hotel, catering and tourist industries recruit additional employees to cope with the holiday rush.

In order to take account of these natural variations in the number of people employed each year unemployment statistics are often presented in a *seasonally adjusted* form. This means that the natural peaks and troughs in the number of people employed are smoothed out over the year to provide a more realistic account of the underlying rate of employment or unemployment (*see* Fig 4.2).

The term *cyclical unemployment* is used to refer to changes in the number of people employed which arise as a consequence of fluctuations in a country's economic fortunes. In general we would expect a country which was experiencing an economic boom to have higher levels of employment and lower levels of unemployment than a country which was in the midst of an economic recession. The United Kingdom has experienced a number of economic booms and recessions since the end of the Second World War. During the recessions unemployment has increased before declining again during periods of economic growth.

Fig 4.2 Hypothetical example of a graph to show seasonally-adjusted unemployment

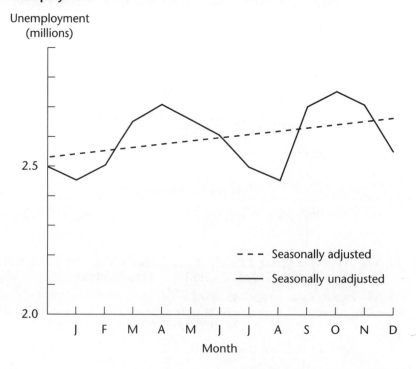

Structural unemployment, unlike seasonal and cyclical forms, tends to be more persistent and enduring. It arises from the long-term decline of specific industries as a consequence of competition, technological change, or shifts in consumer demand (e.g. coal, shipbuilding, typewriter manufacture). Since the early 1970s, the UK, like many other countries in Europe, has witnessed the emergence of high levels of structural unemployment. The number of unemployed within the civilian labour force rose above 1 million in 1975, passed 2 million in March 1981 and reached a peak of 3.12 million in July 1986. Between 1986 and March 1990 the number of unemployed workers fell rapidly to reach 1.6 million before increasing to over 3 million again between 1990 and 1993. Although the level of unemployment has decreased again since the early 1990s a number of economists have expressed a concern that after each period of recession the underlying rate of unemployment has increased.

Despite these increases in the number of unemployed, it is important to remember that this is not a static pool of people. The vast majority of the unemployed will be out of work for less than six months. Nevertheless, in 1993, nearly one half of unemployed males and a third of unemployed females had been out of work for more than a year. Throughout the 1980s and 1990s the highest rates of unemployment have been recorded among those under 20 years of age, although the duration of unemployment was highest among older workers especially men between the ages of 50 and 64. This has led some commentators to question whether the UK is seeing a compression of people's working lives. In future, it has been suggested that many people will start their careers/jobs later in life and find themselves retired or unemployed earlier.

Exhibit 4.1

What do the terms 'employment' and 'unemployment' mean?

According to Charles Handy (1991), the traditional world of work is increasingly breaking down. The vast majority of employees can no longer expect to pursue a career with one employer from the age of 16 to 65, 48 weeks a year, Monday to Friday from 9 am to 5 pm. He suggests instead that the emergence of higher levels of part time work and other new forms of employment requires people to stop talking and thinking about employees and employment. In future we should define work as an activity, some of which is paid for. By this definition everyone is a worker, for nearly all their natural life. Similarly, if everyone is treated as self-employed during their active years then, by law and logic, they cannot be unemployed. They can be poor but that can be put right. The words 'retirement' and 'unemployment' used only as a contrast to 'employment' cease to be useful.

Certainly there are signs that the ownership of careers is being transferred from the organization to the individual. To cope with the uncertainty that this entails Handy encourages us to think about our work as a portfolio of five types of job which will constantly alter in composition as we grow older.

- **Wage or salary work** – where individuals are paid according to the time they devote to a particular organization.

- **Fee work** – where money is paid for a specific piece of work.

- **Homework** – which includes the whole catalogue of tasks that go on in the home, from cooking, shopping and cleaning, to caring for children; maintaining and improving the home.

- **Gift work** – where work is done for free outside the home for neighbours, charities, local groups and the community in general.

▶

- **Study work** – education or training designed to improve skills and increase knowledge, e.g. learning a language, studying for a qualification, reading to gain a better understanding of a hobby or pastime.

As Handy suggests, if we adopt these definitions we can begin to organize our working lives more fruitfully, gain a better division of work within dual-career families, and begin to remove the stigma associated with unemployment.

Occupational change

Overall, employment in non-manual occupations has increased steadily since 1984. The Labour Force Survey in 1990 demonstrated that this growth had been strongest among managerial and professional jobs. Between 1984 and 1990, the number of people employed in these occupations increased by 24 per cent to reach 8.5 million. Over the same period the number of people in clerical and related occupations grew by 19.5 per cent from 3.5 million in 1984 to 4.2 million in 1990. Employment in manual occupations also showed a slow upward trend, increasing from 10.9 million in 1984 to 11.1 million in 1990. By way of contrast, the number of general labourers fell by 51 per cent from 302 000 to 148 000 over the same period. These movements reflect general changes in the organization of UK industry, which have favoured high-skill, white-collar, non-manual jobs and low-skill, service occupations at the expense of high-skill, manual, blue-collar occupations and low-skilled labouring jobs. According to forecasts produced by the independent Institute for Employment Research, this trend is expected to continue until the end of the century (IER, 1993) (*see* Table 4.2).

Table 4.2 Detailed projected change in occupations 1991–2000

Occupational group	Percentage change
Corporate managers and administrators	+27
Managers/Proprietors in agriculture and services	+12
Science and engineering professionals	+24
Health professionals	+17
Teaching professionals	+1
Other professional occupations	+44
Science/engineering associated professionals	+19
Health associate professionals	+7
Other associate professionals	+24
Clerical occupations	−3
Secretarial occupations	−8
Skilled construction trades	−1
Skilled engineering trades	−11
Other skilled trades	−20
Protective services occupations (security)	+9
Personal services occupations	+11
Buyers, brokers and sales representatives	+2

Table 4.2 (*continued*)

Occupational group	Percentage change
Other sales occupations	+9
Industrial plant and machine operatives	–24
Drivers and mobile machine operators	–8
Other occupations in agriculture	–16
Other elementary occupations	–14
All occupations	+2

Source: IER (1993)

In addition to changes in the occupational structure of employment, the UK also witnessed a 56 per cent increase in the number of self-employed people during the 1980s and early 1990s. By 1995, 3.3 million people were self-employed and according to the Institute of Employment Research this figure is to expand by a further 200 000 by the year 2000, with almost half of this increase accounted for by increases in the construction, distribution, catering and repairs sectors of the economy (SEN, 1995; *Labour Market Quarterly*, 1995). Despite these increases there is evidence to suggest that this type of work is less secure than more traditional forms of employment. For example, between 1990 and 1993 the number of people in this category fell twice as quickly as the general decline in the level of employment.

Sectoral change

Over the past 25 years, there have been significant changes in the relative balance of employment between different industrial sectors. Since the beginning of this century, the number of people employed in primary industries (mining and agriculture) has steadily declined. In the late 1960s, this trend was added to by the absolute and relative decline of employment within the UK's manufacturing sector. Between 1971 and 1990, the number of employees in manufacturing industries fell by more than one third, while the number of staff employed in service sector industries increased by a corresponding amount.

During the recession of the early 1990s the decline in manufacturing employment accelerated, but was not offset by increases in the service sector. This recession was the first in which service sector employment declined markedly.

This pattern of decline in primary and manufacturing employment and growth in the service sector is expected to continue during the 1990s. In total, primary and manufacturing industries are projected to lose over 825 000 jobs by the turn of the century. The main increases are expected in the service sector where employment growth is expected to exceed 1 325 000.

Changes in the sectoral distribution of work over recent years have been accompanied by substantial changes in the balance between public and

Table 4.3 Projected employment change by broad industrial sector (1991–2000)

Sector	Percentage change
Primary and utilities	−24
Manufacturing	−12
Construction	−3
Distribution and transport etc.	−0.5
Business and miscellaneous services	+16
Public services	+8
Whole Economy	+2

Source: IER (1993)

private sector employment. In 1961, approximately 24 per cent of the workforce were employed in the public sector; by 1981 this figure had risen to 30 per cent, only to decline again to 22 per cent in 1990. Most of the decrease in public sector employment since 1981 has been accounted for by a fall in employment in public corporations, mainly as a consequence of privatization.

Among the more substantial changes have been the reclassification from public to private sector of nearly half a million workers. This change in status affected over 200 000 British Telecom employees in November 1984, 100 000 British Gas employees in December 1986, 53 000 British Steel staff in December 1988 and 60 000 polytechnic staff in April 1989.

Hours of employment

In 1993, approximately three-quarters of UK employees worked on a full-time basis. By industry this figure ranged from 60 per cent in the hotel, catering, distribution and repairs industries to 96 per cent in the energy and water supply industries. The Labour Force Survey of 1993 estimated that four out of five male employees had basic weekly hours of work (excluding meal breaks) of between 35 and 45 hours per week. The high level of part-time work among women employees was reflected in this hours-at-work data, which showed that half of all female employees worked for less than 35 hours per week and two-fifths for between 35 and 40 hours per week. Although these figures appear relatively low, it should be remembered that they refer to basic hours at work and do not include overtime working. If we include data on levels of overtime and number of hours actually worked, it would appear that male employees in the UK have an average working week which is longer than any of their counterparts in other European Union countries. By contrast, for those women in work, the predominance of part-time work means that their working week is shorter than women in all other EU countries with the exception of the Netherlands.

When considering employees' hours at work, it is important to consider some of the factors that may cause these individuals to be absent. The traditionally high level of strikes in the UK led some commentators to refer to this as the British disease. During the 1980s and 1990s, however, the level of industrial action declined significantly and, in 1992, the number of working days lost through industrial action reached an all time low. Despite this change the number of individuals who reported being absent from work for one or more days in a month due to illness remained very high. The vast majority of this absence was accounted for by avoidable complaints, e.g. non-genuine sickness, back problems and stress-related illnesses. In international terms the UK's strike record in 1993 places it in the lower half of a table of European Union countries. However, when it comes to sickness absence the UK has the second highest number of working days lost. Perhaps in the 1990s, the British disease is really the illness of its workers.

The 'demographic time bomb'

The relatively high birth rates in the 1960s had the effect of increasing the number of 16-year-old entrants to the civilian labour force in the second half of the 1970s. However, this effect reached its peak in 1981 after which the number of 16-year-old entrants fell. In 1990, 16 to 24-year-olds made up 21 per cent of the civilian labour force; by 2001 this is projected to fall to 17 per cent, while the proportion of those aged 55 and over is expected to remain static at around 12 per cent.

In the late 1980s, many employers expected that the changing age structure of the labour force would produce recruitment problems for those employers who rely on school leavers as their principal source of new staff. In the 1990s these fears appear to have evaporated as the recession has led employers to focus on the problems associated with redundancy rather than recruitment. At present it appears that the size of the recruitment problems faced by employers before the end of the century will depend upon the general health of the UK economy. If economic growth continues, many more employers will move away from their traditional reliance on young recruits and may consider other groups more favourably (e.g. women and older workers).

Exercise 4.1	**The effects of labour market trends on Grimbles and Timpanies**

How have the case study companies, Grimbles and Timpanies, been affected by the labour market trends outlined above?

Exercise 4.2	**UK labour market statistics**

The labour market trends described in the preceding section are apt to change. In order to ensure that you and your organization are prepared for these changes, it is important to monitor developments regularly within the UK labour market.

This exercise is designed to make you more familiar with some of the most commonly available sources of labour market statistics. By answering the following questions you should become more acquainted with the variety of statistics currently available, as well as some of the definitional problems associated with collecting this information.

By consulting the labour market reports and periodicals listed in the further reading section, compile the most recent figures for the following labour market indicators.

(a) The UK civilian labour force (seasonally adjusted).
(b) Unemployment in Great Britain (seasonally adjusted).
(c) Unemployment in your region (seasonally adjusted).
(d) Nationally recorded notified vacancies.
(e) Male employees in employment in the UK (seasonally adjusted).
(f) Female employees in employment in the UK (seasonally adjusted).
(g) Male part-time employees in employment in the UK (seasonally adjusted).
(h) Female part-time employees in employment in the UK (seasonally adjusted).
(i) The number of working days lost per thousand employees.
(j) Percentage of manufacturing firms expecting a lack of skilled labour to limit output over the next four months.

LABOUR MARKET SEGMENTATION AND SEGREGATION

Having outlined six general trends in the UK labour market, we now move on to consider the treatment of different groups of workers within this national pool of current and potential employees.

Since the beginnings of the Industrial Revolution, a number of social scientists and policy makers have commented on the immense variety in the conditions and prospects of different groups within the labour market. These differences, it has been argued, arise because of a number of visible and invisible barriers which prevent certain groups of people from realizing their full potential. As a consequence the labour market is in effect segmented into a series of sections. While employees in some sections of the labour market can look forward to stable, well-paid employment with training and career advancement, other sections are consigned to a lifetime of insecure and poorly paid work in unpleasant surroundings with little or no opportunities for further development.

Three of the most important forms of this labour market segmentation are *horizontal, vertical* and *national* segregation.

- *Horizontal segregation.* This is a term used to describe situations where particular jobs within an industry or organization are seen to be the preserve of certain groups of workers. For example, surveys by the Equal Opportunities Commission have suggested that the following occupations are typically undertaken by women rather than men: clerical, secretarial, catering, cleaning, hairdressing, education, nursing, welfare, retail selling and in the manufacturing industry, painting, repetitive selling and product packaging.

- *Vertical segregation.* This describes situations where certain groups of workers predominate in senior positions within an organization or industry. In the UK, research studies have demonstrated that white, middle-aged and middle-class men occupy the majority of middle and senior management positions. By contrast, women, ethnic minorities, older workers and the disabled are under-represented at this level.

- *National segregation.* According to a number of writers, existing trading relationships and the staffing policies of multinational enterprises have produced an *international division of labour*, with the high-skilled knowledge-intensive activities reserved for developed western countries, while the routine tasks are exported to third world countries (Frobel *et al*, 1980; Reich, 1991).

Exhibit 4.2

The glass ceiling

Although women currently account for almost half of the UK workforce only 11 per cent of managers are women and a mere 3 per cent are directors. In recognition of this under-representation, the term 'glass ceiling' was coined to describe the invisible barriers which prevent women and a variety of minority groups from reaching the top in business and politics. Two of the most commonly cited of these invisible barriers are the uneven division of household work and prejudice and discrimination by senior male managers.

To help overcome these problems, Opportunity 2000, an independent pressure group, was established in 1991. Drawing on the example of the 'Glass Ceiling Commission' in the USA, the organizers of Opportunity 2000 have sought to promote awareness and better practice among Britain's leading employers. To advance the position of women this new group and other older established pressure groups have advocated the use of flexible working practices and family-friendly policies to help working parents and others achieve a better balance between their lives at home and at work.

Among the specific initiatives proposed by Opportunity 2000 and other groups have been the following changes to company personnel policies and practices:

- Formal adoption by the Board of Directors of a written commitment to the advancement of women within the organization.
- The use of positive images of women in all recruitment and company promotional literature.
- Analysis of statistics monitoring the number of women in different job grades and sections as well as measures of female job applicants, recruits and promotees.
- Targeting of recruitment channels to boost the number of women applicants for specific jobs within the organization.
- Establishment of committees of networking arrangements to encourage women to meet, exchange experiences, provide feedback to the organization and plan their own career advancement.
- Reviews of current working arrangements in order to consider the feasibility of flexi-time, job-sharing, home-working, teleworking and other forms of flexible employment.
- The introduction of career break schemes, carer leave, crèche and nursery provision or vouchers.
- Specific targeting and training for potential senior women managers.

Exercise 4.3 **Labour market segmentation and segregation**

With reference to the case study at the beginning of the chapter comment upon whether the way in which Grimbles and Timpanies manage their staff exhibits any signs of labour market segmentation.

EMPLOYERS' APPROACHES TO ACQUIRING AND ORGANIZING THEIR WORKFORCES

A brief comparison between any two organizations will quickly demonstrate that managers faced with similar problems will adopt very different solutions when it comes to organizing their workforces. There are likely to be different balances between managerial and subordinate staff, generalists and specialists, tasks performed by a machine and those carried out by other organizations. When it comes to analysing these differences it would be almost impossible to list all of the possible forms of variation. However, there are two important elements of variation which capture many of the differences between organizations.

1 The degree of planning undertaken by the managers of the organization ranging from informal 'off-the-cuff' decisions to complex systems of corporate manpower planning.

2 The extent to which the organization relies on external sources to supply candidates for internal vacancies or, alternatively, uses internal systems of staff development and promotion to meet future staffing needs.

If these two sources of variation are combined we have a powerful analytic tool for distinguishing between the approaches adopted by various organizations, and a mechanism for classifying theories which attempt to describe and explain the approaches of employers.

The combination of the two dimensions produces the triangular arrangement illustrated in Fig 4.3. These three points of the triangle enable us to distinguish between three different organizational approaches: poachers, gamekeepers and contractors. The fourth approach – the flexible firm – represents a hybrid form of organization which combines elements of the gamekeeper and contractor approaches. (The terms 'poacher' and 'gamekeeper'

Fig 4.3 Employers' approaches to organizing their workforces

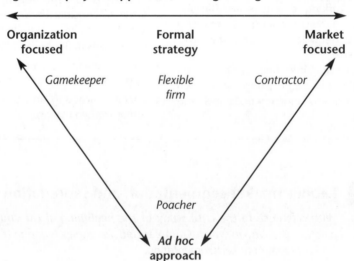

were originally coined by Diana Winstanley (1992) and the phrase 'flexible firm' was used by John Atkinson (1984).

Each one of these four approaches has formed the focus of discussion and analysis in a range of academic disciplines including sociology, economics, organization and management theory. As each discipline has its own peculiar language and writers have a vested interest in creating new labels, there are a number of different names which have been used at various times to describe the same phenomena. The rest of this section is devoted to describing the four approaches in more detail, reducing the confusion of terminology and drawing together the insights from researchers working within different academic traditions.

Poachers

Poacher-type organizations do not spend a lot of time planning to meet their future staffing needs. They devote few if any resources to planning their manpower needs or staff training and development. If they need staff with new skills or an increased number of employees to deal with a larger work load, they will look for the quickest and easiest solution. If a member of staff cannot be transferred from another department within the company, managers will probably look outside for a person with the right skills to plug the perceived gap (*see* Fig 4.4). Examples of organizations adopting a poacher approach can be found in most industries, although this style of operations is most characteristic of small and medium-sized firms.

Because poachers spend very little money or time on manpower planning or training to meet their future staff needs, when they have to recruit they

Fig 4.4 Organization adopting a poacher approach

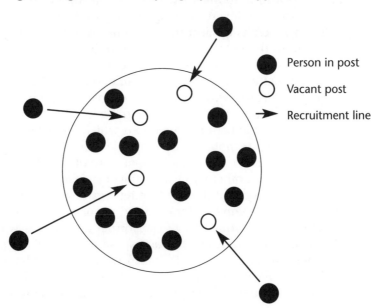

tend to look for staff that already have the experience or skills they need. This task may be hampered by the lack of formal job descriptions (spelling out what the job entails) or person specifications (detailing the ideal characteristics of a new member of staff).

In the search for experienced staff, poachers have one significant advantage over other firms that have spent time and money, training and developing staff. Because they have spent less on training and development they may be able to offer higher wages and benefits to prospective staff. Another feature of poacher-style companies that reflects their lack of attention to planning, is that they tend not to have clearly thought out how they will recruit and select staff. As a consequence these companies will tend to use a variety of recruitment and selection methods, e.g. hotel walk-ins, press advertisements, recruitment agencies, etc. The reasons for using these methods will probably not have been fully or properly thought out and as a consequence the organization will frequently chop and change between these different tactics. Once staff have been selected their future development is left in the hands of the staff themselves. Formal training, when provided, is unlikely to be linked to a careful consideration of the future direction and objectives of the organization or the individuals it employs. Finally, it is worth mentioning that these types of organization will often dispense with employees as quickly as they are prepared to take them on; as a consequence staff are likely to be fired or made redundant at short notice.

Gamekeepers

The term 'gamekeeper' is used to describe the same features of an organization which economists have traditionally referred to as an internal labour market, and sociologists have been apt to call a bureaucracy. Unlike poachers, gamekeeper organizations tend to spend a considerable amount of time and money planning to meet their future staffing needs. They are more likely than poachers to invest in manpower planning as well as training and developing raw recruits to meet the future needs of the organization. These firms will tend to prefer to recruit young school leavers and graduates and then train and develop these staff over a number of years. They expect their staff to be committed to frequent training and development and in return offer these employees a career with a series of possible promotions up a predetermined grading structure. At each level or grade within the organization there are likely to be a number of defined jobs which are formally described through the use of job descriptions and job evaluation. Job evaluation involves determining the relative worth and importance of a particular job by systematic comparison with other jobs within the organization.

Examples of organizations adopting a gamekeeper approach include large private sector companies and public sector services. The recruitment and development of armed forces personnel and nurses within the National Health Service provide one of the best examples of this approach in practice.

Because gamekeeper organizations invest in developing the knowledge and skills of their staff, they are less worried about the skills staff have when first recruited. Attitude, intelligence, aptitude and the right motivation are often

Fig 4.5 Organization adopting a gamekeeper approach

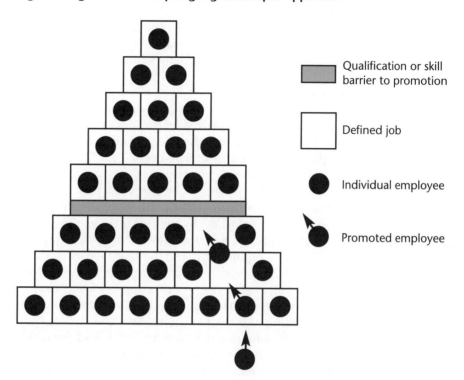

deemed to be more important. The organization's commitment to training and development, with all the costs that go with this, may mean that there is less money to spend on staff wages and other benefits; therefore, the organization may have trouble retaining staff once they have received their training. In order to ensure that they attract staff with these characteristics, gamekeepers will tend to spend more time and money on developing integrated and cost-effective recruitment and selection procedures, for example the use of assessment centres. These organizations are also more likely to evaluate regularly the success of their recruitment and selection policies and procedures. Finally, because gamekeepers approach the development of their staff as an investment, they are apt to want to hold on to them until this investment is repaid, as long as this is consistent with the needs of the business and the desire to manage a steady flow of staff through the organization. (*See* Fig 4.5.)

Contractors

The third category – 'contractors' – refers to organizations who meet their demands for labour without employing people on permanent contracts of employment. For many of these organizations, uncertain surroundings and doubtful future prospects provide the impetus for decisions which are designed to ensure that the employer pays only for work which helps to further the organization's goals in the short term.

In the UK there are a range of ways in which an organization can seek to limit its labour costs in this way. At one extreme, the organization's managers may choose to replace permanent staff with employees on temporary contracts. This arrangement may be useful when managers are unsure about future demand for the company's products, or, when there are small, relatively short-term projects which need to be completed without leading to a permanent increase in the size of the organization's workforce. Examples of this approach in the leisure industry include staff who are employed on temporary contracts to cover the peaks in demand during the holiday season. Similarly, in the education sector, research staff may be employed to complete specific short-term projects.

At the other extreme of contractor behaviour, an organization's managers may abandon the provision of a particular product or service and decide that in future these functions will be either provided by a sub-contracted supplier or alternatively performed by the customer.

The employees of a sub-contracted supplier may use the organization's premises and equipment, but will not be directly employed by them. Traditionally, this form of employment has been confined to the construction industry, but in recent years this approach has been extended to a range of other settings. The store within a store concept has revolutionized high street retailing and frequently involves the staff of these concessions being employed by one organization and managed by another. Similarly, many public services have been opened up to sub-contractors through compulsory competitive tendering, market testing and other initiatives. Indeed there are few contemporary organizations who do not employ sub-contractors of one form or another, whether as contract catering and cleaning staff or head-hunters and other management consultants. Despite the growth of sub-contracting arrangements, however, this does not relieve the contractor's managers of the need to manage staff. Council administrators and retail managers have realized that if this system is to work effectively, desired service levels have to be tightly specified and effectively monitored.

Another related development has been a move to get customers to perform some of the work for themselves. Whether it is self-assembly furniture, dispensing money from banks via automatic teller machines, or collecting groceries from large out-of-town food stores, customers often play a bigger part in making products or providing services. Even in universities, services are being done away with or turned into products. These types of change have profound effects on the type of work left for the remaining employees. Reductions in direct face-to-face interaction with customers have changed the nature of the jobs performed by many banking and financial services staff as well as employees in supermarket stores.

Flexible approaches

The last category of organization outlined in Fig 4.3 refers to a variety of practices which according to a number of writers have been adopted in recent years by an increasing number of organizations (Piore and Sabel, 1982; Atkinson, 1984; Lash and Urry, 1987; Handy, 1989).

In the early 1980s, the work of Piore and Sabel drew attention to changes in the way organizations plan production and as a consequence structure their labour forces. They argued that the structure and organization of developed economies were changing rapidly from the late 1970s onwards. Of particular importance in this context were the onset of high and persistent unemployment, a rapidly changing balance of international economic power, greater political reliance on market forces, changing consumer preferences and the widespread adoption of micro-electronic technology. Because of these changes, companies could no longer rely on Fordist methods of mass production with their emphasis on the strict division of labour within large bureaucratic (gamekeeper) organizations in which semi-skilled and unskilled workers were employed to assemble standardized products for mass markets. Instead, they suggested that a new method of organizing production was emerging which they termed *flexible specialization*; other writers have described similar trends under the heading post-Fordism. This new approach led manufacturers to focus on developing adaptable production techniques and *flexible* workforces to serve a growing number of specialized markets (*see* Chapter 2 for further discussion of these issues).

Shortly after the publication of Piore and Sabel's work, Atkinson (1984) published a number of papers based on case studies undertaken in the southeast of England. According to these studies, companies were responding to economic recession, uncertainty about the future, job loss and technological change by searching for flexible ways of staffing their organizations. Atkinson identified three forms of this flexibility:

- *Numerical*. The number of staff employed by the organization (head count) was varied in line with changes in the product/service market demand. In addition, the employment practices of organizations had changed in order to allow them to make rapid changes in the number of their employees, as trading conditions fluctuated.

- *Functional*. Employers were adopting policies which actively encouraged employees to develop a range of skills and competencies which would enable these staff to be deployed quickly and smoothly between a range of activities and tasks. The development of these new aptitudes was seen as a way of gaining the maximum return and benefit from the staff employed.

- *Financial*. There appeared to be a general shift away from pay systems which gave staff uniform increases towards new arrangements in which pay was related to local market conditions, individual performance and/or the range of skills possessed.

According to Atkinson (1984) the adoption of these three forms of flexibility lay at the heart of a new approach which he has called the 'flexible firm model' (*see* Fig 4.6).

Figure 4.6 illustrates the distinction between three groups of employees within Atkinson's model of the flexible firm.

Fig 4.6 The flexible firm

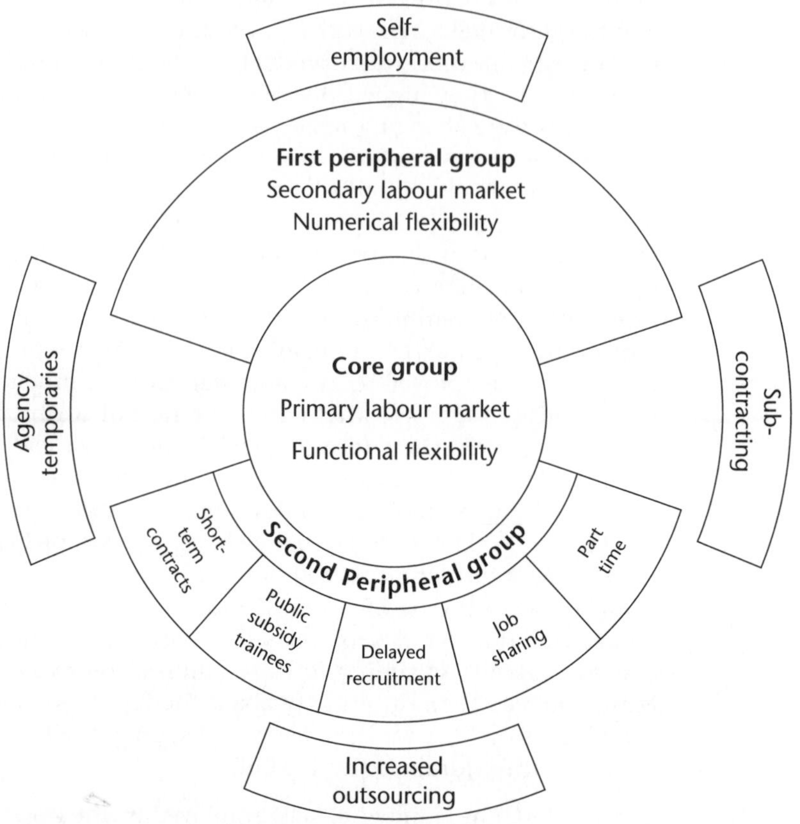

Source: Atkinson, *Personnel Management*, August 1984

1 Core Group This group consists of full-time permanent career employees, e.g. managers, designers, technicians and craftsmen. These staff are offered employment security in exchange for being flexible about the work they perform (*functional flexibility*). For example, office workers and machine operators might be expected to take on a wider range of duties including supervising some aspects of their own work, ordering materials, and checking the quality of products and services which they produce or deliver. In the personnel department staff might be encouraged to take responsibility for all the human resource issues of a particular group of employees rather than concentrate on one set of issues like pay, training or sickness and holiday leave monitoring. In the longer term employees may be encouraged to change careers and retrain for other jobs within the organization. The main characteristic of the core group is that their skills cannot be bought in.

2 First periphery Employees within this group are employed full-time, but have lower levels of job security and fewer career opportunities than staff in the core. The number of staff employed in this group is varied in response to changes in the demand for the products or services provided by the organization (*numerical flexibility*). Examples of the types of staff employed in this category include clerical, supervisory, assembly and sales occupations. Workers in this category have general skills rather than skills which are specific to the firm. According to Atkinson, functional flexibility is not sought from this group.

3 Second periphery This section is made up of workers or sub-contracted staff with jobs designed to combine numerical and functional flexibility. Part-time work provides the best example of this as it allows numbers to be varied easily and deployed at times which suit the company, e.g. twilight shifts. Job security for this group of employees is minimal. Atkinson also maintains that companies are making increased use of outsourcing, e.g. sub-contracting, self-employment and agency temporaries. The skills of these jobs are not at all firm-specific because they are either very specialized, e.g. systems analysis, or very mundane, e.g. office cleaning. Outsourcing is seen as a means of increasing numerical flexibility as the firm can decide precisely how much of a service it needs at any particular time. It is also a means of increasing functional flexibility as a result of the greater commitment of self-employed staff to get the job done.

Atkinson's model of the flexible firm has been subject to considerable criticism in recent years. The most important of these criticisms were:

- It has been argued that the model is based on practice in a small and statistically unrepresentative group of companies.

- It has been suggested that wider evidence does not support Atkinson's belief that organizations in all sectors of the economy will adopt the flexible firm approach. Changes in the number of part-time and temporary workers reflect the UK economy's growing reliance on low-paid service-sector employment and female staff, rather than concerted strategy on the part of employers; traditional homeworking has decreased in recent years, reflecting the decline of the manufacturing industry; and the growth of teleworking, outsourcing and self-employment do not necessarily reflect a general and planned movement in the direction of the flexible firm. Similarly, studies of functional flexibility initiatives in the manufacturing industry have revealed that these schemes are invariably associated with reducing the level of skill in particular jobs, rather than improvements in the range of jobs performed by employees. For example, studies in the manufacturing industry suggest that workers are more likely to be asked to assume responsibility for organizing the cleaning of their own work areas, rather than assume responsibility for the supervision and inspection of their own work.

- It has been argued that Atkinson's model is ambiguous, in that it says that each firm must find forms of flexibility and ways of achieving them which are appropriate to its own ends. This leaves Atkinson's analysis open to the interpretation that these developments are a good thing. As Anna Pollert has forcefully commented, further expansion of an insecure, poorly trained and cheap 'periphery' of employees is the last thing the United Kingdom needs to do to improve its productivity and competitiveness (Pollert, 1988). Rather than representing new and innovative practices these developments may just be evidence of further labour market segmentation and segregation.

Despite these criticisms, Atkinson's model remains a powerful guide to management practice and the lessons implicit in its construction have informed the recommendations of countless management consultants. Indeed, it has been suggested that Atkinson's threefold typology of flexibility should be extended to include *temporal* and *geographical* flexibility.

The first of these terms refers to the increasing willingness of employers to move towards new forms of work scheduling so that the most productive use is made of their investments in property and machinery. Examples of this trend include the adoption of nine-day fortnights in the telecommunications industry, annual-hours contracts in the engineering industry, fourth-term working in the education sector and Sunday opening in the retail industry.

Geographical flexibility is used to refer to the willingness of multi-plant companies to shift production and people between sites and on occasion between countries.

Exercise 4.4   ## Analysing employers' approaches

With reference to the four basic approaches outlined in the preceding section classify the approaches adopted by the two case study companies, Grimbles and Timpanies. When answering this question try to be specific about the features of each organization's approach which correspond to elements of the poacher, gamekeeper, contractor and flexible models.

DEALING WITH LABOUR SHORTAGE AND SURPLUS

Having considered some of the variety of ways in which employers choose to organize their workforces and acquire new employees, the following section moves on to consider some of the tactical and strategic alternatives available to employers faced with a surplus or shortage of possible new recruits.

Dealing with shortages and surpluses of staff presents many modern organizations with considerable problems. Fluctuations in the level of growth within the economy in general and variations in the fortunes of specific organizations present managers with the task of adjusting the number of employees within the organization to meet the demand for the company's products and services.

Labour shortage

Despite the continued presence of high levels of unemployment within the UK economy, many employers still experience considerable difficulties in attracting and retaining staff of the right calibre. According to John Atkinson there are a number of possible solutions to this problem (Atkinson, 1989). Basing his analysis on the results of research among British companies in the late 1980s, he suggests that managers are often faced with two types of choice. The first of these forms of choice is between either altering the organization's demand for labour or alternatively attempting to draw upon previously untapped supplies within the labour market. The second type of choice is between short-term tactical measures and longer term strategic initiatives. By combining these two dimensions of choice, managers within any organization may take one or more of the four options outlined in the quadrants which make up Fig 4.7.

According to Atkinson, the simplest option is to 'take it on the chin' by doing nothing, reducing output or constraining growth in order to prevent the shortage of available labour from undermining the work of the organization. In the longer term, however, this solution may not always work as other employers may try to tempt staff to leave the organization with the promise of higher pay, better conditions, or improved promotion prospects.

Faced with these pressures, an alternative option is to attempt to 'compete' with other companies in order to attract the best possible recruits from traditional sources. This may be achieved by reviewing the organization's recruitment and selection procedures to ensure that recruitment brochures and visits are targeted at the right people, and that the administration of open days, interviews and offer letters does not deter potential applicants. Another typical response from organizations faced with these difficulties is to increase the starting pay and improve conditions of new recruits.

In the longer term the two options outlined above are unlikely to be effective for individual companies or the wider economy. Most organizations can make their recruitment procedures more effective and the most profitable businesses can improve pay and conditions. However, neither of these measures will remove the fundamental problem of the demand for employees exceeding the supply available from traditional sources. In response to this dilemma Atkinson suggests that organizations could do more to exploit the

Fig 4.7 Employers' responses to labour shortages

talents of people who have traditionally been discriminated against. By directly targeting these untapped sources of labour, organizations may find that they are able to recruit high calibre staff at little additional cost. Among the potential sources of these recruits are women returners, older workers, ethnic minorities, disabled people and the long-term unemployed. It may even be appropriate to target suitably qualified staff from overseas.

Finally, Atkinson suggests that if labour shortages persist, despite attempts to access alternative pools, there are only three effective choices left open to managers. They may decide to make a long-term commitment to the training and development of their staff in order to ensure their employees are able to work more efficiently. Alternatively they may decide that services provided by their staff can be replaced by machines or the sub-contracting of work. Finally, if all else fails the only remaining option is to consider relocating the organization's operations to another region or country where the supply of suitably skilled labour is more plentiful.

Labour surplus

For organizations which are experiencing a decline in the demand for their products or services, with knock-on effects upon the number of staff they can sustain, there are also a number of options available. These options are outlined in Fig 4.8 using Atkinson's distinctions between the demand and supply for labour and tactical and strategic decisions. This diagram also draws on the work of Leonard Greenlagh who has conducted research into how organizations respond to labour surpluses (Greenlagh, 1991).

Fig 4.8 Employers' responses to labour surpluses

The four quadrants in Fig 4.8 illustrate a few of the ways in which either the demand for labour may be maintained or increased while the overall level of supply is reduced.

One of the quickest and cheapest ways of reducing staffing costs within an organization is through the stopping of overtime, reduction in hours of work and the non-renewal of temporary contracts of employment. It is important to note that it is rarely possible or sensible to introduce these changes without prior consultation and agreement from the members of staff concerned. Where employees are members of a union, this process should include discussion with their representatives.

The official announcement of business difficulties may be sufficient to encourage other members of staff to leave the organization voluntarily in order to pursue their career with another employer. Where this does not happen, it may be appropriate to halt recruitment, and call for voluntary redundancies.

Within larger organizations, it may be possible to avoid the need to lay off staff by 'redeploying' staff within the organization. An increasing number of companies have used internal career counselling and job notification systems in order to encourage these types of movement. The most sophisticated forms of this approach take advantage of open access databases where staff can register their qualifications, skills and experiences so that managers in other departments or divisions can fill vacancies without incurring the cost of advertising externally.

If these measures do not work, more radical options include encouraging staff to take a career break or temporary secondment with another employer. The advantage of this option is that it allows the employee the option of returning to the employer if business conditions improve. It will also mean that the employer is not forced to lose a valuable member of staff. The organization may even benefit from the development and training the employee receives while away from the organization.

Finally, where all of the preceding options have been tried and have failed or where the organization is experiencing very severe difficulties, managers may be forced to engage in a fundamental review and 'refocusing' of their business operations. In these circumstances it may be appropriate to sell elements of the business to other companies or to encourage the employees themselves to organize a management buy out.

Exercise 4.5   ## Dealing with labour shortages and surpluses

With reference to an organization known to you specify which of the steps outlined above have been taken in any recent attempt to deal with either a shortage or a surplus of labour.

SUMMARY AND CONCLUSION

This chapter began with a review of recent trends within the UK labour market. Among the changes noted in this section were the continuing increase in the number of women at work, enduring long-term unemployment, shifts in the industrial and occupational composition of the workforce and the gradual emergence of part-time, shift and other forms of flexible employment.

These developments have important implications for organizations and their employees. The UK labour market is moving away from a system of employment characterized by employers competing to attract male employees who will work full-time for most of their adult years. In years to come it seems probable that a more diverse pattern of employment will continue to emerge in which men and women compete for a variety of forms of employment.

In the longer term, whether these changed forms of employment will be spread evenly across the workforce remains to be seen. At present the prospects do not seem good. As we saw in the second section of this chapter, there are still considerable differences in the employment prospects available to different sections of the workforce. Women, ethnic minorities, older workers, the long-term unemployed, and the disabled still face significant barriers when searching for employment and a career. For these workers the 'flexible' label applied to temporary, part-time and other non-traditional forms of employment may be no more than a more palatable way of describing poorly paid and insecure work.

Despite the widespread nature of changes to the overall pattern of employment in the UK and the persistence of poor pay and conditions for some groups of employees, the third section of this chapter sought to demonstrate that managers still have choices over the way in which they staff their organizations. As we noted in this section, there are a number of options available to managers in the way in which they structure jobs and career opportunities within their organizations. For example, they may decide to adopt a gamekeeper approach and focus on the development of their own staff. Alternatively, they may choose to avoid the costs of training and development and concentrate instead on poaching staff from other companies; or alternatively sub-contracting work to temporary staff, consultants or suppliers.

For most established organizations it is important to remember that these choices will rarely be presented in such stark terms. It is more likely that decisions made in response to short-term shortages and surpluses of labour will set the tone for general developments in the way in which managers deal with their staff. As the final section of this chapter indicated, managers are often faced with tactical and strategic decisions which can have profound implications for those who are employed and the work that they carry out.

CHAPTER 5

Economics and the UK economy

INTRODUCTION

The citizens of all developed countries are faced with difficult choices about how to organize their activities. An important area within which these decisions are made concerns the planning of work and the creation of wealth. Over the past three hundred years, economics has developed as a field of study devoted to analysing these decisions and their consequences. Derived originally from the Greek word for 'housekeeping', the term 'economics' is generally used today to refer to the study of firms, industries, regions, nations and international trading relationships.

When applied to the UK in the post-war period, this form of analysis has typically sought to explain the reasons for the country's relative economic decline, and to outline ways in which policy could be improved to prevent a continuation of this decay. The main focus of this debate has been upon the steps which national governments can take to maintain and enhance the economic well-being of people and companies in this country. As this chapter aims to demonstrate, governments of different political persuasions have adopted different priorities and policy instruments in their pursuit of this objective of increased economic growth.

FOCUS AND SCOPE

This chapter aims to explain some key economic concepts and to describe the current operation of the UK economy. Throughout this analysis the principal focus is the national economy although, as noted in earlier chapters, the increasing globalization of business means that considerable attention is also devoted to key features of the emerging international economy.

LEARNING OBJECTIVES

Once you have read through this chapter and completed the associated exercises, you should be able to:

- comment on the three principal questions in economics;
- outline the principal features of market and command economies;
- describe six key economic indicators currently used to measure the performance of the UK economy; and
- comment critically on the economic goals pursued by the UK government in recent years.

FIRST PRINCIPLES IN ECONOMICS

Despite tremendous growth in the economic wealth of developed countries over the past three hundred years there is little evidence that the wants of individuals within these societies have been satisfied. In the last century, cars, telephones and colour televisions have been added to the list of goods and services that many people feel they need.

By contrast, more than half the world's population live in countries where people continue to die each year from starvation and a lack of basic health care. Despite calls from some socialist and environmental campaigners for individuals in rich countries to reduce their demands, it seems likely that the mismatch between the limitless wants of people and the world's scarce resources will continue for the foreseeable future. These contradictory pressures give rise to the fundamental problem at the heart of economics – how to reconcile unlimited demand by consumers with the world's limited supply of resources.

The limited supply of resources forces those who make decisions to answer the following three important economic questions:

- What goods and services should be produced?
- How will these goods or services be produced?
- How can these products be distributed?

In tackling these questions the people involved are deciding how resources will be used and how they will not be used. Allocating resources to meet one set of consumer wants will inevitably mean that another set of demands are not satisfied. For example, an individual deciding how to spend his or her wages may have to choose between having a holiday or buying a new car. Similarly, an employer may have to choose between giving employees a pay rise or investing in new equipment. Economists refer to this type of choice as the *opportunity cost* – that is, the cost of the options given up in order to pursue the preferred course of action. For example, the opportunity cost of a government decision to cut taxation on petrol may be a cutback in, or delay in the improvement of, public transport.

When analysing how the basic problems of economics are tackled, it is possible to discern two basic approaches: market and command economies. In practice there are few countries in which either of these systems operate in its pure form; most developed economies have struck some balance between the two and operate what is called a mixed economy.

Market economies

The market system works on the basis of people deciding for themselves what, when, how and where they are going to produce and consume goods and services. Under such a system what will be produced, how it will be produced and the method of distribution is determined by individuals and companies. These different groups within the economy choose what to do by comparing the price of different options and considering which course of action will lead to the biggest improvement in their level of satisfaction.

Many economists use demand and supply analyses to examine the operation of this market system. This approach begins by recognizing that consumers will place different values on different goods and services. These differences will be reflected in the prices that they are prepared to pay.

Demand

Some people will value a particular good or service so much that they will be prepared to pay considerably more than others to ensure that they satisfy their demands. Similarly, with other categories of goods some people will be prepared to buy more of the goods as the price of this product falls. For example, if we look at the demand for apples in the UK over a one-week period, we might find that when the price is £1 per kilo the overall demand is 200 tonnes. When the price falls to 20p per kilo, the overall demand increases to 1000 tonnes. This relationship between the price and demand for apples is mapped out in the form of a demand function in Fig 5.1.

In addition to the price, the demand for apples, as set out in Fig 5.1, will also respond to movements in the price of other goods, changes in consumer preferences (fashion) and shifts in the size and distribution of household income. Change in any one of these variables can alter the shape of the demand function. Figure 5.2 illustrates how the demand function responds when the consumption of apples goes out of fashion.

As Fig 5.2 demonstrates, at any given price the quantity demanded by consumers has decreased. This relationship is represented by the shift in the demand function from D1 to D2. Thus at a constant price of 0P1, the quantity of apples demanded by consumers has fallen back from 0Q1 to 0Q2.

Apart from uniform shifts in the demand curve, as denoted by the movement from D1 to D2 in Fig 5.2, the slope of the demand function may also

Fig 5.1 The demand function

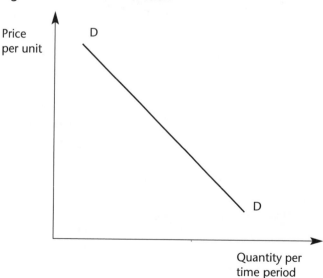

Fig 5.2 Shift in the demand function due to a change in consumer preferences

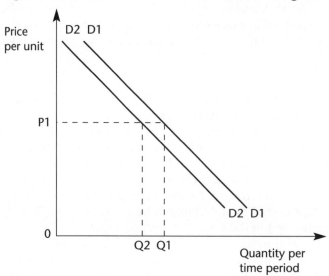

change. The gradient of the demand function is referred to by economists as the *price elasticity of demand*. If the demand function becomes steeper, as illustrated by the movement from D1 to D3 in Fig 5.3, the demand for the goods being sold will become less price sensitive. In these situations people will continue to buy similar quantities of the good despite large increases or decreases in its price. This phenomenon is referred to by economists as *inelastic demand*.

Fig 5.3 The elasticity of demand

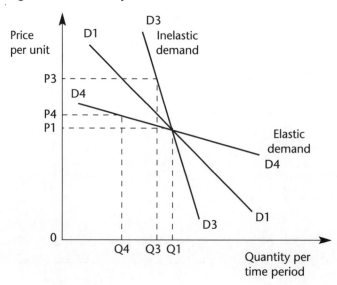

If we reverse these changes and the slope of the demand function becomes less severe, as illustrated by the movement from D1 to D4 in Fig 5.3, the quantity of goods demanded will become much more sensitive to price changes. Thus, if the price increases marginally, the quantity of goods demanded may decrease markedly. Economists refer to this form of relationship as *elastic demand*.

Supply

The supply of goods and services in any market also responds to fluctuations in the price. Other things being equal, when the price of a particular good or service increases in relation to the costs of production, more resources will be devoted to supplying this product. Among the other important variables affecting the supply of a particular product are the prices and profits available from producing other products, the cost of raw materials, the objectives pursued by company managers and, finally, the state of the technology available. If we return to the previous example, the general relationship between the price and supply of apples over one week in the UK is demonstrated by the supply function in Fig 5.4.

Like the demand function, the gradient of the supply function may change giving rise to *elastic* or *inelastic supply*. For example, the supply of many precious metals and stones is relatively inelastic because there are limited amounts of these materials and it is not possible to increase the supply markedly, even if the price rises substantially. By contrast, the quantity of magazines and newspapers supplied may be more sensitive to changes in the price of these products. Thus, other things being equal, an increase in the price consumers are prepared to pay may lead to a substantial increase in the quantity supplied.

Fig 5.4 The supply function

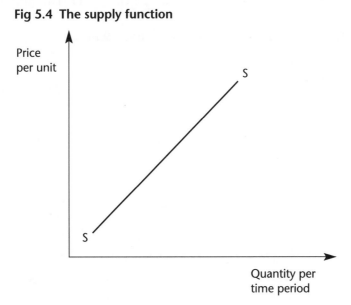

The interaction of demand and supply

If we now bring together the two sides of the equation and examine the interaction of supply and demand we find that where the two lines intersect supply equals demand. Economists refer to the intersection of the demand and supply functions as *the equilibrium position*. At this point the market should clear. In other words everything that is supplied will be purchased. In Fig 5.5, at the equilibrium position the quantity of apples actually supplied is 0Q1 at the price 0P1. The total revenue available to suppliers from all these sales can be calculated using the following formula 0P1 × 0Q1.

Thus according to free market economists, prices respond, more or less, to the forces of demand and supply. The end result tends to be the equilibrium of demand and supply and therefore the coordination of the economic activities of countless individual consumers and companies. In the words of Adam Smith, 'the invisible hand of the market' guides the best utilization, production and distribution of goods and services.

However, the market system is not without its failings and critics. Among the most commonly cited problems are the following.

Market domination

The free interaction of demand and supply may be subject to distortions caused by the collusion of a few producers or consumers. In these situations prices may be kept artificially high, or the quantity of goods supplied may be restricted, in order to ensure that a few firms or individuals make very substantial profits or gains.

Inequality

This may arise because goods and services are distributed according to ability to pay, rather than the need of the consumer. This will mean that poorer

Fig 5.5 The interaction of demand and supply

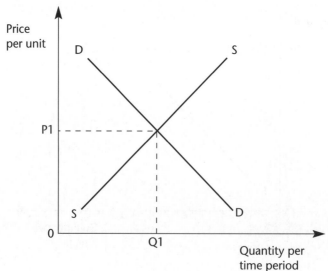

members of a society may not receive the goods and services they need. In the short term, this may appear economic, but in the longer term the costs of dealing with the crime and disease which result from poor housing, education and health will be considerable.

Economic dislocation
Rapid changes within a particular market may have very detrimental effects upon the employees or immediate neighbours of a particular business. For example, a fall in the international price of coal has led to the closure of a number of collieries. These closures have meant that not only have many miners lost their jobs, but also that other local shops and companies have experienced significant losses of business.

Externalities
The market system provides an ineffective means of controlling and reducing the environmental and social costs associated with modern business activity. For example, individuals and companies who pollute the atmosphere may be able to avoid the costs of this activity. In these situations the final costs of dealing with the consequences of this pollution may have to be met by people who live many miles away.

Public goods
There are many goods and services which are best provided collectively, either because the costs would be prohibitive if they had to be borne by small groups or individuals, or, alternatively, because it would not be possible to enjoy fully the benefits of these products unless everyone else had access. Examples of public goods include the fire, health and sanitation services. In a market system it may be tempting for an individual to avoid paying for these public goods because they rarely, if ever, need them, or alternatively, because they feel that the services provided by other people's contributions are sufficient to ensure that they are covered. However, this so-called *free-rider* approach only works if the number of people who avoid paying for the service is relatively small. When the number of free-riders increases there is a danger that the limited cover provided by a few people will be insufficient to cover the needs of those who have opted out.

The failure of the price mechanism
Market systems do not work perfectly because there are limits to the availability of information about the prices of particular goods and services. Furthermore, even when price information is available, people rarely, if ever, have the time, capacity or ability to react and alter their behaviour as a consequence (Omerod, 1994). For example, when people choose a job, they rarely conduct their own comprehensive survey of the relative wages on offer before deciding upon which employer to work for.

Price is not the only indicator of worth
Traditional economic analysis suggests that consumers and producers are motivated primarily by the cost or price of a product. Thus workers will seek

the highest wage, consumers will hunt for the lowest prices, and producers will pursue the lowest costs. However, reducing all human behaviour to this form of economic calculus has its dangers. As a number of social commentators have pointed out, this form of analysis ignores wider social and ethical motivations in human behaviour (Etzioni, 1988). For example, wages are affected by feelings of fairness, established internal pay scales, the cost of living, general wage increases, and a number of other factors which are not related to the state of the employer's capital, labour or product markets. As a consequence employers will rarely lower or increase the pay of their employees purely in response to changes in the general price of labour, costs of their raw materials, or the price of their finished goods and services.

The myth of the free market

The operation of market economies relies on a system of law and social customs which defines ownership rights, regulates the exchange of property, and controls the exchange of labour for wages. In the absence of these legal and social regulations there would be considerable incentives for people to steal, renege on commercial agreements, or engage in fraud. Thus the view that markets are part of the natural order and that they would emerge in their present form without any regulation is misplaced. Instead it is more appropriate to see markets as relying on centralized controls or cultural norms which ensure that everyone knows and abides by the rules of the game. The presence of these laws, regulations and customs in turn create their own anomalies which prevent markets from behaving in the manner suggested by traditional economic analyses.

Exercise 5.1 | ## Market economies

Draw a diagram to map out the effects of the following changes to the demand for and supply of apples:

(a) A change in fashion which leads to an increased desire for apples.
(b) An improvement in technology which makes it cheaper to grow and supply apples.

Command economies

Command economies are managed by a central authority which determines what, when, how and where goods and services should be produced and consumed. This central authority decides what resources to use, what to produce and how to distribute on the basis of cost, anticipated demand and wider economic, social and political objectives. For much of the twentieth century, countries within the Communist Bloc operated as command economies.

The advent of *glasnost, perestroika* and the gradual break-up of the USSR and its satellite states in Eastern Europe have generally been viewed as signalling an end to the centrally planned system. The old warnings of Nikita Khrushchev, leader of the USSR in the early 1960s, that Communism would bury Capitalism, appear to have been turned on their head. Today, no country in the world operates a pure command economy. Indeed in recent years all of the former communist states have adopted some form of market-based approach modelled on established practice in western economies. This movement away from command economy structures was based upon a recognition of the following problems associated with centrally planned systems.

- *Difficulties in forecasting future demands.* The problems associated with producing accurate centralized forecasts of consumer demand led to the over-provision of some goods and chronic shortages of others. The gaps in supply were then frequently filled by the growth of black market activity.

- *Lack of focus on the customer.* Increasing wealth leads to a wider variety of tastes and a more discerning approach by consumers. It is therefore difficult for central planners to anticipate and accommodate these changes in fashion.

- *Lack of incentives for producers.* The central determination of the level of supply and the prices that will be charged means that local managers and employees have few economic incentives to operate more effectively and efficiently. As a consequence the quantity and quality of products may be lower than expected.

- *Low investment.* The desire to minimize costs leads to a lack of investment in improving technology.

- *Bureaucracy.* The need to produce complex central plans may increase bureaucracy as a large number of staff are employed to draw up and issue these documents. Furthermore, if these planners are not democratically accountable the plans will not only ignore the demands of consumers, but may also fail to take account of the environmental and social concerns of the wider population.

Mixed economies

Mixed economies combine elements of the market-based and centrally planned systems outlined above. Thus some areas of economic activity are centrally planned, e.g. the armed services and police force, while others are left to centrally or locally regulated markets, e.g. groceries and telecommunication services.

The relative balance between these two forms of provision usually reflects political decisions about the best means to provide certain goods and services. As we have seen in earlier sections, markets tend to respond more quickly to changes in consumer demands because they provide strong incentives to producers to alter their output as tastes change. However, democratically accountable centrally planned systems tend to provide a more effective means of taking social and environmental costs into account when deciding what to produce, how it is to be made and what is the most effective means of distributing it.

In the UK, despite concerted efforts by recent Conservative administrations to introduce the discipline of the market into an increasingly wider sphere of economic activity, the State oversees the planned provision of goods and services in a number of areas. Thus the UK can still be characterized as a mixed economy. The areas of economic activity within the UK which are still planned or heavily regulated by the State include:

- *Provision of essential services*. The government provides health, education, sanitation, policing and national defence for everyone, regardless of their ability to pay. These services benefit all members of society and there is a general political consensus that a market system would not produce the same level of provision.

- *Transfer payments*. Various forms of taxation and government borrowing are used to redirect resources within the economy to more desired ends, e.g. pensions and social security payments.

- *Regulation of monopolies and cartels*. Whether privately or publicly owned, the government monitors, regulates and places limits on the activities of monopolies in the UK, e.g. Ofgas, Oftel, Monopolies and Mergers Commission and the Office of Fair Trading.

- *Social costs and benefits*. The government intervenes in the market to protect consumers from certain goods and services which are deemed to produce high social costs, e.g. drugs and alcohol. In addition, a growing awareness of the damage done to the environment by the activities of industry has led to government proposals to control pollution by taxing or prosecuting polluters.

- *Support for industry and commerce*. Regional, industry and organization-level grants may be made by governments to support economic or social goals, e.g. assisted areas and small business grants.

- *Management of economic activity*. Governments intervene in the economy to encourage balanced economic growth, control the level of inflation and to promote acceptable uses of the nation's scarce resources. This area of government activity is commonly referred to as *macroeconomic policy*. The following section examines government activity in this area in more detail.

THE GOALS OF MACROECONOMIC POLICY

Governments normally pursue a number of economic objectives simultaneously, although the importance of each and the trade-offs between them vary, reflecting the political orientation of the people in power and the external pressures facing these policy makers. Furthermore, most countries are subject to international economic pressures as a consequence of trade with other nations and the movement of capital across borders. The list below sets out some of the more commonly sought objectives of macroeconomic policy.

- *Economic growth*. As measured by national income and other indices, consistent economic growth usually leads to increases in the living standards of the general population.

- *High employment*. Persistent unemployment represents wasted resources and may be politically damaging to the political party in power.

- *Low inflation*. High levels of inflation create uncertainty and may erode standards of living and the value of investments and savings.

- *A sound balance of payments coupled with a strong and stable currency value in foreign exchange markets*. The balance of payments refers to the flows of money in and out of a national economy. Governments normally strive to avoid a deficit balance.

In addition to the above list, at different times in post-war UK history, governments have pursued their own subsidiary goals. Among the more noteworthy have been attempts to influence the distribution of wealth and income and increase or decrease the level of state ownership of industry and commerce.

In order to measure progress towards their preferred economic goals, governments use a range of economic indicators. The definition and calculation of six of these measures – economic growth, inflation, money supply, balance of payments, exchange rates and employment – and the operation of associated policy instruments form the focus of the remainder of this section.

Economic growth

Economic growth is the term used to describe expansion of the productive capacity of an economy. In general it is assumed by most economic commentators that economic growth will lead to a general improvement in people's living standards, if the population of a country remains relatively stable. As a consequence, in the post-war period, governments of all political persuasions have sought to promote economic growth within the UK. In determining specific objectives for this economic growth these administrations have relied upon one or more of the following three measures of economic growth.

- *Gross domestic product (GDP)* measures what is produced in the domestic economy.
- *Gross national product (GNP)* adds to GDP property income from abroad.
- *National income* deducts capital consumption, including the sale of investments in housing and shares, from GNP.

Despite their apparent simplicity and common usage, there are three important problems associated with the use of these measures as an indication of the economic performance of a country.

1 *There are difficulties associated with the measurement of these indices.* Gross domestic product and the other two measures of economic growth can be measured in three ways: either by counting output, expenditure or income. In theory all three measures should produce the same result, but in practice they rarely do. For example, between 1980 and 1992 differences between the highest and lowest of the three measures of annual growth in GDP averaged 0.6 per cent (Kennedy, 1992). This may appear to be a small figure, but when we consider it in the context of the average annual rate of GDP growth in the UK over the last 50 years the effects are more marked. The addition or subtraction of 0.6 per cent to the 2.2 per cent average annual rate of GDP growth produces significantly different perceptions of the performance of the British economy in recent years. (*See* Table 5.1.)

2 *Some important areas of productive human activity are excluded.* For example, the official measures take no account of housework, do-it-yourself, volun-

LIBRARY
BISHOP BURTON COLLEGE
BEVERLEY HU17 8QG

Table 5.1 National and domestic output (1993)

	£ million
Gross domestic product at market prices	570 722
Net property income from abroad	9 496
Gross national product at market prices	580 218
Net transfer income from abroad	−4 874
Terms of trade effect	3 334
National income	578 678

Source: *United Kingdom National Accounts: The Blue Book*, p 11, Office for National Statistics. Crown Copyright 1995. Reproduced by permission of the Controller of HMSO and the Office for National Statistics.

tary work or any other form of work which is not sold for money. Similarly, in the UK, but interestingly not in Italy, these figures ignore the contribution of the 'black economy' and other unlawful or illegal activity. If measures of the contribution made by these forms of activity were included in the country's national accounts it is possible that different conclusions could be reached about the performance of UK PLC in recent years.

3 *The primacy attached to these measures by government ministers and other policy makers can have negative consequences.* According to a number of critics this focus upon economic growth has detracted attention from other important gauges of the social well-being of the population. Although measures exist to monitor people's health, education, housing, general satisfaction and the state of the natural environment, these have not generally been given the same priority as economic growth. As a consequence a number of economists have suggested alternative measures of economic and social progress. For example, the United Nation's Human Development Index, which ranks countries by a measure combining life expectancy, educational attainment and basic purchasing power, placed the UK in 17th position in a list of 174 countries compiled in 1995. The top three positions in this league table were held by Canada, the USA and Japan (UN,1995).

Despite these problems with measures of the UK's economic performance, GDP, GNP and National Income remain the principal yardsticks for estimates of improvements in the UK economy. By these measures in the post-war period UK economic growth has been very variable. As Fig 5.6 indicates, the level of economic growth within the UK has been subject to periodic booms and cyclical recessions. During the nineteenth century this economic or business cycle appeared to occur every seven to ten years. After the First World War this pattern ceased and for nearly twenty years the UK and much of the western world experienced a sustained depression in economic activity. This economic collapse was reversed in the USA and much of Europe during the 1930s by massive programmes of public spending and rearmament. The recovery resumed after

Fig 5.6 Economic growth in the UK: 1951–1993 (at factor cost)

Volume index (1990 = 100)

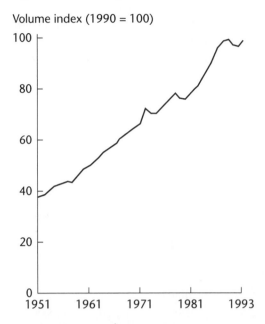

Source: Social Trends 1994, No 24: 98, Office for National Statistics. Crown Copyright 1995. Reproduced by permission of the Controller of HMSO and the Office for National Statistics.

the Second World War and continued until the early 1970s. Although the UK experienced declines in economic growth over this period they never lasted more than one year, and rarely involved more than a 1 per cent decline in GDP. In most of these downturns GDP merely grew at a slower rate, rather than declining in real terms. This pattern changed again in the early 1970s and for the last 20 or more years the UK has once again experienced alternating periods of economic growth and recession on a seven- to ten-year cycle.

Apart from wrestling with the problems of managing cyclical variations in the economic growth rate, post-war governments of the UK have also been concerned with the overall level of growth. Although the economy has grown, the rate of this growth is lower than that of many competitor nations. As Table 5.2 indicates, this relative decline continued during the 1980s and 1990s. According to recent figures compiled by the Organisation of Economic Cooperation and Development (OECD) – a grouping of 24 of the world's largest industrial nations – although the UK remains the world's sixth largest economy, it lies in 17th position in terms of GDP per head of population. Furthermore, there are few signs of this relative decline abating. Several economies in the Far East have recently experienced economic growth rates which are twice those of the UK. In addition, recent studies of international corporate and national competitiveness appear to indicate that the UK is falling even further behind. According to the World Economic Forum, between 1994 and 1995 the UK slipped from 14th to 18th position in the league table of global competitiveness (WEF, 1995). If these trends continue, it appears to be only a matter of time before the relative wealth of the UK's population declines even further.

Table 5.2 Gross domestic product in OECD nations

	GDP at current prices and exchange rates ($ bn) (1993)	GDP per capita at current prices and exchange rates ($ bn) (1993)	Average annual GDP growth (%) (1982–92)
Australia	278.8	16566	3.1
Austria	181.2	23495	2.5
Belgium	207.5	21829	2.2
Canada	548.9	20541	2.8
Denmark	135.4	27551	2.1
Finland	81.8	21058	1.5
France	1254.4	23006	2.1
Germany	1712.9	27592	2.9
Greece	74.2	7562	1.8
Iceland	5.8	25451	1.8
Ireland	44.7	13729	3.9
Italy	999.7	21122	2.4
Japan	4198.0	29525	4.0
Luxembourg	10.3	27073	4.0
Netherlands	309.4	21102	2.6
New Zealand	43.4	12099	1.3
Norway	103.2	26343	2.8
Portugal	75.1	8551	2.7
Spain	482.8	14708	3.2
Sweden	185.3	28489	1.6
Switzerland	232.8	34962	2.0
Turkey	138.4	1914	5.2
United Kingdom	927.4	18027	2.3
United States	6245.4	23215	2.8

Source: OECD (1994)

In order to cope with the twin problems of variable and low rates of economic growth, government ministers and policy makers in the UK have looked to economists for proposals to improve the situation. Economists' views of how to increase a nation's economic growth may be divided roughly into two schools of thought: *Keynesian* and *Monetarist*. The ideas of the first group evolved from the work of John Maynard Keynes and had a profound effect upon the economic policies of governments of all political persuasions between 1945 and 1976. Put simply, Keynesian economists believe that the level of economic growth within an economy is determined by the overall level of consumer demand for goods and services. Today, Keynesian economists still believe that when an economy has spare productive capacity (people and capital), investment and output can be stimulated without increasing inflation by changing levels of government expenditure. They argue that this can be achieved by altering taxation or government borrowing in order to finance public projects which will inject money into the economy and therefore fuel demand.

The apparent failure of Keynesian policies in the mid-1970s, when both inflation and unemployment remained persistently high (circumstances referred to as *stagflation*), led policy makers to focus their attention on an alternative Monetarist approach. Monetarist policies owe much to the work of Milton Friedman in the USA. He conducted a number of studies examining the relationship between the supply of money in an economy and the overall level of inflation and economic growth. He argued that increasing government expenditure inevitably led to increases in the money supply which rather than fuelling growth merely led to an increase in inflation in the longer term. As a consequence of this line of thought, Monetarists have argued that you cannot buck the market. The proper job of government is twofold: first, to limit the growth in the money supply to changes in the level of productive capacity in the economy; and second, to ensure that there are few barriers to the effective operation of markets within the economy. The second of these objectives can be achieved by reducing taxation, benefits and regulations on the free movement of labour and the competitive behaviour of organizations. In addition, the operation of the market may be improved by regulating the behaviour of large companies, trade unions and professional associations to ensure that they do not engage in restrictive practices. By adopting this approach, inflation may be limited and appropriate conditions for the growth of private enterprise can be created.

Although the Monetarist approach was initially successful in reducing inflation in the late 1970s, in 1979 international and national economic pressures coupled with the tight monetary stance of the UK's new Conservative administration led directly to a deep recession between 1980 and 1982. Having recovered from this recession, the UK enjoyed a period of rapid growth during the mid-1980s.

In 1987, the UK economy began to experience new problems. The combination of an international stock market crisis, the relaxation of controls on individual credit; and inadequate or inaccurate measures of the economy's performance conspired to produce an unsustainable consumer spending boom. In the fallout from the so-called Lawson boom, the government once again pursued a policy of attempting to control inflation through the combination of interest rates and maintaining a specified exchange rate against the Deutschmark. By 1990, however, separate wrangles about the role of the UK within the European Community led directly to the resignation of Margaret Thatcher and a fundamental switch in government economic policy. When the UK joined the exchange rate mechanism (ERM) in October 1990, the primary policy goal became the maintenance of a stable exchange rate. Unfortunately, the decision to enter the ERM coincided with the onset of recession in the UK and elsewhere in the western world. This recession was prompted, at least in part, by austerity measures introduced in Germany to ease the process of reunification with the East, and concerns about government debt in the USA. The ensuing recession became the longest, although not the deepest, in UK post-war history and together with uncertainty about Britain's commitment to the European Community led to speculation about the government's ability and commitment to sustain the chosen Sterling/

Deutschmark exchange rate. In early September 1992 increased speculation on the international money markets led to the UK's withdrawal from the ERM. With the abandonment of this policy the Conservative government at that time reaffirmed its commitment to moderate and sustainable economic growth within strict inflation targets.

Inflation

In general there is agreement between economists about how inflation manifests itself. In essence, it is seen as an increase in the price of any factor of production or output, e.g. price or wage inflation. Thus an annual rate of inflation of 10 per cent will increase the price of a £300 fridge by £30 to £330 over a twelve-month period. However, this general agreement between economists masks some important areas of disagreement: how to measure inflation; what is an acceptable level of inflation; what causes increases in prices and wages; and how to control inflation.

Measures of inflation

In the UK economy a range of indices are used to measure inflation; these include the Retail Prices Index (RPI), the Tax and Prices Index (TPI), the Consumers' Expenditure Deflator and the Producer Output Prices Index.

The *RPI* is sometimes referred to as the headline rate of inflation as it is most commonly quoted in the media. As an index it measures the total cost of a notional basket of goods and services of the sort bought by the great majority of UK households (excluding pensioners dependent on state benefits and the wealthiest 4 per cent of the population). It is constructed by collecting the prices of around 600 items on a specified day every month (including mortgage interest payments and council tax). These are then weighted according to their importance within household budgets. To avoid seasonality in the figures (the effect of changes in the price of fruit and vegetables, etc.), the increase in retail prices is expressed as a percentage change since the same month a year earlier (*see* Fig 5.7).

Although the RPI is the measure of inflation most commonly referred to there are a number of problems with this index which may be overcome by alternative measures.

First, the RPI takes no account of changes in direct taxation. This means that reductions in personal tax allowances and increases in income tax rates or the level of national insurance contributions are not reflected in changes in the RPI's measure of inflation. This failing is overcome by the *Tax and Prices Index* which takes account of these changes and is therefore often favoured by trade union negotiators who are anxious to protect their members' real standards of living in annual wage negotiations.

Second, the RPI is based upon the contents of a notional basket of goods and services which is updated infrequently and may therefore not be representative of an average family's purchases. More worryingly this measure tends to exaggerate the effects of inflation during periods of rapid price increases, because it fails to take account of the fact that consumers alter their buying behaviour by purchasing fewer of the most inflationary goods and services.

Fig 5.7 The components of the Retail Prices Index (RPI)

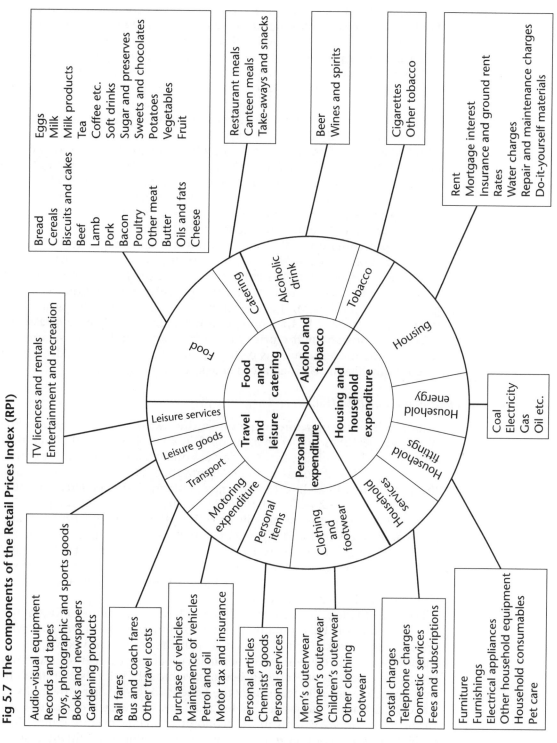

Source: Economic Briefing. Crown copyright. Crown copyright is reproduced with the permission of the Controller of HMSO.

These problems are overcome by the *Consumer Expenditure Deflator (CED)* which provides a measure of real purchasing activity within the economy. In addition, this measure has the added benefit of including an estimate of housing costs which is based on notional rental values of owner-occupied housing rather than mortgage interest payments. This is beneficial because a reliance on interest payments may mean that the inflation rate as measured by the RPI will increase at a time when governments are using interest-rate changes as a means of reducing inflation. In these circumstances the cure (higher interest rates) may appear to make the symptoms (the level of price inflation) worse.

Third, the RPI only deals with consumer prices and therefore does not deal with inflation as it affects the price of wholesale goods. As these price rises may feed through into the rest of the economy at a later date, the RPI is best treated as an historic measure rather than as an indication of what might happen in the future. For these reasons many management negotiators may prefer to focus their attention on the Producer Output Prices Index as this may give an indication of future trends in inflation.

As the preceding discussion has illustrated, there are a variety of ways in which inflation can be measured. It is not surprising, therefore, that these different measures produce different indications of the level of inflation in the economy. Obviously, the combination of estimates of future economic growth and inflation will have an immediate effect upon decisions within many organizations. In the short term we might expect these measures to affect decisions about the price of products and the level of salaries and wages. In the longer term, it is perhaps more important to consider what, in an economy like the UK's, an acceptable level of inflation is.

What is an acceptable level of inflation?

Inflation is not a new phenomenon in the UK. In 1990, the Retail Prices Index was 45 times higher than its level in 1900. However, this significant increase in the level of consumer prices conceals variations in the rates of increase at different points in time. During the first 90 years of this century the level of inflation fell in 13 years, most notably during periods of recession or depression – 1920–23 and 1925–33. Meanwhile, during the periods of moderate and sustained economic growth in the 1950s and 1960s inflation stood at averages of 3 and 4 per cent respectively. It was not until the mid-1970s that inflation became really serious, with a record rate of 25 per cent in 1975 and an average rate for the decade of 13 per cent. During the 1980s the inflation rate fell from 19 per cent to 3 per cent in 1986 before rising again to 9 per cent at the end of the decade.

These fluctuations in the rate of inflation have led a number of economists to suggest that the UK economy is inherently inflationary – a tendency which appears most marked when compared with the consistently lower levels of inflation experienced by some of our main economic competitors. According to this view, periods of economic boom have brought price rises in their aftermath which eventually wipe away the benefits of the earlier growth. By this standard, inflation should be avoided at all costs because it erodes the benefits of earlier improvements in the economy as well as making it difficult for employers and employees to predict how their production or living costs will alter in the near future. By contrast, a number of other economists suggest that moderate levels of inflation may be acceptable or even beneficial. They argue that if the level of inflation is predictable, producers and consumers can adjust their behaviour to take account of possible future price rises. Furthermore, the presence of low levels of inflation is preferable to periods of sustained price falls, because rising prices can increase consumer confidence. The recent decline of the UK housing market is used as one example of how falling prices can undermine this confidence and thereby restrict or delay a more general expansion of the economy.

This disagreement between economists about what is an acceptable level of inflation reflects deeper seated differences in their analyses of the causes of inflation. Here, once again, there are a variety of different views; however, the most fundamental differences exist between Keynesian and Monetarist economists.

Causes of inflation

For many Keynesian economists the fundamental cause of inflation is excess demand (*demand pull*) or cost increases (*cost push*); therefore, the most efficient means of reducing inflation is through one or more of the following mechanisms: limiting demand via taxation, quotas and rationing, or constraints on cost increases through prices and incomes policies. Under these arrangements in periods of relatively high economic growth and rising inflation, excessive consumer spending is reined in by increases in indirect purchase taxes and direct income taxes. Similarly, mortgages and other forms of credit which might create inflation are controlled through strict limits on the availability of this form of finance. Meanwhile, incomes policies are used to limit the level of pay rises in the economy by setting national guidelines or going rates. Finally, price controls discourage companies from passing on to the consumer the effects of increases in the price of their raw materials and labour.

By contrast, Monetarist economists argue that inflation arises from the presence of too much money in an economy. If the presence of paper money exceeds the real value of goods and services in any economy then the price of goods, in terms of paper money, will increase giving rise to inflation. Thus Monetarists argue that governments can reduce inflation by restricting the money supply through the use of interest rates (increasing the cost of money) and tight controls on public spending.

Money supply

Any attempt to restrict the supply of money requires an accurate measure of the money supply so that the success of policy can be determined. In a modern economy like the UK, however, a universal definition of money is not available, as money exists in several different forms, e.g. cash (notes and coins), bank deposits and credit arrangements. In order to cope with this diversity of forms the government has developed a series of ways of measuring the money supply. These different measures are known as the *monetary aggregates* (*see* Table 5.3).

Balance of payments

The UK economy relies heavily on trade and the international flow of capital to generate the nation's income and meet the demands of the country's

---

Table 5.3 Money aggregates and their components

M0   Cash in circulation, in banks' tills, money deposits and deposits with the Bank of England. (Non-interest bearing component of M1.)

M1   M0 plus private sector interest-bearing sterling bank deposits.

M2   M0 plus private sector interest-bearing retail sterling bank deposits plus private sector holdings of retail building society shares, deposits, national savings bank ordinary accounts.

£M3   M1 plus private sector sterling bank deposits and private sector holdings of sterling bank certificates of deposit.

M3c   £M3 plus private sector holdings of foreign currency bank deposits.

M4   £M3 plus building society shares, deposits, sterling certificates of deposit and holdings of foreign currency bank deposits. Less building society holdings of bank deposits, bank certificates of deposit, notes and coin.

M5   M4 plus holdings by the private sector (excluding building societies) of money-market instruments (bank bills, treasury bills, local authority deposits) certificates of tax deposit and national savings instruments (excluding certificates, SAYE and other long-term deposits).

---

consumers for goods and services. The balance of payments provides a summarized statement of a country's international trade transactions in goods and services and capital transactions with all other countries.

The UK's balance of payments account is divided into two parts.

- *The current account.* This records visible and invisible import and export activity. Visible imports and exports are those goods which can be physically seen and counted, e.g. aeroplanes, cars and hairdryers. The invisible balance consists of the sale and purchase of services between the UK and other countries, plus interest on investments, profits and dividends paid and transfer payments. The term 'transfer payments' refers to non-trading and non-commercial payments, e.g. private gifts, international aid and subscriptions to international organizations.

- *The capital account.* This is the balance of payments statement and covers changes in a nation's external assets and liabilities including foreign exchange reserves and borrowings.

By definition, the sum of these two parts of the balance of payments must be equal to zero (the overall balance of payments always balances). Thus media reports of a balance of payments deficit refer only to the current account and are always financed by a reduction in foreign currency reserves or an increase in borrowings from overseas so that the overall balance remains zero.

At the bottom of the statement of the UK's balance of payments account is the *balancing item*. This relates to discrepancies between the total value of recorded transactions and the actual flow of money, i.e. it is the total of errors and omissions arising within the balance of payments accounts. A positive value shows there have been unrecorded net inflows and a negative value that there have been unrecorded negative outflows. The size of the balancing item from any one period can be huge highlighting the difficulties in interpreting the data, for any one single period (*see* Table 5.4).

An imbalance in the UK's current account balance of payments will have the following implications. In the case of a deficit, the country will face a drain on its foreign currency reserves and is likely to find itself getting into more and more debt with overseas monetary agencies and authorities. By contrast, a country experiencing a continuing balance of payments surplus will be accumulating reserves at the expense of the deficit countries. Eventually this inflow of currency may create inflationary pressures as the foreign currency is converted into own currency increasing the overall money supply. Given these possible problems there are four policy measures available to control the overall balance of payments.

- *Demand management policies.* Expanding demand will generally lead to an increase in imports reducing a balance of payments surplus. Similarly, contracting demand should reduce the level of imports and consequently decrease a balance of payments deficit.

- *Supply side policies.* As previously mentioned these policies focus on improving the efficiency and effectiveness of an economy. If successful, these policies will improve the international competitiveness of an economy and consequently gradually move the balance of trade into surplus.

- *International trade policy and protectionist measures.* Artificial barriers to trade with other countries will obviously reduce the level of imports. However, limits on imports are likely to lead to retaliatory action by the governments of the exporting countries. Furthermore, the growing globalization of

Table 5.4 The UK balance of payments 1993 (current account) (£ million)

Visible trade		
Exports	121 414	
Imports	134 623	
Visible balance		−13 209
Invisibles		
Credits	116 000	
Debits	113 102	
Invisibles balance		2 898
of which:		
Services balance		4 942
Investment balance		3 062
Transfers balance		−5 106
Current balance		−10 311

Source: United Kingdom National Accounts: The Blue Book, Office for National Statistics. Crown Copyright 1995. Reproduced by permission of the Controller of HMSO and the Office for National Statistics.

business activities has to lead to increased cooperation between the governments of different countries designed to reduce the barriers to international trade and thereby foster economic growth. There have been two important developments in this direction:

1 attempts by the World Trade Organisation (formerly known as the General Agreement on Tariffs and Trade) to promote free trade between all countries of the world;

2 the establishment of a number of international customs unions or trading blocks including the European Union (EU), North American Free Trade Area (Nafta) and the Asia-Pacific Economic Cooperation Forum (APEC).

● *Exchange rate management policies*. The final option available to governments is the management of their exchange rate. The following section deals with the mechanisms by which countries attempt to manage their exchange rate in more detail.

Exchange rate

Exchange rates exist because one country's currency is not acceptable in another country and this leads to the need to exchange or convert money from one currency to another. Most developed western countries permit this form of exchange, but not all currencies may be freely traded. Some countries have non-convertible currencies, and others, like the UK before 1979, operate exchange controls which limit the amount of currency that may be traded or taken out of a country.

Exchange rates may be managed/fixed or free-floating. Over the past one hundred years, the UK has experimented with both of these approaches.

Under a managed or fixed exchange rate system, government ministers make a commitment to maintaining the value of their currency against another specified currency or international standard. This value is then defended by the country's central bank which buys or sells the domestic currency on international money markets. In the short term, the value of the currency may be reduced by sales on the international money markets; similarly, the value of the currency may be increased by buying the domestic currency with foreign currency reserves. It is in the longer term, however, that fixed exchange rates are supposed to help a country's economic planning. The main virtue of fixed/managed exchange rates is that they impose a discipline upon a country's economic policy makers ensuring that governments do not use short-term currency devaluation to fuel short-term economic growth. In the long term, within a fixed or managed exchange rate system, currency stability may only be achieved by improvements in a country's international competitiveness whether this is achieved through deflationary policies or economic restructuring.

There have been three periods over the last one hundred years during which the UK has been a member of a fixed or managed exchange rate system: the Gold Standard (linking the value of sterling to the value of gold) from the late nineteenth century until the 1930s, The Bretton Woods Exchange Rate System (linking sterling to the value of the dollar) from 1944 to 1971, and the Exchange Rate Mechanism (ERM) (linking the value of sterling to the ECU and Deutschmark) from October 1990 to September 1992 (*see* Exhibit 5.1).

Fixed or managed exchange rate systems work most effectively when the economies of member states are performing in similar ways. When one or more countries is experiencing higher rates of growth, inflation or public debt than other members, problems are likely to arise. For example, as one member's currency appreciates that country's economic policy makers will be forced to sell their currency on the foreign exchange markets. This approach will inevitably lead to an expansion of the money supply and may force up the inflation rate. These problems confronted the UK in the late 1980s when the then Chancellor of the Exchequer, Nigel Lawson, pursued a policy of maintaining the UK exchange rate at £1=DM3. By contrast, when one member's economy experi-

Exhibit 5.1

European Monetary Union

The Maastricht Treaty, agreed in 1992, contained a commitment to promoting 'an ever closer union among the peoples of Europe'. A central component of this treaty was a three-stage plan to create monetary union between member states. The first two stages of this plan involved wider membership of the European Exchange Rate Mechanism (ERM) and the creation of a Central European Bank in Frankfurt, Germany.

The Exchange Rate Mechanism (ERM)

The ERM works on the following basis. The currency of each member state is allotted a central rate against the European Currency Unit (ECU). The ECU is a 'basket' of *all* member state currencies, and consists of specified amounts of each country's currency. The relative amounts of component currencies roughly reflect the countries' relative economic weight and are reviewed at least every five years. Although the central rate is formally expressed in ECUs, most media coverage of the ERM refers to a currency's exchange rate against the Deutschmark because this is the European Union's strongest currency.

Members of the ERM limit movements in their exchange rates in relation to other member currencies by coordinated intervention in the international money markets. Several members are allowed to fluctuate their exchange rates within a margin of 2.25 per cent above or below the central rates (the *narrow band*). Other countries are allowed more discretion within a so-called *wide band*. When one currency strays from its margins against another member currency, the central banks in both countries are under an obligation to intervene in the foreign exchange markets. For

example, if the Franc/Deutschmark exchange rate reaches the limit of its range the French central bank must sell Deutschmarks to buy francs and the Bundesbank must sell Deutschmarks to buy francs. In the short term, there are central credit facilities available under the ERM to ensure that this intervention can take place.

A single European currency

The Maastricht Treaty envisaged that each member state of the European Union would join the ERM and progress to the narrow band before adopting a single currency in 1997. However, since the treaty was signed a number of events have produced setbacks to this timetable. The date for monetary union has now been put back to 1999 and member states are no longer required to be members of the ERM before signing up for the new 'Euro' single currency, although the participant states will still be required to meet a number of economic *convergence criteria*. These criteria cover measures of economic performance including the inflation rate, the size of the budget deficit and the accumulated level of government debt.

At present there are some doubts about whether all member states will achieve the convergence criteria by the spring of 1998 – the deadline date for countries wanting to take part in the creation of a single currency in 1999. Meanwhile, the governments of the UK and Denmark have reserved the right to opt out of EMU in 1998 if they believe the adoption of a single European currency would be inappropriate for their national economies. When the decision is finally made in the UK, there have been suggestions that this will be on the basis of the results of a national referendum.

ences problems leading to a fall in its exchange rate, policy makers will be forced to buy their own currency through the money markets. In the long term this policy will not be sustainable as foreign currency reserves may become exhausted. Unless other more fundamental steps are taken to address the decline in the exchange rate, this member's currency will be forced to devalue against other currencies in the system. This problem confronted the UK in September 1992 when Norman Lamont, the then Chancellor of the Exchequer, decided to remove sterling from the ERM and allow it to float freely.

The term 'floating exchange rate' refers to situations where the exchange rate is determined by the interaction of supply and demand for a particular currency in international foreign exchange markets. Under this system the exchange rate reflects the relative price competitiveness of an economy and speculation about its future performance. This system offers governments the benefit of rapid movement in the exchange rate to reflect changes in the balance of trade and investment. For example, if a country experiences balance of payments problems reducing the exchange rate may help to bring the balance back into equilibrium. Decline in the value of the currency will make exports more attractive to overseas buyers, while imports to the home country will increase in price and decline in number. However, whether the effects of this devaluation can be maintained in the longer term depends upon the ability of governments, employers and employees to prevent these gains being lost through inflationary increases in domestic wages and prices.

Floating exchange rates also have political as well as economic benefits for national governments. Under a fixed or managed exchange rate system governments are required to sanction any change in the international value of their currency. In the UK these changes have typically involved a politically embarrassing devaluation of sterling. For example, the official devaluation of sterling by Harold Wilson in the late 1960s and Britain's exit from the ERM in 1992 were widely treated with dismay by many journalists and economic commentators. Meanwhile, between 1972 and 1986, when sterling was allowed to float relatively freely in foreign exchange markets, the gradual devaluation of sterling was arguably just as damaging, but less contentious because it happened slowly.

For business people and tourists, floating exchange rates produce considerable extra costs as they are forced to pay in order to transfer money from one currency to another. Furthermore, there are additional risks for companies involved in doing business between countries with variable exchange rates. For example, the British car manufacturer Jaguar made considerable profits in the USA during the mid-1980s when the value of sterling was relatively weak vis-à-vis the dollar. When sterling subsequently strengthened, American consumers were less willing to buy what had become expensive British cars and Jaguar's profits declined markedly. The risks associated with these types of currency movement can be offset in the short term by speculation in foreign exchange and futures markets, but this activity merely adds to business costs. In the longer term, companies can avoid these costs of foreign exchange dealings by building production facilities in overseas markets. However, this type of activity may be seen by national governments as damaging to the level of employment in the company's home country.

Exercise 5.2   **A single European currency?**

Outline the principal arguments for and against the adoption of a single European currency.

Employment

It is common sense to suggest that stable and high economic growth depends on the most effective and efficient use of a nation's human resources. Therefore any level of unemployment reflects an inefficiency. However, economists disagree about what is a sustainable level of employment and what is an unacceptable level of unemployment.

Between 1945 and 1976, a broad consensus existed between all political parties about the importance of maintaining very low levels of unemployment. This political position drew on Keynesian analysis in which full employment was deemed an achievable goal, as unemployment was seen to represent a shortfall in the demand for goods and services.

From 1976 to the late 1980s the adoption of Monetarist economic policies led successive British governments to attach a lower priority to the maintenance of high levels of employment. According to many Monetarists, there is a link between the level of inflation and the level of unemployment. Adapting earlier arguments by non-Monetarist economists, Monetarists argue that, other things being equal, when the rate of inflation increases the level of unemployment will tend to rise. Similarly, when the rate of inflation decreases the level of unemployment will generally fall. By this reasoning there is, at least in the short to medium term, a natural rate of unemployment. This so-called *natural rate* is often referred to by economists as the non-inflationary-inflation rate of unemployment (NAIRU).

For Monetarist economists, the natural rate of unemployment in the UK during the 1980s and early 1990s was judged to be between 6 and 8 per cent – higher than the 1 to 3 per cent experienced between 1950 and the early 1970s. It was therefore not surprising that the official rate of unemployment consistently exceeded 1.5 million from the late 1970s onwards and reached a peak of 3.12 million in July 1986. This figure may have been even higher if account is taken of changes in the way unemployment statistics were collected over this period.

The theory of the NAIRU is a re-interpretation of the more famous, but now discredited, Phillips Curve which proposed that there was a straight trade-off between inflation and unemployment. Economies throughout the western world did appear to work like this in the 1950s and 1960s, but the relationship then broke down with the emergence of *stagflation* in the 1970s. In order to account for these new circumstances economists developed the theory of the NAIRU. This new approach suggested that there was a relationship between unemployment and the rate of change in inflation; and only one rate of unemployment is consistent with inflation that is neither rising nor falling. If unemployment is below this critical rate, workers will push for bigger pay increases, inflation will rise and keep rising. If it is above it, inflation will fall.

Believers in this natural rate of unemployment concede that it is not set in stone. It will vary with supply side policies. For example, minimum wages or more generous job benefits will tend to raise the rate. Indeed some have suggested that the high level of unemployment in Europe over the last two decades reflects the influence of these policies.

Critics of the theory of a natural rate of unemployment suggest that two recent changes in western economies have undermined the validity of this model. First, they suggest that the rapid globalization of business has reduced inflationary pressures within domestic economies, by removing the bottlenecks in production which used to arise because of scarce labour during periods of low unemployment. They maintain that firms are now less reliant on local labour markets to supply their needs. If they cannot employ local staff to make a product, they can always buy the item from another firm in another country. Second, they argue that the rate of technological change has accelerated in recent years with the more widespread adoption of information technology. This computerization has led to rapid increases in productivity which mean that firms can increase their output without increasing their staffing levels.

On the basis of these arguments a number of economists have suggested that full employment is once again a feasible economic objective. With appropriate international co-operation, governments can develop the skills of their domestic workforces and stimulate consumer demand, in order to promote non-inflationary growth with low levels of unemployment. Despite this optimism, however, there are few signs of national or international political initiatives in this direction. The vast majority of western government finance ministers remain committed to a belief that there is a limit to the steps which can be taken to reduce unemployment.

SUMMARY AND CONCLUSION

This chapter began with an outline of three important questions for economists, politicians and the wider population of any country. What should be produced? How should it be produced? And how should the results of productive activities be distributed? As we noted in the first half of this chapter, the answers to these questions vary.

For some, free markets provide the most effective means of deciding what to produce, ensuring that the productive activities of millions of people are coordinated and maintaining an efficient distribution system. The market may create temporary hardship for some, but it also provides incentives for entrepreneurs, encourages innovation by employees and offers choice for customers.

For others, markets provide an ineffective method for deciding what to produce and how to produce it. In the market place, things only have a value if they have a price and therefore there is a tendency to overlook important social and environmental objectives. Furthermore, markets do not distribute the results of economic activity fairly. To overcome these problems governments and other bodies are needed to regulate economic activity to ensure that everyone benefits.

In practice, despite continued disagreement between economists, most, if not all, economies are organized on the basis of some mix between market and planned provision of goods and services. The balance may vary between countries, and the emphasis may change over time, but today there are few politicians or business people who would seriously advocate a purely market-based or planned system.

In the second half of this chapter we moved on to consider the economic goals of politicians overseeing macro-economic policy in mixed economies like the UK. Here we argued that the primary goal of UK economic policy in the post-war period has been sustained economic growth. Politicians of all political persuasions have explicitly or implicitly suggested that if everyone becomes wealthier they will be better placed to choose what they want to produce and how they wish to produce it. Despite this consensus, there has been disagreement about the balance to be struck between this objective and the other goals of containing inflation, maintaining high levels of employment and safeguarding a stable balance of trade and exchange rate. Here once again policy prescriptions have varied. While Keynesian economists and politicians have emphasized the importance of reducing unemployment, Monetarist economists have been more concerned with controlling and reducing inflation.

In recent years British governments have experimented with Keynesian and Monetarist approaches and as a consequence have used different economic policy instruments and indicators to map and chart their progress. Thus the emphasis on demand management in the 1950s, 1960s and 1970s gave way to monetary controls and supply side reforms in the 1980s, which in turn were replaced by a brief experiment with fixed exchange rates in the early 1990s. These policies enabled, or, alternatively, did not prevent, the UK economy from growing in absolute terms. However, its relative position in international economic league tables has continued to deteriorate. Whether this decline can be arrested in the future remains to be seen. At present the British government has returned to Monetarist economic controls and supply side policies, but there is a possibility that more economic decision-making power will be ceded to the European Union at the end of this century if a single European Currency is created.

Exercise 5.3 Economic indicators

Choose one of the seven economic indicators listed in Table 5.5 and plot the movement of this variable over the last ten years on a graph. You should be able to collect the raw data for this exercise from one or more of the statistical series listed.

When the graph is complete, write a very short account of the trends it reveals and the implications for a specified organization if the trends continue.

Table 5.5 Some economic indicators and their sources

Economic indicators	Statistical series
1 UK annual aggregate GDP	*Annual Abstract of Statistics* or *Economic Trends*
2 UK annual aggregate retail price index	*Autumn Statement* or *Social Trends*
3 London Clearing Banks Base Rate *or* selected retail banks base rate	*Financial Statistics*
4 Growth in the monetary aggregate M0	*Economic Trends*
5 Annual average UK unemployment	*Economic Trends* or *Social Trends*
6 UK annual aggregate current account balance	*Annual Abstract of Statistics*
7 UK effective exchange rate *or* annual average sterling exchange rate index	*Financial Statistics*

CHAPTER 6

Technology and technical change

INTRODUCTION

Technological developments have literally and metaphorically provided the motor for much of human development. In the last two hundred years the pace of this technological change has accelerated continuously. With each successive wave of innovations the lives of people as employees and citizens have been altered. Cars have offered people greater mobility, medical advances have provided relief from illness and disease, while telephones and computers have enabled people to gain access to enormous quantities of information. For many people these inventions and discoveries represent progress. The human race now has a better understanding and mastery of the world within which it lives, and this knowledge has been used to improve the health, wealth and well-being of societies across the globe. For others, these same innovations present problems as well as solutions. Industrialization threatens to exhaust the natural resources of the planet; information technology threatens to reduce employment opportunities and dehumanize work; and medical advances pose difficult questions about the value of different people's lives.

FOCUS AND SCOPE

This chapter begins the task of assessing and evaluating the effects of new and established technologies upon the lives of individual employees, the organizations they work for, and the societies of which they are a part. To this end, the following chapter is arranged into two main sections. In the first section we attempt to define what is meant by the term technology and to analyse the nature of technological change. The second section then moves on to consider the characteristics of three recent technological changes: industrialization, information technology and bio-technology. Here, as well as spelling out some of the benefits of these developments, we attempt to outline some of the many dangers.

LEARNING OBJECTIVES

Once you have read through this chapter and completed the associated exercises, you should be able to:

- explain what is meant by the term 'technology';
- describe the nature and causes of technological change;
- outline some of the problems associated with industrialization, information technology and bio-technology; and
- critically evaluate the introduction of new technologies within an organization known to you.

THE NATURE OF TECHNOLOGICAL CHANGE

What do we mean by the term 'technology'?

If we are to examine the effects of technology on employees, organizations and society in general we need to be clear about what we mean by the term. According to Winner (1977), the term technology is now used to convey such a wide range of meanings that it has become ambiguous. He suggests that the vagueness of traditional definitions can be overcome by differentiating between the following three distinct uses of the term:

- *Apparatus*   The tools, instuments, machines and other appliances which may be applied to a specific task. Examples include combustion engines, computers and chemical testing techniques.

- *Technique*   Technical activities such as skills, methods, procedures or routines which people perform to achieve particular purposes. The focus here is the human agent that adopts new ways of accomplishing tasks.

- *Organization*   The social arrangement of work and machines designed to produce specific products and services. Examples include offices, factories, laboratories and other ways of organizing the work of a large number of people.

When has technological change occurred?

Researchers examining the historical development of technology usually take the Industrial Revolution as their starting point. For example, Gill (1985) describes three phases of technological change in the UK since the late eighteenth century along the following lines.

- *Primary mechanization*   The use of machinery driven by steam power to replace human labour in the transformation of raw materials into products.

- *Secondary mechanization*   The use of machines powered by electricity to accomplish the transfer of materials between machines and to run continuous flow assembly lines.

- *Tertiary mechanization*   The use of electronics-based computing and information technologies to coordinate and control the transformation and transfer of tasks.

The distinction between these three stages in the technological development of western societies is based upon the assumption that the invention of steam-powered machinery produced a radical transformation in the way people lived and worked. While there is truth in this assertion, technological innovation did not begin with the Industrial Revolution in the late eighteenth century. The developments at this time were merely an acceleration of the pace of invention and discovery. For example, progress in the development of energy sources had already led people to use horses, water and wind power as alternatives to their own muscles and brawn. The subsequent development of steam and petro-chemical engines as well as gas, electrical and nuclear turbines were a natural extension of these earlier innovations.

What causes technological change?

An important question for policy makers in government and business is, what causes technological change? The answer to this question has important implications for the research and development strategies pursued by different countries and companies. New inventions and discoveries offer people the opportunity of better standards of health and education. They also provide the physical basis for an expansion of the wealth of nations and their citizens.

Conventionally, the opinions of scientific and economic historians about the causes of technological change could be divided into roughly two groups. One group of writers believed that the role of scientists and engineers engaged in pure research was central. The breakthroughs made by these specialists, they argued, produced the technological push for the development of new products, processes and organizational forms. By contrast, another group tended to highlight the role of customers and financial backers who, they suggested, provided the demand for new ways of doing things. This approach emphasized the power of the market place and the importance of the final consumer, who, they maintained, provided the demand pull which inspired new approaches.

In recent years, this polarization of the debate between advocates of the technological-push theory and believers in market pull has been superseded by more complex explanations which combine elements of each approach. Freeman (1987) provides a good example of this approach with his distinction between four forms of innovation:

- Incremental innovations
- Radical innovations
- Changes of technology system
- Technology revolutions.

Incremental innovations

Incremental innovations happen continuously in any industry or service activity. They arise as a consequence of engineers, managers and workers making suggestions to improve the goods or services being produced. A number of research studies have demonstrated how this form of continuous improvement by quality circles, team briefing groups and individual suggestion schemes can lead to improvements in the efficiency and effectiveness of organizations. Although the effects of these changes often go unrecorded, the cumulative effect of these innovations can often be very dramatic.

Radical innovations

Radical innovations occur irregularly and often as a result of deliberate research and development activity by companies, universities or government laboratories. The causes of these developments are difficult to ascertain. Radical innovations often provide the stimulus for the development of new markets and industries. Thus, while the immediate effects of these inventions or discoveries may appear at different times in different industries over a period of time, they can have a profound influence over the way we live and work. For example, the invention of the semiconductor in the early 1960s is still revolutionizing the work of many companies and industries. Evidence of market pull is much weaker than in the case of incremental innovation, since by definition no established market exists. However, those responsible for these developments clearly have some idea of the potential applications of their research and the possible markets for its exploitation.

Changes of technology system

In this case a number of related innovations appear simultaneously and they can provoke fundamental changes in the corporate structure and composition of specific industries. Comprising of a combination of incremental and radical innovation, these developments can give rise to the emergence of new industrial sectors as well as rapid and turbulent restructuring or decline within established industries.

A recent example of this type of technological change is provided by the development of multi-media forms of entertainment which combine digital communication with established television and computer technologies. According to a number of futurologists, one effect of these changes within the next 20 years will be the gradual replacement of television by entertainment and communication boxes which can be used to perform the following functions:

- broadcast programmes from a variety of sources (cable, satellite and video);
- play interactive games;
- visually and verbally communicate with other people;
- retrieve text, audio and graphical information from a variety of sources including national and local libraries;
- manipulate images and text; and
- store material.

Exercise 6.1 ## Multi-media technology

What do you anticipate to be the likely consequences of multi-media technology for people's working lives and leisure habits.

Technology revolutions

In these circumstances changes in technology are so substantial and far reaching that they have the capacity to change the way in which people think and behave within an entire economy. These revolutions happen relatively infrequently and take many years to affect everyone; however, when they occur, they necessitate changes in the knowledge, skills and systems of working for entire populations.

A number of writers have suggested that technological revolutions occur in cycles or waves. These waves, it is argued, provide the impetus for economic growth as people find ways of exploiting these technologies.

One of the earliest and best known proponents of this approach is Krondratieff. A Soviet economist, he observed in the 1920s that it took the world economy approximately 50 years to move through a boom-to-slump-to-boom cycle. Subsequently, economists have traced the development of 'Krondratieff cycles' into the latter part of the twentieth century (*see* Fig 6.1).

According to this long-wave theory, the world economy in the mid-1990s is beginning to emerge from the bottom of the slump in the fourth Krondratieff cycle. As a consequence a number of economists have devoted their attention to spotting the technologies which will provide the stimulus for the upturn of the fifth Krondratieff cycle. One of the most promising contenders at this stage appears to be the emerging bio-technologies.

Research by the Science Policy Research Unit has demonstrated that the upturns in Krondratieff cycles are stimulated by the adoption of new technologies by pioneering new firms (Freeman, 1982). These new technologies are then transferred to other parts of an economy, either by spin-off companies from the original pacesetter, or by the adaptation of existing mature firms who respond to the competition from new firms. These established companies are apt to rely upon external consultants and training programmes to provide expertise in the new technologies.

Fig 6.1 Krondratieff cycles and innovation waves (1775–2000), showing innovation peaks in troughs of long wave

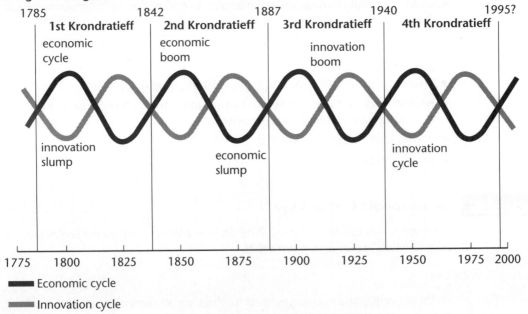

Source: Open University, T362 Course Team (1986) Innovation Waves, T362, Block 5, Unit 13, reproduced by permission of the Open University Press, Milton Keynes.

According to Miles and Snow (1978), organizational approaches to technological development vary and can therefore be categorized into one of the following three basic types: prospectors, analysers and defenders (*see* Table 6.1).

Prospectors actively search out and develop new technologies, products and markets. The leaders of these organizations are not averse to taking risks and actively promoting flexible forms of work organization and devolved decision-making to encourage innovatory behaviour by employees. *Analysers,* by contrast, may be characterized as firms which study and follow technological, product and market developments. The senior managers of these firms are keen to develop their business, but are anxious that new initiatives fit neatly within the existing organizational structure and methods of operating. The last category – *defenders* – as the name implies, strive to attain the most efficient use of relatively stable technologies. The emphasis here is upon ensuring that customers are provided with value for money, rather than state-of-the-art technology. To achieve these goals managerial planning and decision making tend to be highly centralized.

Exercise 6.2	**Corporate approaches to technological innovation**

Which of Miles and Snow's categories most accurately describes an organization known to you? Try to justify your answer by giving examples of the way in which recent problems or issues were handled.

Table 6.1 The influence of different types of organizational culture on approaches to technology and strategic decision making

Organization type	Characteristics of strategic decision making		
	Dominant objectives	*Preferred strategies*	*Planning and control systems*
Prospectors	Location and exploitation of new product and market opportunities.	Growth through product and market development, use often in spurts. Constant monitoring of environmental change. Multiple technologies.	Emphasis on flexibility and decentralized control of *ad hoc* measurements.
Analysers	Desire to match new ventures to present business.	Steady growth through market penetration; exploitation of applied research; followers in the market.	Functional and matrix mostly centralized, but decentralized in marketing.
Defenders	Desire for a secure and stable niche market.	Specialization; cost efficient production; marketing emphasizes price and service to defend current business. Vertical integration.	Centralized, detailed planning. Emphasis on cost efficiency. Extensive use of product planning.

Source: Adapted from Miles, R E and Snow, C C (1978) *Organizational Strategy, Structure and Process*, McGraw Hill.

THE HUMAN AND ENVIRONMENTAL COSTS OF INDUSTRIALIZATION

The adoption and exploitation of mechanical, chemical, electrical and electronic technologies from the late eighteenth century onwards led to the gradual spread across the globe of new forms of work and patterns of leisure activity. As sophisticated technologies have been turned to the provision of goods and services, in the west at least, industry and commerce have replaced agriculture as the main source of income and wealth. Accompanying this industrialization have been massive increases in population, urbanization and the commitment of considerable resources to further innovations, inventions and discoveries.

Today one fifth of the world's population are fortunate enough to live in highly developed western economies. Meanwhile, a further fifth of the world's population live in abject poverty as they toil on subsistence wages to produce many of the raw materials which feed western industry and commerce. Between these two extremes, the remaining three fifths of the world's population live in developing countries with standards of living that provide for more than subsistence, but which would still be considered impoverished in the west.

In recent years, a number of writers have begun to question whether the relentless pursuit of technological progress and industrialization should be tempered by a consideration of the physical and human effects of these changes. The following sections explore some of the more profound of these changes under the following headings: non-renewable resources; pollution; the greenhouse effect and ozone holes.

Non-renewable resources

The generation of power and the production of manufactured goods require large amounts of raw materials. Although many of these raw materials renew themselves, many more are scarce and cannot be replaced. In recent years, the realization that the earth's supply of fossil fuels, minerals, wood and many species of animals are limited has led to campaigns to increase awareness of the dangers associated with the uncontrolled use of these resources.

Fossil fuels

According to current projections the earth's stocks of crude oil and natural gas will not last more than another century. Stocks of uranium and coal reserves are more plentiful, but the environmental costs associated with these forms of energy may make their use uneconomic in the foreseeable future.

Forests

Forests currently cover a little under one fifth of the earth's land surface. This vegetation is crucial to the stability of soil systems and to the survival of innumerable animal and plant species as well as millions of people.

Fauna and flora

The number of animal species facing extinction increases every day. In 1992, the World Wildlife Fund for Nature (WWF) estimated that there were approximately 380 000 species of plant and between 5 and 10 million species of animal. In the same year, according to the WWF's World Conservation Monitoring Centre 4589 species of animal were known to be in danger of extinction and close to 60 000 species of plant.

The destruction of these animal and plant species threatens to reduce the variety of life on earth (*bio-diversity*) with serious consequences for the stability of eco-systems around the world. This contraction threatens to rob us of a number of species which may have provided important new medical remedies and other innovations. Without a rich assortment of different plants and animals, the self-regulating stability of eco-systems may be in jeopardy. The extinction of natural predators may free some species to become dangerous new pests to people and their activities.

While the quality of life on earth is being denuded, the quantity of animals available for farming and fishing is threatened. Despite improvements in modern trawling techniques, the catch from modern fishing has levelled off. In response to these pressures, international agencies have attempted to regulate some forms of fishing, e.g. whaling, drift netting and herring fishing.

On the land, despite the conversion of increasing areas of land to arable and cattle farming, there are signs that advances in farming may not be able to keep pace with the exponential growth of the world's human population. Of particular importance is the declining availability of fresh drinking water in areas of the Middle East, Africa and Asia.

Conservation, managed farming, recycling and the exploitation of alternative resources have all been offered as possible solutions to the depletion of the world's natural resources. However, for a number of environmental campaigners these initiatives do not go far enough. They suggest that the fundamental problems are the exponential growth of the world's population and the rapid spread of industrialization. Without more effective programmes of population control and limited or sustainable development they argue that famine, pestilence, war and disease will increasingly blight the lives of people across the globe.

Pollution

While consuming the earth's limited natural resources in order to feed and equip a burgeoning population, the human race has also been responsible for creating massive quantities of pollution. Chemical wastes and other byproducts of human activity belch onto the land and into the air and seas. As these contaminants build up in the environment they threaten the continued lives of countless species of plants and animals. Two of the most damaging of these forms of pollution are high levels of acidity (acidification) and excess nitrogen and phosphates (eutrophication).

Acidification

Acidification is caused by sulphur and nitrogen oxide emissions from fossil-fuel burning power stations, motor cars and heavy industry. Winds can disperse these pollutants over great distances until they eventually come down to earth as rain, snow, dry particles or gases.

Increases in the level of acid in the world's soils, rivers, lakes and seas have had dramatic effects on the types of plants and animals which are able to live and prosper in these environments. For example, the acidification of rivers and lakes in Northern Europe and Scandinavia has meant that many are unable to support fish life.

On land, low levels of acidification can produce beneficial effects for plants as it helps to free nutrients trapped in the soil. However, as the acidity level increases vital chemicals are leached out of the earth while other more toxic chemicals are freed. The net effect of these changes is that increased acidification may kill or severely curtail plant growth and can have effects on the health of animals further up the food chain.

The worst effects of acidification can be temporarily neutralized by treatment with lime or other agents. However, this is an expensive and difficult process which is rarely applied to the areas of natural wilderness most seriously affected by acidification.

Eutrophication

Modern fertilizers and other artificial soil and plant treatments have greatly improved crop and cattle yields, but the full costs of these innovations have only recently been realized.

One of the most damaging side effects is eutrophication. This is mainly caused by the over-use of chemical fertilizers. When rain falls after these nutrients have been applied, any surplus nitrogen or phosphates in the fertilizer is likely to be dissolved and will then leak into adjoining rivers or lakes. In euthrophied waters, algae and weeds feed on the nitrogen and phosphate and as they grow and multiply they use up oxygen killing fish and other aquatic life.

The greenhouse effect

All living things need carbon to survive and grow. Carbon is a chemical element which forms a component part of sugars, fats and the amino acids that form proteins. Without these nutrients animal and plant life would not be possible.

The level of carbon in the sea, underground and in the air is regulated by the carbon cycle. Plants convert carbon dioxide in the atmosphere into oxygen and sugar through the process of photosynthesis. When these plants die the carbon is further converted into soil, peat or coal. If the plant is eaten, the carbon-based sugars may be used to create energy, releasing carbon dioxide in the process. Alternatively, if the sugars are stored, when the animal dies the carbon will return once again to the soil.

The rapid process of industrialization over the past two hundred years has disturbed the carbon cycle. The extraction and burning of the earth's reserves of coal, gas and oil have released vast quantities of carbon dioxide into the atmosphere. In addition, the destruction of many of the world's forests and pollution of the sea have meant that there is not enough plant life to convert the increased levels of carbon dioxide back into oxygen or soil-based carbon.

The increased levels of carbon dioxide cause the atmosphere to allow sunlight through to the earth's surface but prevent heat from escaping. This phenomenon has been referred to as *the greenhouse effect.*

Many scientists are worried that if the emission of greenhouse gases is allowed to continue unchecked it will ultimately disrupt the earth's climate. A number of forecasts have already predicted that this may lead to an increase in the world's temperature of two or three degrees over the next century which would produce the following effects:

- create famine by reducing rainfall in farming areas;
- produce tropical storms and hurricanes; and
- partially melt the polar ice caps, increasing the sea level, and flooding many low lying, heavily populated areas.

The suggestions which have been put forward to limit the emission of greenhouse gases include:

- a carbon tax on those fuels most responsible for the release of carbon dioxide;
- restrictions on the use of carbon-based fuels and the promotion of energy conservation, e.g. speed limits for cars, insulation for houses, recycling initiatives and the expansion of public transport;
- the exploitation of new sources of energy which do not involve the release of carbon-based gases, i.e. nuclear, wind, wave, solar and geo-thermal energy.

Exhibit 6.1

Gaia

In the early 1970s James Lovelock and others formulated the influential *Gaia Hypothesis.* According to this proposition, on any planet where life is found, the living organisms themselves maintain the conditions they require for their own survival. By adopting this perspective, the whole of the planet Earth may be regarded as a single living organism (Gaia).

Lovelock uses this approach to attack some widely held assumptions about the effects of human activity. He argues that current concern about the effects of pollution on the environment over-emphasize the scale of the effects that man can have on the planet and ignores more significant developments in the history of Gaia. He maintains that the parts of the earth responsible for planetary control are the vast hordes of micro-

organisms in the soil and sea. For example, these algae, bacteria and other microscopic flora and fauna are responsible for turning over more than half the earth's supply of carbon. Large animals and plants may have important specialist functions to perform but they are largely irrelevant when considering the planet's self-regulating activities.

Furthermore, he suggests that the use of the term pollution is misleading because it involves drawing artificial distinctions between different types of waste product so that naturally decaying vegetation might be seen as better for the environment than the smoke emitted by a large power station. As Lovelock points out, all living things produce waste and much of this is toxic. Seen in this context the activities of man are not as significant as they might at first sight appear. For

▶

example, the greatest pollution disaster to befall the earth occurred one and a half aeons ago with the emergence of free oxygen gas into the atmosphere. When this happened, all the earth's surface in contact with the air and tidal seas became lethal to a large range of micro-organisms. These creatures were therefore forced to retreat to the mud at the bottom of rivers, lakes and seabeds.

Lovelock is optimistic about the future of the human race. He suggests that developments in technology should enable us to monitor changes within the environment and take evasive action where necessary. Even if this fails, he stoically reminds us that humans will not end all life on Earth, although they may end human life on the planet.

Ozone holes

The ozone layer in the earth's upper atmosphere provides protection from harmful ultraviolet rays from the sun, while letting enough light in to support the growth of plants and animals. However, this protective screen is beginning to break down. The major causes of ozone depletion are man-made chlorine and bromine compounds – notably chlorofluorocarbons (CFCs). These CFCs are found in aerosol cans, refrigeration coolants, fire extinguishers and the byproducts of plastic foam manufacture. When CFC molecules reach the upper atmosphere, ultraviolet light causes them to break down releasing chlorine atoms. Each of these chlorine atoms can then destroy up to 100 000 ozone molecules.

The appearance of a hole in the ozone layer over the South Pole in 1985 and over the North Pole in 1994 drew the world's attention to the possible damaging effects of CFCs. Each year these holes have widened and every spring they now cover several million square miles in the southern and northern hemispheres. Doctors and ecologists are worried that the depletion of the ozone layer will increase the level of ultraviolet light reaching the earth's surface causing skin cancer and cataracts among humans, as well destroying a number of species of plants and animals. In response to these worries the heads of several western governments signed the Montreal Protocol in 1989 which includes targets for the phased reduction of CFC production. In 1994, the UK and other members of the European Union took further steps by committing themselves to a complete ban on CFC production. Despite this progress, a number of other ozone-depleting agents remain unregulated, e.g. methyl bromine and HCFCs.

Exhibit 6.2

Green accounts and audits

In the United States companies are required to inform the government authorities about their prospective environmental liabilities and their use of chemicals listed as toxic. As a result of these regulations, a growing number of American companies include some environmental information in their financial statements.

Outside the USA there are few regulations governing the types of environmental information companies must release. Those companies that voluntarily choose to release information have adopted a variety of approaches as the following examples demonstrate.

● Dow Europe – a division of an American multinational chemicals company – produces tabulations of the pollutants to air, water and soil from its individual plants and lists the extent to which they have been reduced or increased in recent years. They also list unwanted events, including accidents, spills, complaints and fines imposed.

- Union Carbide – the company responsible for the Bhopal disaster in India – tracks its performance against the 'Responsible Care' programme devised by the American chemical industry. Their reports give details of pollution prevention, safety and targets for future improvement.

- Kunert – a German textile manufacturer – has published an 'eco-balance sheet' for the past four years. This document weighs up the company's use of raw materials including electricity, air and water against its output of tights, socks and waste.

- B&Q – Britain's biggest chain of do-it-yourself retailers – has recently augmented its own annual green audit by requiring its suppliers to complete a tough environmental questionnaire. Managers at this company believe that their customers are concerned about conserving the environment and are prepared to change their shopping habits in order to buy from companies that share these beliefs.

In the near future these voluntary arrangements are likely to be superseded by national regulations. As a consequence, several organizations including the United Nations, the International Chambers of Commerce and the European Union as well as a variety of industry groups are now trying to develop guidelines in an attempt to influence national regulations. The effects of these regulations will doubtless depend upon the force of the law attached to these rules.

The European Union's proposals will require companies to evaluate and improve their environmental performance. It is expected that these guidelines will be based on the 'Valdez Principles' drawn up by the Coalition for Environmentally Responsible Economics (CERES) in the USA.

CERES was formed in 1989 when a number of environmental groups, religious organizations and investors came together in response to the disastrous oil spill by the *Exxon Valdez* oil tanker in the Prince William Sound on the Alaskan coastline. This coalition represented the largest cooperative effort by social action groups to campaign for the adoption of conservation policies by large companies. One of the first actions of this group was to lay down a code of conduct which it has called the 'Valdez Principles'. This code encourages companies and other organizations to abide by the following ten proposals:

1 *Protection of the biosphere* – to strive to eliminate the release of harmful pollutants.

2 *Sustainable use of natural resources* – such as water, soils and forests.

3 *Reduction and disposal of waste* – to minimize the creation of waste and, wherever possible, recycle materials.

4 *Wise use of energy* – to make every effort to use environmentally safe and sustainable energy sources; invest in improved energy efficiency.

5 *Risk reduction* – to minimize risks to employees by employing safe technologies and operating procedures and by being constantly prepared for emergencies.

6 *Marketing of safe products and services* – to inform consumers of the environmental impact of products and services.

7 *Damage compensation* – every effort to be taken to restore the environment and to compensate those persons who are adversely affected.

8 *Environmental directors* – to have at least one member of the board of directors qualified in environmental issues.

9 *Disclosure* – to disclose to employees and to the public incidents relating to operations that cause environmental harm or pose health and safety hazards. To disclose potential environmental, health or safety hazards posed by operations and not to take any action against employees who report any condition that creates a danger to the environment or poses health and safety hazards.

10 *Assessment and annual audit* – to conduct and make public an annual self-evaluation of progress in implementing these principles and complying with all applicable laws and regulations.

Exercise 6.3 | **Eco-friendly organizations**

How does an organization known to you measure up to the Valdez Principles listed above?

INFORMATION TECHNOLOGY

Having examined the effects of industrialization and commercial activity on the environment that surrounds us, we now move on to consider the effects of information technology – the most recent technological revolution to affect people's work and social lives.

A post-industrial society, an information or a computer revolution, whatever we call it, most people agree that the invention, exploitation and diffusion of microchip technologies have had a profound effect on people's lives over the past 30 years. For some people, this new technology offers us all the prospect of more enjoyable jobs and more fulfilled lives. For others, these advances are less worthwhile as they threaten to increase unemployment and create sharp distinctions between the information haves and the information have-nots; the technologically literate and the technologically illiterate; the gods and the clods.

Whether these developments are seen as good or bad often depends upon the perspective of the commentator. The following section aims to define what it is we mean when we talk about new technologies and to examine their effects upon employment and the skills of the workforce.

What is information technology?

According to Buchanan and Boddy, computer-based information technologies have four unique characteristics which set them apart from older and more established technologies (1983).

- *Information capture*   Sensing, gathering, collecting, monitoring, detecting and measuring information.

- *Information storage*   Converting text and numeric data into a digital form which can be stored and retrieved when required.

- *Information by manipulation*   Organizing large quantities of data and analysing this information, performing standard calculations or operations

- *Information distribution*   Digitally stored information can be transmitted rapidly over large distances to be used by other computerized systems or displayed in a variety of forms, e.g. video display screens, printed documents or audio announcement.

The introduction of information technology can have two implications. First, people may lose their jobs as the tasks they previously performed are now undertaken by machines. Second, the knowledge, skills and attitudes required from those staff who are fortunate enough to retain their jobs are likely to change as the new technologies call for people with different aptitudes and abilities. The scale and nature of these two effects will depend upon a number of factors.

Information technology and employment

In the 1960s and 1970s, it was widely believed that the newly emerging computer-based technologies would herald an era of unmanned factories and people-less offices. It was argued that machines and robots would be able to take over the work of humans. Working around the clock in unlit buildings, these machines would be able to increase production levels and lower costs. These changes promised to solve the problems of production, leaving policy makers and business leaders free to worry about how the vast numbers of newly unemployed people would be able to afford to buy these manufactured goods. Thirty years later, despite the widespread adoption of computers, there is little evidence that this vision of the future is any nearer realization. According to Huczynski and Buchanan (1991), a number of compensatory mechanisms have prevented the introduction of new technology being accompanied by massive and sustained unemployment.

- *New products and services.* Technical innovation generates new products and services, like video cassette recorders, telephone answering machines and personal computers. These inventions change the pattern of consumer demand and this leads organizations to invest in factories and offices which in turn leads to new employment opportunities.

- *Productivity.* Higher productivity means producing more or the same level of output with the same or fewer resources. As productivity increases, the associated savings may be passed on to the consumer as lower prices; kept by the employer with increased wages and other expenses; or transferred to shareholders in the form of rising share prices and dividends. Whichever way these gains are distributed there will be more money available to be spent on other goods and services within the economy.

- *Investment costs.* Many new technologies are still very expensive. Unless a company expects the demand for its products and services to expand it may not be able to justify the expenses associated with the investment in new technology. Automating production and information flows does not guarantee profitability. Indeed, a number of studies have confirmed that the relationships between the adoption of information technologies, productivity and product quality are not straightforward. For example, some of the most effective and efficient automobile plants in the world have low levels of automation.

- *Technical limitations.* New technologies may not always live up to the claims of their inventors, champions or salespeople. The new machines may not be able to do everything that the old technology was capable of doing. For example, it is common to find electronic typewriters next to word processors in many offices and no craftsperson would be without a screwdriver or hammer.

- *Time lags*. It takes time for existing organizations to adopt new technologies. They need to be made aware of the development, train their staff and carefully appraise the risks before investing in new equipment. Because of the time lags associated with these developments, technical changes take a long time to permeate all areas of industrial and domestic life. The result of these delays is that employment losses caused by the introduction of a new technology take many years to have their full effect.

Information technology and skill

According to McLoughlin and Clark (1994) there are three competing views of the effects of information technology upon job content, skill levels and status. They label these three different perspectives: technological determinism, labour process and strategic choice.

Technological determinism

The work of Joan Woodward (1970) perhaps best exemplifies this approach. On the basis of a number of research studies in the early 1960s, she argued that technology determines the nature of the work people undertake and the systems of control they are subjected to by management. While she conceded that different technologies require different approaches, she maintained that competition determines which technology is the most economic. At the time of her investigations, Joan Woodward suggested that the emerging highly automated technologies of assembly line operations (characteristic of consumer goods factories) and continuous process production (common in refineries and large chemical works) would increasingly require impersonal management control systems. Under these new regimes, employees would be engaged in work which involved monitoring production processes, rather than directly intervening in them.

Labour process

Advocates of this approach argue that technology does not determine the form of managerial control systems or the nature of employees' work. Instead they argue that technology provides a means by which managers seek to impose control over the work of employees. Seen from this perspective, technology embodies management control systems which themselves arise from the class-based conflict between capital and labour. According to Braverman (1974), information technology is used to cheapen labour and deskill job content. Furthermore, this new technology is used to remove control over the execution of work from the worker, and place it in the hands of management. As a direct consequence of these processes the work of employees is degraded.

Strategic choice

Writers adopting this perspective argue that the effects of introducing information technology are not predetermined in any way. Instead they suggest that the outcomes of technological change are the products of choice.

Different groups within the organization – managers, unions and individual employees – will all have a preferred set of objectives for the new technology. The eventual outcomes will depend upon negotiations between these groups and will reflect the values, power and determination of these various parties (Child, 1972). Thus the introduction of electronic tills and price-scanning equipment in a supermarket may be undertaken in a human-centred or technology-centred way. Human-centred design begins with the needs of the employee rather than the needs of the equipment. Adopting this approach, technology will be designed to deal with the most laborious elements of the work, freeing the employee to engage in the more socially and intellectually rewarding aspects of the job. Furthermore, the layout and design of the new machinery will be determined by the physical and social needs of the operator, rather than the economic and technical demands of the equipment.

A more human-centred approach to technological innovation provides benefits for companies as well as employees. As Walton and Susman (1987) have argued, although the primary motive for the adoption of advanced manufacturing technology tends to be the search for cost reductions, many manufacturers still look for ways to enhance employees' capabilities and improve labour relations. They suggest that concern with these human aspects is based on a realization that the adoption of new technology increases:

● the interdependence between different functions in the production process;

● the requirement for skill and commitment from employees;

● the need for capital investment;

● the speed, scope and cost of errors; and

● the sensitivity of overall organizational performance to changes in employees' skills and attitudes.

If the needs of human operators are overlooked, the introduction of new technology will merely increase the likelihood and cost of operator errors and poor performance.

Information technology and health and safety

The effects of information technologies upon employees' health and safety has received considerable attention in recent years. Eye strain, migraine and repetitive strain injury (RSI) are just a few of the medical conditions which doctors have suggested are caused or aggravated by prolonged use of personal computers and other machines that make use of keyboards and video display screen equipment (*see* Table 6.2).

In response to the perceived health hazards accompanying the use of some forms of information technology, the UK government, as a result of pressure from the European Union, introduced regulations governing the use of display screen equipment (DSE). These regulations contain detailed advice on appropriate computer design, operator seating and general work station layout as well as advice on how to monitor the health and welfare of PC users.

Table 6.2 Office automation hazards: a summary from the literature

Typical symptoms	Probable causes	Ergonomic solutions	Organizational solutions
Reproductive disorders			
Male infertility	Repetition	Work design	Job enlargement/enrichment
Abnormal pregnancy	Radiation	Screen filters	Job rotation
Miscarriage	Static electricity	Equipment earthed	Training
Still birth			
Eye sight			
Eye strain	Poor lighting	Good lighting	Office layout
Blurred vision	Screen glare and flicker	Good displays	IT audits and assessments
Flickering eyelids	Intense concentration	Work schedule	Working hours
Migraine			
Musculo-skeletal			
Stiff neck and shoulders	Repetition	Check posture	Exercise routines
Arm and wrist pains	Inadequate desk and chair	Desk design	
Backache and headache	Work pace	Chair design	Check rest periods
Repetitive strain injury	Poor posture		More rest periods
	Badly designed keyboard	Properly designed keyboard	Increased job variety
Personal			
Heightened levels of stress		Job design	Organization and work design
Disturbed domestic life			

Source: adapted from Huczynski, A and Buchanan, D (1991) *Organizational Behaviour: An Introductory Text*, Prentice-Hall, Hemel Hempstead. Reproduced by permission of Prentice-Hall.

Exercise 6.4 ## Information technology and health and safety

What steps has your organization taken to ensure compliance with the Display Screen Equipment Regulations and to reduce the health and safety risks associated with the use of personal computers?

Information technology, control, surveillance and data protection

Information technology allows managers and employees greater access to information about their organization, its employees, suppliers, customers and other stakeholders. When used appropriately, this information can be turned to competitive advantage over rival firms in the market place. This information can also be used, among other things, to match employees' skills and expectations to job opportunities, protect employees from health hazards, and tailor reward packages to individual demands.

Buchanan and McCalman (1989) suggest that computerized information systems offer the following benefits.

- They encourage managers and employees to share information previously protected in manual systems.

- This technology may enhance the motivation and confidence of managers as they now have access to accurate and shared information. The visibility of individual employee's work performance is increased as tasks may be monitored more effectively.

- The enhanced confidence of managers and visibility of work performance increase the pressure on managers to react quickly and appropriately to business opportunities and problems.

- Shared information, shared confidence, shared visibility and shared pressure encourage a cooperative approach to management decision making, reducing opportunities for power struggles and inter-departmental conflicts.

Other writers are more pessimistic about the effects of increased access to information (Zuboff, 1988; Sewell and Wilkinson, 1993). As they point out, there are dangers associated with unregulated access to information. The following five problems are among the most important mentioned by these authors.

- Information technology may enable managers to gain access to previously confidential records about their employees, customers and other parties. For example, computerized databases can provide people in positions of authority with easy access to personal information about credit ratings, school performance, housing and medical histories.

- Unrestrained access to information increases employees' fears and worries about what their employers know about them and their personal lives.

- Surveillance techniques enable managers to keep their workforce under surveillance, monitoring work rates and comparing employees. The information produced by these techniques may not take sufficient account of differences between employees, and the contexts within which their work has been performed.

- Surveillance increases the pressure on employees to ensure that the performance indicators they are measured against show favourable results. It may also prevent employees from devoting attention to other issues, i.e. customer service and productivity improvement suggestions.

- Access to private information and secret surveillance may alienate employees, reduce their trust in managers and decrease commitment to the organization. As employees become increasingly disgruntled and worried about their job security, there is a possibility that cooperation within teams will break down and power struggles will increase.

Data Protection Act 1984

The Data Protection Act was introduced in order to control the use of computerized personal information by employers and other organizations. This

Act places an obligation on these 'data users' to ensure that the information they collect on 'data subjects', i.e. employees, customers or other individuals, is:

- registered with the Data Protection Registrar every three years;
- used only for pre-specified and lawful purposes;
- accurate, relevant, up to date and not excessive;
- processed fairly and lawfully;
- protected by appropriate security measures and not disclosed to others without prior permission;
- kept only for as long as is necessary; and
- available for inspection by the data subject.

Data users are exempt from these general principles, however, if the computerized information deals with an individual's medical records and if disclosure would lead to the identification of other people, or if it is likely to cause serious harm to the physical or mental health of the data subject.

Data users are also exempt if the information relates to the calculation of an individual's pay and pension, or relates to the accounts of any business carried out by the data user.

If a data user fails to comply with the general principles listed above, the Data Protection Registrar is empowered to order rectification or erasure of the information being held. Furthermore, where a data subject is able to prove that he or she has suffered damage or distress as a consequence of the use of inaccurate or misleading information, the courts may award compensation.

BIO-TECHNOLOGY

While managers and employees are still wrestling with the opportunities and problems presented by the new information technologies, another wave of technological change is beginning to take shape in laboratories and research establishments across the western world. These new bio-technologies offer the prospect of new products and services which will create new businesses and industries in the twenty-first century.

Since the discovery of DNA by Crick and Watson in the early 1950s, scientists have been engaged in the mammoth task of mapping and understanding the operation of the genes which form the building blocks of all life. The strands of DNA in each animal or plant cell contain unique codes which control the growth and reproduction of the organism. In recent years, biochemical research has established links between certain DNA sequences and specific physical characteristics, susceptibility to disease and more contentiously particular patterns of behaviour. As a consequence of these advances, scientists have been able to genetically engineer more productive farm animals and create disease-resistant crops as well as discover new pharmaceutical products, diagnostic tests and therapeutic procedures. Despite the obvious benefits associated with these new bio-technologies a number of writers have expressed their concerns about the possible consequences of these developments.

Genetic profiling

The development of genetic profiling techniques raises the possibility that within the not too distant future people will be able to assess their susceptibility to a range of common diseases and conditions, e.g. cancer, heart disease and mental illness. If this information is used to provide affected individuals with better health care it is possible that the length and quality of their lives may be extended. However, if the information concerns diseases or conditions that are untreatable and unavoidable, being aware of the fact that you will develop a particular disease within the next ten years is unlikely to improve the quality of your life. Furthermore, unrestricted access to this information could present problems. For example, once employers have obtained this material, they may decide not to recruit certain individuals, while mortgage and insurance companies may decline to accept the risks associated with granting them a policy.

Agribusiness

According to some writers, when scientists manipulate the genetic make-up of plants and animals they are artificially accelerating and altering the course of evolution with possibly dangerous consequences. As scientists strive to increase the yield of new crop strains and cattle breeds, older established species are left to die out. This, coupled with deforestation and other attacks on bio-diversity, reduces the variety of plants and animals and may diminish the size of the gene pool – the number of different genes available to a particular species from which new offspring can be produced. Without the constant support and assistance of man these new breeds and strains would be unlikely to survive for long. Thus, for critics of agricultural biotechnology, the continued existence of viable arable crops and livestock necessitates the maintenance of a rich diversity of different species and breeds.

Bio-hazards

Advances in genetic engineering techniques have produced useful new types of bacteria, plants and animals. However, these developments have also raised people's fears about the prospect of generating dangerous organisms which could damage the environment or human health. Past experiences give little cause for comfort. Experiments with anthrax on islands off the Scottish coast during the Second World War have left at least one island uninhabitable to this day. Popular dramas, like *The Andromeda Strain*, have also outlined the possible risks associated with the release of new organisms which mutate or interact with other agents in the environment to produce dangerous side effects.

SUMMARY AND CONCLUSION

In this chapter we have sought to demonstrate that technological change is an ambiguous term which can be used to describe new tools, ways of working and organization. Over the last two centuries the pace of this change has accelerated as humans have adopted mechanical, electrical, electronic and biological technologies to improve the quality and productivity of their work. Each new wave of technological change has affected the numbers of people employed in different occupations and the skills they are required to use. These changes have also influenced the structure of employing organizations, the wider pattern of social relations and the physical environment within which these firms operate.

However, these changes were not inevitable. As individuals, organizations and governments develop, assess and implement new technologies they are faced with important choices which will have important direct and indirect effects. For example, computers can be used either to intensify, deskill and degrade, or alternatively to improve, enhance and enrich the work of employees. Similarly, organizations can actively seek out new technologies or defensively protect established ways of operating. At a societal level, new technologies can be developed which either protect or undermine communities and the natural environment.

In practice these choices are rarely presented in such stark terms. New technologies slowly permeate organizations and gradually alter the way in which people work and live their lives. It is therefore important that managers in general, and human resource managers in particular, are constantly involved in questioning the way in which new technologies are designed, implemented and evaluated within the workplace.

CHAPTER 7

Society and social trends

What does the word 'society' mean? According to Halsey (1995), this term should be used to refer to patterns and structures of relationships between people who share a common place in time and space. This rather vague definition highlights some of the problems confronting sociologists and others interested in gaining a better understanding of the social arrangements that surround them.

A wider reading of sociology textbooks and other sources suggests that 'society' has two distinct and opposite meanings. On the one hand, it refers to the things that people share in common: work, leisure, families and faith. On the other hand, it is used as a heading under which to examine the divisions and differences between people, e.g. class, gender and ethnic origin. Sociologists and other social scientists are interested in documenting and analysing these patterns. Their task is to describe and comment upon how patterns of difference and similarity between people change or remain the same. Where possible they also seek to explain why these patterns have emerged and to map out the possible consequences of these arrangements.

FOCUS AND SCOPE

The aim of this chapter is to outline recent social trends and to comment upon their causes and implications for the management of people at work. To this end we concentrate on five of the more important changes that have affected British society since the end of the Second World War: demographic trends and changes in the overall population of the UK; the family and the changing make-up of households; the shifting balance of income and wealth; developments in educational provision and attainment; and the health of the nation. The chapter ends with a summary of some of the explanations that have been offered for the persistence of inequality in society. Here we consider class- and status-based accounts of stratification and division within British society.

LEARNING OBJECTIVES

Once you have read through this chapter and completed the associated exercises, you should be able to:

- describe recent population trends;
- report on the changing composition of British households;
- comment upon the distribution of wealth and income within the UK;

- **summarize recent changes in educational provision and attainment within the UK;**
- **summarize changes in the health of the nation; and**
- **outline different methods of analysing social class and status.**

DEMOGRAPHIC TRENDS

In 1994, the population of the world was estimated to be 5.7 billion and rising rapidly. Over the next 30 years current projections suggest that the total population will reach 6 billion by 1999, 7 billion in 2010 and 8.5 billion in 2025. Most of this expansion is expected to occur in the poorer developing countries of Asia, Africa and South America, while the population of richer countries in the North and West will remain stable, or rise only modestly.

The population of the UK grew rapidly in the early twentieth century, but is now growing much more slowly. In 1993, the total UK population was 58.1 million – an increase of approximately 50 per cent on the figure of 38.2 million in 1901. Over the next 30 years this expansion seems set to carry on, albeit at a reduced rate. As Table 7.1 demonstrates, if present trends continue, the population of the UK is expected to reach a peak of 62.2 million in 2031.

Table 7.1 Total and estimated population of the United Kingdom, 1951–2031

	1951	1961	1971	1981	1991	2001	2011	2021	2031
Total population (millions)	50.3	52.8	55.9	56.4	57.8	59.2	60.0	60.7	62.2

Source: Social Trends 1994, No 24, Office for National Statistics. Crown Copyright 1995. Reproduced by permission of the Controller of HMSO and the Office for National Statistics.

The changing size of the UK's total population reflects changes in the country's life expectancy and birth rates, as well as the effects of emigration and immigration.

Life expectancy

The elderly population of the UK is expanding rapidly. In 1993, there were 9.2 million pensioners in the UK – a rise of over one tenth since 1971. By 2031, the numbers are expected to increase by a further third to 14.6 million. This expansion has its origins in the high birth rates of the past and the increased life expectancy of the elderly. While the maximum length of life remains obstinately set at about 115 years, a greater proportion of the population are surviving childhood and middle age to reach 'the third age' of the 60s, 70s, 80s and beyond. If present trends continue, men and women born in 1991 can expect on average to live for 80 or more years. This is a considerable increase over the comparable figures for 1901 when the average life expectancy for men was 45 years and for women 49 years.

Birth rates

Since the Second World War, the UK birth rate has varied on a cyclical basis with peaks in the late 1940s, early 1960s and mid-1990s. These peaks reflect the impact of the Second World War which delayed the birth of a generation of children and had consequent knock-on effects upon subsequent generations. The current upturn in birth rates is projected to peak at 790 000 in 1996. Thereafter, the number of births is expected to fall as the 'baby boomers' of the early 1960s pass their peak child-bearing years. Over the next 30 years, although the birth rate will decline, it is projected to remain higher than the death rate leading to a natural increase in the overall population.

Although the birth rate has varied on a cyclical basis, the average number of live births in each decade has decreased. This fall in the number of babies being born reflects a steady reduction in average family size and a slight increase in the age at which women choose to become pregnant. Today the average age at which women give birth to their first child is 28 and an average family (if such a thing exists) will include 1.8 children.

Similar changes to the pattern of childbirth have been reported from other developed countries and it is generally thought that these developments reflect increases in family income and wealth, the wider availability of effective contraception, and increasing rates of divorce.

Emigration and immigration

The measurement of emigration (people moving overseas) and immigration (people coming to the UK) is difficult. Unlike births and deaths, there is no single standard system for the registration and monitoring of flows of people into and out of the UK. Increased international travel and the relaxation of cross-border controls within the European Union have added to the problems associated with collecting accurate statistics. Nevertheless, estimates based upon the International Passenger Survey suggest that over the period 1987 to 1991 slightly more people moved to the UK than emigrated to live in other countries. The bulk of these immigrants were British citizens from Ireland and New Zealand, as well as African and Asian Commonwealth countries. By contrast the chief beneficiaries of emigration from the UK, in order of importance, were Australia, the USA, Canada and the European Union. Although emigration to the European Union is only 7 per cent of the total annual exodus to the USA, it is growing in importance. In 1992, 392 000 UK nationals were living in other European Union countries. Two fifths of these people were resident in either Germany or Spain.

Age structure of the population

It is anticipated that the combination of declining birth rates, increasing life expectancy and a slight net inflow of immigrants, will produce a steady 'greying of the population'. In the year 2021, it is projected that nearly one in five of the population will be over 65, compared to only one in ten in 1951. These developments have profound implications for the wealth of the nation. If the current retirement and pension policies of the government and private sector employers remain unchanged, it seems likely that a progressively smaller proportion of young employees among the population will be responsible for generating sufficient income to pay the pensions of an increasing number of elderly people. Furthermore, the needs of elderly people are likely to be different from those of their younger fellow citizens. For example, their tastes in clothes, furniture and leisure activities will, if present trends continue, tend to be different. As a consequence, we can expect to see changes in the structure of industry and employment in the UK which reflect the changing supply of labour and demands of the wider population.

Households and the family

One of the most persistent and enduring of all post-war social trends in the UK has been a change in the make-up of a typical household. The last 50 years have witnessed a gradual breakdown of households containing traditional nuclear families (a married couple with dependent children) and a steady increase in the number of lone parents with dependent children, single men under pensionable age and single pensioners. These and other changes have contributed to a gradual increase in the number of households, but a decline in the number of people in these units (*see* Table 7.2).

Table 7.2 Household by type in Great Britain, 1961–93

	1961 %	1971 %	1981 %	1993 %
One-person households				
Under pensionable age	4	6	8	11
Over pensionable age	7	12	14	16
Two or more related adults	5	4	5	3
One-family households				
Married couple with:				
No children	26	27	26	28
1–2 dependent children	30	26	25	20
3 + dependent children	8	9	6	5
Non-dependent children	10	8	8	7
Lone parent with:				
Dependent children	2	3	5	7
Non-dependent children	4	4	4	3
Two or more families	3	1	1	1
All households (per cent)	100	100	100	100
Total number of households (millions)	16.2	18.2	19.5	22.9

Source: *Social Trends 1994*, No 24: 41, Office for National Statistics. Crown Copyright 1995. Reproduced by permission of the Controller of HMSO and the Office for National Statistics.

LIBRARY
BISHOP BURTON COLLEGE
BEVERLEY HU17 8QG

The growth in the number of individuals living on their own or with dependent children, but no other adults reflects a number of developments.

More single elderly women

A combination of women's longer life expectancy (five years on average) and the tendency for women to marry older men produces an increasing number of single elderly women. Although 95 per cent of retired people live in their own homes, they often receive significant care and support from younger relatives and friends.

Geographic dispersal

Although the vast majority of people continue to live within five miles of their original place of birth, a sizeable minority have moved to find employment elsewhere in the country. This trend has meant that the geographical distance between successive generations of the same family has tended to increase over time.

Declining marriage rates and increased divorce rates

Between 1971 and 1994 the number of weddings in the UK fell by one quarter. Accompanying this decline in the marriage rate has been an increase in the divorce rate. Between 1971 and 1992 the divorce rate doubled. In 1992, 173 000 decrees absolute were granted and this contributed to a decline in the average length of marriages. Most divorces now occur within five to nine years of the original wedding day.

The decline in the marriage rate and increase in the divorce rate have been matched to some extent by a growth in the number of people who either cohabit before marriage, or alternatively forego a wedding and live as common law husband and wife. Despite this increase, however, there is little evidence that the length of these relationships exceeds that of traditional marriages. As a consequence the length of time during which couples live together has been steadily decreasing in recent years. Sociologists refer to this new pattern of human relationships as *serial monogamy*. By this they mean that people continue to live in monogamous relationships, but that they are more likely to separate or change their partner.

Increased divorce and separation rates have contributed to the growth in the number of households containing lone parents with children. Between 1961 and 1993 the number of people in this category more than tripled. This increase in divorced lone parents considerably outstripped the growth in the number of unmarried lone parents.

| Exercise 7.1 | ## The consequences of demographic changes |

List five possible consequences of the changes in the structure of population and the composition of families for the personnel policies of an organization known to you.

LIBRARY
BISHOP BURTON COLLEGE
BEVERLEY HU17 8QG

INCOME, EARNINGS, TAXATION AND WEALTH

Sociologists and statisticians typically make a distinction between wealth and income because of the manner in which statistics are collected. Income refers to an individual's flow of earnings, e.g. wages, salary or interest on investment, while wealth refers to the stock of riches accrued by an individual. Adopting this distinction, this section examines changes in the pattern and distribution of incomes before going on to consider general variations in the level of wealth.

Income

Total household disposable income per head in the UK rose by 80 per cent between 1971 and 1993. Within this general trend, pensions and social security benefits contributed an increased share of household income, reflecting changes in the age profile of the population and increases in unemployment over the period (*see* Table 7.3).

Table 7.3 Household income in the UK, 1971–93

	1971	*1981*	*1993*
Sources of income (percentages)			
Wages and salaries	68	63	56
Income from self-employment	9	8	10
Rent, dividends and interest	6	7	7
Private pensions and annuities	5	6	11
Social security benefits	10	13	13
Other current benefits	2	2	3
Total household income (£ billion)	44.7	202.1	546.8
Direct taxes (percentages of total household income)			
Income taxes	14	14	12
National insurance	3	3	3
Pension contributions	1	2	2
Total household disposable income (£ billion)	36.4	162.4	453.2

Source: Social Trends 1994, No 24: 85, Office for National Statistics. Crown Copyright 1995. Reproduced by permission of the Controller of HMSO and Office for National Statistics.

Accompanying the increases in the level of total household income have been marked changes in the distribution of income. Between 1979 and 1991 the share of total incomes going to the worst-off 20 per cent shrank from 10 to 6 per cent (*see* Table 7.4). Despite this relative fall, however, the overall

LIBRARY
BISHOP BURTON COLLEGE
BEVERLEY HU17 8QG

increase in total income meant that even the most disadvantaged experienced some material improvement in their standard of living. For example, 69 per cent of the people in this category now have central heating in their houses – up from 29 per cent in 1979. Similarly, 73 per cent have telephones – up from 47 per cent; and 49 per cent have cars – up from 39 per cent.

Table 7.4 Distribution of disposable household income in the UK: net income after housing costs (%) (1979–92)

	Quintile groups				
	Bottom fifth	Next fifth	Middle fifth	Next fifth	Top fifth
1979	10	14	18	23	35
1987	8	12	17	23	40
1992	6	11	17	23	43

Source: *Social Trends 1994*, No 24: 94, Office for National Statistics. Crown Copyright 1995. Reproduced by permission of the Controller of HMSO and the Office for National Statistics.

In 1992, as the figures in Table 7.4 demonstrate, only the top 20 per cent of the population had a bigger share of total income than they had in 1979. This gradual redistribution of income reversed the egalitarian trend of the post-war period. Between 1945 and 1979 income differences between the highest paid and the lowest paid had gradually narrowed. During the 1980s and 1990s, however, incomes once again became more unequally divided. Today, although average income is approximately £19 000 per annum, the gap between the highest and lowest income groups is greater than at any time since records were first kept in 1886 (Commission on Social Justice, 1994).

Will Hutton has powerfully illustrated this disparity by using an analogy based on the height of people in an imaginary parade of Britain's working population. If, as he suggests, the population of Britain were divided according to income, if income were made equivalent to height and if the population then marched past for an hour, it would take a full 37 minutes before the first adult of average height was seen. For the first 15 minutes there would be a parade of dwarves. Stature would increase gradually thereafter, but 57 minutes would have passed before we saw people of twice average height. Giants of 90 feet or more would appear in the last few seconds, with the last one or two literally miles high (Hutton, 1995:193).

Over the last 15 years the main cause of these increases in income inequality has been changes in earnings and variations in the tax and benefits system. As mentioned previously, earnings in the form of a wage or salary may be just one element of an individual's income. Other elements might include social security benefits, pension payments or interest on investments. Each of these different forms of income is itself subject to different tax regulations.

Earnings

The main source of earnings for most households is waged or salaried employment (*see* Table 7.3). These earnings from employment vary from year to year reflecting the level of overtime, bonuses, shift allowances and annual pay reviews. Changes in the level of earnings do not affect all sections of society equally, and so over a period of years the distribution of earnings between regions, occupations and demographic groups will vary. While the pay available for certain jobs and people will rise, for others it will decline.

Over the last 25 years there have been three distinct trends in the earnings of British employees.

- The highest earners remain heavily concentrated in the south-east of England where pay levels are at least 25 per cent higher on average than elsewhere in the country.

- The gap between average female and male earnings has remained fairly constant since the early 1970s. On average women's pay is 29 per cent lower than that of men.

- The earnings of the higher paid have risen more rapidly than those of the lower paid. For example, in the five years to 1992, the average pay of the top directors of the FTSE 100 companies rose by 133 per cent to £535 000 per year, while average earnings in general rose by only 48 per cent.

Taxation and benefits

While pay awards have fluctuated in recent years, the level of take-home pay (gross salary less income tax and national insurance contributions) and disposable income (net salary less living expenses and associated VAT) has been affected by changes in the tax and benefits system. Here too, the highest income groups in Britain have received more favourable treatment than their poorer colleagues. The net effect of these changes has been to further reduce the income of the poorest groups. As Chris Pond has pointed out, between 1945 and 1979 the UK operated a *progressive* tax and benefits system which redistributed money from the rich to the poor. During the 1980s, what little effect this system had on the distribution of income was wiped out (Pond, 1989). Today, when all taxes are taken into account (VAT and other indirect taxes, as well as direct taxes like income tax) the poorest 10 per cent of the population pay a higher proportion of their income in tax than the richest 10 per cent – 43 per cent versus 32 per cent respectively. As such the current taxation system in the UK can be characterized as *regressive* because it takes proportionately more income away from the low earners than it does from the high earners.

The effects of changes in the taxation system upon the distribution of income have been further compounded by alterations to the benefits system. When the welfare state was created after the Second World War, its founders believed that a universal system of benefits would remove the social stigma previously associated with collecting benefits. They also believed that if everyone was entitled to social security, unemployment benefit and free health care, they would all have an interest in ensuring that the level of these benefits was adequate. Finally, it was felt that the costs associated with targeting selective benefits through means tests or other mechanisms would significantly reduce the overall amount of money available and would merely produce additional administrative costs. Over the last 20 years many universal benefits have been replaced by selective payments. Furthermore, although the level of these benefits has increased in *absolute terms* in line with price inflation, it has fallen in *relative terms* when compared with average increases in take-home pay and disposable income. As a consequence many of the poorest sections of society have suffered most. While universal entitlement to free university tuition remains in place, maintenance grants are now provided on a selective and much reduced level. Similarly, while universal mortgage income tax relief and child benefit remain available to the most affluent, tougher regulations have been introduced to govern the distribution of many social security payments.

Exhibit 7.1

Top executive pay

Since 1979, the pay of managers in the private sector has risen dramatically against a background of cuts in income tax and the removal of statutory restrictions on pay rises. Between 1974 and 1979, the pay of all managers lagged behind inflation, while in the period 1984 to 1995 the net pay of UK-based chief executives rose at more than twice the rate of inflation. The recession in the early 1990s reduced the pace of pay increases for executive board members, but they continued to fare better than their subordinates. The scale of these increases is revealed by recent surveys by Hay management consultants.

The figures in Table 7.5 understate the scale of the overall changes in income because they do not take account of annual bonuses, share options, car allowances and other long-term rewards.

According to the Norman Lowndes Consultancy, basic salary accounts for only 70 per cent of average top executive remuneration in the UK.

Table 7.5 Hay salary scales (1971–92)

	Pay Index		
Job level	1971	1981	1992
Directors	100	304.7	906.7
Senior management	100	323.0	908.1
Middle management	100	351.1	933.4
Senior clerical	100	381.6	871.9

Source: Hay (1992)

Exercise 7.2 **Top executive pay**

What explanations might be used to support the case for the present high levels of executive pay? Do you believe these justifications are well founded?

Exhibit 7.2

A statutory minimum wage

In September 1993 the government abolished 24 of the UK's remaining 25 wages councils, thereby ending Britain's established but patchy system of statutory minimum wage regulation.

Originally established by Winston Churchill in 1909, wages councils were charged with setting minimum rates of pay and conditions for employees in industries where unions were traditionally weak. The councils were made up of workers' and employers' representatives and were chaired by independent conciliators. The terms and conditions set by the councils were specific to particular industries and were enforced by wages inspectors who were empowered to compel employers to increase their wages and conditions to the minimum rates.

When they were initially formed, it was hoped that wages councils would be temporary bodies which could be disbanded when trade unions and employers extended collective bargaining to cover employees in poorly paid industries. This hope proved ill-founded; at the beginning of 1993 wages councils still set rates of pay for 2.5 million workers in industries as diverse as retail trades, catering, hotels, clothing manufacture and hairdressing. The only one of these bodies to escape abolition in 1993 was the Agricultural Workers' Wages Council. This body remained in operation as a result of campaigning by the National Farmers Union – a powerful employers' association with considerable political influence.

The abolition of wages councils encouraged the TUC and Labour Party to reaffirm their commitment to the introduction of a statutory national minimum wage. This legislation would establish a mechanism for determining a basic minimum rate of pay which would apply in all sectors of the economy. The original conference motions calling for this legislation suggested that the minimum wage should be pegged at half male median hourly earnings (a figure which equated to between £3.70 and £4.15 per hour in 1994). It was also hoped that within a few years of introduction this rate could be raised to a figure of two-thirds of male median hourly earnings.

Reference to a specific earnings figure was dropped in 1995 due to pressure from Tony Blair and the Labour Shadow Cabinet. They feared that the publication of a headline figure would be an electoral liability which would only lead to attacks on this policy by Conservative MPs and supporters.

Despite the removal of any reference to specific figures, both the TUC and Labour Party remain committed to the need for legislation in this area. Rather than set one blanket rate for the whole economy, however, it now seems likely that a future Labour government would establish a National Wage Commission which would set different minimum wage rates for employees in specific industrial and commercial sectors. In effect, this mechanism would operate as a reformed system of wages councils.

Exercise 7.3 A statutory minimum wage

Outline the arguments for and against a national system of statutory minimum wages along the lines currently proposed by the Labour Party.

Wealth

As mentioned earlier, wealth refers to the stock of riches accrued by an individual. These riches may be held as cash or invested in a house, pension, life assurance, share holdings or other valuable items.

Like income, the overall wealth of the UK population has been steadily increasing since the end of the Second World War. Despite this increase, however, the distribution of wealth between different sections of society has remained remarkably stable. Since 1976 the percentage of marketable wealth held by the top 50 per cent of the population has remained constant at about 92 per cent. Similarly the share of the richest 1 per cent was stable at 18 per cent.

An examination of the composition of the wealth held by different groups reveals some intriguing patterns. The very wealthy tend to hold a significant proportion of their wealth in the form of investments in the sphere of companies and other investment instruments. By contrast the less wealthy are more likely to have the bulk of their wealth invested in their own housing, pensions, life assurance and savings accounts. Halsey (1995) distinguishes between these two forms of ownership as property for power and property for use. The former involves some control over the lives of other people, the latter does not.

EDUCATION

The increased birth rate of the late 1940s and early 1960s led to increases in the number of pupils in public sector primary and secondary schools in the 1960s and the mid-1970s. Between 1976 and 1986 this trend reversed and the overall number of children in state schools declined. Despite these falls in the total number of pupils aged 5 to 16 engaged in compulsory schooling, the number of pupils enrolled in voluntary education increased throughout the late 1970s, the 1980s and early 1990s. As a consequence of this expansion children now start their studies earlier and complete them later. Over the last 25 years, the number of children under the age of five attending nursery schools on a full-time or part-time basis has more than doubled and now accounts for over half the population of four-year-olds. At the other end of the age spectrum, two-fifths of 16-year-olds currently choose to continue their studies at school or further education college, while a further fifth elect to take up some other form of vocational education or training.

Over the next five years this expansion of the number of people in voluntary education seems set to continue, as government-sponsored reforms designed to increase student numbers and the quality of education begin to have an effect.

During the 1980s and early 1990s, the system of education and training qualifications in the UK was subject to three substantial reforms.

1 The Education Reform Act 1988 introduced a National Curriculum for all pupils between the ages of 5 and 16 attending state-funded schools in England and Wales. The National Curriculum covers ten foundation subjects of which English, mathematics and science are treated as core study areas. Pupil performance within these subjects is monitored by means of a series of standard assessment tests (SATs) at the end of four key stages – at the ages of 7, 11, 14 and 16.

2 The range of courses and examinations available to pupils over the age of 14 was broadened. For example, the General Certificates of Secondary Education (GCSEs) were introduced to provide a route to qualification suitable for the majority of 16-year-olds. These new qualifications replaced the more narrowly targeted GCE O levels and CSE examinations. Meanwhile,

the Advanced Supplementary (AS) level examination was introduced to supplement A Levels and broaden the range of subjects which could be studied by pupils over the age of 16.

3   A range of vocational courses and examinations were introduced to school curriculums to provide an opportunity for pupils to develop work-related skills in parallel with, or as a replacement to, the traditional academic focus of GCSEs and A-Levels. In the late 1980s the government sponsored the introduction of a unified system of National Vocational Qualifications (NVQs) which were designed to provide a standard system for the assessment and accreditation of work-based training. More recently a number of General National Vocational Qualifications (GNVQs) have been introduced to provide students enrolled in full-time education with high-status vocational courses as an alternative to A-Levels.

Today, as a consequence of these and other changes, many more people are studying for longer and leaving school or college with some form of qualification. For example, approximately 60 per cent of 16-year-olds and 31 per cent of 18-year-olds now choose to continue their studies at further and higher education institutions respectively.

Much of this growth in the number of students in further and higher education has arisen because of increases in the number of female students. Furthermore, women are now more likely to leave school with a qualification of a higher standard than men of the same age, although they do not tend to study the same subjects. Girls tend to outperform boys in English, biology, French and history, while boys do better in mathematics, physics, chemistry and geography.

The higher performance of girls in schools examinations is gradually affecting the composition of undergraduate courses in British universities. Between 1981 and 1991, the proportion of female students in higher education increased from 40 per cent to 48 per cent. If present trends continue, the number of women in higher education will overtake the number of men within the next five years. However, even here there are differences between the sexes in terms of the subjects they choose to study. While an increasing number of women have enrolled on undergraduate courses in law and medicine, they remain under-represented on engineering and information technology courses. These differences contribute to the horizontal segregation of women at work. While women look set to improve their representation among the professional classes of lawyers and doctors, in addition to established positions in nursing and education, they will probably remain under-represented within technical occupations in the engineering and computing industries.

For most people the massive expansion in the number of people obtaining educational qualifications is to be welcomed as a sign of social and economic progress. However, a small number of critics have suggested that this expansion has merely led to an escalation in the level of qualification expected by employers and professions. According to Dore (1976), who christened this phenomenon the *diploma disease*, employers often raise their qualification requirements merely to cut down on the number of applicants for a given job, to increase the age at which candidates are employed, or to improve the social position of members of a profession vis-à-vis other groups in society. As the number of graduates increases, therefore, society has either to ensure that there is an increase in graduate-level job opportunities or consider how to alter the aspirations of new graduates.

Exercise 7.4

How might the changes in the number of students gaining qualifications at school and university affect the personnel policies of an organization known to you?

HEALTH AND WELFARE

As mentioned in the opening sections of this chapter, the life expectancy of people in the UK has been significantly extended over the last century as a consequence of improvements in medical practices, health education, housing, sanitation and nutrition. Today, many of the infectious diseases and medical conditions which previously killed people can be cured or prevented. For example, cholera and typhoid have been virtually eradicated as a consequence of improvements in sanitation. Tuberculosis and diphtheria have been controlled by immunization programmes. Rickets and scurvy are very uncommon because of improvements in diet.

As the traditional diseases of poverty have declined a new set of diseases and conditions have grown in significance. Today the biggest killers of men and women are circulatory disease and cancer.

- *Circulatory disease*, including coronary heart disease and strokes, account for nearly 40 per cent of all deaths in the UK. These conditions are the single largest causes of premature death and are responsible for an estimated 42.7 million lost working days per year.

- *Cancers* are the second largest cause of premature death, accounting for 25 per cent of all deaths. Although the overall figures are large, there are substantial differences between the sexes. Lung cancer is the single largest cancer affecting men. Breast cancer accounts for the majority of cases among women.

Although genetic and biological processes play a part in the development of these conditions, there are social and lifestyle factors which can significantly heighten the risk of contracting a circulatory disease or cancer. In particular, smoking, excessive alcohol consumption, inappropriate diet and lack of exercise have been singled out as major contributors to the development of these diseases. The rest of this section considers these factors in more detail and outlines some of the steps employers have taken to counteract their effect.

Smoking

Smoking is the single largest preventable cause of disease and premature death in the UK. It has been linked to the onset of lung cancer, coronary heart disease, bronchitis and emphysema. At present in the UK, approximately a third of people over the age of 16 smoke regularly and more than 100 000 people die prematurely each year as a result.

Over the last 25 years the total number of smokers has declined by 25 per cent, but some sub-groups within society appear to be more resistant to change than others. The British Social Attitudes Survey in 1990 revealed that, in general, older people were less likely to smoke than those under the age of 55. Similarly, women are on the whole less likely to smoke than men, although the number of young women taking up smoking has not decreased as rapidly as it has among men. Furthermore, smoking is rather more common among the working classes and the less well qualified than among the educated middle classes.

Recognition of the dangers associated with passive smoking appears to have accelerated the rate at which people stop smoking, and to have hardened people's attitudes towards smoking in public places. Today, even a majority of smokers are in favour of greater restrictions on smoking.

Table 7.6 Attitudes to smoking in public places (%)

	Total	Current smoker	Ex-smoker	Never smoked
Smoking at places of work should be:				
• freely allowed	5	13	2	2
• restricted to certain areas	60	75	63	48
• banned altogether	33	9	33	48

Source: Ben-Shlomo et al (1991:173)

In response to changes in people's attitudes towards smoking a growing number of employers have introduced smoking policies which seek to limit or restrict smoking within the workplace. Pressure for these controls have come from employers, employees and more recently the government. The *Health of the Nation* White Paper (1992) declared a goal of 'a large majority of employers' implementing a no-smoking policy by the year 1995. In addition, the European Union has recently introduced health and safety regulations which require all employers by 1996 to provide smoke-free rest rooms for their staff. The organizations that have recently introduced a smoking policy include the Automobile Association, ICI, Black and Decker, Royal College of Nursing, the Civil Service, Body Shop and the Metropolitan Police. In general, these policies limit smoking to designated areas only or, alternatively, there is a complete ban on smoking at work (IDS, 1993).

Alcohol and drug misuse

An estimated one in ten of the UK's adult population is a problem drinker. These people do not leave their problems behind when they come to work. Alcohol Concern estimates that around 75 per cent of problem drinkers are in full-time employment at all levels within business organizations. The statistics on drug taking are less accurate but there has been an acknowledged growth in drug dependence in recent years and many drug addicts are employees. Alcohol and drug misuse cause ill-health, accidents and death. They are also major factors in law and order problems, family breakdown and industrial inefficiency. It is estimated that alcohol-related absences from work account for 8 million days lost a year – three times the number lost through industrial action. In terms of lost production, this is costing the British economy approximately £1.7 billion per year.

Research by the Health Education Authority in 1991, and Industrial Relations Services in 1992, revealed that 70 to 76 per cent of the organizations surveyed had some form of alcohol policy. However, the success of these policies has been difficult to gauge because people tend to underestimate the amount of alcohol they consume. Nevertheless, two recent surveys designed to measure the effects of the relaxation of licensing laws in 1988 reveal that overall alcohol consumption has changed little in the last five years. In response to concerns about the high levels of alcohol consumption among the population, the government plans to take steps to reduce the proportion of men drinking more than 21 units of alcohol per week from 28 per cent in 1990 to 18 per cent by 2005. The government also aims to reduce the proportion of women drinking more than 14 units per week from 11 per cent in 1990 to 7 per cent by 2005. (One unit is equal to half a pint of beer, a single pub measure of spirit or a glass of wine.)

Diet and exercise

Consistent overeating and insufficient exercise combine to produce obesity. In 1987, it was estimated that 8 per cent of men and 12 per cent of women were obese. Obesity is determined by calculating an individual's body mass index. This involves dividing body weight in kilograms by height in metres. A body mass index of more than 30 is considered obese.

In addition to the generally damaging effects of excessive body weight, it is important to consider what is eaten. High concentrations of cholesterol in the blood are associated with increased risk of circulatory disease, and high intakes of saturated fatty acids increase blood cholesterol. At present doctors estimate that approximately two thirds of the British adult population have blood cholesterol levels above the desirable range.

In order to control body weight and reduce blood cholesterol levels it is important that people consume a healthy and varied diet. Employers can play a crucial role in encouraging their employees to eat sensibly. The Health Education Authority's 'Look after your Heart' campaign suggests that employers should provide a healthy choice of foods and publicity about them in staff canteens and public eating places.

In attempting to reduce obesity and blood cholesterol levels the other half of the equation involves increasing the amount of physical exercise people carry out. In recognition of the benefits of a fit and active workforce, a number of companies have installed gyms or made arrangements with local health clubs. Among the well known British-based companies with exercise facilities freely available to staff are IBM, Kelloggs, Marks & Spencer and United Biscuits.

Stress

Many of the illnesses, conditions and behaviours listed above may merely be symptoms of deeper-seated stresses in the lives of people at work. The term 'stress' is now part of the regular vocabulary of managers and employees. While some stress is a normal feature of everyone's working lives, high levels of prolonged stress can give rise to one or more of the following symptoms.

- tension and anxiety;
- excessive alcohol, tobacco and drug misuse;
- sleep problems;
- reduced job satisfaction;
- high blood pressure;
- eating disorders and digestive problems;
- forgetfulness;
- increased absenteeism.

Traditionally the analysis of stress at work has concentrated on the problems experienced by senior executives, but a number of more recent studies indicate that levels of stress tend to be highest among employees in the lowest echelons of an organization. The causes of this stress may be many and varied but typically include poor job design, difficult working relationships, lack of communication, work overload, time pressures and business reorganizations. These occupational pressures will heighten the stress that individuals experience as a consequence of tensions in their home and personal lives.

A number of recent court cases have demonstrated that an employer's duty of care towards his or her employees extends to reducing and controlling the level of stress they experience. In response to these decisions as well as direct pressures from employees and other sources, a number of organizations have established counselling services to ensure that this aspect of their employees' welfare is catered for effectively. These services are often referred to as Employee Assistance Programmes (EAPs).

Exercise 7.5

A health awareness audit

Employers can do a lot to help improve the health and fitness of their staff. Whether their organization is part of a large multinational or a recently established small business there are a number of steps that can be taken to increase health awareness. The following list sets out some of the measures available to employers. Read through the list and tick those steps which have been taken by an organization known to you. What steps could be taken to improve the organization's performance?

1. *Use offices to put across health information and distribute information to staff about healthy living.*

2. *Publish articles in the company newsletter or magazine promoting health consciousness.*

3. *Provide smoke-free offices and other work areas.*

4. *Provide a healthy choice of food in staff canteens.*

5 *Introduce training and education programmes for employees in exercise, nutrition and stress management.*

6 *Provide more opportunities for staff to take exercise.*

7 *Arrange for staff to have a general medical and fitness testing including blood pressure monitoring and cholesterol testing.*

8 *Adopt practical, company-wide policies on smoking, nutrition, exercise, alcohol and stress management.*

9 *Take steps to encourage regular eye sight testing, dental check-ups, hearing examinations and screening for breast and cervical cancer.*

10 *Establish an Employee Assistance Programme (EAP) to provide confidential counselling, advice and welfare support for staff experiencing high levels of stress or other work and non-work related problems.*

SOCIAL STRATIFICATION AND MOBILITY

In earlier sections of this chapter we have described and documented a number of recent social trends which have affected the behaviour and attitudes of the UK population in general. At various points in this discussion comments have been made about the distribution of these changes. In short, it has been noted that these changes have not had a uniform effect upon all sections of society. This should not be surprising because, as countless historical and contemporary research studies have demonstrated, all societies are to a greater or lesser extent stratified so that some people obtain more resources than others for legal, religious, economic or social reasons. For example, the feudal legal system which operated in medieval England and Wales provided a justification for the unequal distribution of material rewards and rights for different groups within society. Thus, lords had more than freemen and freemen had more than serfs. Similarly in modern India traditional religious rather than legal differences between various groups have been used to justify dividing people at birth into castes with distinct privileges and opportunities in life.

Today, in the UK, legal and (with the exception of Northern Ireland) religious explanations of the position of specific groups within society are increasingly less important. However, there are still considerable differences in the status and prospects of different sections of the community.

In this final section of the chapter these differences will be discussed. More specifically we will be considering why certain groups expect to live longer, earn more, receive a better education and enjoy better health? In examining these questions we will be drawing upon insights derived from a number of mainstream economic, political and sociological debates. The aim here is not to provide a definitive answer to these questions, but instead to highlight factors which may explain the current and evolving structure of UK society.

Class

The concept of social class has been one of the mainstays of sociological analysis in the UK for over 150 years. Despite the endurance of this concept, however, the meaning of the term and its implications for the study of the structure of society and the behaviour of groups and individuals have been hotly contested.

Early attempts to define social class focused on the jobs and labour market position of different groups within society. According to these definitions the social class of particular groups and individuals reflected their position within the jobs hierarchy of companies or the pattern of market relationships between large and small organizations. For one of the most radical of these writers, Karl Marx, society could be divided into several classes of which the most important was a powerful and monied *bourgeoisie* (the upper class) who were able to use their position in order to exploit the poorer labouring *proletariat* (working class). Between these groups lay the *petty bourgeoisie* of shop keepers and managers.

Marx used this analysis of class differences to explain the historical and political changes which had given rise to the unequal distribution of wealth and income in Victorian Britain – a situation in which the majority of the population were poor, unhealthy and ill-educated, while a tiny minority of people enjoyed the benefits of large incomes, medicine and good education. He believed that if the working class became more aware of the wider social processes which had caused their predicament they would be better placed to take action and change things.

Although Marx was among the first to draw attention to these class differences, he was not the last. Efforts to measure and map class differences have led to the production of a variety of different schemes. One of the most influential of these approaches has been the Registrar General's classification of socio-economic groups. Revised on a number of occasions this classification system places people into categories according to the occupation of the head of their household. The most commonly used version of this scheme appears in Table 7.7.

Table 7.7 The Registrar General's classification of socio-economic groups

I	Professional occupations
II	Intermediate occupations
III (N)	Skilled non-manual occupations
III (M)	Skilled manual occupations
IV	Partly skilled occupations
V	Unskilled occupations

Source: *Social Trends 1994*, No 24, Office for National Statistics. Crown Copyright 1995. Reproduced by permission of the Controller of HMSO and the Office for National Statistics.

Another popular scale of class positions was first used for the National Readership Survey and is now commonly used by market research companies. This index divides the population into one of six alphabetical categories (A, B, C1, C2, D and E) according to occupation. Although not strictly comparable with the Registrar General's scheme, the list of occupations in each category is similar.

Commonsense measures of class like those of the Registrar General and the National Readership Survey have been subject to considerable criticism by a number of academics and researchers. They have suggested that ranking people according to their occupations merely produces an index of people's income and wealth and therefore it does not help to explain how classes are formed, the reasons for the different class positions, who belongs to these classes, and whether individuals are conscious of their class position. In response to these criticisms a number of sociologists have developed class maps which they believe provide a better explanation of patterns of control at work and the class position of different occupations (*see* Crompton (1993) for a review of alternative approaches).

Regardless of the way in which class is measured, a range of studies has demonstrated that there is a relationship between social class, life expectancy, education and health. Put simply, the middle and upper classes are more likely than the working classes to enjoy good health, live longer and achieve higher educational qualifications, as well as having high incomes and owning more.

Because of these differences in life chances considerable attention has focused on recent changes in the overall distribution of people between classes. Here, because of differences in the methods of classifying classes, as outlined above, different conclusions have been drawn. At one extreme there are a number of optimistic commentators who suggest that the 'pyramidical' class structure which characterized British society at the beginning of the twentieth century has broken down. They argue that Britain should no longer be seen as a society in which a large working class supports a small middle class and a still smaller upper class. Instead, they maintain that this old order has been replaced by a diamond shaped structure. There are now fewer members of the working and upper classes and correspondingly more members of the middle classes (Halsey, 1995). As a consequence there is also much greater mobility between classes as individuals are able to improve their position by education and diligent work (Saunders, 1990).

More pessimistic commentators suggest that these changes are more apparent than real. While the number of managerial and professional occupations has increased, the economic and market position of these jobs has changed. Jobs which were once considered middle class, therefore, have been devalued and degraded as new technology and changing management practices have lowered the relative position of these occupations (Wright, 1985). More worryingly, these developments have been accompanied by a steady increase in the number of the long-term unemployed. This change has helped to create an 'underclass' with low levels of education and training, poor health, negligible income and no wealth (Murray, 1990).

Status and citizenship

Other analyses of the changing class structure of the UK have more profound implications. According to a growing group of commentators with a variety of political beliefs, social changes over the past 50 years have been so significant that the traditional concept of class is no longer as important as it once was. Class, they suggest, should no longer be the main focus for explanations of the economic position, attitudes and behaviours of the individuals and groups within British society. Analysis should focus instead on other differences of status and citizenship within the population. Amongst the specific criticisms which have been levelled at traditional class analysis the following five are worthy of special attention.

1 It has been claimed that most studies of social class confuse class structure and class consciousness. Thus there is a tendency to assume that people who are defined as members of a particular class will be aware of this fact and therefore able to see areas of common interest with others in the same position. One commonly cited example of the failure of this assumed relationship is the decline of the assumed relationship between social class, trade union membership and voting intentions during the 1970s, 1980s and 1990s. As more professional and managerial employees in the public sector joined trade unions, and more working class people voted Conservative, the view that class position translated into class consciousness and action became less tenable.

2 It has been suggested that increases in the material well-being of the vast majority of the population has meant that people are more likely to define themselves in terms of the things they buy and the lifestyles they aspire to, rather than the job that they hold. With the steady development of a more openly consumerist culture it has been suggested that modern marketing terms such as yuppies, dinkies, wrinklies and generation X'ers are at least as effective as occupational categories in explaining people's attitudes and behaviour. Even in situations where people are out of work, the persistence of the welfare state and various social rights to housing, education and health care mean that their relationship to the tax and benefit system as contributors or claimants is more important than their previous occupation in explaining the divides that exist in modern society (Saunders, 1990). In short, it has been suggested that consumer choices are as important as people's position in the production process.

3 It has been argued that the increasing number of women active in the labour market calls into question the practice of categorizing an individual's class according to the occupation of the male 'head of their household'. As women have advanced their position in the world of work, independently of their partners, class has begun to be seen as an unsophisticated mechanism for explaining differences in the life chances of individuals and groups. Today, independently of their class position, women live longer than men, achieve higher educational qualifications, and enjoy better health. Despite these benefits, however, they earn less and own fewer assets. Indeed women at all ages are more likely than men to live in poverty. This problem is particularly acute for single and divorced mothers, widows and female pensioners. A number of important contributions to the second wave of feminism from the late 1960s to the early 1990s have explained these disadvantages by reference to the lower status attached to women's role in society. This, they suggest, has been reinforced by a patriarchical (male-dominated) system which has traditionally accorded women fewer civil, political and social rights than their male counterparts.

4 The influx of immigrants into the UK from the commonwealth countries of Africa, Asia and the West Indies has exposed other divisions within

modern British society. Although it is dangerous to assume that members of these different ethnic minorities share a common sense of identity or similar prospects, on average regardless of their educational achievements they are more likely to be unemployed or on lower incomes. Explanations of the relative disadvantage of these groups have focused upon the discrimination and prejudice they experience.

5 There has been a growing awareness in recent years of other sources of individual identity and status difference including age, health, physical ability, previous criminal record, sexuality, height, weight, looks and intelligence. Furthermore, a range of studies by social scientists have demonstrated that people often suffer discrimination and disadvantage because of these differences. While many of these forms of discrimination are currently unlawful or generally seen as unethical, the limits to what is acceptable and unacceptable are constantly being redrawn. Thus, whether or not it will be unlawful in the future to discriminate on the grounds of weight, looks or intelligence remains to be seen.

In summary, the combination of declining class consciousness, growing consumerism and the heightened visibility of status differences between men and women, as well as black and white people, has called the traditional centrality of class analysis into question. Although class remains important in explaining inequalities in the UK, it is not the only explanation. Status differences based on other forms of discrimination and prejudice are also important.

SUMMARY AND CONCLUSION

In this chapter we have described a number of general trends in the structure of British society. Among the recent changes singled out for attention have been the continued growth in the world's population, increasing life expectancy in the UK, the demise of the traditional family unit, growing inequalities in income, improvements in general educational achievement and altering patterns of disease within the population.

These trends affect each and every one of us in different ways as members of British society. They also have indirect implications for us as employees and managers in British-based organizations. As people change the way in which they live their lives, policy makers within organizations are forced to respond. As in other areas of business practice, these policy makers have choices. They may decide to ignore these changes and continue to use established policies which worked well in the past. Alternatively, they may act on an *ad hoc* basis as general trends become evident when individual employees present the organization with specific problems. However, it is our belief that more proactive managers and organizations will ensure that they are aware of these general and emerging trends so that they are in a position to think out the implications for their personnel policies before problems emerge. By anticipating the possible future direction of these changes and being aware of different explanations of their causes, managers and employees should be better prepared to deal with their consequences.

CHAPTER 8

The political context

INTRODUCTION

A country's political system is concerned with the exercise of power. Although some people find politics and politicking distasteful, most see institutionalized political processes as necessary and preferable to anarchy or war. By setting down ways in which decisions should be made in a framework of laws, rules and conventions, conflicts of opinion are consequently handled in more predictable and manageable ways.

FOCUS AND SCOPE

This chapter explores a number of contemporary issues relating to the operation of Britain's political system. These issues are, to varying degrees, matters of concern for both employers and other interest groups within society (voters, employees, trade unions and pressure groups).

The three contemporary issues selected are:

- the extent to which Britain can be said to be a representative democracy;
- the significance for Britain of membership of the European Union;
- the nature of the law-making processes within Britain.

These issues are interrelated. Decision making (including law making) in a representative democracy is expected, in theory, to reflect the interests of citizens in that society. As we shall see, however, the concept of 'representativeness' is not easy to define.

Furthermore, the British political system is now locked into the European Union. Membership of the Union affects both political decision making and law making. Consequently, there can be tensions about the policies advocated and pursued. Questions can arise as to whether such laws and policies are in the interests of the British people as a whole or just particular segments of society. It is also frequently argued that the institutions of the European Union are not fully democratic and so cannot fully reflect the interests of European citizens.

LEARNING OBJECTIVES

Once you have read through this chapter and completed the associated exercises, you should be able to:

- understand the concept of representative democracy;
- understand the significance of Britain's membership of the European Union;

- understand the processes used for law making by the European Union and the British Parliament and the extent to which these might be influenced by employers', consumers' and employees' organizations;
- understand the impact of political activity on private, public or voluntary sector organizations;
- advise on how employers might lobby within the political system.

THE CONTEXT OF THE POLITICAL SYSTEM

Of course, a political system does not exist in a vacuum. It operates in an economy, which will influence it and which will have its own balance of power between employers, on the one hand, and employees and trade unions on the other. It operates in a society and so will be influenced by developing social attitudes. The political system is also affected by the legal system, which can determine the legality of certain political actions.

Of course, influence does not flow in one direction. Those operating in the political system, in their turn, invariably seek to influence the economy, society and the legal system. This reciprocal interplay of relationships can be seen in various ways.

In the economy, government policy may be affected by multinational companies. For example, Nissan, the car manufacturer, negotiated favourable investment incentives to locate its manufacturing base and entry into the European Union market in Britain. Government, on the other hand, can try to influence the behaviour of employers – either through law or taxation or through the advocacy of policies. In the mid-1980s, for example, the Conservative government, to promote a free labour market, successfully encouraged many employers to rescind industry-wide collective bargaining and to relate pay either to the business's economic performance or that of individual employees.

In terms of society, reciprocal influence is often quite complex. For example, as we shall see in Chapter 10, the enhancement of women's status in society derives from a number of factors. On the one hand, some women have challenged (through direct action and political campaigning) their subservient position – by demanding the right to vote, the right to equal pay and the right not to be discriminated against on grounds of sex, marital status and pregnancy. Legislation was eventually enacted to achieve certain standards of equal treatment. This legislation, in its turn, generated further demands for action to eradicate entrenched discriminatory practices by employers and within society at large.

Finally, in terms of the legal system, legislation is enacted by Parliament. This statute law frequently reflects the views and ideology of the predominant political party. In the 1980s, the Conservative governments introduced a rolling programme of legislation to curb trade union power and to limit the definition of lawful industrial action. In turn, the legal system, through the courts, can affect the actions of politicians by determining the legality of certain actions by government ministers or certain pieces of legislation. For example, in 1994, the House of Lords, under judicial review, ruled that the

qualifying periods necessary for employees to invoke unfair dismissal complaints were contrary to European Union law.

The areas of contemporary debate

Three areas of contemporary debate concerning the British political system
have been selected for examination. These are:

1 *The nature of representative democracy* – Britain's status as a liberal democracy; securing constitutional rights; the structure of government and the
separation of powers; the values and policies of the main political parties;
the role of pressure groups; and reforming the political system.

2 *Britain's membership of the European Union* – perceptions of the European
Union; the philosophy underpinning social legislation; principal institutions of the EU; processes for implementing EU law.

3 *Making statute law in Parliament.*

BRITAIN'S STATUS AS A LIBERAL DEMOCRACY

To consider this, it is necessary to explore the nature of 'liberal democracy',
and examine it in comparison with other political systems. It is possible to
categorize these systems in different ways. In this chapter, we use the model
shown in Fig 8.1.

This links two broad characteristics:

● the fundamental ideological perspective embodied in the political system
(on an axis ranging from 'liberal democratic' to 'totalitarian');

● the predominant form of participation by citizens (on the 'individualist'/
'collectivist' axis).

Fig 8.1 Political systems

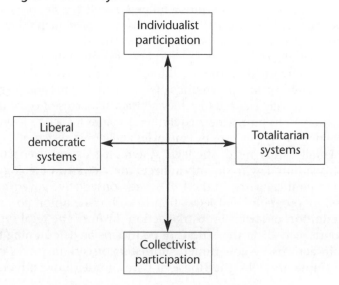

The extremities of each axis refer to theoretical 'ideal types'. Political systems are unlikely to conform precisely to such 'pure forms'. Using this model, however, we should be able to plot the location of a country's political system by examining the extent to which it measures up to the characteristics set out below.

It should also be possible, broadly, to compare one country's political system with that of another and identify any shifts that may take place within any one country – that is, is a particular political culture becoming less 'collectivist'? Is it tending to adopt more 'totalitarian' measures?

Each of these axes will be considered in turn.

Liberal democratic societies

Liberal democratic societies are pluralist – in accepting the expression of various opinions – and they acknowledge a range of rights and duties for both the governors and the governed. The rights can be categorized as human rights, social rights, economic rights and political rights.

Human rights

These include the following basic rights:

- Freedom of thought, conscience and religion; and the right, individually and collectively, to practise such beliefs (provided this does not interfere with the freedom of others in a democratic society).
- Freedom of peaceful assembly and freedom of association with other people to join together in organizations (e.g. political pressure groups, political parties and trade unions).
- Freedom from arbitrary arrest; and access to effective judicial remedies to enforce all rights.

Political rights

Issues of economic, social and political policy are debated and opinions are sought from the electorate; and pressure groups are able to organize and influence the political process.

The electorate is widely drawn and the right to vote is not limited on grounds of, for example, property ownership, educational qualifications or sex. Political leaders are elected in individual secret ballots, free from intimidation. More than one political party competes for power and it is expected that opposing parties may replace governing parties from time to time.

Political power is spread across a number of different bodies. This may include the devolution of some power to local and/or regional government. There are safeguards to prevent the abuse of power (e.g. an independent judiciary, committees of inquiry, and the existence of investigatory agencies, like 'Ombudsmen').

Economic rights

These generally comprise a right to work and to job security; a right not to be conscripted into forced labour; a right to fair remuneration for work performed; a right to 'just conditions' at work; and also, adequate social security benefit protection (e.g. pensions, sickness, unemployment and disability).

Furthermore, there should be effective judicial remedies to deal with complaints about infringement of these economic and employment-related rights.

Social rights

These include basic provisions for all citizens, equally, in respect of education, healthcare and accommodation. Furthermore, there is the right not to be discriminated against on such grounds as 'sex, race, colour, language, religion, political or other opinion, national or social origin, association with a national minority, property, birth or other status' (European Convention for the Protection of Human Rights 1950, Article 14).

Duties

It is generally acknowledged in liberal democratic societies that such rights should coexist with duties and obligations that, on the one hand, citizens owe to each other and to society in general and, on the other hand, the government owes to citizens. Some of the principal duties are:

- *Compliance with 'the rule of law'.* Members of society are expected to obey laws passed by democratically elected legislatures and adjudicated by an independent judiciary. They are likewise expected to co-operate with enforcing agencies, like the police service.

- *Restrictions on the exercise of rights.* Rights like freedom of thought, belief, speech, association and assembly may be qualified in various ways. The European Convention on Human Rights 1950, for example, refers to restrictions that 'are necessary in a democratic society in the interests of national security or public safety, for the prevention of disorder or crime, for the protection of health or morals or for the protection of the rights and freedoms of others' (Article 11).

- *Non-discriminatory speech and behaviour.* A further example of restricted rights can arise in respect of freedom of speech. This can be limited if it is to result in, for example, unfair discrimination and racist behaviour.

Totalitarian societies

At the other end of this axis are totalitarian societies. Countries which have been described this way include the former Soviet Union, Nazi Germany, Fascist Italy and, currently, the People's Republic of China, Iran and Iraq. The characteristics of such political systems are:

- The society is committed to one overriding secular ideology or religious ideal – usually embodied in an all-powerful authoritarian leader (e.g. Stalin, Hitler, Mussolini, Mao Tse Tung, Ayatollah Khomeni and Saddam Hussein).

- A power élite exists that expects full compliance by the population to the ideology or religious belief. Dissent and critical questioning is not permitted. Citizens are required to follow the will of their political masters.

Education, literature, the arts, the professions are likely to be subordinated to the ideology or religious dogma.

- Enforcement of the power élite's ideology is carried out by the police, armed forces and other agents of the government. The techniques used to ensure compliance can include a secret police force, surveillance of the population, the torture and murder of dissenters, and imprisonment in concentration camps.

- Commitment to the ideology or religious belief is reinforced by identifying an external enemy who must be mobilized against and destroyed (e.g. the United States of America has been demonized by Iran). Often, an enemy is also identified as disruptive or seditious within the particular society (e.g. the Jews in Nazi Germany).

- Any alternative focus of loyalty – e.g. non-approved religious organizations, trade unions, opposition political groups – is either suppressed or subverted. For example, in the former Soviet Union, trade unions became an administrative arm of the Communist power élite. They did not engage in free collective bargaining and the right to strike was deemed unnecessary.

- The right to vote freely in elections does not exist. If elections take place, they will be restricted in various ways. For example, voters may be physically intimidated; they may be required to ask for a separate ballot paper to oppose the governing party; or their choice may be restricted to rival candidates of the governing party.

The other axis in Fig 8.1 refers to participation within political systems – that is, the extent to which 'individual' as against 'collective' participation is actively encouraged or discouraged.

Individualist participation

Under a 'pure' individualist approach to participation, engagement in the political process will be as an individual citizen (e.g. by voting periodically in an election). Any collective involvement – through pressure groups – is likely to be minimal or non-existent.

The economic system in such a society will also perceive the individual as of paramount consideration as either consumer or worker. Individuals are expected to pursue their own economic well-being and ownership of private property is widely dispersed. Collective expressions of economic concern (e.g. in consumer groups and trade unions) will be of minimal significance.

As for the notion of 'society', its existence is denied. Margaret Thatcher exemplified this by stating that: 'There is no such thing as society. There are individual men and women and there are families' (quoted in Wedderburn, 1991:209). This attitude reinforces the atomization that is evident in the political and economic arenas.

Collectivist participation

The 'pure' collectivist approach sees individual participation within the political system as minimal – possibly restricted to voting occasionally in elections.

Most major political and economic decisions are likely to be taken by organizations, groups and committees established within the political process.

In liberal democracies, these may comprise the principal pressure groups (like employers' associations, consumer groups and trade unions). In totalitarian regimes, the collective groups will represent supporters of the power élite at particular levels. For example, in the former Soviet Union, such groups would involve Communist Party committees, Communist-run trade unions, and committees of local and regional Communist officials.

In the social arena, collective action is seen as the normal and legitimate form of participation. In liberal democracies, this may be reflected in the establishment of community groups, for example. In totalitarian societies, collective social activities may be designed to reinforce commitment to the political or religious 'ideal'.

(You may choose to undertake the following two exercises now or, alternatively, keep them in mind as you read the remainder of the chapter and complete them at the end.)

Exercise 8.1   ## Liberal democratic rights

Consider the extent to which you think Britain provides human, political, economic and social rights for particular social groups. Draw up a matrix similar to that shown in Table 8.1. Mark with a tick, a cross or, if you think the existence of the right is unclear, with a question mark.

Table 8.1

	Human rights	*Political rights*	*Economic rights*	*Social rights*
Men				
Women				
Pregnant workers				
Ethnic minorities				
The elderly				
The unemployed				
Full-timers				
Part-timers				
Trade unionists				
Homosexuals				
Religious groups				
Disabled persons				

| **Exercise 8.2** | **Political systems** |

Using your general knowledge, indicate on the model in Fig 8.1, by inserting the appropriate number, the location of the following political systems:

1 *Britain in the 1980s and early 1990s.*

2 *Britain in the 1970s.*

3 *the United States of America.*

4 *the former Soviet Union (1917–91).*

5 *the People's Republic of China (1949 to date).*

6 *Nazi Germany (1933–45).*

7 *the Federal Republic of Germany (1949 to date).*

8 *Japan (since 1945).*

9 *Sweden.*

10 *Iran.*

11 *Iraq.*

SECURING CONSTITUTIONAL RIGHTS IN A LIBERAL DEMOCRACY

As we have already seen, liberal democracies are characterized by the provision of various fundamental rights. Such societies can of course be differentiated by both the ways in which they secure these rights and also the nature of their democratic procedures. One important distinction is between those countries that have a written constitution (like the United States, France and Germany) and those which do not (like the United Kingdom).

This distinction can be important in respect of employment policies and law. For example, in France, Germany and Belgium, written constitutional provisions guarantee a core of fundamental rights and freedoms. These include the right to engage in collective bargaining and the right to form and join a trade union. Such rights come within the jurisdiction of a constitutional court. This can provide a protection against any government which seeks to infringe them.

In Britain, on the other hand, there is no written constitution nor any Bill of Rights guaranteed by a supreme court. Each democratic right, enacted into statute law by one particular Parliament, can, technically, be repealed by a subsequent Parliament. For example, the wide protections for trade unions (when organizing industrial action) that had developed over the past century were considerably eroded by successive Parliaments during the 1980s. With no constitutional 'right to strike' and no constitutional court, the actions of the government could be neither modified nor constrained.

The debate in favour and against a Bill of Rights has been quite extensive over the past decade. Keith Ewing (1990), in considering the possible impact on trade unions, signalled a cautious approach. It would mean transferring power from Parliament to the courts. These would have to determine whether legislation passed by Parliament was consistent with such a Bill of Rights. If this Bill was vague and unclear, it would be for the judges to determine the meaning. Clearly, this would have profound implications for the separation of powers (*see* below).

Having said this, however, British governments do not have unfettered power. There are three possible constraints that can be brought to bear: the European Union, international conventions and the process of judicial review by British courts.

Britain, as a result of its membership of the European Union (since 1973) is obliged to conform to *European law*, whether it concerns competition, the free movement of labour or employment protection for individual workers.

For example, as far as individual employees are concerned, the EU has set certain principles which should govern their treatment. Most significant in effect is the principle of equal treatment on grounds of sex. This principle has had a profound effect on British legislation and case law. It has ensured that these protections were guaranteed despite the Conservative governments' pursuit of free market deregulation. In the 1980s and early 1990s, the principle of equal value was introduced into equal pay law; pregnant workers' rights were enacted; and access to unfair dismissal and redundancy rights could not be restricted to disadvantage part-timers, who were predominantly female, because this was held to constitute indirect sex discrimination.

International conventions, on the other hand, have provided a much weaker safeguard of rights. The most significant in respect of employment are those adopted by the International Labour Organisation (ILO). During the 1980s, Britain was found to have infringed certain of these conventions (Ewing, 1994) – for example, the removal of school teachers' collective bargaining rights. The weakness of these international standards lies not so much in the conventions themselves but in two related issues. First, governments can voluntarily subscribe to the conventions; and, second, the ILO has no enforcement mechanisms. It can investigate non-compliance and publish a report, but action beyond that is not possible.

In the European Union, by contrast, the Commission can initiate infringement proceedings against a government which fails to comply with EU law. In 1992 Britain was taken before the European Court of Justice for failing to implement fully the Directives on Collective Redundancies and on Transfers of Undertakings.

A final form of potential constraint on a British government is the *process of judicial review*, whereby the legality of certain policy decisions can be challenged – initially in the High Court.

A significant example of this process in the employment arena was the action of the House of Lords in declaring qualifying thresholds for unfair dismissal compensation and redundancy pay to be contrary to EU equal treatment law because of their differential impact upon women as against men. One writer has commented that this case has given Britain 'the taste of a constitutional court' (Szyszczak, 1995).

Direct and effective guarantees of civil rights, therefore, whether in employment or in society at large, are dependent on the attitudes and decisions of each successive British Parliament (apart from those specifically deriving from the European Union). They will be affected by the results of elections and political decision making.

The separation of powers

In liberal democracies there are four principal elements of government: the head of state; the executive; the legislature; and the judiciary.

The head of state oversees the political system and can be guardian of the constitution. The powers of the head of state can vary significantly from being largely ceremonial – either as a monarch or elected president – to being an important political actor, as in the elected presidencies of the United States and France.

The executive is charged with the formulation and implementation of policy. In Britain, Ireland and Germany, for example, the head of government is the Prime Minister who appoints a Cabinet of ministers to carry out executive responsibilities. Normally, the Prime Minister is the leader of the largest party in the country's Parliament. In recent political analyses of Britain, it has been commented that the Prime Minister has at his or her disposal considerable patronage in terms of Cabinet and other political appointments. The Prime Minister is also central to the management of government business. Possible limitations on this power may arise when a political party is part of a coalition and, therefore, daily negotiations are required to determine policies and legislative priorities.

A further constraint can arise when the governing party has a slim parliamentary majority. Given that political parties are themselves 'coalitions of interests', well organized minority groups of MPs can influence the direction of specific policies – for example, the 'Euro-sceptic' MPs in the Major government.

Generally, however, the role of the executive in Britain has been enhanced by two interlocking developments during the Thatcher/Major governments. Both these developments have promoted considerable centralization, a reduction in democratic accountability and a broadening of the scope for ministerial patronage.

1 *Local government has become increasingly subject to central government direction* – for example, changes in local government financial management, requirements to put out services to competitive tendering, and the fragmentation of local control over education.

2 *There has been a growth in unelected quangos.* By 1996, there will be 7700 unelected quangos with 40 000 appointees. This growth has resulted from the theory that 'management' tasks can and should be organized outside the political arena and be run on 'business' principles. For example, Michael Howard, as Home Secretary, stated in 1995 that while he was responsible for policy matters in respect of the Prison Service, the head of that service was concerned with operational matters. It is, of course, arguable whether such a fine theoretical distinction can exist in practice.

The legislature or parliament discusses, scrutinizes and amends legislative proposals. Such measures are normally approved by a simple majority vote. In Britain, it has been usual in most of the post-war period for one political party, either the Conservatives or Labour, to form a majority government. Other western democracies have been characterized by coalition governments for most of their recent histories, e.g. Ireland and Germany.

The judiciary is responsible for interpreting law and adjudication on cases. Judges may have to decide whether particular laws are themselves lawful as well as whether they have been breached in specific circumstances.

The separation of powers in Britain

While the concept of 'separation of powers' is useful as a theoretical tool to analyse political systems, in practice the constitutions of most western democracies allow for overlap between these four functions. This can be considered by looking at the operation of certain parts of the British political system: the sovereign, the government, the official opposition, the House of Commons and the House of Lords.

The sovereign

Since the constitutional settlement of 1688, the powers of the monarch as head of state have been limited. Although the Queen keeps in touch with political developments, not least through weekly meetings with the Prime Minister, her only remaining substantial constitutional role is the formal granting of a dissolution of Parliament prior to a general election at the request of the Prime Minister. Technically, she gives the Royal Assent to any legislation passed by Parliament. However, the role of the monarch today is largely ceremonial and confined to providing a unifying figurehead for the different nations and cultures that comprise the United Kingdom.

The government

Most post-war British governments have been drawn from the party with a majority of seats in the House of Commons. If no party has a majority, then a coalition government can be formed. Alternatively, the largest party might govern as a minority government – making *ad hoc* deals with other parties to ensure that government business and legislation is approved – for example, the Wilson government in 1974 and the Callaghan government between 1977 and 1978.

A government comprises about 100 individuals. Most are drawn from the House of Commons. However, some are members of the House of Lords. These Secretaries of State, ministers and parliamentary secretaries are responsible for developing policy and tactics. The most senior members are the 20 or so members of the Cabinet, who include the Prime Minister, the Chancellor of the Exchequer, the Foreign Secretary and the Home Secretary. These senior ministers collectively discuss and agree policy – frequently in various Cabinet committees of a few members – before it is proposed to Parliament.

The Prime Minister appoints members of the Cabinet and presides over it. To this extent he or she exercises considerable control and patronage and can influence the political perspective of the government. He or she is the main public presenter of government policy and gives a government its identity. Prime ministers usually take a special interest in economic, foreign and defence policy issues. Although the Cabinet is expected to operate on the basis of collective responsibility – by publicly accepting agreed courses of action – disagreements, sometimes quite strong ones, can exist between ministers from different wings of the governing political party.

In Britain, therefore, the separation of the executive and the legislature is blurred. Members of government are clearly part of the legislature and responsible for the organization and control of its business. Individual MPs have little freedom of action. They are 'whipped' to support their political party. They are only likely to succeed in promoting a Private Member's Bill – e.g. in the early campaigns for disability discrimination legislation – if the government is supportive.

The official opposition

The official opposition comprises MPs from the second largest party in the House of Commons. The main roles of the opposition are to challenge the government, to make it explain its policies, to check that it undertakes the task of government properly and, of course, to defeat it in Parliament or at a general election. The Leader of the Opposition presides over a 'Shadow Cabinet' of MPs, each of whom is charged with following the work and department of a government Cabinet minister.

The House of Commons

There are 659 Members of Parliament representing different geographical constituencies. The House of Commons performs five major functions:

- *Law making.* Most of the proposed legislation is submitted by the government of the day (*see* below).
- *Controlling finance.* Before the government can raise or spend money, it must have the permission of the Commons. Each year, usually in November, the Chancellor of the Exchequer presents a Budget Statement and Public Expenditure Estimates which cover both taxes and spending together.
- *Scrutinizing public administration.* This takes two forms. First, the government is required to explain its actions to the Public Accounts Committee and to Select Committees. Second, questions are asked of specific ministers and debates are organized, particularly by the opposition, on issues of concern.
- *Examining European Union proposals.* The Select Committee on European Legislation examines proposed European laws before they are passed into UK law.
- *Protecting the individual.* Petitions to the House of Commons from members of the public, together with the lobbying of pressure groups and opinions as monitored in the media, help ensure that Parliament is informed of the electorate's concerns. Furthermore, MPs may take up issues on behalf of individual constituents with the relevant minister.

The House of Lords

There are approximately 800 hereditary and life peers in the House of Lords. Only a small number of 'working peers' are usually involved in the day-to-day business. This chamber has limited legislative powers – and no power in relation to financial measures. It can vote against entire Bills and specific clauses. This is only a delaying power, however, because the House of Commons can subsequently return measures to the Lords and require them to be approved. Effectively then, the executive branch of government has considerable indirect control over this House.

The second important function of the Lords is to act in its judicial capacity as the supreme court – except in relation to European Union law where appeal is possible to the European Court of Justice. Law lords, who can sit as legislators in the House of Lords, can also adjudicate on appeals from lower courts.

Political parties

Different views about social policy, economic management and the nature of the political and legal systems are characteristic of liberal democracies. These divisions of opinion are reflected in the policies of political parties. The successful implementation of particular policies can depend on either the extent to which particular views are dominant within the governing party – e.g. the Thatcherite free market ideology of the 1980s – or, alternatively, reflect strongly articulated public opinion – e.g. in respect of disability discrimination.

Political parties, both within Parliament and at constituency level, are organized expressions of specific political opinions. It is a mistake, however, to see such parties as homogeneous. They, themselves, are coalitions of different interests. It is better, therefore, to think of these bodies as broad-based organizations encompassing a range of different values and attitudes rather than narrowly focused monolithic structures. To illustrate this point, we will look at the two political parties which have formed post-war governments in the UK.

The Conservative Party

According to Dunleavy (1993), current members of the Conservative Party can be divided into four groups reflecting two interlocking dimensions of conservative thought: 'wet' versus 'dry', and one 'nation' versus individualist' (*see* Fig 8.2).

Wets, on the first axis, believe that some degree of state intervention is desirable to reduce the social inequities that result from the market system.

Fig 8.2 Political perspectives within the Conservative Party

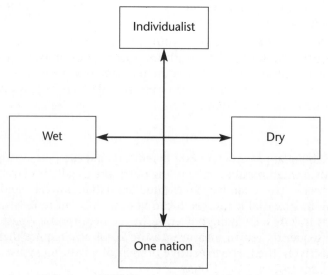

Source: P Dunleavy (1993) *Developments in British Politics* (4th edn). Reproduced by permission of Macmillan Press Ltd.

This intervention may be in the form of social security benefits, financial assistance to industry to ensure job protection and creation, and protective employment laws, to promote minimum standards of fair treatment. Their view is that if government fails to redress the imbalance against the economically disadvantaged, then, social conflicts and tensions may develop. For example, many adherents to this view see unions playing a legitimate and constructive role helping to solve workplace discontent.

The *dry* wing of the Conservative Party, by contrast, sees it as natural and desirable that wide differences in wealth, income and social status that arise in a market economy are not 'distorted' by government action. They believe that these differences provide motivation for people to work hard and to better themselves. They view intervention by government as rarely working. For example, subsidies to declining industries merely delay the final day of reckoning; and social benefits for the unemployed provide an incentive for people to stay at home and avoid work. Employment protection legislation is seen as a distortion of the free labour market.

The second axis reflects the difference between one nation conservatism and *individualism*. *One nation conservatism* reflects those values and attitudes of the aristocracy and upper middle class who dominated the party until the 1950s. They believed in promoting social cohesion across social classes and encouraging the gradual evolution of British democracy. Loyalty to the sovereign and to the Empire, particularly in the first half of the twentieth century, adherence to the Christian religion and commitment to a natural hierarchical social order were used to reinforce such cohesion. This group down-played social divisions of wealth and status and inequalities of opportunities. They responded slowly to social change.

At the other end of this dimension are those who set the individual at the centre of policy-making (*individualism*). The proponents of this view see collective social representation as of marginal importance.

The interlocking of these dimensions produces a four-way ideological split within Conservative Party attitudes and values.

- *The traditional right.* The pre-Thatcherite, aristocratic wing of the party, this group places the defence of hierarchy, deference to social superiors and tradition at the core of its opinions. It is committed to national sovereignty, national defence and strong government.

- *Tory paternalists.* They accept the need for a welfare state and are pragmatic in their economic thinking (i.e. they will adjust policies to respond to changing circumstances).

- *Tory technocrats.* They believe that the welfare state is inevitable and the job of government is to run the public sector efficiently. They are interventionist in economic, industrial and social policies. They see Britain's future as intimately linked with the European Union and, generally, share the values propounded by the European Union.

- *Thatcherites.* Their chief commitment is to free market economics and cutting back the role of government to an absolute minimum. They promote deregulation, privatization, curtailing the powers of trade unions and professional associations, and reorganizing the public sector to achieve greater cost-effectiveness. This group has been most active in combating further integration within the European Union.

These groups are, of course, not of equal size or significance within the policy-making organs of the party. The influence of each group can shift over time as party membership changes, as particular individuals are selected to be prospective Members of Parliament, and as particular individuals are chosen to be either Cabinet members or 'Shadow Cabinet' members. Of even greater importance is the person elected to be party leader, as he or she can strongly promote particular values and views.

The Labour Party

According to Dunleavy (1993), current members of the Labour Party can be divided into four groups reflecting two interlocking dimensions in thought (*see* Fig 8.3): a continuum from support for public ownership – '*the left*' – to support for a mixed economy – 'the right' – and the existence of two wings – an 'industrial' wing and a 'social welfare' wing.

The horizontal axis in Fig 8.3 concerns different attitudes to economic ownership. '*The left*' has traditionally supported fairly widespread nationalization of larger private sector companies and also state intervention in the running of private companies. This was seen as essential for ensuring that business organizations take account of both the national economic interest and also the social cost of their decisions.

'*The right*', by contrast, has traditionally believed in the importance of a mixed economy. It favours nationalization only for certain key industries which have a strategic significance for the national economy, e.g. water supply, the railways, electricity supply and distribution, etc.

Fig 8.3 Political perspectives within the Labour Party

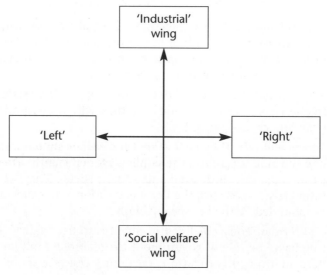

Source: P Dunleavy (1993) *Developments in British Politics* (4th edn). Reproduced by permission of Macmillan Press Ltd.

This traditional division within the Labour Party is now less clear-cut. The commitment to nationalization is limited. The emphasis within the party has shifted from the issue of ownership to that of regulation. A strict regime of regulation is favoured to control the operation of those private sector companies which occupy monopoly or quasi-monopoly positions within an industry.

The second division within the Labour Party is between the industrial wing and the social welfare wing. The *industrial* wing created the Labour Party in 1900 as a means of representing the interests of trade unions and working people, particularly manual working men, in Parliament. It reflected, principally, the interests of those in large-scale manufacturing, such as engineering, and extraction industries (coal-mining) – some of which, were taken into public ownership after the 1945 Labour election victory.

The *social welfare* wing comprises mostly the white collar salariat who, in the post-war period, worked in what was a growing public sector, i.e. in health care, education, local government, and administration in public sector corporations.

The interlocking of these dimensions produces a four-way ideological split of attitudes and values.

- *The trade union right.* This does not support the wide extension of public ownership. It defends free collective bargaining as a central form of regulation for terms and conditions of employment. It is also, generally, sceptical about government intervention.

- *The trade union left.* This advocates wide extension of nationalization and a number of democratic reforms of the Labour Party itself. For example, this group was successful in removing the sole right of Labour MPs to elect the party leader and to broaden the constituency to party members. This group of trade unionists has now diminished in numbers since the 1980s.

- *The welfare state left.* This wants to reposition the party away from its old industrial and trade union ties towards the wider representation of the disadvantaged within society – the unemployed, ethnic minorities and women. It advocates greater public expenditure on health, education, housing, public transport and less defence expenditure.

- *Fabianism.* The Fabian Society reflects the views and creative thinking of intellectual supporters of the party. They are moderate in approach. They rejected internal constitutional reform as a distraction and prefer to focus on pragmatic economic policies designed to alleviate poverty and promote growth. However, it has been commented that 'the traditional Fabian conception of society was one in which people were profoundly dependent on government. Problems were to be solved by experts, and there were few mechanisms for ordinary people to participate in decisions affecting their own lives' (Commission on Social Justice, 1994).

However, this four-way split cannot adequately explain the intricacies of Labour Party internal politics over the past two decades. During the 1970s and 1980s, the party experienced the influence of groups that owed allegiance to *far left* organizations – particularly the Militant Tendency and the Socialist Workers Party (both of which were Trotskyist organizations) and the former Communist Party. They infiltrated the Labour Party and sought to influence its policies. They were significant in the recession-hit inner cities of, for example, Liverpool and Manchester. By the end of the 1980s, their power and numbers declined as they were expelled from the party or marginalized by internal party reforms initiated by Neil Kinnock.

The election, in 1994, of Tony Blair as Leader of the Labour Party has resulted in the acceleration of various 'modernizing' trends that had been initiated or developed under Neil Kinnock and John Smith. It is arguable that the policy consequences of these changes are disrupting the model set out in Fig 8.3. The four key areas of development identifiable at this stage are: internal Party democracy; the Party's statement of values; the attitude to the European Union; and policies on economic ownership.

1 *Internal democratic reforms* within the Labour Party are increasingly providing a considerable range of opportunities for membership (as opposed to activist) participation, e.g. in direct elections for the Leader of the Party, in the selection of Parliamentary candidates, in elections to the National Executive Committee. The voting strength of affiliated trade unions within the Party Conference is diminishing and that of constituency parties growing.

2 In 1995, after a wide debate among members, the Labour Party rescinded the commitment to take wide sections of the economy into public ownership. It approved *an updated statement of values*. This recognizes, among other provisions, both individual and collective interests, the continued existence of the mixed economy, and the need to develop policies promoting social justice.

3 The Party supports *continuing membership of the European Union*. It is committed to adopting the Social Chapter. It has expressed concerns, nevertheless, about various aspects of EU policy – e.g. value for money in the use of EU funds and the need to make EU institutions more democratic.

4 *The issue of economic ownership* is no longer a central concern of the Labour Party. It accepts the mixed economy and pursues policies to promote more efficient economic management and wealth creation, e.g. encouragement of private investment and the development of training schemes. Nationalization is seen as of specific value only where social need is a primary consideration – e.g. the railways and water supply. This approach to economic policy is reflected in the following, rather simplified pen-portrait set out by the Commission on Social Justice describing the 'Investors' approach' to economic management:

> The Investors believe we can combine the ethics of community with the dynamics of a market economy. At the heart of the Investors' strategy is a belief that the extension of economic opportunity is not only the source of economic prosperity but also the basis of social justice. The competitive requirement for constant innovation and higher quality demands opportunities for every individual – and not just an élite – to contribute to national economic renewal; this in turn demands strong social institutions, strong families and strong communities, which enable people and companies to grow, adapt and succeed.

The role of pressure groups

In Fig 8.1 the nature of participation within political systems was outlined: individual and collective. In Britain, there are two principal forms of individual participation – voting in general elections and activity as a member of a political party.

In the post-war period, both these forms of participation have been gradually seen as less significant forms of influence on political decision making, both in central and local government. For example, the turnout in general elections has dropped since 1950 by about 10 per cent. There are estimated to be 1 million eligible voters who do not register. In terms of political party membership, these stand at approximately 750 000 (Conservative), 330 000 (Labour) and 100 000 (Liberal Democratic Party). (Marr, 1995:40–42.)

By contrast, activity in pressure groups and political campaigns is buoyant. There are numerous pressure, or interest, groups, many of which are widely acknowledged as a legitimate and valuable part of democratic society. These can be differentiated in the following ways: in terms of whether their organizational structure is 'formal' or 'informal'; and whether their primary activity is 'lobbying' or 'political campaigning' (*see* Fig 8.4).

Groups that are *formal* tend strongly towards the *lobbying* end of the spectrum. They include broad-based interest groups like employers' organizations, (such as the Confederation of British Industry and the Institute of Personnel and Development), trade union organizations (such as UNISON and the Trade Union Congress – an association of some 60 individual trade unions) and professional bodies (such as the British Medical Association).

It is, of course, possible that from time to time such groups might additionally engage in political campaigning. This might be through published survey reports, publicity and/or public demonstrations. In the early 1980s, for example, when the trade union movement was generally excluded from any discussions

Fig 8.4 Pressure groups

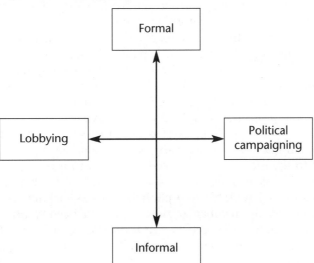

with the Thatcher government, it used marches and demonstrations against unemployment and privatization as vehicles to influence public attitudes.

Formal organizations can develop a strong institutional link with government. Between elections, they manage the flow of influence between society and the government of the day. They articulate policy demands and opinions. Some pressure groups (particularly those which are professional associations, like the British Medical Association) are reservoirs of considerable expertise that can make constructive contributions to the legislative and policy-making process. As a consequence, in their activities, they give much attention to senior civil servants and departmental ministers. Furthermore, there are quangos, such as the Equal Opportunities Commission and the Commission for Racial Equality, which have a statutory duty to put proposals for legislative reform to the appropriate Secretary of State.

There are also some formal organizations which are more specifically focused upon *political campaigning*. One such group is the *think tanks* which review economic, social and judicial policies and make recommendations. Normally, their aim is to influence the policies of either government or the opposition. During the 1980s, for example, the Adam Smith Institute and the Institute for Economic Affairs were particularly influential in promoting free market ideas and deregulation policies with the Thatcher governments. On the left of the political spectrum are organizations like the Fabian Society and Demos, which promote the welfare state and a social justice model of political policy.

There have been occasions, in recent years, when *ad hoc* organizations have been established to campaign against a specific issue. For example, protesters against various motorway extensions and bypasses (Twyford Down, the M11 extension, the Newbury bypass), using modern telecommunications, have developed sophisticated forms of physical obstruction to these works. Their objectives are twofold: to prevent the specific new roadworks and to raise public consciousness about the nature of transport policy. Such 'organizations' do not have the permanence of formal organizations, with premises and staff. However, in their activities, using the experience of previous campaigns, they are far from informal.

Furthermore, there are circumstances where existing formal groups create coalitions to push for particular policy changes – for example, in lobbying for disability discrimination legislation or improvements in overseas aid. Some groups involved see political lobbying as an ancilliary activity. For example, they may be a charity primarily, raising funds and promoting particular services and projects, e.g. Age Concern or Oxfam.

Finally, pressure can be exerted upon the political process in a generally informal, unorganized way – arising from various sources, i.e. letters to politicians and to the media, MPs' conversations with party activists and constituents, public opinion polls, newspaper editorials, etc. This amorphous concerted protest can arise from well publicized and shocking criminal activities – for example where members of the public have been victims of knife attacks and the government is expected to implement new, tougher policy measures.

Pressure groups operate principally at the following access points in the political system:

- within the media to generate public support for a particular policy, as campaigning groups did to achieve disability discrimination legislation;
- within political parties to mould policy objectives;
- lobbying government departments in favour of particular economic or social policy or legislation – for example, employers' organizations trying to influence government tax and interest rate policies which affect economic activity and employment levels;
- responding to consultation opportunities provided by government through Green and White Papers (the case study towards the end of this chapter illustrates the opportunities available);
- pressing for specific legislative provisions and amendments as a Bill proceeds through Parliament;
- monitoring the implementation of legislation and administrative action and seeking consequential amendments as in the work of environmental groups such as Greenpeace and Friends of the Earth.

Exercise 8.3 Using pressure groups

Has your employer ever lobbied government – directly or through an employers' organization – about any particular issue? If so, what was it? How did the organization go about putting over its point of view?

If you were a member of a pressure group, e.g. a consumer group, a political campaigning group or a trade union, how would you go about representing specific interests?

REFORMING THE POLITICAL SYSTEM

The prolonged period of Conservative government in the 1980s and 1990s provoked a number of questions about the character and operation of the British political system and about whether reform was necessary. These concerned, principally, the following issues:

- *The extent to which British parliamentary democracy was truly representative of the views of the electorate.* For example, no post-war British government has achieved over 50 per cent of the popular vote in elections. This issue was brought to a head when the Thatcher/Major Conservative governments only achieved about 43 per cent of this vote and, on occasion, introduced some controversial measures which were often opposed by a majority of the electorate. The Commission on Social Justice (1994) referred to 'the confusion of democracy with majority rule'. Inevitably, it resulted in debates about forms of proportional representation.
- *Whether there should be some move towards a written constitution and the development of both a Bill of Rights and a Freedom of Information Act.* These would be designed to safeguard the basic freedoms of liberal democracy (as outlined earlier) for individuals and for minority interest groups.

- *Whether there should be a reconstitution of the House of Lords as the second chamber in Parliament to make it more representative of different interests within society.*
- *Whether the United Kingdom should move from being an increasingly centralized unitary state.* The directions for reform could be either the creation of a federal state or, alternatively, the creation of much greater decentralization of decision-making for Scotland, Wales, Northern Ireland and the English regions. A key issue in this debate is the appropriate level of decision making.

In some matters, such as transport policy, there are calls for decentralization to local government at regional and city level; by contrast, in the case of environment or macroeconomic policy, a European level of debate is essential. This is the 'double-shift' faced by all advanced industrial societies. (Commission on Social Justice, 1994)

A broad coalition of interest groups and political parties is debating these issues. Principally, those involved include the Labour Party, the Liberal Democratic Party and pressure groups like Charter 88.

These debates have also been overlaid by a further constitutional concern arising, particularly, within the Conservative Party. This derives from Britain's membership of the European Union and, in shorthand terms, is about *sovereignty*.

The European Communities Act 1972, passed by the British Parliament, approved the country's membership of the (then) European Economic Community from 1 January 1973. This resulted in Britain becoming subject to European law and Treaty obligations in a number of areas of economic and social activity. Consequently, by submission to both European Union law – which Britain can influence in discussions – and the jurisdiction of the European Court of Justice, British governments and Parliament have foregone some freedom to legislate – that is, some sovereignty.

Furthermore, this debate now concerns the extent to which there might be further erosions of sovereignty particularly in economic, monetary and taxation policy decisions (*see* below).

Exercise 8.4   Is political reform necessary?

1 What are your views about the issues that have been proposed for reform?

2 Alternatively, in class, you might like to debate the following motion:

'The unwritten British constitution has demonstrated in recent years that strong, representative government can be provided that protects the rights and interests of the electorate.'

BRITAIN'S MEMBERSHIP OF THE EUROPEAN UNION

The European Union (known, variously, in its history, as the European Community, the European Economic Community and, colloquially, the Common Market) was given this title in 1993. It was originally created by

France, Germany, Italy, Belgium, the Netherlands and Luxembourg on 1 January 1958 under the Treaty of Rome 1957. It now comprises 15 member states covering a population of almost 350 million people and a labour force of 140 million.

The European Economic Agreement, which came into force on 1 January 1994, now extends the *single market* to certain non-EU states – namely Norway, Iceland and Liechtenstein. They are covered by a majority of EU law including social legislation.

This section will explore various perceptions about the nature of the European Union, the philosophy underpinning social legislation, the principal institutions of the European Union and the processes for implementing European Union law.

Perceptions of the European Union

The concept of European 'union', developed under the Treaty of Rome, is founded on the principles of liberal democracy – the provision of basic rights and plurality of opinion (*see* the discussion relating to Fig 8.1). New members are expected to conform to these principles. This determines the fundamental character of the present-day European Union. In terms of specific economic and social purposes, there are three broad 'schools of thought'. These perspectives are: the *single market* view, the *federalist* view, and the *integration* view.

The single market view

This view encompasses those who see the EU principally in economic terms – that is, as a single market of goods, services, labour and capital. The regulatory framework of law should be limited to that necessary to make this economic entity function effectively. Some members of the 'Euro-sceptic' right within the British Conservative Party generally accept this view.

The federalist view

The *federalist* view supports a European Union in which there are active and creative European political institutions and, counterbalancing these, independent nation states who constitute the membership of the Union. This perspective sees economic and social regulation throughout the Union as indissolubly linked. The issue which is often in contention, however, is the location of both decision-making and legislative authority.

In recent years, debate on this issue has revolved around the issue of *subsidiarity*. This concept relates to the question of which is the most appropriate level for legal regulation and decision making within the Union – that is, should these functions operate at the level of the member state or at the European Union-wide level.

For example, individual employment rights and laws on competition and the free movement of labour have tended to be adopted at Union level and, ultimately, enforced through the European Court of Justice. By contrast, economic decisions on taxation and public expenditure are generally the responsibility of individual governments in member states. Furthermore, collective rights – for example, relating to trade union status and membership, collective bargaining and the conduct of industrial action – have generally been determined at the level of each member state. This position is gradually changing, however, as the Union develops measures on the 'collective' issue of consultation.

Political debate in Britain in the 1980s and 1990s has been strongly affected by tensions between 'federal' decision making and subsidiarity.

The integration view

This sees a long-term shift in sovereignty from the governments and parliaments of member states to European institutions. The Maastricht Treaty 1992 was formulated to provide impetus in this direction. For example, it created forums for co-operation on police, crime, immigration and defence matters. It established European citizenship.

Of particular fundamental significance, the Treaty enacted the Economic and Monetary Union (EMU) which is to be achieved by 1999. It refers to 'the irrevocable fixing of exchange rates leading to the introduction of a single currency, the ECU [named the Euro in 1995], and ... a single monetary policy and exchange-rate policy' (Article 3a). A main consequence of this will be the alignment of the economies of member states and the transfer of economic decision-making power from the member states to central European institutions.

Member states proposing to join the EMU have to achieve four economic policy objectives. These 'convergence criteria' are designed to ensure that all EMU members are performing similarly. For each member, they are as follows:

- *Inflation*. Its rate should be within 1.5 per cent of the three best performing countries.
- *Budget deficit*. This should not exceed 3 per cent of Gross Domestic Product.
- *Debt*. This should not exceed 60 per cent of Gross Domestic Product.
- *Interest rates (long-term)*. These should be within 2 per cent of the average of the three countries with the lowest inflation.

The achievement by a member state of these economic objectives will also have social and political consequences. In France, in 1995, attempts to reduce the budget deficit by cutting public expenditure resulted in large demonstrations and prolonged strikes in opposition to the government.

The philosophy underpinning social legislation

The social policy of the European Union has developed since 1957. It comprises two broad sets of measures: general policies to influence the labour market and employment protection for individual employees.

The emphasis given to these social policies has varied over different periods. For example, the framework of employment protection expanded considerably under two substantial Social Action Programmes (1972–80 and 1987 to date). Since 1994, there has been some shift in focus towards specific labour market policies designed to assist job creation – that is, investment in education and training and the promoting of labour market flexibility.

The philosophy of European social policy comprises a number of important strands.

- *Improvements in working conditions and standards of living.* The promotion of these by member states is a commitment in the founding Treaty of Rome.

- *Harmonization.* This is an established Treaty goal associated with the aim of economic convergence.

- *Equal treatment for men and women.* This is a fundamental principle of the Treaty which has been elaborated in a 1976 Directive. It has radically influenced equal opportunities for women – particularly as a result of interpretations and rulings by the European Court of Justice.

- *Specific protections for individual workers.* Examples of these are maternity rights, display screen equipment regulations, working time restrictions and protections during collective redundancies and transfers of undertakings.

- *Social partnership.* Both employers' organizations and trade unions are defined as 'social partners' and are consulted widely in the formulation of, for example, new Directives (*see* ECOSOC below).

- *Employee participation.* Social partnership is elaborated further in employee participation measures. At present, the most notable is the European Works Council Directive 1994. This involves requirements on information disclosure and consultation in prescribed multinational companies. Consultation with employee representatives is also required in collective redundancies and transfers of undertakings.

The Social Chapter

Exhibit 8.1 on pp 200–1 gives the background to the Social Dimension and a summary of the Social Chapter.

The arguments in favour of the Social Chapter of the Maastricht Treaty include:

- Employee protection, job security and health and safety;
- Help for employees in coping with technological change and relocation to new jobs;
- Common standards across the EU;
- Decent standards of terms and conditions of employment ensured;
- Disclosure of information and consultation with employees;
- Better informed employees and more understanding of business issues;
- Promotion of more harmonious employment relations.

The arguments against the Social Chapter include:

- Cost of employment protection;
- Unemployment and job creation minimized;
- Enterprise discouraged;
- International competitiveness jeopardized;

Exhibit 8.1

The Social Dimension and the Social Chapter

From its inception in 1957, the European Commission of the EEC, and more latterly the EU, has sought to encourage greater alignment and harmonization of the regulations governing social and employment matters in member states (the Social Dimension). However, it was not until the early 1970s that significant progress was made in this field. The Community's first Social Action Programme in 1974 heralded the implementation of a number of directives which added to the employment rights of female employees, bolstered health and safety provisions, and strengthened the position of all workers affected by major organizational change.

In the early 1980s, the pace of the EEC's social reforms slowed markedly in the face of persistent opposition from the UK's Conservative Government. Although directives dealing with health and safety issues and the equal treatment of men and women were adopted, UK employment ministers consistently vetoed draft directives covering workers' rights to information, consultation and participation; part-time work; temporary work; parental leave and leave for family reasons.

In 1987, in response to the lack of progress in the field of employment rights, plans were drawn up for the Community Charter of the Fundamental Social Rights of Workers, otherwise known as the Social Charter. The Charter was designed to ensure the creation of a Single European Market in 1992 was accompanied by the establishment of a floor of basic employment rights.

Among the measures contained within the Social Charter were proposals to ensure:

1 the right of free movement within the EU becomes a reality;

2 workers are paid a sufficient wage to enjoy a decent standard of living;

3 adequate social security protection is provided in all member states;

4 basic law on working time, the provision of employment contracts, treatment of part-time and temporary workers and collective redundancies is improved and harmonized;

5 all workers have a right to join or not to join a union, negotiate collective agreements and take collective action, including strike action;

6 all workers have access to continuous vocational training throughout their working lives;

7 equal treatment and equal opportunities between men and women are developed to enable men and women to reconcile family and work responsibilities;

8 information and consultation rights are developed along appropriate lines taking into account national practices, and particularly in European enterprises;

9 health and safety protection is improved;

10 young workers are given fair treatment and access to training;

11 the elderly are guaranteed a sufficient income; and

12 measures are taken to improve the social and professional integration of people with disabilities.

Although the Charter was merely expected to be a statement of intent, and was not intended to be legally binding, the UK was the only member state which declined to sign the final document.

The broad aims of the Social Charter were taken up in the second Social Action Plan in 1989. This document proposed more than 20 new directives and a similar number of non-binding initiatives. However, the Social Action Programme did not cover all of the areas listed in the Charter. For example, there were no proposals for legislation guaranteeing the right to union membership and collective action.

The Second Social Action Plan, like the Social Charter, was opposed by the UK government. While Conservative ministers were prepared to agree some additional health and safety regulations, they were not prepared to implement new employment rights. To overcome this opposition, the Maastricht Treaty in 1992 included a Social Chapter which provided for qualified majority voting in many of the areas initially covered by the Social Charter. The main areas covered by this new treaty are as follows:

- Health and safety
- Equal treatment and opportunity
- Social security
- Representation and collective defence (excluding trade union rights)

- Working conditions
- Persons excluded from the labour market
- Employment protection and termination
- Conditions of third country nationals

- Information and consultation rights for employees

- Measures to promote greater social dialogue between the social partners (e.g. trade unions and employers' associations)

- Financial contributions by the governments of member states to promote employment

Because of the UK's opposition to these proposals, the final Social Chapter of the Maastricht Treaty specifically excluded the UK from its remit.

- Cost of consultation and information disclosure;
- Interference with management's freedom to make decisions;
- Restriction on freedom of countries to set own laws recognizing their diversity.

Social policy is affected by four, often interlocking, contextual factors: the views of member states about the balance between supra-national and national interests; different social and political philosophies between governments of member states and within the European Union; different traditions of legal regulation; and the differences of interests between employers and trade unions.

- *Supra-national and national interests*. A fundamental tension exists within this supra-national organization about the extent to which national interests are acknowledged and accommodated and the extent to which they are subsumed under a 'European' approach.

- *Social and political philosophies*. European social policy aims to achieve harmonized employment protection. The political philosophy underpinning this approach – deriving from Social Democrat, Socialist and Christian Democrat traditions – is markedly at variance with the free market ideology adopted by Conservative governments in Britain. Consequently, in the debates on social protection in the 1980s and early 1990s, several issues were dominant: the extent to which employment protection measures were both a burden on business, and were costly and impeded competiveness; and the appropriateness of European-wide regulation as against subsidiarity.

- *Traditions of legal regulation*. Employment protection measures within the European Union are being implemented across 15 member states which have different traditions of legal regulation. This can be an additional source of tension. The original six member states were more accustomed to a prescriptive and interventionist legal approach to employment relations.

Britain, on the other hand, has a more voluntarist tradition based on either the exercise of the management prerogative or, if an employer agrees, free collective bargaining.

- *The interests of employers and trade unions*. Throughout employment relations within the European Union, there is also evidence of the usual differences of interest between employers and trade unions. These differences of interest usually focus around three sets of issues:

  1 *Economic considerations* – for example, the extent to which EU policy facilitates or impedes job creation, the extent to which unit labour costs are perceived to rise as a result of employment protection laws and are seen to reduce business efficiency.

  2 *Balance of power considerations* – for example, the extent to which EU employment protection constrains the right to manage, the extent to which employee interests are accommodated, through employee participation, in corporate decision making.

  3 *Predominant values* – for example, the extent to which equal treatment, job security etc. are promoted within an organization's employee relations.

The principal institutions of the European Union

Five principal institutions within the European Union will be considered: the Commission, the Council of Ministers, the European Parliament, the European Court of Justice, and the Economic and Social Committee.

The governments of member states operate directly and regularly through the Council of Ministers and can, consequently, have considerable influence over policy-making. Additionally, they are responsible for nominating people to join such bodies as the Commission and the European Court of Justice. Their influence in the nomination process can shift the political emphasis either towards greater federalism or towards a greater recognition of subsidiarity. By contrast, the only direct influence exerted by citizens of the European Union is through elections to the European Parliament.

Governments of member states, of course, can have differing views about the relative powers of these institutions, e.g. should more power be granted to the European Parliament? Should the jurisdiction of the European Court of Justice be curtailed?

- *The Commission*. This is the executive body of the Union. Its principal functions are to propose measures for discussion by the Council and to secure the implementation of decisions. It comprises 20 members, representing the 15 member states. Larger member states, like Britain, have two commissioners. Each commissioner is responsible for one or more of the 23 Directorates General, e.g. DG5 is responsible for social and employment policy.

- *The Council of Ministers*. This is the decision-making body of the Union. It 'adopts' measures proposed by the Commission for enactment by member states. The Council comprises several levels. Principal among them are:

  (a) *The European Council*, which comprises heads of government of member states, who hold summit meetings twice a year to discuss major issues and decide broad policy.

    (b) *The Presidency*, which is held by each member state in turn for a period of six months. As President, the member state sets Council agendas and can determine to some extent, therefore, which Commission proposals are progressed and prioritized.

    (c) *The Council of Ministers*, which comprises appropriate government ministers from each member state. The minister varies according to the subject under discussion. For example, an appropriate British employment minister attends meetings to discuss the free movement of labour, health and safety, or employment protection rights.

    (d) *COREPER*, which is the Committee of Permanent Representatives of each member state in Brussels. It acts as a national embassy to the EU and negotiates on the details of Commission proposals in preparation for Council of Ministers' meetings.

- *The European Parliament*. Unlike the parliaments in member states, this is a consultative rather than a legislative body. It advises on proposals from the Commission. It comprises 626 members directly elected within member states every five years. The UK has 87 Members of the European Parliament. The next elections are in 1999.

- *The European Court of Justice*. This is the legislative body of the Union. It rules on the interpretation and application of European law. It comprises 15 judges, nominated by member states for a six-year term. The rulings of the ECJ on appeals lodged with them from cases arising in specific member states are binding on all members of the EU. The Court is assisted by nine Advocates-General. These provide reasoned submissions (an Opinion) in open court and help the ECJ reach a decision by identifying points of law and by referring to relevant precedents.

- *The Economic and Social Committee (ECOSOC)*. This is an advisory body to the Council of Ministers. It is unelected and comprises 222 members – primarily employers, trade unionists and other interested parties, including consumers. It suggests amendments to proposed legislation. It has few formal powers. Three representative industrial and public sector bodies contribute to this committee: UNICE (the Union of Industrial and Employers' Confederations of Europe); CEEP (the European Centre of Enterprises with Public Participation); and ETUC (the European Trade Union Confederation).

Processes for making EU law

All EU policy proposals must be based on an Article in the Treaty of Rome 1957 (as amended). There are two principal procedures in the Treaty of Rome, for the making of European Union employment law (*see* Fig 8.5).

- *The Consultation Procedure* – for proposals on employment rights made under Article 100. Unanimity is required on the Council of the EU to approve such proposals.

- *The Co-operation Procedure* – introduced by the 1986 Single European Act, as an amendment to the Treaty of Rome, to strengthen the European Parliament in law-making. It is used for proposals on health and safety of

Fig 8.5 Consultation and co-operation procedures in EU law

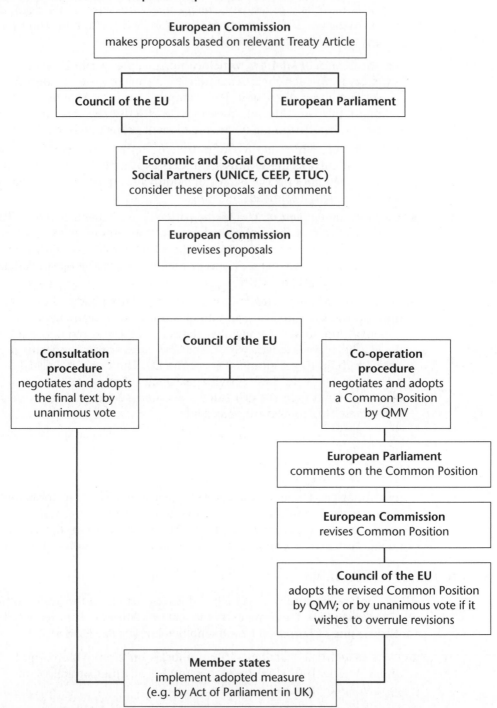

workers made under Article 118a and free movement of workers made under Articles 7 and 49. Such proposals can be adopted by *qualified majority voting* (QMV).

Within these procedures, there are considerable opportunities for the governments of member states to influence proposed legislation. The unanimity procedure provides an effective veto. One member state in the Council of the EU, therefore, may be in a strong position to achieve concessions from others to ensure that a consensus view is achieved. British Conservative governments in the 1980s and 1990s, concerned at the cost of employment protection legislation and the constraints imposed in a free labour market, frequently used this veto threat to achieve some concessions.

The wider public is represented by the European Parliament. As indicated, this is not a legislative body; it is consultative. This means that it is only able to persuade the Commission and the Council. It can generate publicity about particular policies in an effort to influence public and sectional opinion and indirectly pressurize governments.

Sectional interests, like employers, trade unions and consumers, are formally represented on the Economic and Social Committee. This provides a direct opportunity to influence proposals. Indirectly, lobbying of the individual governments will also take place, by these groups, in favour of particular courses of action.

MAKING STATUTE LAW IN PARLIAMENT

The preceding discussions have shown that law-making is affected by political tensions both within and between political parties and also between member states of the European Union. There are, invariably, clashes of values and differences of interests to be taken into account.

This section and the related case study will consolidate the preceding discussion. We will first focus on the processes through which statute law is made in the British Parliament. By means of a case study, we will then show how different political interests and pressure groups can influence the character of specific legislation.

Passing an Act of Parliament

Within Britain, most legislation originates in government departments and progresses through a number of stages, some of which are optional and some obligatory.

Publication of a Green Paper

This is an optional stage. A Green Paper is a consultative document for interested parties, such as employers' organizations, trade unions and pressure groups, to consider. It will set out the case for new legislation and the pros and cons of various courses of action. These Green Papers are prepared by government ministers and civil servants.

Publication of a White Paper

This is a firmer statement of government's legislative proposals. Again, it is an optional stage. Interested parties can still make representations. Sometimes, a government minister may change proposals as a result of reactions to the White Paper by either campaigning or other interest groups.

Publication of a Bill

This is a debating document, produced for Parliament to consider, amend and, if there is a sufficient majority of support, to enact. A Bill may reflect the results of consultation on Green and White Papers. Alternatively, it may be a direct reflection of government policy. Some Bills are introduced to give effect to EU directives. A Bill comprises various clauses and schedules and is drafted by specialist lawyers in the Parliamentary Counsel's Office. These parliamentary draughtsmen must ensure that the law is certain and unambiguous for judges and others who will interpret it and that no loopholes exist within the proposed legislation enabling certain groups to avoid the effect of the law.

A Bill must pass through the following formal stages of Parliamentary procedure.

- *The First Reading.* This is the formal presentation of the Bill to the House of Commons.

- *The Second Reading.* There is usually a full debate on both the principles and outlines of the Bill – rather than on its finer details. This is the most important stage through which a Bill has to pass. If a government has a working majority in the Commons, the result is usually predictable.

- *The Committee Stage.* Most Bills are dealt with by Standing Committees of between 15 and 20 MPs representing proportionately the various political parties in Parliament. At this stage detailed scrutiny of the Bill takes place and amendments may be proposed and voted upon. Some of these may represent the views of outside interests groups. If the government has a large majority in Parliament, it will control the committees and the Bill is likely to emerge with very few changes. Sometimes, government ministers, themselves, will initiate amendments at this stage.

   Occasionally, with particularly important draft legislation – e.g. the Bill which subsequently became the European Communities Act 1972 – the Committee Stage can be taken on the floor of the whole House.

- *The Report Stage.* The amended Bill then returns to the House of Commons for scrutiny. Amendments can be made, or unmade, if the government has been defeated in Committee.

- *The Third Reading.* This is the final stage in the Commons. It usually follows the Report Stage immediately, and is often taken without debate.

- *The House of Lords.* The Bill is then passed to the Lords and progresses through substantially similar procedural stages. The Bill may be altered in the Lords. The Lords may, of course, reject a Bill. Under Parliamentary procedure, however, it may be presented again in the following session and must be passed by the Lords. Effectively, then, this chamber has a delaying power only.

- *Final reconsideration by the House of Commons.* This will involve consideration of whether to accept or reject amendments made in the House of Lords.
- *The Royal Assent.* This is the final stage of enactment. Normally, assent is signified on the sovereign's behalf by specially appointed commissioners. It is a formality – the last monarch to reject a Bill was Queen Anne. The Bill then becomes an Act of Parliament. Depending on the provisions in the legislation, it may be effective immediately or at a later date under a *Commencement Order.*

CASE STUDY

The politics of industrial action ballots

In 1984, the Conservative government, led by Margaret Thatcher, enacted a requirement that individual secret ballots of union members should be held before any industrial action to obtain their approval. The trade union(s) could be sued for damages and served with an injunction (a court order to stop the unlawful action) if they did not obtain this approval.

The political process that produced this legislation highlights some important issues in British Parliamentary democracy.

The standards in a liberal democracy

The International Labour Organisation affirmed the fundamental liberal democratic freedom of association in stating that governments should not interfere in any internal rule-making (Convention 87, to which Britain is a signatory). This balloting requirement, therefore, raised the question, 'To what extent should the state in a liberal democracy interfere in the internal affairs of a voluntary organization like a trade union?'

Responsibility of government for 'the public interest'

The ILO principle can pose certain dilemmas. Although trade unions are self-regulating voluntary organizations, their actions can have a 'public' effect – for example, disruption to services or the supply of goods to consumers and to other employers because of strike action.

Politicians then may ask, 'Have strikers willingly consented to and participated in the action? To what extent are the strike organizers' aims related to "industrial relations" or to "politics"?'

To answer these questions, others are raised:

(a) How far do union internal decision-making processes allow for full democratic participation?

(b) Are union members too heavily influenced by workplace and national leaders?

(c) Do individual union members fully understand the implications of industrial action?

The Thatcher government had these issues in mind. In a Green Paper, it stated that the external harms which unions could cause made it 'essential for their internal affairs to be conducted in a manner which commands public confidence' (para 3). Unions were being told that they must consider the 'public interest' as well as the 'sectional interests' of their members.

Conservative Party ideology

The Conservative Party has had a long-standing preoccupation with the economic consequences of industrial action. This became directly linked with concerns to *depoliticize* the trade union movement and reduce *militancy.*

Party policy on balloting developed during the 1980s. In 1980, James Prior, as Secretary of State for Employment, rejected compulsory strike ballots in favour of policy of cash reimbursement of expenses. He believed that, in practice, it was difficult to achieve a uniform arrangement for all unions. He also preferred unions to develop their own democratic arrangements voluntarily.

Indeed, in the 1970s and early 1980s there had been a general political debate about, on

▶

the one hand, the promotion of self-regulation and voluntary reform through the TUC and, on the other hand, the desirability of legislative action by government.

Public and pressure group attitudes
Generally, however, there was little public confidence in the effectiveness of TUC self-regulation and voluntary reform.

A Green Paper
In January 1983 a Green Paper, *Democracy in Trade Unions*, was published. It stressed the need for basic minimal protections for union members and for the government now to consider action in view of the lack of voluntary reforms.

It weighed up the pros and cons of employer-triggered and member-triggered ballots. The initial preference was for 'non-mandatory', 'member-triggered' ballots. There was 'considerable hesitancy' by the government for the idea of simply linking a ballot requirement to loss of union immunity, i.e. making unions liable to be sued.

Employer responses
Employer organizations like the Engineering Employers' Federation, the Confederation of British Industry, and the Institute of Personnel Management responded. Generally, these organizations did not see strike ballots as a central reform. If compulsory ballots were adopted, however, then these should be triggered by union members. Employers were lukewarm on the issue of improving union democracy. Their greater concern was strikes in essential services. Only the Institute of Directors advocated that loss of immunity should be a sanction for refusing to ballot.

1983 Conservative election manifesto
Despite the general reservations set out above, this manifesto stated that, 'We shall ... curb the legal immunity of unions to call strikes without the prior approval of those concerned through a fair and secret ballot'. This commitment was part of a wider undertaking to reform unions, ensuring that they acted democratically and

responsibly. Simultaneously, it enabled the Conservatives to demonstrate publicly their intention to tackle the economic consequences of union militancy. The views of the IOD seemed to have prevailed.

The new legislation would mark 'a key shift in legislative technique from restriction to regulation' (Auerbach, 1990:153). Whereas, in the previous four years, the government had restricted various industrial action – secondary action, political strikes, action to support workers overseas, inter-union strikes – it was now regulating the way unions behaved in calling and organizing industrial action.

Proposed legislation on union democracy – July 1983
Following the manifesto commitment, ballots were to be a prerequisite for the preservation of immunity for all forms of industrial action.

The Bill
This included the ballot requirement. The government said it was a minimum level of intervention. Immunity was to be subject to certain minimum standards of conduct. The sanction would be action in the courts by employers, seeking an injunction and damages. Consumer actions were also contemplated. Member-triggered ballots were not to be introduced.

The continuing impact of the legislation
The Conservative Party continued to develop the regulation of balloting in subsequent legislation and also introduced a *Code of Practice on Balloting* which became ever more complex.

The Labour Party shifted its attitude in favour of accepting the principle of statutorily required ballots before industrial action. However, it has considered amending certain provisions.

Public opinion, on the whole, was reconciled to statutory ballots as a fair means of determining the views of trade union members.

The International Labour Organisation criticized the complexity and some of the details of this British employment legislation. The principle of balloting was, however, consistent with freedom of association.

SUMMARY AND CONCLUSION

This chapter has considered the British political system as a liberal democracy and a member state of the European Union. It has explored the complex network of different interests that exist in such a society and in political parties. It has considered the ways in which they may or may not be accommodated. It has, also, provided an outline of the context in which employment law is both formulated and enacted, which will be examined further in Chapters 9, 10 and 11. The case study is designed to illustrate some of these tensions and the processes within the political system.

Exercise 8.4 **Review**

Go back to Exercise 8.1 and 8.2 and consider any changes you would make in the light of what you have read in this chapter.

CHAPTER 9

Employment law in context

INTRODUCTION

This chapter opens up a consideration of the importance of employment law. It examines the context in which it is developed. In Chapters 10 and 11 the individual and collective frameworks of employment law will be discussed and their significance for employers explored.

It is important to remember that employment law does not emerge in a vacuum. It is moulded by various economic, political and social factors. These standards and requirements are subject to constant pressures. For example, governments may change and so may promote different values. Under one government, the economic interests of employers may predominate over the social and welfare interests of employees. Under another, more attention may be given to employee protection and fair treatment. Employment law is, therefore, enacted and implemented in a state of flux.

FOCUS AND SCOPE

This chapter provides an understanding of the nature of the employment relationship, the 'politics' of employment law, the regulation of the employment relationship, the institutions for enforcing employment law and the impact of employment law on the managing of people.

LEARNING OBJECTIVES

Once you have read through this chapter and completed the associated exercises, you should be able to:

- describe the main characteristics of the employment relationship;

- understand the political and economic context in which employment law develops;

- be aware of the balance between voluntary regulation and legal regulation of the employment relationship;

- understand the different forms of legal regulation;

- appreciate the impact of European Union law on legal regulation in Britain;

- be able to identify the processes that might be used for dealing with infringements of employment rights.

THE EMPLOYMENT RELATIONSHIP

What is the nature of the employment relationship?

In historical terms, the concept of 'employment' is of relatively recent origin. From the beginning of the eighteenth century, in those societies that were transformed by the Industrial Revolution, it emerged as the dominant way of organizing work. Before the development of a sizeable manufacturing sector, work was carried out by people having different statuses – as self-employed artisans and craftsmen, merchants, peasants subject to feudal relations, slaves, etc. Indeed, even today, the nature of work relations varies between societies. Compared with industrialized market economies, some developing societies are characterized less by employment and more by some of these other statuses.

As the nature of work relations has evolved, so the form of law governing workers has also changed over the past two hundred years. It has come to be based on *contract*. Previously, workers had their relationships

> ... shaped in part by criminal law, operating through a line of statutes which imposed compulsory labour and gave magistrates the power to fix wages and, in part, by civil law regulating the status of different categories of persons. (Napier, 1986)

At the heart of this concept of status was the relationship of 'master and servant' – a relationship of submission. The jurist, Blackstone, writing in 1765, analysed this relationship as similar to the relationships of 'parent and child, guardian and ward, and husband and wife [*sic*!]'.

This submissive master and servant relationship contrasted with the *contractual relationship* which, in theory, was arrived at freely between two equal, independent parties. Progressively, *status* was superseded by *contract* as the basis for regulating the employment relationships. By 1875, the Master and Servant Acts had been repealed.

It is, of course, questionable whether the notion of equality underlying contract is realistic. This will be discussed later (*see* Chapter 10). It is necessary, first, to explore in more detail some views about the nature of the employment relationship.

By the late nineteenth and early twentieth centuries, various social scientists had begun analysing this relationship, identifying various aspects and proposing some theoretical perspectives to explain its character. These theories are concerned with the extent to which employees are motivated by purely economic concerns and the extent to which social values contribute to behaviour in the employment relationship. The analyses also considered such concepts as authority, control, power and conflict.

'Economic man'

In the nineteenth century, neo-classical economists in their model of the labour market put forward the concept of 'the economic man'. The implication of this notion was that:

> ... the employment relationship is a relationship between individual actors which can be understood largely without reference to the network of other social relations in which such actors might be involved; and that such actors will act in a self-interested way as utility maximisers. (Brown, 1988:34)

Under this model, individualism and self-interest were seen as the fundamental ingredients of the employment relationship and any notions that collective interests were of significance were disdained. Employees were seen as factors of production to be controlled. The *scientific management* of *Taylorism* provided the management techniques aimed to achieve this. This was based upon the detailed study of work processes to promote the more effective and efficient use of labour by breaking jobs up into narrow component tasks.

Social factors

Throughout the twentieth century, various social scientists evaluated this 'economic man' model critically. They drew attention to other key elements in the employment relationship. However, there is, as yet, no synthesis of these critiques into a single model.

In broad terms, the essential observations of these studies can be summarized as follows. Working people enter the employment relationship as social beings. They have been socialized through the family, the education system, possibly, religious organizations, community bodies, etc. They have learned social norms of behaviour; they have accepted certain values; and they bring to the employment relationship a range of expectations – some social, some economic.

Elton Mayo's research in the 1930s – *the Hawthorne experiments* – was the first to throw doubt on the economists' 'economic man' model. It was found that because of social norms, people might behave in economically non-rational ways.

Subsequent work by *systems theorist*, Talcott Parsons, argued that the employment relationship is clearly located in a social system. Brown (1988:40) suggests that four features of his discussion of the employment relationship can be regarded as of particular value:

- the emphasis on the employment contract as involving more than just an exchange of wages for labour (i.e. it has a social as well as an economic dimension);
- the recognition that individual employees commonly enter employment as members of households towards which they have important responsibilities;
- the importance of the values which surround and support employment relations;
- the identification of significant differences in the employment relationship for workers making different types of contribution to the organization and/or with different positions in the employment hierarchy.

Further work – deriving from social psychology – has also contributed to this analysis. This work has elaborated on the needs and motivations that employees bring to the employment relationship.

Pre-eminent in this area is the work of Maslow, who asserted that basic human needs were organized in a *hierarchy of needs*:

- physiological;
- security and safety;
- love, affection and belongingness;
- self-respect and self-esteem; and
- self-actualization, developing one's full potential.

He accepted that such a hierarchy was not fixed in all circumstances. In this context, then, the social psychologist, Schein, has proposed the existence of *a psychological contract* between the employee and his/her employer.

Overall, four general points can be made from sociological studies about working people's attitudes to the employment relationship:

- Individuals are already 'socialized' on entering the employment relationship as a result of their experiences in their family, schools, with friends and, possibly, religious and community organizations.
- Social influences on employees' expectations and priorities at work are important.
- Employees' attitudes and actions towards their employer are influenced by their orientation to work – that is, do they come to work for money alone and to what extent do they achieve other personal objectives at work?
- An employee's orientation to work derives from non-work life as well as from his/her experiences in the labour market and in employment itself.

If this social dimension is acknowledged, then a fuller understanding of the employment relationship can only be arrived at if certain other social phenomena are explored. These are authority, control and power relations; conflicts of interest; and individualism and collectivism.

Authority, control and power relations

There are differing views about the significance of power relations within employment. The question at the heart of this debate is whether the employment relationship should be seen as a continuing power relationship wherein the individual employee normally has little power relative to the employer. Some subsidiary questions might assist in coming to a view. For example:

- Who is responsible for formulating the terms and conditions of employment?
- Who is responsible for initiating changes to existing terms and conditions of employment?
- Who is responsible for organizing the deployment of the workforce?
- Who is responsible for determining manpower requirements?
- Who is responsible for terminating the employment relationship?
- What degree of influence do employees, individually and collectively, have in the making of these decisions?

| Exercise 9.1 | **Power relations** |

1 *What answers would you give to these questions in relation to your own organization?*

2 *What overall view do you come to about the balance of power between employees, both individually and collectively, and their employer?*

The view adopted in this text is that the balance of economic and social power is clearly in favour of the employer. The employer also can – and does – exercise considerable authority in this relationship.

In his discussion about the formulation of contracts of employment, Wedderburn (1986) illustrates the fundamental imbalance. He comments that:

> The 'individual' employer is from the outset an aggregate of resources, already a 'collective power' in social terms ... In reality, save in exceptional circumstances, the individual worker brings no equality of bargaining power to the labour market and to this transaction central to his life whereby the employer buys his labour.

Such a power imbalance would probably be of minor importance if the employment relationship could be characterized as entirely consensual and harmonious. Even casual observation of the employment relationship reveals endemic conflicts of interest between the employer and the employee – for example, in pay claims, in redundancies, and in the implementation of health and safety standards.

Conflicts of interest

The issue of whether there is consensus or conflict at the heart of the employment relationship has been widely discussed by sociologists and industrial relations academics. Alan Fox (1974) contributed to the discussion by defining three perspectives:

- *The unitarists*. People adopting this view believe that the interests of employees and of employers are fundamentally the same. Conflict is not seen as inherent. It arises from various distortions such as poor communications or the existence of 'troublemakers'.

- *The pluralists*. People adopting this view believe that, within limits, the interests of employees and employers differ. However, there is likely to be agreement on such fundamental issues as the survival of the business. Conflicts, such as they are – about pay, hours and conditions of employment – can be 'institutionalized', i.e. processed through grievance procedures, through consultation mechanisms, or through negotiations, conciliation or arbitration.

- *The radicals*. People adopting this view believe that the balance of power is fundamentally unequal. Even negotiated settlements will reflect that imbalance of economic power, so they are more likely to be resolved in the employer's interests.

If the existence of conflicts of interest is accepted, it is possible, then, to distinguish between different sources of conflict which occur in the employment relationship. Allan Flanders (1968) suggested that they arise around three sets of issues:

- *Economic issues*. This source concerns the allocation of financial resources between pay and other labour costs, on the one hand, and investment, taxation, interest payments and dividends, etc. on the other hand.

- *Political issues*. This concerns the distribution of power and authority within an organization. Such conflict usually concerns the question, 'Who has decision-making power to determine aspects of terms and conditions of employment?' It involves the extent to which management is prepared to share power or be influenced. For example, should there be negotiation and agreement with unions about pay, manning levels, working practices, etc., or should there be meaningful consultation with employee representatives about conditions of employment?

- *Values*. This relates to those standards that are used for judging management decision making. The most graphic conflict, in this respect, surfaces where a dispute involves, on the one hand, the employees' concern about security of employment and, on the other hand, the employer's pursuit of cost-effectiveness and efficiency.

Individualism and collectivism

The discussion so far has considered some of the context in which legal standards and rights are located. One further dimension and area of debate that needs to be identified concerns *individualism* and *collectivism*. A proper appreciation of the employment relationship, it is argued, recognizes that it has both an individual and a collective dimension.

There has been a tendency in the past 15 years or so to downplay the importance of collective interests and to see individual interests as the primary focus of the employment relationship. This view was driven both politically and as a result of the employment policies of some employers. The anti-union philosophy of Thatcherism stressed individualism as central to its overall policy of *decollectivization*. Simultaneously, at the workplace, the concept of *human resource management*, in its pure form, emphasized individualism and a unitarist approach to employment relations.

However, in their exploration of contemporary human resource management and industrial relations, Storey and Sisson (1993:4) argue that 'the handling of both collective and individual issues (in unison) is likely to be the essential management requirement during the forthcoming period'. Certainly, any realistic assessment of the employment relationship must take into account both dimensions.

Asserting employees' interests

Having explored these characteristics of the employment relationship, we now consider the mechanisms available to employees to exert countervailing influence, power and control in this relationship.

There are two ways in which employees can attempt to rectify the power imbalance and deal with conflicts of interest – one depends on legal action and the other on voluntary action:

- by taking legal action through courts and tribunals against the employer, claiming the infringement of either an individual or collective right, e.g. unfair dismissal or consultation with employee representatives about redundancies;
- by organizing collectively at the workplace, through a trade union or through a non-union committee of employee representatives.

The nature and effectiveness of these will be considered in more detail in Chapters 10 and 11.

The stakeholders in the employment relationship

From the discussion so far, it is possible to see that, arising out of the operation of the employment relationship, there are likely to be various issues of fundamental concern to the different stakeholders in employee relations. Principally, the stakeholders with a direct interest will be employers (and their associations), employees, and trade unions; and, those with an indirect interest will be customers (internal and external), government and the European Union.

The questions that are likely to arise, in varying ways, for these stakeholders are:

- What is the appropriate balance of power between an employer and his employees?
- What countervailing protections in law does an employee need in relation to his/her employer?
- Should there be a right to express collective interests at work?
- Should there be a complementary right to express collective interests in the political system?
- How might collective interests be expressed in the workplace and in the political arena?
- What values and standards should be promoted in the conduct of employee relations?
- What mechanisms need to be adopted to help in the management of employment conflict?

The answers to these questions will inevitably reflect a person's view in relation to a number of issues:

- the extent to which employers and employees, and trade unions, should voluntarily regulate themselves;
- the extent to which public policy should set standards to judge managerial behaviour;
- the extent to which employees should be entitled to job security and protection;
- the extent to which the collective interests of employees should be protected;
- the extent to which trade unions should play a role in employee relations;
- the extent to which employees are permitted to engage in industrial action.

In the next section, the political context of employment law will be discussed. The issues that have just been outlined will be considered against the backdrop of different ideological perspectives.

Exercise 9.2	## Stakeholders

At this point think about the list of questions for stakeholders which appears above and make a brief note of how you would answer these questions.

THE 'POLITICS' OF EMPLOYMENT LAW

The legislators

The legislators in UK employment law are Parliament, European institutions and the judiciary. In understanding employment law, it is essential to recognize that it originates in a political context. There are three aspects to this: statute law, Treaty articles and case law.

Statute law is clearly created in a political process. It can, and frequently does, reflect government policies, which themselves may be influenced by pressure group interests (*see* Chapter 8). These policies may not necessarily reflect a wide consensus of opinion in society and indeed may be partial to one interest group as against another.

In the past 20 years, fundamentally differing political views – for example, about the legitimacy of industrial action, the right to be a trade union member, minimum wages protection and, in some respects, equal opportunities – have resulted in certain pieces of employment law being highly contentious.

The judiciary provides another aspect of the political context of employment law. Judges are appointed after soundings made by the Lord Chancellor – a Cabinet member and a political appointee.

Anthony Scrivener QC, a former Chairman of the Bar, is reported as being critical of this secret appointments system:

> Judges were chosen mainly from barristers who had concentrated on prosecuting cases for the government rather than defending civil liberties ... the secret appointments system was known only to involve taking soundings from the Bar Chairman and the heads of four High Court divisions ... You can only make representations. (Reported in *The Guardian*, 21 September 1991.)

The appointments system, however, has begun to change. For example, it has become open to application, as a result of advertisements. Lord MacKay, as Lord Chancellor, said that the bench in 10 or 20 years' time should look very different in terms of racial and gender composition (reported in the *Financial Times*, 7 November 1990).

However, the concerns about the judiciary are not usually related to direct political control. They are about two sets of related issues: attitudes and values; and the use of certain legal mechanisms which enable particular attitudes and values to become entrenched.

LIBRARY
BISHOP BURTON COLLEGE
BEVERLEY HU17 8QG

Attitudes and values

In a profile of the judiciary, John Griffith (1985:27) drew attention to their educational background, class, gender and age:

> In broad terms, four out of five full-time professional judges are products of public schools and of Oxford or Cambridge ... the age of the full-time judiciary has remained constant over many years [52 on appointment and 60 as the average age for all judges].

Such a profile has provoked critical questions about the extent to which the judiciary is accommodating to changing social attitudes, to the changing role of women in society and to the evolution of a multiracial society. Furthermore, questions are asked about their understanding of intricate social sub-systems like employee relations.

There can be no simple appropriate response. Some judges, irrespective of this profile, show great facility in appreciating social changes. Others show a lack of understanding and, occasionally, marked prejudice.

To help promote an understanding of employee relations within the legal system, one innovation has injected some appropriate workplace experience decisions on certain employment issues. In 1975, the, then newly created, Employment Appeals Tribunal was established with panels of High Court judges and lay members representing experience of both sides of industry. Some commentators have advocated the extension of this model into a system of Labour Courts (McCarthy, 1989).

Precedent and tests

The second area which occasionally raises some concern, in respect of the judiciary, relates to the continuing influence of judicial decisions, unless they are overturned by Parliament. This arises in two principal areas: under the doctrine of *precedent* and, as a result, the creation of *tests*.

Precedent refers to the use by a court of a previous judgement or court decision, normally recorded in approved law reports, which can be used as an authority for reaching a decision in subsequent cases. For example, the decisions of the House of Lords are binding upon the Court of Appeal and all lower courts. Under appropriate employment law, the Employment Appeals Tribunal can bind industrial tribunals, unless a superior court – for example, the House of Lords or the Court of Appeal – has previously ruled on the matter. In these circumstances, the EAT must follow the superior court.

In reaching decisions, judges may also formulate *tests* to help determine particular cases. These continue to influence employee relations under the doctrine of precedent. For example, a test has been developed, over a number of years, to determine whether or not a person is an employee and, consequently, is entitled to make certain claims before an industrial tribunal (*see* the discussion in Chapter 10 on contracts of employment).

This judicial role in creating precedents and formulating tests can be helpful and influential in the longer term implementation of employment law. Such tests may not necessarily ossify. The law-making process is dynamic after all. Tests may be amended in the light of changing circumstances indicated in new cases; precedents may be overturned by an Act of Parliament or a ruling of the European Court of Justice.

The politics of employment law: three models

Parliament, the European institutions and judges, then, are the legislators. They operate in arenas where there are likely to be conflicts of values and ideological perspectives. Any brief consideration of the policies of the Conservative and Labour parties in recent years will show clear divergences concerning the aims and character of employment law. Likewise, there has also been a similar marked conflict of view between recent Conservative governments and the European Union about social policy and its economic effects.

The approaches, ideologies and attitudes of government, particularly, to the framework of employment law can be encapsulated in three different models:

- The *free collective bargaining* model
- The *free labour market* model
- The *employee protection* or *social justice* model.

Each model addresses, in differing ways and with significantly different emphases, a range of important economic, social, political and civil rights issues – for example, the management of the economy, the economic consequences of collective bargaining, the concept of social justice, the entitlement to job security, anti-discrimination policies, the civil rights of freedom of association and representation.

The free collective bargaining model

This might be characterized as the traditional British model. It became increasingly predominant following the First World War. Its central process for handling employee relations was collective bargaining. Consultation was seen as comparatively marginal, although occasionally it may have been supportive of collective bargaining. In part, this model also reflected the international standards on freedom of association set in the 1940s and 1950s by the International Labour Organisation (*see* Chapter 8).

Philosophically, this model emphasized *voluntarism*, which was characterized by the general, though not complete, 'abstention of the law' (Kahn-Freund, 1954) and limited state intervention, primarily in helping resolve industrial disputes.

The limited law that was enacted had two principal functions. First, it provided a permissive framework which enabled trade unions to exist lawfully, to operate, to engage in collective bargaining and, also, to call for and organize industrial action. For example, in the public sector and through the statutory duty of the Advisory Conciliation and Arbitration Service (ACAS), between 1974 and 1993, the State aimed to promote collective bargaining. The second function was to provide limited support for workers in vulnerable situations, e.g. through minimum pay set by Wages Councils (until 1993) and through health and safety legislation.

A consensus on voluntarism was broadly subscribed to by employers, unions and governments of both major political parties. The accepted view was that employers and trade unions should be free voluntarily to negotiate and agree both terms and conditions and also the procedures for handling their industrial relations.

Voluntarism was subject to numerous strains in the post-war years. Government increasingly tried to balance sectional interests and the public interest. For example, when the level of pay settlements through free collective bargaining was perceived to be inflationary and economically damaging, governments, both Conservative and Labour, enacted statutory incomes policies and introduced legislative attempts to limit trade union power. Since 1979, this free collective bargaining model has been subject to a major political onslaught.

The free labour market model

From 1979, this Thatcherite model was gradually implemented in Britain. It broke the prevailing consensus on a range of important industrial relations issues. The principles underlying this model emphasized the following:

- deregulation of the labour market, removing certain protective measures for employees, which were seen as 'burdens on business';
- the primary importance of individualism in the employment relationship (and the consequential marginalization of collective interests);
- the curbing of trade union power;
- the advocacy of policies promoting cost-effectiveness, competitiveness, and flexibility in the use of labour;
- the limiting of external constraints (especially from the European Union) on the operation of this model – through both a commitment to the principle of *subsidiarity* and also through the *opt-out* mechanism.

In terms of employee relations, the following were the key consequences:

- Statutory recognition rights for trade unions were repealed.
- Non-unionism and derecognition of trade unions were encouraged.
- Lawful industrial action became increasingly difficult to undertake.
- Various statutory employment protections were rescinded.
- The individual employment relationship was emphasized in preference to collective representation.

In addition, large public sector organizations (which had provided the traditional base for trade union organization) were fragmented by policies designed to promote competition and cost-effectiveness – for example, the introduction of profit centres, the contracting out of local authority services, the establishment of trusts in the National Health Service and agencies in the Civil Service.

These policies were principally driven by the economic interests of employers. Arguably, the countervailing interests of working people received little consideration – except, perhaps, in the areas of sex, race and disability anti-discrimination policies, and health and safety at work. To a considerable extent, however, in the areas of both sex discrimination and health and safety at work, the extended protections were a result of European Union policies and rulings by the European Court of Justice.

The employee protection or social justice model

This third model reflects the approach adopted, largely, by the European Union. As a consequence of Britain's membership, and obligations to implement EU Directives, it infuses certain pieces of legislation enacted in the UK.

In devising its legislative framework, the European Union places considerable emphasis on consensus – not only between member states, but also between employers' organizations and trade unions. Both are described as *social partners* and are explicitly involved in preliminary consultations about proposed new legislative initiatives. Under the Maastricht Treaty 1992, European Union-wide collective agreements were permitted and encouraged as a means of promoting EU social policy objectives. The negotiators and signatories of these deals would be UNICE, CEEP and the ETUC. An agreement on paternity rights was signed in 1996.

The principles underlying EU law are as follows:

- protection of employees throughout the employment relationship by creating a regulatory framework;
- a recognition that employees have both individual and collective interests and that these have to be accommodated in a framework of employment law;
- harmonization of conditions of employment across member states – an aim which complements the objective of economic convergence;
- an acceptance of the principle of subsidiarity – that is, that some issues are more appropriately regulated at the level of the member state rather than at the level of the European Union;
- some regard paid to the economic issues of cost-effectiveness, competitiveness and labour flexibility.

As a consequence, various EU policies, outlined in Articles in the 1957 Treaty of Rome and in a range of Directives, have been enacted which provide for the equal treatment of women and men, for equal pay, for the protection of pregnant workers, for the establishment of health and safety standards, for restrictions on working time, for job security and for the protection of part-timers.

As far as the procedures of employee relations, such as trade union recognition, collective bargaining, dispute resolution, etc. are concerned, the European Union has been less interventionist, leaving the detailed arrangements to be devised in accordance with practice in each member state.

For example, it has established only the principle of consultation with employee representatives in respect of collective redundancies, business transfers and health and safety. The detailed mechanisms are a matter for determination in member states. One exception to this more voluntarist approach is the prescriptive Directive on the establishment of European Works Councils by multinational companies operating within at least two member states and with a given number of employees.

The interlocking of the models

None of these models exists in its pure form. Contemporary employment relations in Britain are, in fact, governed by the inter-penetration of the three models.

There is evidence of the free collective bargaining model continuing to cover about half the workforce. However, the major tension over recent years has been between advocates of the free labour market and employee protection models. In terms of domestic politics, this ideological dissonance is broadly reflected in the policies and perspectives of the Conservative and Labour parties. On a European level, it has been a marked source of conflict between the European Union and the Thatcher/Major governments.

Since Britain's entry into the European Community in 1973, no government has been a free agent in respect of certain policies that it wishes to pursue. To that extent sovereignty has been limited. In terms of social policy, of which employee relations is a major part, signatories to the EC's founding Treaty of Rome (1957) must conform to Articles of that Treaty and to Regulations and Directives of the Union.

Inevitably, this obligation to conform can cause tensions and conflict between the government of a member state and the EU – particularly if there is a fundamental ideological gulf between them. The continuation and intensity of Britain's tensions are dependent, in large part, on which party will be in power in the coming years. The Conservative Party will continue its advocacy of the free labour market model; while the Labour Party will rescind the opt out and propose a charter of employee rights which will reflect EU policies and principles.

REGULATING THE EMPLOYMENT RELATIONSHIP

During the past century, as we have seen, when governments have attempted to regulate the employment relationship, different interests have prevailed at different times. Employer interests were dominant in some periods; at some times, trade union and employee interests were influential. On other occasions, a more consensual approach was attempted.

The interlocking of the three models outlined above has resulted, in practice, in a system of regulation of the employment relationship that combines both voluntary action and action deriving from law. Indeed, at any time, in any workplace, it is possible to see the coexistence and interplay of these two different methods.

Voluntary action

Traditionally, voluntary action to regulate the employment relationship was seen as the preferred approach by employer, trade unions and government. This was reflected in three principal ways:

- *Promotion of collective bargaining.* The process of collective bargaining was entered into voluntarily by employers. The range of issues to be bargained about – pay and various conditions – could be determined by the employer. Collective agreements were (and continue to be) voluntary, rather than legally enforceable, agreements.

- *Adoption of voluntary codes of practice.* Such codes have been adopted by bodies, such as the Institute of Personnel and Development, in order to set standards in the various stages of the employment relationship, e.g. in recruitment, occupational testing, equal opportunities, employee involvement.

● *Observance of international standards*. Principal among these standards have been those promulgated by the International Labour Organisation (*see* Chapter 8). These tend to reflect a free collective bargaining perspective.

So significant was this voluntary approach that, in the early 1950s, Kahn-Freund stated that collective bargaining was more important as a form of regulating the employment relationship than statute law (Kahn-Freund, 1954).

Legal regulation

Forty years on, the predominant form of regulation has changed substantially. It is now, clearly, the law. It infuses every term and condition of employment – for example, pay, health and safety standards, criteria for redundancy selection – and also, many of the processes used in the employment relationship – for example, disciplinary and dismissal procedures, consultation about redundancy and health and safety. In addition, it regulates trade union membership and various forms of industrial action.

Of course, to talk about 'the law' is an over-simplification. Lord Wedderburn (1986) has remarked that:

> It is never enough to call an act 'unlawful'. We must know what kind of illegality is in issue. Nor, for parallel reasons, should we speak of 'the law' without distinguishing what kind of obligation and sanction is involved.

The legal regulation of the employment relationship derives from a number of sources – some of which are long-standing and others of which are of more recent origin. These are common law, statute law, European Union treaties, the 'direct effect' of EU Directives, rulings of the European Court of Justice and ministerial rules and regulations.

● *Common law*. This embodies the principles and precedents derived from judicial decisions over many centuries and used in the interpretation of statute law.

● *Statute law*. This describes Acts of Parliament. These laws govern people's behaviour and are enforced by various agencies, e.g. government departments, local authorities, the police service, the Health and Safety Executive. Compliance with or infringement of these laws are generally determined by the courts. Case law is created as a consequence. Some statutes give effect to EU Directives.

On occasion, under employment law, Parliament may approve a statutory code of practice. Notable examples are the ACAS Code on disciplinary procedures, the Equal Opportunities Commission Code on Sex Discrimination, the Commission for Race Equality Code on Race Discrimination. Such codes are not enforceable as statute law. They are for practical guidance only. However, a tribunal or court may take into account any evidence of an employer's breach of the standards or guidance set out in a code.

● *European Union Treaties*. These have provided a new source of law since Britain became a member in 1973. Where a provision of the Treaty of Rome

1957 and the Treaty of the European Union 1992 (the Maastricht Treaty) is 'sufficiently clear, precise and unconditional as to require no further interpretation' it becomes a direct right enforceable by an individual in the national courts. One notable Treaty provision is Article 119 which provides for equal pay. It can be relied on directly by a person claiming infringement of equal pay rights before a British court of tribunal. It has been used in several influential cases.

- *Direct effect of Directives*. Generally, these are not enforceable between individual persons but only against the State. They must be enacted, therefore, in national law and enforced in national courts. However, where an employee is employed by the State or 'an emanation of the state', then the individual can directly invoke the Directive in his or her national courts where that directive is 'sufficiently precise and unconditional'.

- *Rulings of the European Court of Justice*. These are binding on all member states, irrespective of where a case originates. They are concerned with the interpretation of and compliance with EU law. For example, Article 119 of the Treaty of Rome has been interpreted in various cases to encompass a wide range of remuneration.

- *Ministerial rules and regulations*. Statute law may confer powers upon ministers to adopt rules and regulations to suit changing circumstances without using full Parliamentary procedures. The regulations removing the ceiling on compensation in sex discrimination claims were made under European Communities Act 1972. Other regulations (on display screen equipment) have been made under the Health and Safety at Work Act 1974.

Under the unwritten British constitution, through convention, Parliament has been seen as sovereign. This means that statute law stands above judge-made law or ministerial regulations, because statutes can overturn these other two sources of law.

However, Britain's membership of the European Union has modified this position. In those policy areas where the EU is empowered to act, then both Parliament and the British courts are bound by the EU Treaties and rulings of the European Court of Justice.

Common law and statute law

The differences and functions of these two sources of law can be seen by considering two broad types of law: criminal law and civil law.

Criminal law

Criminal law is mainly statutory. It deals with wrongs against society in general – for example, theft, burglary, actual bodily harm, public order offences – for which someone is prosecuted. In order to convict someone of a crime, the prosecution – usually, the Crown Prosecution Service (the Procurator Fiscal in Scotland) – has to prove the case *beyond all reasonable doubt* – a high standard of proof. Such offences are primarily dealt with in magistrates' courts or in the Crown Court. Punishment can be a fine, a probation order, a community service order or imprisonment.

Criminal law has various implications for the employment relationship. For example, under an organization's disciplinary procedure, certain acts of gross misconduct are likely to be specified under disciplinary rules, e.g. theft or acts of violence. Both are also crimes. An employee who commits such an offence may, therefore, face two consequences:

- arrest by the police, prosecution, and a penalty imposed by the court; and

- disciplinary action by the employer – possibly dismissal without notice which, in turn, depending on all the circumstances and the conduct of the dismissal, could lead to an application by the ex-employee to an industrial tribunal alleging unfair dismissal.

Employers, themselves, are also subject to criminal law in some employment relations matters. For example, an employer can be prosecuted by the Health and Safety Executive, under the Health and Safety at Work Act 1974 (s39) for using unsafe machinery.

Civil law

This is a mixture of statute law and common law. It concerns disputes between private individuals (including organizations). In these cases someone is sued. There are two branches of civil law: the law of contract and the law of tort.

The *law of contract* determines that a contract is an agreement between two or more parties. These parties voluntarily decide the content of the contract, i.e. create their own rights and duties. Courts may be involved in discovering the intention of the parties when they agreed particular provisions.

A civil wrong is committed when one party breaches the contract. In establishing whether or not a breach occurred, the standard of proof is *the balance of probabilities*, i.e. whether something is more likely to have happened than not.

The *law of tort* relates to civil wrongs other than breach of contract. This branch of law concerns the interests of one person that may be injured by another. Usually, it is related to obligations imposed by law. For example, a person may be injured by another's negligence, his/her property may be injured by nuisance or trespass or his/her reputation by defamation.

The bulk of employment law in Britain is civil and so is subsumed under either the law of contract or the law of tort. The most obvious example of contract law is the contract of employment or those contracts offered to self-employed workers. Courts and tribunals may be called on to consider allegations of breach of contract, and other complaints relating to variation and termination of contracts. (The contract of employment is discussed further in Chapter 10.)

The law of tort is especially important for trade unions in relation to industrial disputes, where Parliament has prohibited certain forms of industrial action (*see* Chapter 11). As far as employers are concerned, they may have allegations for negligence (a tort) made against them for failure to provide proper standards and procedures for health and safety at work.

The principal remedies for an aggrieved party under civil law are damages – compensation for the injury sustained – and an injunction – a court order to stop the unlawful act.

THE INSTITUTIONS FOR ENFORCING EMPLOYMENT LAW

In the discussion so far, references have been made to particular courts and tribunals. The next section provides short descriptions of these bodies and their relationships. The administration of employment law is undertaken in two sets of bodies:

● courts and tribunals; and

● statutory agencies.

The court and tribunal system is set out in Fig 9.1. This shows the location of those dealing with employment rights.

Fig 9.1 The court and tribunal system

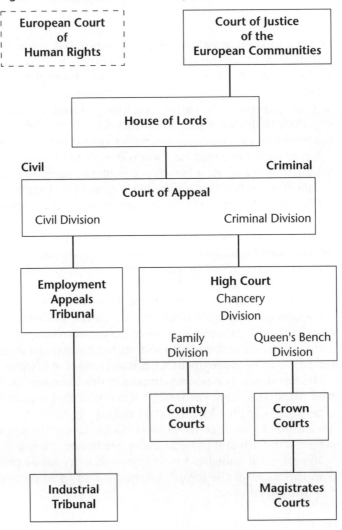

Normally, complaints on individual employment rights are made to an industrial tribunal and may proceed, through appeals on points of law, from the Employment Appeals Tribunal up to the House of Lords. A complaint may go to the European Court of Justice if the case involves specific European Union law – for example, on sex discrimination, redundancies or transfers of undertakings.

The statutory agencies have responsibilities for various pieces of employment law. Among such bodies the most notable are the Advisory Conciliation and Arbitration Service, the Equal Opportunities Commission, the Commission on Racial Equality and the Health and Safety Commission.

Courts and tribunals

Industrial tribunals

Originally set up in 1964, the scope of industrial tribunals has been extended to cover a very wide range of employment rights. For example:

- unfair dismissal
- sex discrimination
- race discrimination
- equal pay
- discrimination on the grounds of disability
- maternity rights
- trade union membership rights
- unlawful pay deductions.

A tribunal comprises three people – the chair being legally qualified and the two lay members being drawn from either side of industry.

Some 90 000 applications are made each year, 60 per cent of which are unfair dismissal claims. Two-thirds of these are either withdrawn or settled by conciliation. Of those that proceed to a full hearing, about 20 per cent result in success for the applicant. (The role industrial tribunals play in the enforcement of individual employment rights is discussed in Chapter 10.)

The Employment Appeals Tribunal

This was established in 1976 as a superior court of record to hear appeals on points of law from industrial tribunals. It comprises judges, nominated by the Lord Chancellor, from the High Court and Court of Appeal, together with other lay members who have experience of employee relations as either an employers' or employees' representative.

The House of Lords

A panel of Law Lords – either three or five – sit to hear appeals from 'inferior' courts. For most British cases, this is the final court of appeal. However, if the law derives from European Union law, then there is a further stage of appeal to the European Court of Justice.

There is no automatic right of appeal to the House of Lords. Leave, or permission, must be granted by the Court of Appeal or the House of Lords itself. It has, in recent years, produced a number of significant judgements on employment law in relation to business transfers, sex discrimination and equal pay and on the access of part-time employees to statutory rights.

European Court of Justice

Located in Luxembourg, it is officially known as the Court of Justice of the European Communities. It has jurisdiction in Britain under the European Communities Act 1972. It deals with appeals on matters within its competence. In terms of employment law, this includes, for example, collective redundancies, the rights of part-time workers, health and safety, working time, pregnant workers, sex discrimination, transfers of undertakings. In matters of European Union law it is superior to the House of Lords. Its rulings on points of law are binding (*see* Chapter 8).

European Court of Human Rights

Located in Strasbourg, this court exists under the Council of Europe, which is separate from the EU, although many member states do participate in this Council. Its responsibility is to adjudicate on alleged violations of the 1950 European Convention on Human Rights, of which Britain is a signatory. Its decisions do not automatically become part of British law. It has dealt with employment-related matters which have been said to be breaches of civil rights – for example, the British Rail closed shop and the withdrawal of union recognition rights from GCHQ.

Statutory agencies

Advisory Conciliation and Arbitration Service

Established in 1974, the Advisory Conciliation and Arbitration Service (ACAS) is an independent service, charged with a general duty to promote the improvement of industrial relations. It is governed by a Council, comprising a full-time Chair, three members appointed after consultation with the Confederation of British Industry, three after consultation with the Trade Union Congress, and three appointed by the Secretary of State for Trade and Industry. It publishes an Annual Report.

Among its functions are the following:

- to offer conciliation in disputes over individual statutory employment rights between individual employees and their employers (e.g. unfair dismissal, equal pay, discrimination);
- to provide collective conciliation for industrial disputes;
- to provide facilities for arbitration, mediation and committees of investigation;
- to issue codes of practice providing guidance, e.g. on disciplinary rules and procedures.

Equal Opportunities Commission

Established in 1976, under the Sex Discrimination Act 1975, the duties of the Equal Opportunities Commission involve:

- working towards the elimination of discrimination;
- promoting equality of opportunity between men and women;
- keeping relevant legislation under review and making proposals for change.

It is headed by a Chair and Deputy Chair and has 13 part-time commissioners. It operates through a series of committees and working parties.

It advises people of their rights in law and, in certain circumstances, can assist them to take cases to a tribunal or court; this is usually where there is a legal point to be tested. It can conduct formal investigations, issue non-discrimination notices enforceable in the courts, issue codes of practice and institute proceedings both in relation to advertising and in cases where there have been instructions or pressure to discriminate. It publishes an Annual Report.

Commission for Racial Equality

The Commission for Racial Equality was established in 1977 (replacing the previous Community Relations Commission and the Race Relations Board). Its objectives include working towards the elimination of discrimination and to promote equal opportunity and good relations between different racial groups. It has similar powers and duties to the Equal Opportunities Commission. It provides advice to employers, unions and other bodies. It supports and co-ordinates the work of about 100 local community relations councils operating in areas with significant ethnic groups. It publishes an Annual Report.

Health and Safety Commission

The Health and Safety Commission was established in 1974 under the Health and Safety at Work Act. It is responsible to the Secretary of State for the Environment for taking appropriate steps to secure the health, safety and welfare of people at work and to protect the public generally against dangers to health and safety arising from work activities.

It is headed by a Chair and up to nine commissioners. In formulating its policies, the Commission organizes widespread consultation on all aspects of health and safety. It is advised by a number of Industry Advisory Committees as well as by experts within its own Executive. It publishes an Annual Report.

National Disability Council

This is a statutory, independent body to advise government on general issues relating to disability discrimination. These issues include the drafting of codes of practice, measures to reduce or eliminate discrimination, and the right of access to goods and services. It does not have powers comparable to those of the EOC and the CRE in relation to enforcement of the legislation and assistance with individual discrimination claims.

THE IMPACT OF LAW ON THE EMPLOYMENT RELATIONSHIP

In this chapter, we have discussed the nature of the employment relationship, the sources of employment law and the political, economic and social context in which it develops. This concluding section is in two parts. First, it draws out some general comments on the impact that the law has had on the employment relationship. Second, it will outline a case study that brings together a number of elements from the context within which employment relations operate – both British and European.

The development of employment law in Britain has been a gradual process. The present framework owes its origins to a number of key phases:

- the legalization of trade unions and industrial action in the 1870s;
- defining the legal status of industrial action in 1906;
- the introduction of some piecemeal employment rights in the 1960s, e.g. on employment contracts and redundancies;
- a substantial growth of individual employment rights in the 1970s, e.g. sex and race discrimination, health and safety;
- legal constraints on trade union power in the 1980s;
- the significant expansion of European individual employment rights in the 1980s and 1990s, e.g. in transfers of undertakings, redundancies, working time, pregnant workers, health and safety, part-time workers.

The major expansion has been within the past 25 years – so much so that nowadays, employment law is a significant influence on the responsibilities of both personnel departments and line managers in their dealings with staff. The significance of this influence is seen in three ways:

- the standards used for determining managerial behaviour and action;
- proceduralization;
- sources of advice.

Standards of practice

In the past, managers tended, usually, as part of day-to-day managerial decision making, to set voluntarily their own standards of practice, and their own rules and procedures for dealing with staff. Sometimes these reflected agreed standards of good practice; sometimes they were standards incorporated in collective agreements negotiated with trade unions; sometimes they were bad standards reflecting managerial prejudice and unfairness.

Increasingly, however, managers take account of those norms, standards and procedures set by Acts of Parliament and in case law. This tendency is called *juridification* – that is, the extent to which the behaviour of employers and unions is determined by reference to the law. It is a trend in all western industrialized countries and is strongly evident in Britain, where it can be seen in the following areas:

- *Individual rights*. There has been legislation in respect of dismissal, employment documentation, discrimination, the payment of wages and the legal regulation of health and safety.
- *Collective relations*. Collective relations between employees and their employer have been influenced by the law on such issues as discipline, redundancy, union membership and non-membership, equal pay and consultation rights.
- *Collective industrial disputes*. These have been made subject to a range of legal restrictions and requirements, including balloting provisions.

Proceduralization

Recent industrial relations surveys have commented on the growth of formal procedures for handling certain individual employment issues. By 1990, formal grievance and disciplinary and dismissal procedures had become universal in all but the smallest employments.

As far as collective employment issues are concerned, the situation is less clear-cut. The removal of statutory recognition rights for collective bargaining has been one factor in the decline of trade unionism. In the 1990 Workplace Industrial Relations Survey (WIRS), 53 per cent of establishments recognized unions, as against 64 per cent in 1980 (Millward *et al*, 1992).

The incidence of joint consultation on employment issues, according to the WIRS survey, remained a minority activity – in only 29 per cent of establishments. The 1995 regulations on consultation rights in redundancies and transfers of undertakings (and those proposed for health and safety consultation) may result in greater attention to this process.

Finally, procedures on industrial action developed to a high degree of intricacy under the legislation of Conservative governments in the 1980s and 1990s. This regulatory framework created conditions in which lawful industrial action became increasingly difficult to organize. Although the Labour Party, if elected, would modify this framework of law, it is likely to retain some of the procedures for balloting and legal redress.

Sources of advice

The 1990 Workplace Industrial Relations Survey showed that in terms of external advice to managers, 'the most striking increase was in relation to outside lawyers, whose use almost doubled over the decade' – 19 per cent consulted lawyers in 1990 as against 10 per cent in 1980. The survey also reported 'increasing recourse' to ACAS and other government agencies – up from 9 per cent to 15 per cent (Millward *et al*, 1992:357).

For employees, there are three significant sources of advice. Trade unions continue to play a significant role in providing advice for their membership. Unions have continued to develop the advisory and representative service to members pursuing legal redress. This has been successful in respect of, for example, negligence claims about safety standards, equal pay issues, rights when business transfers take place, and unfair dismissal and redundancy cases.

Given the decline in trade union membership and the consequential expansion of non-union workforces, other sources of advice are being sought by working people. Two widely known sources have reported increasing requests and queries: ACAS and the Citizens' Advice Bureaux. For example, in 1994, ACAS reported that its public enquiry points received 526 189 enquiries – an increase of 9 per cent over the previous year, 56 per cent of which were made by individual employees. The National Association of Citizens' Advice Bureaux reported in 1993 that it was dealing with increasing levels of enquiries about employment problems – 856 855, involving a 10.5 per cent annual increase (NACAB 1993).

CASE STUDY

The Marshall cases

This case study draws on a pair of related influential cases – known as the Marshall cases. These involve a complaint about a discriminatory retirement age (as between men and women) and the available level of compensation for sex discrimination in British tribunals and courts.

The two Marshall cases deal with incompatibilities between British and European law. They also reveal the processes used to enforce the law. Furthermore, they provide examples of how British law had to be amended to comply. In the first case, British differential retirement ages for men and women were tested against European law. In the second case, the level of available compensation was determined.

EU equal treatment law

In 1976, the European Community implemented the Equal Treatment Directive. This concerned the eradication of discrimination on grounds of sex or marital or family status in access to employment, vocational training and working conditions.

Member states were required, by 1978, to enact legislation in their own Parliaments to ensure there was no provision contrary to the principle of equal treatment in:

- all legislative provisions;
- the terms of collective agreements;
- individual contracts of employment;
- the internal rules of undertakings.

If so, such a provision would be declared null and void or amended.

The Equal Treatment Directive, like all Directives, imposes obligations on the member state – not on private persons such as employers. Consequently, to regulate the behaviour of employers, trade unions and working people, the member state must enact the Directive into its own legislation. If a Directive is not fully implemented by a member state, then the EU Commission may start *infringement proceedings* against the member state before the European Court of Justice. In respect of equal treatment, Britain did have legislation (The Sex Discrimination Act 1975).

The first Marshall case

Up to the early 1980s, the policy of the South-West Hampshire Area Health Authority was that 'normal retirement age will be the age at which social security pensions become available' – that is, 60 years for women and 65 for men. Miss Marshall argued, before an industrial tribunal, that this policy constituted less favourable treatment under the Sex Discrimination Act. Her case was dismissed by the industrial tribunal and, on appeal, by the Employment Appeals Tribunal. British legislation, at that time, permitted these differential retirement ages.

However, Miss Marshall made an alternative claim that her compulsory retirement, at 62 years, was also contrary to the EU Equal Treatment Directive. She was able to invoke this, directly, because she worked for 'an emanation of the State' – that is, an organization subject to state control and regulation. Had she worked

▶

for a private company, she would not have been able to.

The industrial tribunal agreed with this claim. The EAT rejected it, however, arguing that the Equal Treatment Directive did not have *direct effect* in Miss Marshall's case. The matter was referred to the European Court of Justice for a ruling. This ruled that direct effect was appropriate in this case.

The consequence of this first Marshall case was that those who worked for the State, or an emanation of the State, were entitled to harmonized retirement ages between men and women, under the direct effect of EU law. Those who worked for private organizations were exempt because British law – The Sex Discrimination Act 1975 – permitted differential retirement ages.

The European Union could have started infringement proceedings against Britain for non-compliance with the Equal Treatment Directive. However, the discrepancy was rectified when the Sex Discrimination Act 1986 was enacted. This required harmonized retirement ages throughout all sectors of employment.

The second Marshall case

When the issue of compensation for Miss Marshall's loss was considered, the compensa-tion limit stood at £8500. However, this could not compensate her fully for a loss estimated to be £19 405, including interest. Eventually, after various appeals, in 1991, the House of Lords referred the issue of compensation to the European Court of Justice for a ruling on com-patibility with European Equal Treatment law.

In August 1993, the ECJ gave its historic ruling. It stated that a fixed upper limit on com-pensation, which was awarded for loss and damage suffered as a result of sex discrimina-tion, was contrary to equal treatment law. Compensation must be 'adequate'. It must enable the loss, including interest for reduced value as time passes, and damage actually sus-tained as a result of the discriminatory dismissal 'to be made good in full'.

The consequence of this ruling was that all complaints would benefit from a change in the law in sex discrimination compensation. The compensation limit was repealed and industrial tribunals were also given the power to award interest with effect from 22 November 1993, under the Sex Discrimination and Equal Pay (Remedies) Regulations 1993. Comparable action was taken to remove limits in race dis-crimination complaints, under the Race Relations (Remedies) Act 1994. This came into effect from 3 July 1994.

Exercise 9.3

The implementation of employment law

In this section, we have considered a number of broad trends in personnel manage-ment and employment relations that have arisen from the implementation of employment law. The Marshall case study illustrates the importance for employers of a number of factors examined in this chapter

Read the case study again and note down how the following factors affect the Marshall cases:

(a) social policy standards about equal treatment;

(b) the regulation of the employment relationship;

(c) sources of employment law;

(d) the political and legislative significance of Britain's membership of the European union;

(e) the operation of the judicial process;

(f) the impact of judicial decisions and consequential legislative action for employers.

SUMMARY AND CONCLUSION

Employees are not one-dimensional individuals concerned solely with their own economic interests and rewards. They are social beings who import into the employment relationship values, expectations, experiences, external social and family obligations and differing standards of physical and mental health.

At work, employees will have many individual interests; but they will also have numerous interests in common with fellow-workers. These interests will not always coincide with those of their employer. In such conflicts of interest, employees are disadvantaged because of the scale of their employer's economic power.

The effective working of the employment relationship, therefore, requires reconciliation and accommodation:

- *Accommodation* by the employer to individual employees, with a proper recognition of their wider social concerns as parents, carers, breadwinners, etc. and their interests in both job and income security.

- *Reconciliation* between the values and expectations of employees with those of employers for productive, high quality, cost-effective, flexible working.

Given the underlying imbalance of power in the employment relationship, three questions inevitably arise:

- To what extent should employers and employees be free to work out the necessary accommodation and the reconciliation of interests?

- To what extent should government intervene, setting appropriate standards of public policy to deal with, for example, unfair discrimination and treatment, exploitation in terms of low pay and long hours, poor health and safety standards?

- To what extent should government intervene to promote, by encouragement or by statutory requirements, the representation of both individuals and groups of people at work through either trade unions or non-union employee representation systems?

These tensions between voluntarism and legal regulation have been explored in this chapter. In addition, three models reflecting different political perspectives on the balance between voluntary action and legal regulation were considered. It has been concluded that, at the present time, manifestations of all three models coexist in British employee relations. In addition, it has been noted that, over the past 20 years or so, there has been a marked shift from voluntarism towards considerable legal intervention and juridification.

CHAPTER 10

Implementing individual employment rights

INTRODUCTION

This chapter will concentrate on the context in which three key sets of individual employment rights continue to be developed. The employment rights that will be used to illustrate the importance of these various contextual factors are:

- equal treatment and equal opportunities in employment;
- the creation and operation of the contract of employment;
- the termination of employment.

Together they provide a broad framework of law that reflects the flow of the employment relationship from start to finish. They will also highlight the interaction and importance of both statute law and the common law of contract.

Why have these been chosen?

- The principle of equal treatment is a theme which is fundamental to the entire employment relationship.
- The contract of employment is central to the regulation of the employment relationship.
- The termination of employment is likely to involve considerable loss of benefits to employees and result in a significant deterioration in living standards.

These areas of employment law give some protection for employees, who may otherwise be vulnerable to arbitrary treatment by their employer. This protection is provided, in theory:

- by outlawing unfair discrimination throughout the employment;
- by integrating *natural justice* into the employment relationship, e.g. in relation to dismissal;
- by recognizing the value to employees of job security and the rights and benefits that accrue with length of service, e.g. in relation to redundancy; and
- by requiring *reasonable treatment* by employers.

All these issues have been at the forefront of public policy debates during the past 30 years.

FOCUS AND SCOPE

This chapter is not designed to provide a detailed outline of employment law. The focus will be on the political, social and economic context that has affected employment rights in recent years. The principal issues are:

- social attitudes about good employment practice and fair treatment;

- social attitudes about work and its relationship to an employee's domestic responsibilities;

- social attitudes about women's role in society and the economy;

- employers' economic objectives and the pursuit of cost-effectiveness and flexibility in the use of labour;

- the standards of public policy set by various British governments and the European Union to promote fairness, reasonableness and non-discriminatory treatment;

- the extent to which labour market conditions encourage or discourage observance of these standards of good practice;

In the subsequent discussion, the following issues will be considered:

- the extent to which the law influences the policies and practices of employers in the management of their staff;

- the justifications for developing statutory individual employment rights;

- the costs and resource implications for employers of compliance with the law;

- the enforcement processes and their significance for good personnel management practice.

LEARNING OBJECTIVES

Once you have read through this chapter and completed the associated exercises, you should be able to:

- understand the fundamental importance of equal opportunities as a theme in the employment relationship;

- understand the social and economic factors that influence the development of equal opportunities;

- analyse particular employment policies and practices in terms of equal opportunities and suggest action that might be taken;

- understand the central importance of the contract of employment in the regulation of the employment relationship;

- understand the legal principles underpinning this contract;

- advise an employer on issues to be considered when contractual terms have to be changed;

- understand the concepts of *fairness* and *reasonableness* in termination of employment.

CASE STUDY

Seymour Aerial and Cable Installations

Seymour Aerial and Cable Installations employs about 30 staff at its office in Merton. There are three word processor operators, who carry out some ancillary tasks. Together with four other administrators, they work in the Central Administrative Services Department.

The company was founded in 1955, as Seymour Aerials, by Sid Seymour. It was initially a small business run from his home and then from a lock-up. In the early 1980s, his more entrepreneurial son, Warren, began to expand the business and Sid retired to the Costa del Sol.

The personnel management and employee relations approach of the company reflected Warren's buccaneering attitude. He had no time for formal procedures or policies. He was a great admirer of Margaret Thatcher. Like her, he regarded trade unions as 'the enemy within' and employment protection law as 'a burden on business'. Staff, consequently, were treated in an arbitrary manner. They were well paid when times were good and they were expected to work hard. When times were tough, exercising his right to manage, Warren would change conditions of employment unilaterally – cutting back what he saw as expensive, fringe benefits.

The company expanded considerably during the 1980s and was re-named Seymour Aerial and Cable Installations. In late 1995, however, it put a freeze on recruitment and the Engineering Manager had been overheard by one of the reception staff talking about possible redundancies.

Personnel management, such as it was, was undertaken by Terry Daley, the Administration Manager. He was assisted by Sharon James, a secretary/PA who joined the company in 1993 to handle personnel administration. In her previous job, Sharon had successfully completed the Certificate in Personnel Practice course at the local further education college. She tried to make some simple changes at Seymour's such as providing every employee with a *Section 1 written statement* of their terms and conditions and introducing a disciplinary procedure. Terry said, 'We're not interested in all that stuff; we've got a business to run.'

Selena Charles, aged 23 years, had been employed by the company since 21 November 1994 as a full-time WP operator in the Merton office.

Selena was a moderately good employee. She had only been late twice. Her standard of performance at work was reasonable. She took some time to settle in. Her probationary period of three months was extended by a further three months because some of her work was sloppy and she was slow. By March 1995 she was doing a reasonably competent job.

She was known to the other staff as a friendly and helpful person, although Terry Daley found her surly. He had commented to Warren that 'she's one of those people who are always going on about their rights.' This arose for two reasons.

Selena had mentioned casually at coffee break to the other staff that some new law had been introduced about VDUs. Her father had read about it in an article in his union journal.

A few weeks later, when the company decided to impose a 1 per cent pay increase, Selena had been vociferous in an office discussion. She had said, 'If there was a union here, they wouldn't get away with this exploitation.' She told colleagues that her father was a shop steward at London Underground, where he had worked for 30 years since coming from Barbados. He had said that they should get organized into a union. Terry Daley was passing and said that they 'needn't try that here. Warren wouldn't stand for it.'

Returning from her Christmas holidays, on 2 January 1996, Selena was delighted to tell the other staff in the office that she was pregnant. The baby was due in July. The other staff asked if she was giving up work or taking maternity leave. She said that she wanted to carry on working because she and Winston, her boyfriend, were saving to buy a small flat. Her mother would look after the baby during the day.

Selena did not formally tell Terry about her pregnancy. He found out from Sharon, who, at Selena's request, was looking up the law on maternity leave. 'Bye bye, blackbird,' Terry

▶

commented. 'She's too much of a troublemaker, that one.' He told Sharon to tell Selena that she would have to finish work when the baby was due. Sharon tried to explain that Selena might have some rights. 'Look,' said Terry, 'they're all the same, these people. Their rights – that's all they go on about. It's probably her father putting her up to it. One of these militants, isn't he?' Later Sharon told Selena what he had said.

At the end of February, two weeks after this incident, Selena was late for work three days in succession because she was suffering from morning sickness. Terry seized his opportunity. 'We can't have this,' he told her. 'You'd better leave now. There's work to be done here and you're not up to it. Pick up your P45 and any money owing on Friday. You're finished.'

On the advice of her father, Selena decided to complain to an industrial tribunal about unfair dismissal.

Exercise 10.1 **Individual employment rights**

The case study covers a number of individual employment rights discussed within this chapter. It can be used in various ways, depending on how much detailed exploration is required:

1 *Note the individual rights issues that you think arise from the case study and then check them off as you read through the remainder of the chapter. Think about the importance of the underlying principles of fairness and non-discrimination in the case.*

2 *Check, in an employment law text or guide, the rights that Selena has and how they have been infringed.*

3 *Obtain an IT1 form from a local industrial tribunal office and imagine that you are assisting Selena to complete it.*

4 *Obtain an IT3 form and imagine that you are assisting Terry Daley to complete it.*

EQUAL TREATMENT AND EQUAL OPPORTUNITIES

This section will examine the interplay of social, political and economic factors on the development of equal opportunities law. It will consider, first of all, the responsiveness of the political system to social pressures for change; and, then, it will explore the impact of various contextual pressures on employing organizations. Finally, it will examine those issues that are present within the workplace which facilitate or obstruct the implementation of equal opportunities objectives.

The political context

Equal treatment law concerns the eradication of both policies and practices based on stereotyping and also unfair discriminatory treatment of particular groups, e.g. women, pregnant women, people from various ethnic groups, and disabled people. The law, consequently, advocates effective equal opportunities policies. These are expected to reflect standards of social justice and good human resource management practice.

The concept of *equal opportunities* is set in the context of often negative, long-established, social attitudes, expectations and stereotyping. It is important to remember that, under this concept, it is not implied that, for example, all women must seek promotion and have full-time permanent jobs or even undertake paid employment at all. The concept is not prescriptive. It is founded on the notion of freedom of choice in decisions about employment. Such freedom can, of course, only be genuinely effective if stereotyping and entrenched discriminatory employment practices are eliminated.

Over the past 30 years, there has been a strong political impetus to outlaw discrimination – particularly sex discrimination. This has been derived primarily from the policies of various British governments, and supported by a framework of European Union law. There is no comparable European law on race discrimination, although both the Commission and the Council of Ministers have discussed proposals.

The initial areas of discrimination outlawed in Britain in the 1970s were those on grounds of sex, marital status, race, colour, nationality and ethnic origins. By the mid-1990s, the legal framework has expanded substantially to cover pregnancy, sexual harassment, disability and trade union membership and non-membership. The European Union has also reinforced this legal protection in respect of sex discrimination, pregnancy, maternity and paternity.

Although such legislation has largely been initiated by those sympathetic to the *employee protection/social justice* model (*see* Chapter 9), there has been no concerted attempt to repeal these protective measures by recent free labour market' Conservative governments. John Major, as Prime Minister, publicly supported such developments as Opportunity 2000 and also initiatives to tackle race discrimination. Furthermore, his government eventually, after prolonged and concerted campaigning, introduced, albeit limited, legislation on disability. By contrast, there has been considerable resistance to the extension of statutory paternity rights into Britain.

It might be argued, then, that over the past 20 years or so a loose bipartisan political consensus has existed on some important areas of discrimination. Disagreement has arisen principally on details – the mechanisms used to ensure compliance by employers – and also on the degree of financial commitment necessary to implement them.

The organizational context

In the following section, several issues are explored about employers' attitudes to effective implementation. When implemented in organizations, equal opportunities policies are likely to confront numerous constraints and tensions – particularly financial costs, the degree of managerial commitment and social attitudes. In many organizations, equal opportunities continue to exist on paper only and not in reality.

For example, in 1990 the Equal Opportunities Commission reported that 93 per cent of Health Authorities stated they had an equal opportunities statement or policy. However, 75 per cent did not monitor the policy and 30 per cent did not communicate the policy to staff.

Employer attitudes to the economics of equal opportunities fall under two related headings:

- the degree to which the achievement of equal opportunities objectives is seen as a cost to the organization;
- the degree to which it is seen as a contribution to the business objectives of the organization.

Cost consciousness

A clear tension exists within organizations between the requirements to be cost-effective and competitive and the cost of compliance with social policy standards. The severity of economic pressures confronting employers is dependent on the state of their product markets and the labour markets in which they operate. A highly competitive product market will increase pressure on an organization to trim unit labour costs. Adherence to social policy standards is likely, then, to be a lower priority, particularly for small organizations.

Employer resistance to these standards could, of course, be misplaced. Compliance might result in a better motivated, more creative and productive workforce. Nevertheless, this tension is a reality.

The possible costs facing an employer include both those which are directly quantifiable and those which are indirect and dispersed within the organization.

Directly quantifiable costs can include, for example:

- the cost of compliance with improved terms and conditions of employment set out in law, e.g. equal pay, statutory redundancy pay, and working time requirements;
- resources and time involved in both providing advice and training on standards of good practice;
- establishing and operating monitoring procedures;
- the potential *opportunity cost* of non-compliance, e.g. representation at an industrial tribunal, an award of compensation to a successful applicant, and the likelihood of anyone taking this course of action.

Indirect costs, by their very nature, are much less easy to discern and quantify. On the one hand, low compliance with standards of good practice might have a range of adverse employee relations consequences – low productivity, low quality standards, low morale, high labour turnover, poor attendance records, a sense of job insecurity, etc. On the other hand, compliance might result in higher unit labour costs than competitor companies and consequential difficulties in gaining orders.

Business strategy considerations

Some organizations are taking steps forward in the implementation and evolution of equal opportunities policies. One innovative concept centres around the *management of diversity*. This concept is located within the context of strategic business issues. It is concerned with the management of a workforce as a diverse group of people. It considers not just groups identified in those areas of outlawed discrimination but also includes people with differences on many other grounds – e.g. age, social background, personality, sexual orientation.

Its business focus means that consideration is to be given by all managers:

- to the promotion of greater creativity among staff;
- to problem-solving;
- to the reduction of the costs of staff recruitment and retention by reducing labour turnover; and
- to assistance in marketing goods and services to a diverse range of customers.

As an approach towards operationalizing equal opportunities, the management of diversity is commendably broad. It recognizes the social heterogeneity of British society and is inclusive of wide ranges of groups and is not merely restricted to those defined by anti-discrimination law. However, although described as a step in the evolution of equal opportunities policies, it does not rely on one set of the equal opportunities measures – positive action and targets.

The justification for this has been put as follows:

> ... if managing diversity is truly about creating an environment where everyone feels valued and their talents are being fully utilised, then actions ought to be targeted on any individual who has a particular development need and not restricted to those who are members of a particular group. (Rajvinder Kandola *et al* 1995)

Although its significance must be recognized, the management of diversity is at present in its infancy in Britain. The focus in this chapter will be towards the implementation of equal opportunities policies as conventionally understood.

Implementing equal treatment in employment relations

As indicated earlier, equal treatment must be acknowledged as an ingredient in the entire employment relationship. It infuses the terms and conditions offered under the contract of employment; and it can be a factor in the termination of employment. It is, of course, central to the first stage in the employment relationship – recruitment and selection. It is this first stage, therefore, that will be used as an illustration, in the following section, of the interplay between recruitment policies and equal treatment.

A number of external and internal factors influence an organization's recruitment policy and practice. Principally, these include:

- changes in social attitudes;
- the characteristics of the external labour market;
- the characteristics of the internal labour market;
- the extent to which positive action is promoted to deal with historic patterns of discriminatory treatment;
- the specific requirements that employers have for skill, experience, particular patterns of working-time and the deployment of labour.

The significance of and interplay between these factors is now considered under the following headings:

- Occupational segregation
- Positive action
- Social attitudes
- The external labour market
- Legal provisions
- Good human resource management practice

Occupational segregation

In considering their recruitment policy, employers should identify, first of all, the existing profile of their workforce. This will probably reveal both an inheritance of previous, often inadvertent, discriminatory practice and also prevailing social attitudes that have resulted in occupational segregation.

Within workforces, such segregation exists in respect of both women and ethnic groups. There are two kinds: vertical and horizontal (*see also* Chapter 4).

Vertical segregation describes the situation where, for example, men predominate in the higher graded posts in an organization and women in the lower graded posts.

> For many women there is a glass ceiling blocking their aspirations, allowing them to see where they might go, but stopping them from arriving there. In any given occupation and in any given public office, the higher the rank, prestige or influence, the smaller the proportion of women. (Hansard Society, 1990).

This phenomenon is common to most large organizations.

Exercise 10.2 Vertical segregation

Look at your own organization's workforce profile and see how extensive vertical occupational segregation is.

Horizontal segregation describes the situation where, for example, men and women in an organization may work in different types of jobs – *men's work* and *women's work*. Workforce surveys, published by the Equal Opportunities Commission, indicate heavy concentrations of women workers in relatively few occupations – frequently those with a large demand for part-time labour.

The following occupations are identified as significantly female:

> clerical and related; catering; cleaning; hairdressing; personal services; professional and related in education, welfare and health; selling; and, in manufacturing industry, painting, repetitive assembly and product packaging.

It is interesting to note that this occupational segregation also reflects in large part the stereotypical female domestic responsibilities – caring, cleaning, menial repetitive tasks and the provision of personal services.

Exercise 10.3	**Horizontal segregation**

Look at your own organization's workforce profile and see how extensive horizontal occupational segregation is.

Positive action

If occupational segregation is a characteristic of an organization's internal labour market, then, in preparing for future recruitment initiatives, an employer may consider whether positive action is appropriate. This involves the identification of targets for the recruitment of particular social groups and, consequently, the encouragement of those under-represented groups to apply for particular positions. It is permitted under both sex and race anti-discrimination law.

An organization carrying out such a diagnosis of its workforce profile and proposing a proactive equal opportunities policy does not, of course, operate in a vacuum. The external context includes three related aspects, all of which are inevitably, by their nature, in a state of some flux: social attitudes; the external labour market; and legal provisions. These form the next part of the discussion.

Social attitudes

Social attitudes influence both the size and nature of the external labour market – that is, the characteristics of available recruits. In addition, attitudes and expectations are imported into the organizations and managers have to deal with them. The significance of this can be illustrated by exploring, as an example, the attitudes both of women and towards women.

Historically, certainly for the first half of the twentieth century, apart from during the two world wars, predominant social attitudes regarded women's contribution to society (outside the home) as largely peripheral. In society generally, the emphasis was on the importance of male roles. For example, government and political activity were male preserves. Full and equal civil rights to vote in elections were not granted to women until 1928. Education was seen as more important for boys. Both full-time work and the breadwinner role were usually ascribed to men.

In recent years, particularly with the emergence of greater feminist consciousness in the late 1960s, there have been some marked shifts in social attitudes among both women and men. In large part, this has arisen both from women's own preferences for changing their role in society and also the identification of particular barriers and discriminatory practices that have to be eradicated.

Labour market data provides some interesting evidence of certain social changes. For example, the economic activity rates of married women have grown significantly from 22 per cent in 1951 to 55 per cent in 1995. This has been a major contributor both to shifts in social attitudes as well as a consequence of such shifts.

Economic activity rates by women's age show that increasingly women in child-bearing and child-rearing years are taking much shorter breaks from employment (*see* Table 10.1).

Table 10.1 Women's economic activity by age groups (%)

	1971	1991	2006 (est.)
25–34 years	45.5	69.7	80.6
35–44 years	59.6	76.7	85.2

Source: Ellison (1994)

For example, whereas in 1971 less than half of 25 to 34-year-old women saw themselves as participants in the labour market, by 1991, the proportion was over two-thirds. Two factors are suggested as contributing to this: a decline in child-bearing, together with a stronger preference to continue in employment after a short maternity career break.

Both sets of statistics, then, provide some explanation of the increasing feminization of the labour market. By December 1993 women accounted for 44 per cent of the working population (11.7 million). By 2006, it is estimated that the proportion will be 45.8 per cent (12.9 million).

By contrast, the number of males in the labour force is projected to stay relatively static or decline slightly as the chances increase of men being permanently out of work once they are over the age of 55 years. In 1993, there were 15.4 million men of working age. By 2006, it is estimated that there will be a marginal increase to 15.7 million.

However, although social attitudes are changing and so enhancing women's roles in both society and work, there are two factors that constrain the achievement of equal opportunities. The first is the existence of residual traditionalism among both men and also some women. The second is the generally inferior status of much female work.

An illustration of traditional stereotyping was reported in an Equal Opportunities Commission survey, where a British Rail manager was reported as saying:

> I have a number of ladies in my establishment and they are quite happy being routine booking clerks, travel centre clerks, and that's not to say they don't do a good job. But they're possibly there because it's basically pin money to them. So they do a good job by their pleasant personality and they get job satisfaction from it, but no way do they wish to go forward and take greater responsibility. (Robbins, 1986)

In a further survey in Barclays Bank, Tina Boyden and Lorraine Paddison (1986) commented:

> We recently asked a sample of male managers what they saw as the major factors inhibiting the progress of women in the bank and they replied that women lacked ambition and confidence, were reluctant to obtain professional qualifications, did not make long-term career plans and tended to put their husband and families first. More to the point, women staff, surveyed independently, also volunteered these reasons for lack of progress.

The comparative inferior standing of much female work is seen, frequently but not always, in terms of:

- employment status, much being part-time, temporary and homeworking;
- lower levels of earnings compared with men;
- low levels of skill; and
- limited or non-existent promotion and development opportunities.

The legacy of these attitudes and practices has to be recognized in society generally and also within the cultures of particular employing organizations. The law assists in setting standards of public policy which condemn such attitudes and practices as unacceptable. However, the eradication of bad human resource management practice is, of course, both morally and in law, the responsibility of the employer concerned.

| Exercise 10.4 | ## Social attitudes |

Ask female relatives from different generations about their experiences of work. For example, were they encouraged or expected to work? Were they expected to give up work on marriage or when they had children? If they wanted to work, what barriers and other difficulties were there to employment or to a career?

The external labour market

The interplay between social attitudes to women and the external labour market is particularly important. We will consider two further aspects:

- general levels of employment and the existence of skill and labour shortages;
- the type of employment status required by employers.

One significant facilitator for the overall promotion of equal opportunities is the general state of the labour market and, associated with this, the labour markets experienced by particular organizations. For example, the impetus for tackling sex discrimination and for advancing equal opportunities for women was considerably greater between the mid-1980s and the onset of the recession in 1990–91.

The two principal reasons for this were:

- employers needed to meet immediate skill and labour shortages; and
- their longer term need to anticipate the effect of the *demographic time bomb* which involves a decline in the number of young people (16 to 24-year-olds) in the labour market – from 21 per cent in 1990 to 17 per cent in 2001.

These supply side factors, in terms of the availability of labour, were matched by a range of practices by employers to encourage women to return to employment after maternity breaks or, alternatively, to remain in employment. These measures included either particular working-time arrangements – such as job sharing, term-time contracts, flexible working hours, career-break schemes – or specific fringe benefits – for example, workplace nurseries or other assistance with child-care provision.

Interestingly, there is in many of these arrangements an implicit, and sometimes explicit, assumption about women's continuing established roles as mother, wife and *carer*. Indeed, it can be argued that unless such arrangements are also genuinely available to men, they are not well-founded in a commitment to the principle of equal treatment. They merely reinforce traditional female roles.

The successful integration of female workers into an organization's workforce, then, involves recognition of many considerations. The five most significant are listed below.

- Women are still the predominant family carers in our society.
- The working life of a woman is normally characterized by a career break, for childbirth and/or child-rearing.
- There is a marked overall preference among women (81 per cent of respondents) to work part-time (*Employment Gazette*, April 1994). After maternity leave, there is some evidence that women are now more likely to return to full-time employment and to the same job, working for the same employer than they were in 1981.
- Working-time flexibility is a key feature of employment conditions widely favoured by women workers.

Recognition of these issues and genuine attempts to incorporate them into equal opportunities policies will go a long way to comply with the requirements of sex discrimination law.

Legal provisions

For an employer, there are three factors that need to be considered in respect of anti-discrimination law:

- the extent to which it is a response to changing social attitudes;
- the extent to which it is moulding social behaviour;
- the extent to which it is fixed or is changing.

Responding to social change

Social changes continue to take place which give rise to developing expectations among women. Principal among these are preferences for flexibility in working time; the acknowledgement by employers of the need to reconcile work and domestic responsibilities; expectations of fair treatment and fair rewards; a growing preference for continuous career progression.

As a result of these evolutionary changes in social attitudes, the employment role of women is increasingly being redefined. Consequently, the law will inevitably be further developed and amended. For example, case law has affirmed the right of women after maternity leave to return to part-time employment. In this way, then, the legal framework is responsive.

However, it is important to remember that the law is a technique used to modify social behaviour. Two processes are at work.

- On the one hand, changes in social attitudes develop resulting in new laws and standards of public policy and acceptable practice.

- On the other hand, social behaviour then has to be modified to conform with these new standards of practice.

Moulding social behaviour

The manner in which social behaviour might be influenced by legal standards is seen in the recruitment and selection process. This is a process where choices are made. Discrimination – distinguishing or making choices between people – is a normal part of employee relations. If employers adopt standards of good practice, they will normally discriminate on the grounds of a person's work experience, skills and educational qualifications relevant to the job concerned.

However, any casual review of employee relations reveals that, when choices are made, discrimination is not always carried out using such objective criteria. Employees or potential employees can often be judged according to qualities they are presumed to have because they belong to a particular social group, e.g. single women, Asians, older workers, people of Afro-Caribbean origin, disabled workers. This stereotyping prevents managers from considering objectively the qualities that a person might bring to a job. Such unfair discrimination is generally unlawful if it relates to sex, marital status, pregnancy and maternity, race, colour, ethnic origin, nationality, disability and, in Northern Ireland, religion.

In recruitment practice, this discriminatory treatment can be of two kinds. The first is intentional and direct. For example, an employer may, illegally, tell an employment agency that it does not wish to employ any black or Asian workers.

The second kind of discriminatory treatment may result, unintentionally and indirectly, from an existing employment practice. For example, an organization may recruit staff by 'word of mouth'. In such circumstances, it is probable that those recruited will broadly reflect the gender, ethnic origin and social background of those employed in the organization. The Sex Discrimination Act 1975 and the Race Relations Act 1976 outlaw both *direct discrimination* and *indirect discrimination*.

These provisions on direct and indirect discrimination are central to the effective enforcement of public policy in this area. The legislation, therefore, intervenes to set out principles of behaviour. It does not prescribe detailed practices. It is the responsibility of employers to scrutinize their own policies and practices and, if a complaint is made to an industrial tribunal, to justify their actions and those of their managers and other staff.

Direct discrimination, by its very nature, is more obvious and may, therefore, be more easily tackled. By contrast, indirect discrimination may be more difficult to diagnose and root out. It is a more subtle form of bias and consists of treatment which may appear to be fair, but is discriminatory in operation and in its effect. It is largely the cause of the continuing absence of women and of ethnic minority groups from important areas of employment. Without this provision, the bulk of our anti-discrimination legislation would have been severely weakened and probably discredited.

Law in a state of flux

There is a danger in considering the law governing any aspect of the employ-ment relationship as being fixed. Clearly, there are fixed principles and certain statutory provisions can have a long life-span. It is important to remember, however, that the law is constantly being interpreted in the light of particular circumstances. Case law and Acts of Parliament change year in and year out. As with other elements in an organization's context, change and evolution are critical ingredients.

For example, within the past few years, British courts and the European Court of Justice have:

- refined the rights of pregnant workers;
- developed the framework of maternity rights;
- enhanced some of the rights of part-time workers;
- determined eligibility for pension rights.

In addition, there are current debates on possible anti-discrimination law in respect of age and sexuality.

Good human resource management practice

A number of critical problems can arise for employers at the recruitment and selection stage, in respect of discriminatory treatment. It is a stage which involves a number of steps:

- the drafting and distribution of a job description and a person specifica-tion;
- the publishing of advertisements;
- the drafting of application forms;
- the organization of interviews;
- the establishment of a monitoring process.

Consequently, it requires clear standards of good practice at each step.

These standards are outlined in the statutory codes of practice from the Equal Opportunities Commission and the Commission for Racial Equality. The Institute of Personnel and Development has also published a voluntary code of practice.

The preceding discussion on equal treatment has focused, principally, on statute law – legislation passed by Parliament to achieve some particular eco-nomic and/or social purpose. It has shown that the character of this employment legislation is frequently determined by an interplay between changing social attitudes, public pressure, and a recognition that certain stan-dards of good practice should be adopted and applied.

An additional form of employment regulation derives from common law. This is judge-made law, enunciated through specific cases. Under the common law of contract various principles have been developed. In two respects, these have had a clear impact on the development of the contract of employment: when it is formulated and when it is changed. The next section, will explore these issues.

CONTRACTS TO REGULATE THE EMPLOYMENT RELATIONSHIP

Different forms of contract

In contemporary society, an employment relationship is invariably governed by some form of contract. Usually, this is a *contract of employment*. However, in the current flexible labour market another form of contractual relationship is developing in importance: *the contract for services*. A person working under such a contract is usually described as self-employed. The person who works under a contract of employment is an *employee*; while, the person who works under a contract for services may be called either an *independent contractor* or a *worker*.

An employer's reasons for choosing one contractual form over another are largely economic, deriving from concern about cost-effectiveness. Several factors influence employers. Self-employed workers can be responsible, for example, for their own training, tools, equipment and office overheads and for providing their own benefits, like pensions. They are less likely to be a direct cost for an employer. The employer can also have greater flexibility to terminate such contracts and so limit access to unfair dismissal rights.

Given different forms of employment status, as an employee or a self-employed person, and atypical forms of employment, e.g. part-time or temporary work or homeworking, it is understandable that some uncertainties will arise over a person's access to industrial tribunals to claim infringement of a particular statutory right.

The groups covered by these rights vary. Unfair dismissal protection is limited to *employees*. Anti-discrimination law, however, extends to all *workers*. Over recent years, arising from various cases, judges have developed a test to determine whether or not an individual is an employee and is, therefore, eligible, for example, to submit a claim alleging unfair dismissal.

This test involves a number of factors:

- the degree of control exercised by the employer;
- the integration of the person into the business, including the extent to which the employer bears risk and provides tools;
- the extent to which a person is obliged to work;
- whether the work is on a continuing basis;
- whether the employer deducts income tax and social security.

According to this test, the finding of a contract of employment depends on considering all these factors. None is sufficient in itself and all do not have to be complied with.

An illustration of how the test may operate in practice is seen in the case *Airfix Footwear* v *Cope* (1978). Mrs Cope worked at home making shoe heels. The company provided her with tools and issued instructions. Over a seven-year period, she generally worked a five day-week. She was paid on a piecework basis, without deductions for tax and national insurance. She was held by the Employment Appeals Tribunal to be an employee and therefore eligible to claim unfair dismissal.

Exercise 10.5 ## Contracts

1 Carry out an audit of the workforce in an organization known to you.

2 Find out whether your organization uses both contracts of employment and contracts for services.

3 How many people are on the different forms of contract? What work do they do? What proportions of your workforce are on full-time, part-time and temporary contracts? Does your employer use homeworkers or teleworkers? What proportions of these groups are male and female?

4 What are your employer's reasons for these different employment arrangements?

Despite the gradual increase in self-employment in the past 15 years – now settling at about 12 per cent of the labour market – most working people are individual parties to contacts of employment. It is this form of contract, then, that will be considered further in this section. It will be explored under two headings:

● *What is the contract of employment?* This section will consider the sources of the contract of employment and those key legal principles that infuse it.

● *How can it be changed?* This section will discuss the interplay between contract law and employers' continuing needs to make employment changes.

What is a contract of employment?

The contract of employment is an agreement, legally enforceable in the courts between an individual employee and his/her employer under which the employee promises to be ready, willing and able to undertake the agreed work and the employer promises to pay the agreed wage. The contract may be in writing, verbally agreed or part verbal and part in writing.

The terms of a contract of employment are usually of primary concern in any grievance, disciplinary case, dismissal, redundancy, sex or race discrimination allegation, etc. Attention will quickly turn to the provisions of the individual's contract of employment – whether those terms are in writing or not.

The contract of employment, on the one hand, enables the employer to assert power and control over the employee – for example, in explicitly requiring mobility and implicitly requiring adaptation to new methods of work. On the other hand, it also confers certain limited rights upon the employee – for example, payment for work performed and implicitly a duty of care by the employer.

It is arrived at freely. This is so to the extent that the employee has a choice whether to accept or reject the contract. As discussed in Chapter 8, however, it is formulated and agreed in the context of a power relationship. So significant can this imbalance of power be that the contract of employment has been described, for the employee, as 'a command under the guise of an agreement' (Kahn-Freund, 1983:18). Other writers, however, would contend that it aims at a more accommodating and consensual form of employment relationship by providing an agreed framework of rights and obligations for each party. To help promote a more equitable balance of power, employees have a right to information about certain key contractual terms. This can be of assistance in any claim before a court or tribunal (*see* Fig 10.1).

Fig 10.1

WRITTEN STATEMENT OF PARTICULARS OF EMPLOYMENT

1 Names of the employer and employee.

2 Date employment began.

3 Date when continuous employment began (this may include previous employment with that employer; or the consequences of a business transfer; or the consequences of transfers between companies within a group).

4 Scale or rate of remuneration, or the method of calculating remuneration.

5 Intervals at which remuneration is paid.

6 Hours of work and normal working hours.

7 Holiday entitlement, public holidays and holiday pay.

8 Job title or brief job description.

9 Place or places of work.

10 Terms relating to sickness, injury and sick pay.*

11 Pensions and pension schemes.

12 Notice periods to terminate the contract.

13 If employment temporary, how long it is to last; or termination date of the fixed-term contract.

14 Collective agreements which directly affect terms and conditions.

15 Where employees are sent to work outside the UK for more than one month:
   - the period of work outside the UK;
   - the currency in which they will be paid;
   - special benefits available while they work abroad;
   - any terms relating to their return.

16 Disciplinary rules and procedures, unless the employer employs fewer than 20 employees.*

17 Grievance procedure. *

* In these cases it is possible to cross-refer to other documents, provided there is reasonable access and opportunity to read.

The interplay between the law and employment practice can be seen, in the first instance, in the sources of the contract of employment. These are likely to include all or some of the following:

- managerial decisions on terms and conditions of employment;
- collective agreements negotiated between the employer and recognized trade unions;
- workplace rules;
- custom and practice;
- statute law;
- implied terms deriving from common law.
- *Managerial decisions on terms and conditions of employment.* Employers will want to set specific provisions in a contract of employment. They will want an individual employee to carry out specific tasks, work certain hours and meet other obligations. For example, an employer may require mobility from an employee, e.g. to work between a number of sites, or may require him/her to be available for night work. Within certain limitations, discussed below, an employer has considerable freedom to prescribe terms and conditions of employment.
- *Collective agreements negotiated between the employer and recognized trade unions.* These agreements on substantive terms – that is, pay, working time, holidays, etc. – are not usually legally enforceable. They are voluntary agreements. However, the provisions are *incorporated*, as appropriate, into each individual's contract of employment. For example, if a union recognized by the employer for negotiations agrees increases across a salary scale, the rate of pay of each individual employee will then change. The new rate becomes part of the contract.
- *Workplace rules.* An employer may set certain rules of conduct which an employee agrees to. Often these relate to such serious matters as harassment, theft, drunkenness and substance abuse at work.
- *Custom and practice.* Certain customary ways of working can become binding as contractual if they are well-known, reasonable and the employee is certain of the effect of the custom.
- *Statute law.* Statute law can influence contractual terms in a number of ways. It can set minimum conditions which must be complied with, e.g. notice to terminate employment, maternity leave provisions. It may also set general obligations on employers' behaviour in the employment relationship – e.g. equal treatment, provision of a healthy and safe working environment 'as far as is reasonably practicable'. Finally, statute law may directly intervene into the contract of employment. For example, the Equal Pay Act 1970 states:

  if the terms of a contract under which a woman is employed at an establishment in Great Britain do not include (directly or by reference to a collective agreement or otherwise) an equality clause, they shall be deemed to include one (s1).

- *Implied terms deriving from common law.* Common law provides terms implied into contracts of employment. These are in the form of general duties placed upon both employers and individual employees. For example, employers have duties to pay wages and salaries and not to make unauthorized deductions. Employees have duties to obey lawful and reasonable instructions and to be trustworthy.

As indicated above, then, employers have some considerable freedom to set and implement terms and conditions of employment. However, they are subject to certain specific constraints: statute law requirements, common law principles and duties, and, if appropriate, the provisions of collective agreements. In the circumstances of specific employee relations problems all three can interlock.

For example, this interlocking could be evident in an application to an industrial tribunal where there is an allegation of unfair dismissal relating to redundancy. If unfair selection on grounds of race is alleged, then statute law is brought into play. The common law principle of *reasonableness* will be considered – particularly as to whether the employer behaves like a *reasonable employer*. In terms of dismissal, the tribunal would also need to be satisfied that the ex-employee had been treated in accordance with the principles of *natural justice*. Furthermore, issues relating to collective agreements on the handling of redundancies may also be invoked.

How can the contract of employment be changed?

Both the employer and the employee operate this contractual relationship against a backdrop of change: technology develops; product markets decline; working practices need to adapt; pay rates must be varied. The terms of any contract of employment are, therefore, from the start, subject to continual pressure for change – normally to take account of the economic and operational interests of the employer and in unionized organizations to respond to new pay and conditions settlements.

Tension invariably exists, therefore, between these employer interests and those of employees for job and income security. These conflicts of interest can be reconciled through negotiation with trade unions or by an employee's individual agreement to change. In some cases, however, the problems seem intractable. As a consequence, for employers concerned about cost-effectiveness and product and labour market conditions, a key question has to be: 'How can contracts of employment be varied within the law?'

Two courses of action are available:

- to change provisions in existing contracts of employment by agreement with the employee(s) in question;
- to terminate existing contracts with due notice and offer contracts embodying the changed conditions of employment.

Changing existing contracts

Case law, particularly in recent years, has elaborated a number of principles and practices that employers should adhere to. These relate to such issues as consent, unilateral variation, consultation and negotiation, and reasonableness. In brief, an employer must not change terms and conditions

LIBRARY
BISHOP BURTON COLLEGE
BEVERLEY HU17 8QG

unilaterally. He must obtain consent from the employee(s) in question. He is expected to discuss proposals for change either through consultation or negotiating procedures. Three sets of examples are given below to illustrate how, in recent years, courts have approached the issue of contractual change.

First, in one set of circumstances, courts have tended to support applications by employees. This is where the employer has unilaterally varied a contract without agreement. For example, unilaterally imposed pay cuts have been ruled by the House of Lords as repudiatory, or fundamental, breaches of the contract of employment by the employer. In these cases, the court was not concerned with questions of the employer's economic necessity. Their concern was with the terms of the contract, with the failure to achieve consent to the variation and with the employer's repudiation of the original contract. Damages in the form of back-pay were awarded to the plaintiffs.

Second, in some other cases, the courts have favoured employers' concern about flexibility to introduce change. For example, in one important case the adaptation to new methods and techniques by employees has clearly been determined as an expectation in the contract of employment. In this case, arising from the computerization of certain clerical and administrative tasks in the Inland Revenue, the High Court judge commented that employees could not conceivably have a right to preserve their working obligations completely unchanged during their employment. They could reasonably be expected, after proper training, to adapt to new techniques. All that would happen with computerization was that jobs would remain 'recognizably the same but done in a different way'.

Finally, another set of cases concerns those circumstances where an employee might resign if an employer insists on a particular contractual change. The employee can allege constructive dismissal before an industrial tribunal. Critical to the ex-employee's success will be whether or not the employer breached, fundamentally, the contract of employment. In the case of an unagreed imposed pay cut, the employee would probably be successful. However, if the employer is found not to be changing the terms of the contract but giving new 'lawful and reasonable instructions' then the employee is unlikely to succeed.

Offering new contracts

The alternative strategy that might be adopted by an employer is to terminate existing contracts of employment with due notice, i.e. what is appropriate for each individual employee. It is then open to the employer to offer a new contract incorporating the desired changes. The employee is free to accept or not.

If the employee does not accept the new contract then the dismissal can be tested in an industrial tribunal under the framework of unfair dismissal law. Tribunals have usually accepted 'business need' as 'some other substantial reason' for dismissal – provided that the employer adduces evidence to show why the changes were required. Reasonableness in handling the whole process is also expected – with the employer showing that the employee's interests had been considered and that reasonable procedures had been followed before the employer insisted on the adoption of the changes.

From the preceding discussion, it is evident that employers in handling change are confronted by a complex network of factors: their own economic and operational objectives; the interests of employees for job and income security; statutory employment protection requirements; and the principles relating to contractual variation which have been elaborated under common law. Each individual tribunal/court case will be considered on its own facts and will be tested against the precedents of previous case law and the interpretation of statute law in the present case.

Although there is no failsafe process in respect of contractual change, it is possible to summarize best practice guidelines:

- Plan the process of change.
- Decide on the nature and scale of contractual changes.
- Avoid unilateral variation.
- Decide whether existing contracts are to be varied or, if appropriate, terminated and new ones offered.
- Give information on the proposed changes to each affected individual employee.
- Be prepared to discuss, consult and/or negotiate.
- Try to obtain the employee's consent.
- Be prepared to justify contractual changes against the organization's operational and economic requirements.
- Anticipate some of the arguments that might be put at a court or tribunal in terms of, for example, reasonableness or business need.

TERMINATION OF EMPLOYMENT

When an employment relationship ends a number of factors that have been explored earlier in this chapter can been seen as interacting. These derive from the interests of the employer, from the interests of the employee, from the nature of the contractual relationship and from standards of public policy. Illustrations of these can be summarized as follows:

The interests of the employer
- The need for a cost-effective organization.
- Employees who perform effectively.
- Acceptable standards of conduct by employees.
- Operational flexibility and responsiveness.
- The ability to manage change.

The interests of the employee
- Protection of job security.
- Non-discriminatory treatment.
- Fair treatment and fair decisions.
- Income security.
- Workplace safety.

The nature of the employment relationship

- The exercise of control by the employer.
- The balance of power.
- Differences of interest.
- Accommodation and agreement between the employer and the employee.
- Public policy.
- Equal treatment.
- Natural justice.
- Fair disciplinary procedures.
- Reasonableness of decisions.
- Consent to change.

Nowadays, in any unfair dismissal application before an industrial tribunal many of these issues will, implicitly or explicitly, be reflected in both the presentation of cases and also the cross-examination. The tribunal will then make its decision on the facts of the case, particularly having regard to the standards of public policy. It is only in the past 25 years, however, that this has been possible. It was only in 1971 that the concept of *unfair dismissal* was enacted. Prior to that date, most employees were vulnerable to unfair termination of employment.

Setting standards of public policy

During the 1960s, various proposals for improvements in the legal protections for employees were being put forward. One influential voice was the Royal Commission on Trade Unions and Employers' Associations – the Donovan Commission. In its 1968 Report, it stated:

> there is ... a very general feeling, shared by employers as well as trade unions, that the present situation is unsatisfactory and it was reflected in the submissions of many who gave evidence to us.

The Donovan Commission's review coincided with the publication by the (then) Ministry of Labour of an advisory council's report on dismissal procedures. This drew unfavourable comparisons between Britain and other industrialized countries in terms of procedural arrangements for contesting arbitrary dismissal. It stated that 'in other countries more elaborate concepts of the rights of employer and employee have been developed.'

Indeed, in the early 1960s, the International Labour Organisation had found that in most of the 68 countries they investigated there were provisions by statute or otherwise for protection from unjust or arbitrary dismissal. Subsequently, in 1963, the ILO published a Recommendation on Termination of Employment to which the British government subscribed.

In Britain, then, until 1971, employees were vulnerable to arbitrary and unjustified treatment by their employer – with only limited redress. The available legal redress was at common law and was generally inadequate.

The general legal position of employees was that, as long as the employer gave proper notice, under the contract, to terminate the employment, then he was able to sack the employee for whatever reason he wished. No obligations were imposed upon the employer either to provide reasons for the dismissal or to justify the dismissal. The only remedy available to an employee was to claim wrongful dismissal in the ordinary courts.

Wrongful dismissal is a relatively weak form of redress. Normally, it is alleged in circumstances where the employer gives inadequate or no notice to terminate the contract of employment. The employee may receive damages from the employer – generally limited to pay for the appropriate period of notice. The Donovan Report commented:

> '... beyond this, the employee has no legal claim at common law, whatever hardship he suffers as a result of his dismissal. Even if the way in which he is dismissed constituted an imputation on his honesty and his ability to get another job is correspondingly reduced, he cannot – except through an action for defamation – obtain any redress' (para 522).

As a result of these criticisms and the subsequent debate, a bipartisan political consensus emerged in favour of the principle of limited protection against unfair dismissal. The legislation was introduced by a Conservative government. It has been accepted by subsequent Labour and Conservative governments – although with some modifications, particularly in relation to access. These modifications have reflected commitment to either the *employee protection* or the *free market* model of employment law.

Unfair dismissal protection is available to all employees who have the necessary service qualifications, currently two years' length of service, although this is being challenged in the courts as unfair sex discrimination. There are no such qualifications if the dismissal relates to an automatically unfair reason. The only remedy, for short service employees, may still be a wrongful dismissal claim – if applicable. (*See* Fig 10.2 on p 258.)

Although the majority of employers may aim to behave fairly towards employees, the potential for using arbitrary treatment, victimization and for ignoring the principles of natural justice is still largely present in the legal regime governing the employment relationship.

Arguably, in certain sectors of employment today, the situation does not appear to have moved on much since the beginning of the nineteenth century where 'the legal regime in a factory could fairly be described as that of a private legislative kingdom in which the employer was sovereign, judge, jury and executioner' (Clark, 1970). The employee is vulnerable not just to loss of job but also to loss of income, loss of status and, possibly, loss of reputation.

THE ENFORCEMENT OF PUBLIC POLICY STANDARDS

The individual employment rights cited in the preceding sections of this chapter, were enacted to establish standards of good practice and, accordingly, modify the behaviour of employers, particularly in the employment relationship. Clearly, behaviour will not change if enforcement of these rights is seen to be weak.

Fig 10.2

TESTING THE FAIRNESS OF DISMISSALS

Industrial tribunals, which hear unfair dismissal claims, consider the following issues in assessing fairness.

Reason

- Is the dismissal for a 'fair' reason, i.e. capability, misconduct, redundancy, a statutory bar on employment, or some other substantial reason?
- Is the dismissal for an 'automatically unfair' reason, e.g. sex, race and disability discrimination, or is the dismissal on the grounds of trade union membership or the voicing of certain health and safety matters?

Reasonableness

Whether in the circumstances, including the size and administrative resources of the undertaking, the employer acted reasonably or unreasonably in treating it as a sufficient reason for dismissing the employee; and that question shall be determined in accordance with equity and the substantial merits of the case (Employment Rights Act 1996, s98 (4)).

Procedural fairness

- Compliance with the guidance in the ACAS Code of Practice: Disciplinary Practice and Procedures in Employment (1977).
- Compliance with the organization's disciplinary procedure, if one exists.

There are two ways in which enforcement of these public policy standards will be reviewed:

- the political perspectives of the legislators; and
- the effectiveness of those existing procedures which provide remedies.

Political perspectives of legislators

There are probably three significant elements in this area: the universal application of the standards; the question of whose interests influence public policy enforcement; and political commitment to effective remedies.

Much individual employment law is designed to protect employees against discrimination, infringements of natural justice, arbitrary treatment and victimization. It might be presumed, therefore, that such standards would be available universally. This has not always been so. Remedies available under sex and race discrimination law, certainly, have been available to any employee, self-employed person or contractor irrespective of the number of hours worked each week or the length of service. However, access to unfair dismissal proceedings has been limited by both the number of hours worked (until 1995) and by length of service, though this is being challenged.

The reason for this is associated with the second factor – whose interests influence public policy enforcement? The Major government resisted the extension of unfair dismissal and redundancy rights to part-time employees who worked less than sixteen hours, in three court hearings, in the High Court, the Court of Appeal and the House of Lords. Eventually, the House of Lords ruled that such qualifying provisions were discriminatory against women, who were preponderant in this group. The government's arguments had revolved around two sets of economic issues: the discouragement of job creation and the burdens imposed on business by further regulation. The social justice issues of employment protection and fair treatment were seen as lower order matters.

It can never be presumed that employee interests are of paramount concern for legislators. There will always be a tension between, on the one hand, these standards of social justice and good employment practice and, on the other hand, the economic consequences for employers of employment protection. This tension is also evident in the debates about the European Union's Social Charter Action Programme (*see* Chapter 8). One result, at that level, was the commitment in the 1994 EU White Paper to consider cost factors in relation to any further employment protection measures. Whether this constitutes a balanced approach or an erosion of employee protection is a matter of debate.

Political commitment to effective remedies is inevitably conditioned by a government's attitude to the relative importance of employer and employee interests. Government can, in fact, use two complementary measures. First, it can provide both enforcement procedures and specific remedies for individual applicants. Second, it can use its economic power to ensure compliance with public policy standards.

The procedures available for aggrieved individual employees will be considered more fully below. As far as remedies are concerned, these tend to be financial – in the form of compensation. Until 1993, there was a ceiling on compensation levels. However, this was ruled by the European Court of Justice to be unlawful in sex discrimination cases (*see* the case study in Chapter 9). As a result, the ceilings were removed in both sex and race discrimination cases. However, they still remain in ordinary unfair dismissal cases. Recent median levels of compensation are £1923 for unfair dismissal cases, £1425 for sex discrimination cases and £1185 for race discrimination cases (*Employment Gazette*, 1993).

It has been argued that compensation is an insufficient remedy given the loss of job, income, benefits and status experienced by the former employee. Technically, of course, an industrial tribunal can order the reinstatement of an unfairly dismissed ex-employee. However, if the employer objects, then the only available sanction is to increase compensation.

The use of government economic power can be seen in respect of the adoption of *contract compliance*. In using its purchasing power, government and local authorities could require the providers of goods and services to give assurances that they are complying with, for example, equal opportunities policy in respect of sex and race discrimination.

Such steps were taken, for example, by the United States Federal Government, initially in the 1940s, to contribute to the slow process of eradicating race discrimination. Similar measures were introduced in Britain on a voluntary basis by some local authorities in the 1980s – covering sex and race discrimination.

The general approach of the Thatcher/Major Conservative governments was hostile to these measures. For example, when initiating its compulsory competitive tendering (CCT) policies it was indicated that non-commercial considerations should not be used to determine the award of contracts. Recent evidence from the Equal Opportunities Commission (1995) has pointed to a weakening of equal opportunities as a result of CCT.

Effective procedures?

Standards set in employment law can be enforced at two levels: within the workplace and through the legal processes of the court and tribunal system.

At workplace level, the principal arrangements for implementing, processing and monitoring standards are, as appropriate, equal opportunities policies and disciplinary and dismissal procedures. Both of these areas of employment practice are supported by statutory codes of practice which have been published by the Equal Opportunities Commission, the Commission for Racial Equality and the Advisory Conciliation and Arbitration Service respectively.

Over 90 per cent of establishments have a disciplinary and dismissals procedure (Workplace Industrial Relations Survey, 1990). Evidence about the extent of equal opportunities policies is more sketchy. WIRS reported that about a third of private sector companies collected information on the gender, ethnic and age mix of their workforce. Such data is the first critical step towards effective monitoring; and it is a prerequisite to any decisions on modifications that need to be made to policies or practices.

It is important to remember, furthermore, that this workplace stage can be supplemented by independent assistance, possibly in the form of investigations, from outside organizations like the Equal Opportunities Commission, the Commission for Racial Equality, and the Advisory Conciliation and Arbitration Service.

The legal processes are, of course, available to individual employees. Normally, this will involve an application to an industrial tribunal about a discrimination allegation, dismissal or certain breach of contract issues. The effectiveness of this form of complaint can be considered under a number of headings. The principal concerns that have been raised by various commentators are as follows:

● *The characteristics of the tribunal process.* When they first became responsible for employment rights in 1972, industrial tribunals were seen as offering 'cheapness, accessibility, freedom from technicality, expedition and expert knowledge of a particular subject'. These characteristics, originally expounded by the Franks Committee in 1957 in respect of tribunals generally, have been used frequently as a yardstick to evaluate the current effectiveness of industrial tribunal operation.

Various researchers have commented on the extent to which industrial tribunals have now diverged from these original characteristics (Dickens *et al*, 1985; Leonard, 1987; Lewis and Clarke, 1993). In an extensive survey of unfair dismissal applications it was reported that:

Although the tribunals were found to display the Franks characteristics, the extent to which they were displayed was found to be constrained by the quasi-court nature of the ITs and their location within a legal framework involving the ordinary courts. (Dickins *et al*, 1985)

Clearly, then, there are serious questions about the extent to which the tribunal process can discourage applicants who are seeking quick and simple justice – particularly in the less legally complex unfair dismissal claims. Exploration of this issue led Lewis and Clarke (1993) to propose the option of arbitration for those applicants who preferred it.

- *The insistence on individual application.* The insistence on individual application can cause some concern and difficulties for individual applicants in discrimination cases. Invariably, discriminatory practices affect more than one person and so patterns need to be established.

- *The balance of resources.* The balance of resources between individual employees or ex-employees and the employer is uneven. Although an employer may be concerned about the costs involved in an industrial tribunal hearing, he can bear the cost of legal representation more easily than an employee, who is not a trade union member. Legal aid is not available to tribunal applicants.

- *The standards used by industrial tribunals.* Various comments have been made about the standards used by industrial tribunals. For example, in deciding reasonableness, tribunals are not using their own test. They determine it by reference to 'the range of reasonable employers'. As Anderman (1986) has commented:

    the net effect of this approach is to require industrial tribunals to adopt a standard of fairness which reflects the lower reaches of acceptable managerial practice, rather than to allow tribunals to establish standards which reflect their view of a more objective standard of fair industrial practice.

JUSTIFYING INDIVIDUAL EMPLOYMENT RIGHTS

The framework of employment law considered in this chapter reflects the *employment protection/social justice* model described in Chapter 9. The appropriateness of this model has been at the centre of political debate for the past 20 years or so.

This debate is complex. It does not conform to a conventional left–right divide. A few on the free-market right wing of the Conservative Party argue in favour of the removal of much statutory employment protection legislation. It is said to be a constraint to economic success. They would leave the contract of employment as the only regulatory mechanism containing mutual obligations. However, a broad political consensus of opinion favours some framework of protective employment law. The debate among those subscribing to this view is about degree. In part, it concerns the extent to which such legislation is, and should be, a constraint and a cost upon employers.

Various factors have been highlighted regarding the merits or otherwise of employment protection legislation. These can be summarized as follows:

Social factors

● A democratic society should have standards of fair and equal treatment for its citizens both out of work and in work.

● Social attitudes and expectations change. To help meet these changing expectations legislative action is necessary to tackle traditional attitudes, prejudice and stereotyping.

● Regulation and standards are necessary to ensure that all participants in the employment relationship understand what is expected of them.

Economic factors

● The implementation of fair and equal treatment can improve the quality of working relationships and so make the organization productive.

● Employment protection legislation ensures that employers generally provide terms and conditions comparable with other employers. This ensures that in competitive markets some employers do not achieve their market share by exploitation of their workforce.

● Each employment right has a price tag deriving from the cost of raising standards, the administrative costs of implementation and monitoring and the possible costs of dealing with complaints.

● The cost of employment protection legislation is a deterrent to employment creation.

● Employment protection legislation limits an employer's flexibility in responding to new initiatives, in introducing technological change, and in changing terms and conditions of employment and, therefore, increases an employer's unit labour costs.

Exercise 10.6

Employment protection

If it is accepted that some framework of employment protection law is required in a democratic society, then each individual citizen should think about the following questions. Consider your own answers.

1 What social and economic purposes should such employment protection achieve?

2 What obligations should be placed upon employees and employers?

3 How much weight should be given to employers' concerns about cost-effectiveness and flexible working practices and conditions of employment?

4 What procedures should be adopted for effectively enforcing these individual rights?

SUMMARY AND CONCLUSION

Various aspects of public policy have been examined. Two broad themes have been considered. First, the standards enacted in law are designed in many respects to balance the interests of employees and employers. While this law is designed to protect employees and promote some concept of social justice in the workplace, it also attempts to take account of employers' interests.

This balancing of interests is often most noticeable when employers seek to make changes in contractual terms. Provided they adhere to the principles set out in case law which protect employees' interests, then, the courts will generally confirm an employer's ability to make such changes.

Even in areas of employment protection where employee interests seem to be paramount, there are opportunities for employer interests to be considered. For example, in respect of equal treatment under sex discrimination law, an employer is able to put forward 'justifications' for indirect discrimination. In respect of dismissals and redundancies, the concept of 'fair treatment' still enables an employer to take action in his interest.

The second broad theme is that individual employment law exists in a state of continual flux. This arises from a number of causes. Social attitudes change. The economic demands of employers vary. Different political ideologies are predominant at different times. Case law sets new interpretations and standards. Judges may try to accommodate the law to changing social circumstances. The economic balance of power between employers and employees can change as a result of both economic and political factors.

Despite this state of flux, certain principles and standards of public policy are preserved, e.g. fairness, equal treatment, reasonableness. These will be interpreted in the circumstances of each case and in the changing social, economic and political context.

CHAPTER 11

Collective interests and the law

INTRODUCTION

Historically, working people have organized themselves, either informally or formally, for various purposes. For example, early nineteenth century trade unionism is littered with *ad hoc* groups of workers who petitioned their employers about low pay, hazardous working conditions or long hours. These groups often disbanded quickly. Occasionally, such a group might form the embryo of a more formal, continuing organization – a trade union. Two principal constraints prevented both informal groups and the formal union organizations from becoming effective: employer resistance and legal prohibitions.

These early examples of collective work group pressure and representation find clear echoes in contemporary employment relations. Employers might still restrict collective representation. Legal rights and obligations in respect of collective representation are still subject to political debate.

FOCUS AND SCOPE

This chapter will explore:

- the continuing significance of collective interests in employment relations;
- the influence of law on the ways employers manage their staff;
- the principles underpinning the law on collective representation at work;
- the importance of enforcement processes.

LEARNING OBJECTIVES

Once you have read through this chapter and completed the associated exercises you should be able to:

- **understand the arguments for and against setting up systems of collective representation, unionized or not;**
- **advise your employer on possible forms of collective representation and the implications for your organization;**
- **understand the factors involved in regulating industrial action and providing a right to strike.**

ARE COLLECTIVE INTERESTS STILL IMPORTANT?

One theme of this book is that the character of the employment relationship can only be properly understood if both individual and collective dimensions are recognized. To deny the existence of collectivism is a mistake. It takes many forms – both formal and informal.

Work itself is after all a social, collaborative activity which produces some common interests among groups of working people. Furthermore, on entering the employment relationship, people import into it a considerable range of social ties and the legacy of their social experiences. The social – the group or the collective – dimension is, therefore, inherently important in various ways to the overwhelming majority of employees.

By its very nature, the employment relationship is concerned with issues that affect both individuals and groups of people. Any single issue is likely to reflect both dimensions. This can be seen as we look at the practical steps necessary for managing redundancies.

- *Notice*. Has due notice of the proposed redundancies been given to the trade union or to employee representatives?

- *Alternative policies*. Have alternative policies been considered in relation to each affected individual member of staff? Has there been consultation about these proposals with either union or employee representatives?

- *The selection criteria*. What are they? Are they fair in terms of employment law? Have they been discussed and agreed with union or employee representatives? How does each individual measure up in relation to them?

- *Handling the redundancies*. Has there been consultation with union or employee representatives about the overall handling of the redundancies and also about individual cases? Has the consultation been 'with a view to agreement'?

- *Redundancy pay*. Is it proposed to pay merely the statutory minimum? Has there been consultation about any enhancements? What are the implications for individual employees?

It is simplistic, then, to talk of *individualism* replacing *collectivism*. What can change over any period of time is the balance between the two dimensions. This balance may be influenced by a number of factors – e.g. prevailing economic conditions, the impact of technological change on job design, employer preferences and government policy.

For example, during recent Conservative governments, there was a political drive to emphasize individualism. The expression of collective interests was marginalized as far as possible. Individual performance-related pay heightened the individual dimension. Withdrawal of trade union recognition made collective representation more difficult to express. Employers were encouraged to withdraw from collective bargaining and to introduce personal contracts.

Employer preferences are varied and complex. Small and medium-sized non-union firms will tend to be individualistic in their employment relations. It is rare, however, to find large companies that have constructed coherent employee relations systems that deny any collectivism and promote entirely individually based arrangements. However, there are exceptions.

The most notable is IBM, which has operated a highly individualist employment relations model. Its approach comprises two elements: a strategic perspective and a view that employees should be 'looked after' by management.

Implicitly, IBM sees in the concept of unionisation the assumption that the interests of the employed would inevitably be neglected by the employer in the absence of trade union representation. IBM does not accept this, arguing instead that its record shows that it is possible for a company to be successful, to be managed successfully, and for its employees' best interests to be a central part of that. (Bassett, 1986)

Among the elements of the IBM approach, described in the mid-1980s are:

1 *Contextual factors*: detailed and long-range manpower planning; guaranteed job security; reliance on full-time permanent employment.

2 *Conditions of employment*: single-status conditions of employment for all employees; within centrally determined salary ranges, individual pay recommended by an employee's manager taking into account merit and performance indicators.

3 *The processes of employment relations*:
   - Communications with employees are the responsibility of line managers.
   - Managers receive 40 days per year training on human resource management – covering, for example, performance appraisal, career prospects, etc.
   - Each manager is responsible for small groups of staff, between 9 and 17.
   - A biennial internal opinion survey is undertaken throughout the organization, covering the employees' evaluation of the company, their satisfaction with their jobs, their rating of their manager, their views on their duties and responsibilities.
   - Two complaint systems exist, on business issues and on management decisions, with the emphasis on managers resolving any problems.
   - Trade unions are not recognized for either individual representation or collective bargaining.

Such an employee relations system will probably be tested at times of organizational crisis – that is, when product market problems arise, when technological change is accelerated, when redundancies are necessary. These changes can expose the contradictions inherent in individualized and paternal employee relations systems. For example, how is job security best protected? How are corporate interests and those of individual employees reconciled at times of crisis?

Arguably, then, no employing organization can ignore the interplay between these two dimensions. If it is an organization that approaches its employment relations strategically and systematically, then it is more likely to consider such issues as:

- the balance of individualism and collectivism required within the organization's human resource management and employee relations policies;
- the extent to which individual interests, commitment and performance can contribute to organizational effectiveness;
- the extent to which collective interests can be harnessed towards organizational goals;
- the procedures that could be used to express collective interests – whether the organization is unionized or not.

| Exercise 11.1 | **Employee representation** |

1 Look at the work group of which you are a member. Consider the ways, if any, in which this group makes representations to your employer about terms and conditions of employment, and/or about the ways in which your work is carried out.

2 What views does both your work group and your employer have about the value of such representative arrangements?

HOW ARE COLLECTIVE INTERESTS EXPRESSED?

The collective interests of working people may be expressed either on an *ad hoc* basis or through some form of continuing organization. It is the organized expression of such interests that will be considered in this chapter.

Employees' interests may be expressed on three levels within employee relations using different processes.

- *An individual grievance to the employer*. This may concern an aspect of an employee's conditions of employment, e.g. grading, or the failure of the employer to meet some statutory obligation, e.g. maternity rights. Although the complaint may be specific to an individual, it could well concern a policy that also affects other staff. Consequently, there can be repercussions on the wider group of employees.

- *Consultation with employee or trade union representatives*. This may concern certain conditions of employment, e.g. health and safety, redundancy, technical change.

- *Negotiation with a trade union*. This may concern certain terms and conditions of employment, e.g. pay, hours of work, holidays.

The legal framework in which these three processes – grievance handling, consultation and negotiation – exist will be considered later in this chapter. Here, we will explore two background factors: employer attitudes to these processes, focusing around the concept of *the right to manage*; and the extent to which the various forms of employee involvement and participation reflect different power balances between employers and employees.

The right to manage and employee participation

Before deciding on whether or not to set up arrangements to deal with employees collectively, employers will have in mind a number of critical issues – principally, the balance of power and control in employee relations, and the freedom for an employer to pursue his economic objectives. These issues are often encapsulated into the short hand phrase, *the right to manage*.

While the phrase can be dismissed as part of the rhetoric of management – for example, when faced with a challenge to its power by either trade unions or legislation – it does draw attention to a number of important questions that need to be addressed:

- Should employers have unfettered power to make decisions because of their economic ownership of the organization?
- To what extent should an employer's decisions be influenced by the views of employees?
- Are there specific issues over which employees should have some influence? Are these issues those which are directly related to employment, e.g. pay, hours and working conditions; or those which indirectly affect an individual employment, e.g. introduction of technological change, changes in products or services provided, closures of parts of the organization?
- If employees are to be involved in influencing management decisions, should this be by negotiation – where agreement is reached with union representatives – or by consultation – where, after discussion, management still retains the right to decide?

Exercise 11.2 *Consider these questions on the right to manage and decide what your views are.*

1 The forms of employee participation are usually considered in terms of the degree to which they might modify management's exercise of power. Some forms enable management to retain a considerable degree of power and so exercise 'the right to manage' in a relatively unconstrained manner. Others are based on the notion of power sharing.

2 A spectrum of employee participation is described in Fig 11.1. In outlining these forms, it starts with those where the right to manage is largely retained; and concludes with those that emphasize power sharing.

Exercise 11.3 *1 Look at employee relations in an organization known to you and find out which of the forms of participation (see Fig 11.1 opposite) exist.*

2 How effective are they seen to be by employees and by the employer?

Despite the rhetoric of managerial prerogatives, some employers report that positive economic benefits can accrue from employee participation.

For example, in an analysis of the 1990 Workplace Industrial Relations Survey data, William Brown (1994) found that non-union companies have generally not adopted the best practice standards of human resource management. They are characterized by 'a tired old world of unrepresented labour'. Only unionized companies adopt best practice. He concludes that promoting collective organization and bargaining is the best way to secure increased productivity and to control the growth in pay. Certainly, this analysis reflects other findings of employers' attitudes towards trade unions (Batstone and Gourlay, 1986; Daniel, 1987; Willey, 1986).

Fig 11.1

FORMS OF EMPLOYEE PARTICIPATION

- *Financial participation.* Such systems are likely to provide individual employees with limited influence over corporate policy. They are more likely to be seen as providing additional remuneration through employee share ownership or profit sharing.

- *Communication systems.* These are likely to be one-way channels of communication like videos, Email, notice boards, conference presentations and team briefings. Their purpose is to disclose management information. (Employers are required in law to disclose certain information to employees.)

- *Operational participation.* This deals with ways to improve service delivery and production processes, through working parties, quality circles or team briefings that are two-way. Management responsiveness to any proposals will vary.

- *Consultation.* This process can be found in various forms. It can be pseudo-consultation, often about trivial issues. Here management is unlikely to be influenced. Alternatively, there may be genuine consultation resulting in changes to policies and achieving some consensus. (Employers are required in law to consult employees about certain matters.)

- *Negotiations.* Usually, negotiations about terms and conditions of employment take place where an employer agrees to recognize trade unions. The outcome is a joint agreement between the two parties. (There are no legal obligations on employers to recognize unions.)

- *Co-determination.* This kind of statutory framework exists in the works council system in Germany, where there is joint decision making between employers and employee representatives on specified employee relations issues.

Legal entitlements are discussed later in this chapter.

The significance of employee participation in its wider sense was also outlined in a recent report in the United States. In surveying the small number of high performance workplaces, the Commission on the Future of Worker–Management Relations (May 1994) pointed to a number of issues of relevance to Britain:

- Interest in participation can be expected to grow in future years as the education of the workforce rises, technology creates more opportunities to share information and delegate decision-making authority and the pressures of competition require continuous improvement in productivity and quality.

- Where employee participation is sustained over time and integrated with other policies and practices, the evidence suggests that it generally improves economic performance.

- Many managers, workers and union representatives believe employee participation and labour-management co-operation are essential to being competitive in their industries and to meeting employees' interests and expectations.

COLLECTIVE INTERESTS: THE CONTEMPORARY DEBATE

During the early years of the 1990s, a number of factors began to coalesce to create the first significant debate for over 15 years on how the collective interests of employees might be represented and accommodated in employment relations. The principal contributions to this debate derive from the trade union movement, employer approaches to employee relations, employee attitudes and concerns, existing statutory rights and the impact of European Union law. Each one of these will be discussed.

Trade unionism

Survey evidence shows a continuing decline in both trade union membership and trade union recognition (Millward *et al*, WIRS, 1992). The reasons for this are complex. There has been a decline in employment in a traditional heartland of trade unionism – manufacturing industry. Furthermore, employment in the public sector has been subject to major structural changes and fragmentation arising from, for example, compulsory competitive tendering, the establishment of NHS trusts, the creation of agencies in the civil service. A consequence has been some reduction in the proportion of the workforce in union membership. It now stands at 48 per cent (Millward *et al*, WIRS, 1992).

These downward trends in membership have been compounded by two further factors: employer resistance and a constraining legal framework. Trade unions have had difficulty in making successful recognition claims in developing sectors of the economy. *Win rates* are estimated at about 25 per cent of claims. Furthermore, there has been no legal remedy available if an employer either refuses recognition for collective bargaining or rescinds existing recognition agreements.

One consequence of the considerable expansion of non-union workplaces has been the search by the Trade Union Congress for a credible recognition and representation strategy. In 1995, a Task Group Report was adopted by the Congress. This explored the levels of representation – both collective and individual – and also considered the possibilities of consultation and collective bargaining. In a political climate that was anticipating the election of a Labour government, the report was seen as a means of influencing future legislation.

Employers' approaches

It is difficult to determine a predominant view held by employers. Those which are most concerned about representational issues are larger companies. Their preferred form of representation tends not to be union-based collective bargaining.

Survey evidence has shown the slow but continuing implementation of employee involvement and participation initiatives at the instigation of employers. The focus of these has tended to be towards operational matters rather than consultation about terms and conditions of employment. For example, quality circles and team briefings have tended to attract some employers because they can be associated with cost-effectiveness. Such approaches to employee involvement have been commended and encouraged in, for example, the Code of Practice on Employee Involvement and Participation drafted by the Institute of Personnel and Development (1994).

Some multinational employers have also been establishing arrangements for information disclosure and consultation under the European Works Council Directive, despite the British opt-out from the Social Chapter. Among the motives for setting up such arrangements are consistency of practice across the organization and the preference to achieve a wider understanding by employees of business developments.

Employee attitudes and concerns

Employee attitudes to collective representation are complex. However, two sets of evidence suggest certain trends. The first relates to employees' experiences at work; and the second is their attitude to unions.

By the mid-1990s, many employees' experiences of employment were encapsulated in such terms as job insecurity, stress, overwork, exploitation, vulnerability. Of course, not all employees experienced these phenomena. Nevertheless, evidence suggests that such experiences were sufficiently widespread to provoke debates about the quality of employment relations.

These characteristics might be thought to create conditions under which collective action, and particularly trade union membership, might grow. However, other factors might constrain this: the lack of any legal rights to representation; employer hostility; employees' sense of their vulnerability to dismissal and victimization, despite certain statutory protections; and, in the absence of unions' recognition, doubts by employees about the ability of unions to articulate their interests and achieve improvements.

Although trade unions, therefore, have found difficulties in gaining recognition rights and so demonstrating their utility to members or potential members, they are increasingly seen in a more favourable light. There is some concern that decollectivization has gone too far. For example, opinion poll evidence (MORI and Gallup, 1993) suggests a more positive public view of trade unions. Three out of four people thought trade unions were essential to protect workers' interests; 55 per cent believed the balance of power in industry had tilted much too far in the direction of management (Taylor, 1994).

Existing statutory rights

In tandem with the attitudes and developments described above is a growing recognition that in the light of recent developments, the existing piecemeal statutory framework of employee participation rights could form the nucleus of a more coherent system.

These developments were necessary to implement fully European union law. In 1995, information and consultation rights in relation to collective redundancies and transfers of undertakings were extended to employee representatives, rather than being restricted to representatives of recognized independent trade unions. Likewise, in 1996, under health and safety law, similar rights are to be enacted.

Such developments will create in non-union as well as in unionized organizations a permanent statutory consultation forum. (The specific details of such legislation are discussed in the next section of this chapter.) It is arguable that this could provide an embryonic works council system for information disclosure, consultation and, if agreed with the employer, negotiations on pay and conditions.

European social policy

European social policy has had an impact on British employee relations and conditioned the debate on collective representation in several respects.

1 The general philosophical approach of the European Union reflects commitment to the participation of the *social partners* – that is, representative employer and trade union organizations – in its supra-national policy-making processes. For example, the UNICE, CEEP and ETUC are consulted in the drafting of Directives, e.g. on Working Time or on European Works Councils.

2 Certain Directives require employee participation at organization level in specific circumstances. The principal examples are the Directives on Collective Redundancies and on Transfers of Undertakings. These require the giving of information by employers and consultation with employee representatives 'with a view to agreement'. In addition the Directive on European Works Councils (1994) covering specific multinational companies provides for the development of information disclosure and consultation arrangements (*see* Fig 11.2).

3 As indicated earlier, when the European Court of Justice ruled that Britain was not complying with the Directives on Collective Redundancies and on Transfers of Undertakings, a change in law was required to provide consultation with employee representatives.

Can there be a consensus on employee participation?

The discussion in this section has illustrated the wide range of opinions held by employers, employees, trade unions and government about employee participation. This is likely to be a growing area of political debate. Consequently, the key question is whether a consensus can be fully achieved on the steps to be taken.

To answer this, the different interests and objectives of the key actors in employee relations have to be addressed. These have been explored earlier and are summarized below.

Employers' responses to employee representation tend to stress three factors: the overriding importance of economic considerations, limited constraint on the right to manage and the need for flexibility. For example, the Institute of Personnel and Development Code, in outlining the aims of employee participation and involvement, highlights the success of the organization; the improvement of performance and productivity; and the organization's ability better to meet the needs of its customers and adapt to changing market requirements and hence maximize its future prospects and the prospects of those who work in it.

Fig 11.2

THE EUROPEAN WORKS COUNCIL DIRECTIVE 1994

- Concerns information disclosure and consultation in specified multinational enterprises.

- Covers 14 EU states (except the UK because of the Social Chapter 'opt out') and Iceland, Norway and Liechtenstein (members of the EEA).

- Must be implemented by 22 September 1996.

- The specified 'Community-scale undertaking' must have:
  - at least 1000 employees in the countries concerned; and
  - at least 150 employees in each of two or more of those countries.

  (Part-time employees are included in the calculations.)

- It broadly requires either:
  - the establishment of a European Works Council comprising central management and employee representatives; or
  - an information and consultation procedure.

- Pre-existing agreements in force in undertakings on the implementation date are exempt. (In November 1994, 41 voluntary EWC-type agreements were known to be in force (Hall, 1995) and further examples continue to be reported in both British and foreign MNEs.)

- The purpose of the EWC is to discuss transnational issues.

- The Directive is to be reviewed within five years by the Commission.

(The detailed provisions of this legislation are explored in Hall, 1995.)

The right to manage and employee participation are theoretically incompatible. However, some employers are prepared to concede some limitation in their managerial freedom to achieve other objectives. It could be merely to promote greater understanding of business conditions through communication channels. In other circumstances, it could be to achieve compliance with managerial policies as a result of consultation. If collective bargaining is used, it could be designed to obtain formal consent to jointly determined policies.

Flexibility relates to the nature and form of employee representation. For example, in its response to the extension of employee representation on redundancies and business transfers, the Confederation of British Industry (1995) commented favourably on the Conservative government's approach. This was seen as flexible. It did not prescribe a uniform set of arrangements across industry. It allowed organizations to tailor the introduction of consultation to suit their own workplace circumstances and to accommodate the new requirements into established arrangements.

From the perspective of employees and trade unions, economic success, power sharing and flexibility are likely to be regarded as important ingredients in processes of employee representation. However, other objectives will also be important: employee protection and the achievement of both job and income security.

Underlying these objectives are a range of specific values – fairness, the avoidance of unfair discrimination, victimization and arbitrary treatment. The divergence between employee and employer attitudes may not be wide – particularly in those large organizations that try to adhere to the standards set out in statutory and voluntary codes of good practice.

As far as the form of employee representation is concerned, employees and, particularly, trade unions are likely to be concerned about the following issues: continuity of the representation arrangements, the independence of the representatives and the degree of power sharing or genuine consultation.

For example, in discussing the impact of the European Court of Justice ruling on consultation in collective redundancies and the transfers of undertakings, the Trade Union Congress emphasized that representatives must be independent of employers and that representation must be part of some continuous system of employee participation and not specific to, for example, particular redundancies.

Trade unions would also be concerned to ensure that the character of employee participation was effective. This means that there would be shared decision making with the employer or genuine influence on managerial decision making.

COLLECTIVE REPRESENTATION: SOME LEGAL ISSUES

This section will review the factors that underpin the legal framework governing collective representation. This framework is significantly affected by government policy. In Chapter 8, three models were outlined: the *free collective bargaining* model; the *free labour market* model; and the *employee protection* or *social justice* model. The adoption of a particular model indicates a government's approach to collectivism in various policy measures: employers' duties to inform and consult; collective bargaining rights; trade union power; the balance between a statutory and voluntary approach for the promotion of employee representation and participation.

Clearly, collective employment law is highly political in all societies. It concerns not only the exercise of economic power by employers, but also the power of unions, not just in relation to employers, but in relation to the government of the country. In liberal democracies, this law will probably address itself, at a minimum, to three sets of often interlocking issues.

1 specified representation rights for employees;
2 rights for individuals to join a trade union, to have collective bargaining rights and to take industrial action against their employer;
3 rights for disclosure of information from employers for both employees and for trade unions.

The detailed content of any country's law on these issues depends on a range of factors. Principally these are political and economic interests and concerns about civil liberties.

Democratic governments are expected to balance interests within their society. On the one hand, there will be employers' concerns about their ability to compete efficiently, to achieve cost-effectiveness and high levels of labour productivity and to retain considerable managerial decision-making freedom. On the other hand, there will be the interests of employees, most of whom will also be voters. These interests, as indicated above, concern job and income security, safety standards and the means by which employees can make effective representations about any of these issues to their employers and to the government.

In addition, the government may be obliged to take account of international standards from the International Labour Organisation, to which it is a signatory, and any relevant European Union Directive.

Governments may, of course, choose neither to balance interests nor aim at consensus. They may act in a less even-handed way and impose significant legislative constraints upon one party. Recent Conservative governments in Britain, for example, enacted policies to curb trade union power. Some of these policy measures have been criticized by the International Labour Organisation – for example, the removal of collective bargaining rights from school teachers, the failure to provide an individual right to strike, and the complexity of the law relating to industrial action (Ewing, 1994).

In formulating its policies on collective representation and union membership rights, the questions that these Conservative governments addressed were those that any democratic government must, from time to time, determine.

- Is there a proper role for trade unions in a democratic society?
- Should trade union activities be restricted to the workplace or should they also act within the political system?
- How can democracy within trade unions be ensured?
- How can the accountability of trade union leaders to their members be guaranteed?
- Should there be complete freedom of choice in respect of trade union membership and non-membership or should the *closed shop* be permitted?
- In which ways can industrial action be limited?

The differences that have persisted, over the past 20 years, between the Conservative Party and its political opponents were not about these questions but about the answers. The Thatcher/Major governments' policies were seen as designed to marginalize unions, and to *decollectivize* and *depoliticize* employee relations.

Exercise 11.4   Collective representation issues

Consider the above questions and decide what your views are.

Fig 11.3

Exercise 11.5   Collective representation rights

Figure 11.3 represents the relationships that can exist at work between employers and employees, employers and trade unions, and employees and trade unions. As you read through the remainder of this section, note the legal requirements that exist in relation to these different pairings of participants.

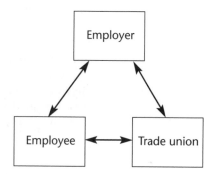

The legal framework in Britain

This section will consider four key aspects of the legal framework: social partnership; the single channel of representation; positive rights and immunities; independence.

Social partnership

The concept of social partnership is central to social policy in the European Union. Although not explicitly so, this view has infused collective representation law in Britain in a piecemeal way. Such statutory rights as exist in relation to information disclosure and consultation might form an embryonic works council system (*see* Fig 11.4).

Fig 11.4

INFORMATION AND CONSULTATION RIGHTS

- *Information to individual employees*: on contracts of employment and any changes; about health and safety hazards, standards and procedures; on reasons for dismissal; on redundancy; right to opt out of Sunday working in shops.

- *Information to union or employee representatives*: on collective redundancies; on transfers of undertakings; in European Works Councils.

- *Information to trade unions*: on collective bargaining matters.

- *Consultation with individual employees*: on changes to contract of employment.

- *Consultation with union or employee representatives*: on collective redundancies with a view to agreement; on transfers of undertakings with a view to agreement; health and safety; equal opportunities policies; disciplinary rules and procedures; in European Works Councils.

(*Note*: Some rights might be qualified by certain conditions.)

The single channel of representation

Traditionally, collective labour law has focused on the rights and obligations of trade unions. They have been perceived, both in law and in practice, as the single channel of representation for working people. In 1995, a significant change was enacted with the introduction of certain rights for non-union employee representatives. At present, these relate to collective redundancies and transfers of undertakings. In 1996, however, it is anticipated that similar rights will be extended to health and safety representatives. This marks a significant break with past practice and may result in a wider reformulation of collective representation across British employment relations.

Positive rights and immunities

The legal framework for collective representation comprises the provision of both *positive rights*, normally for individual union members and officials, and *immunities*, for a trade union as an organization.

The *positive rights* are set out explicitly in legislation and cover a wide range of employment situations and practices (*see* Fig 11.5).

These rights are enforceable in law by lodging a complaint – usually at an industrial tribunal. The remedies variously available to successful complainants include compensation, re-employment if dismissal has taken place, and a declaration of their rights.

At present, in Britain, the law does not provide rights and remedies in certain areas. Examples include the right to individual representation, the right to collective bargaining, and the right to take industrial action.

Immunities are a legal device used to protect specified persons from legal proceedings. This device affects trade unions in the following way. Under common law, trade unions are 'in restraint of trade'. This is because they aim

Fig 11.5

SOME KEY COLLECTIVE RIGHTS

- to be a member of a trade union;
- not to be a member of a trade union;
- not to be excluded or expelled unreasonably from a union;
- to participate in trade union activities at an appropriate time;
- to be protected from dismissal and victimization because of trade union membership and non-membership;
- to vote in elections for the union's principal executive committee;
- to scrutinize a union's accounts and financial affairs;
- to be consulted, through a representative, about collective redundancies, business transfers and health and safety;
- time off for union activities, public duties, prior to redundancies and for antenatal care.

Note: These rights do not extend to the police, armed forces and intelligence services.)

to regulate jointly the pay and conditions of employment offered by employers. By this action they are interfering with employers' economic freedom. In the 1870s, the legal protection of immunity was introduced in statute law to override the common law situation. This meant that the legal status of unions was clarified; they were permitted to exist and function lawfully. Furthermore, they could lawfully negotiate terms and conditions of employment with employers. In addition, the principle of immunities was adopted to enable unions to call for and organize industrial action. Immunities continue to provide the legal base for union activity and are enacted in the Trade Union and Labour Relations Consolidation Act 1992.

Independence

The law in relation to trade unions addresses this critical issue. This concerns the extent to which a union is solely responsible to its members and not under the domination and control of an employer. The Certification Officer will scrutinize the rule book and practice of unions to determine whether they can receive a certificate of independence. All TUC unions have this certificate – as do most outside the TUC. However, the circumstances of a few company-based staff associations has been problematical. In these cases, the employer has provided financial assistance and material support which tends towards control of the organization.

INDUSTRIAL ACTION: THE LEGAL FRAMEWORK

So far, the discussion in this chapter has focused on the primary issue of representation. However, any review of collective employment law would be incomplete without some consideration of the law and industrial action. This area of law changed considerably during the 1980s. This section will review the context within which it developed and also provides a case study to enable you to consider the impact of prevailing legislation.

CASE STUDY

Granny's Pride Bakery

Granny's Pride Bakery is a division of Homely Foods plc. It has a bakery in Liverpool. Due to adverse changes in the market for certain packaged cakes, Homely Foods has decided to close the Liverpool Bakery.

Industrial relations at the bakery have not been good for a number of years. The Food and Bakery Workers' Union is recognized for the production workers. The drivers, who transport the finished products to the retailers, are employed by a separate company owned by Homely Foods plc – Granny's Pride Deliveries Ltd. The Road Transport Workers' Union is recognized for the drivers.

News about the closure of the Liverpool Bakery has not yet been announced. However, rumours, have been spreading through the plant all morning (Tuesday, 5 March). Billy Baker, the FABW Convener, had heard unofficially from a secretary in the Personnel Department. 'It's not on! All the unemployed in this area – and we're going to be added to the heap,' he told the shop stewards' committee. 'We've got to do something now!' At Billy's instigation, the committee decided to call the bakery production workers out on strike.

'What about the drivers?' asked Tracy Jones. 'Can't we get them to support us?' The committee thought this was a good idea and contact was to be made with the drivers' senior steward.

At lunchtime on Tuesday, 5 March, the production workers present in the canteen had a hurried mass meeting. Billy told them about the threatened redundancies and closure and that the Personnel Manager would not discuss the issue with him. He said that the only way to resist the anticipated management action was for the workforce to strike immediately. On a show of hands there was an overwhelming majority in favour of an immediate walkout. By 2 pm, all production workers were outside picketing the plant. The drivers delivering goods were 'persuaded' to go away and those about to transport packaged cakes did not leave the depot.

▶

The Production Manager and the Personnel Manager discussed the situation and made immediate contact with the District Officer of the FABW, telling him to come down urgently and get his members back to work.

After long discussions with the shop stewards' committee, the District Officer, Fred Bland, told the stewards that what they were doing was unlawful and that they must return to work. If they did not, the union would be forced to repudiate them.

Billy Baker, who had been elected Convener because he was the most vocal of the stewards, vehemently opposed this course of action. 'You are not employed by us to implement these laws!' he exploded. 'You are supposed to look after your members' interests. So do it!' Further discussions were fruitless. Eventually, Bland left saying that he was going to report the issue to national level.

The picketing lasted until 5 pm and all present resolved that the strike would continue the next day. At 6 am on Wednesday, 6 March, pickets were outside the gates of the plant and no production took place. A message was received from the senior steward of the drivers, employed by Granny's Pride Deliveries, who said that all the drivers had stopped work in support of the production workers.

The Production Manager had been told by the Managing Director, at the Homely Foods plc Head Office in Berkshire, that it was essential that production was re-started. The previous day's failure to deliver had caused one major supermarket chain to question whether to place further orders with Granny's Pride. Although the plant was to close, the rationalization of the organization was, at this stage, incomplete – so it was essential that production at Liverpool continued for a while longer. The same message was transmitted from the Personnel Director to the plant Personnel Manager.

The Production Manager and the Personnel Manager had a further meeting with the FABW District Officer, Fred Bland, who reported to them that the National Executive Committee had told him to instruct his members to return to work and to open consultations with the management about the prospective redundancies.

Bland went to see the shop stewards' committee to pass on this message. The committee was furious. The committee members told him of the support they had from the drivers as well as among the production workers themselves. 'It won't do you any good. If you don't do what the Union tells you, you're on your own,' Bland told them.

By lunchtime, the strike was still continuing. The Managing Director gave the Production Manager instructions to have the firm's solicitors go to court to obtain injunctions. He told Bland of his intention. This threat was sufficient for the strike committee to call off the action. At 2.30 pm, the production workers were ready to return to work.

The Production Manager told Bland and Billy Baker that he did not want full production to start until 6 am on Thursday, 7 March. The union officials protested that management could not stop them working and prevent them earning any pay. They said that management were breaking their contracts.

The following day full production did start. In their pay packets that week, the production workers had two days' loss of pay.

Exercise 11.6	**The legal framework of industrial action**

As you read through the remainder of this section, consider the case study and determine those points at which particular legal requirements are important and influential.

THE CONTEXT OF INDUSTRIAL ACTION LAW

Political concern about industrial action in Britain has been a continuing theme in both industrial relations and the political system for the past 40 years or so. Advocates of reform have tended to be identified with one of two broad views:

- *Those proposing a reformed voluntary system of free collective bargaining.* Under these proposals more effective grievance and dispute procedures would be established and independent conciliation and arbitration arrangements would be set up by Parliament. Employers and trade unions would be encouraged to review the quality of their industrial relations and introduce the necessary reforms voluntarily. Through these reforms, it was expected that the sources of discontent would be minimized.

- *Those proposing a more detailed and prescriptive legal framework for the conduct of industrial relations.* This would set out rights and duties for employers, trade unions and employees. Industrial relations would be conducted in the context of these public policy requirements. Certain requirements could be enacted to deal with industrial action and its economic effects.

Since 1979, those advocating a legalistic approach have been dominant in political policy making. Concern had been developing throughout the 1970s about the economic consequences of industrial action. Several issues had to be addressed and reformed.

- The voting systems to decide on industrial action were frequently seen as defective. Mass meetings were often used and secret ballots were the exception. There was concern that individuals might be coerced into supporting such action.

- There was some use of industrial action before negotiations had been completed and/or the disputes procedure had been exhausted.

- There was concern about the extent to which it was right for workers to take supportive, sympathetic, secondary action.

- The extent to which trade union leaders controlled their members who were taking industrial action was also a matter of public debate.

- The use of industrial action in essential services, such as hospitals, the fire service, etc., was being challenged.

As a result of the 1979 general election, it became the responsibility of a Conservative government to address these issues. Unlike previous post-war Conservative governments, the Thatcher government was characterized by a radical shift in political ideology and objectives. Its attitude to unions and industrial action was clearly hostile. The policy pursued in relation to industrial conflict reflects this.

It has been described as a *dual-track* policy (Auerbach, 1990), comprising a policy of restriction and a policy of regulation. These policies were framed in the context of the government's economic objectives of deregulated labour markets, the promotion of an *enterprise culture*, greater cost-effectiveness and the assertion of the managerial right to manage.

The *policy of restriction* focused on trade union immunities. These were narrowed, so creating a wide set of circumstances whereby certain forms of industrial action could be declared unlawful. This policy of restriction had two associated underlying components: the promotion of enterprise confinement and the depoliticization of trade union activity.

The notion of enterprise confinement (Wedderburn, 1989) reflected the view that industrial action should only be lawful in respect of employees and their own employer. Sympathetic secondary industrial action was made generally unlawful. This reflected a widely held view in the Conservative Party that trade unions' only legitimate sphere of interest was workplace industrial relations. A corollary of this view was that unions should not pursue political objectives. Industrial action was therefore, deemed unlawful if it was undertaken for political purposes, e.g. to resist privatization.

The policy of regulation involved the use of extensive statutory regulations on trade unions in industrial action. They can be categorized under two headings: those relating to industrial action balloting; and those which concern a union's liability for the actions of its members and its officials.

This policy of regulation used a different technique. Detailed prescriptions on the conduct of ballots for approving industrial action were set out in legislation and a statutory code of practice. While these regulations may appear consistent with improving trade union democracy, they have in fact created a myriad of legal trip-wires. These mean that unions must approach balloting and industrial action cautiously.

As far as liability is concerned, this policy of regulation provided remedies, principally for employers, when unlawful industrial action takes place. An aggrieved employer may apply to the High Court for an injunction (a court order to stop the unlawful industrial action) and for limited damages from the union. Unions can escape liability if they repudiate the members concerned and tell them to return to work (*see* Fig 11.6).

Fig 11.6

WHAT IS LAWFUL INDUSTRIAL ACTION?

1 *Trade dispute.* There must be a lawful trade dispute – between workers and their employer – and it must be 'wholly or mainly' about employment-related matters: for example, pay and conditions, jobs, allocation of work, discipline, negotiating machinery. Industrial action must be called 'in contemplation or furtherance of this dispute'.

2 *Secondary action.* Sympathetic action is not lawful.

3 *Secret ballot.*
- There must be an individual secret ballot.
- Immunity for a union is conditional on approval in such a ballot.
- Code of practice sets specific requirements on organization and timings of balloting process.

4 *Picketing.*
- Attendance at or near own place of work.
- Peacefully to persuade a person to work or not to work.
- Peacefully to communicate or obtain information.
- Police to enforce criminal law.
- A code of practice sets out specific guidance.

The statutory changes outlined above arose from recent political action to deal with trade unions as the organizers of industrial action. In tandem with these developments, the law relating to individual employees continued to be developed. This highlighted, particularly, their vulnerability in the absence of any legal right to strike. Three aspects of the law coalesced to illustrate this: breach of contract; dismissals for industrial action; and pay deduction.

Breach of contract

When an employee takes strike action – or participates in most other forms of industrial action – then he or she breaches the contract of employment. It can be regarded by the employer as a 'repudiatory' breach, so fundamental that it effectively destroys the contract. This will be particularly so if no work is carried out – as in a strike. As a consequence, an employer can dismiss the employee. This has always been the situation under common law.

Britain has been criticized by the International Labour Organisation for failing to enact an individual right to strike. One way of modifying the common law would be to introduce a rule that industrial action suspends rather than breaches the contract of employment. Many European countries have accepted the principle of suspension of contracts in industrial disputes as part of a positive right to strike. In these cases the strike usually has to be lawful. It has to meet some specific statutory requirements, e.g. approval in a secret ballot.

Dismissals for industrial action

Parliament has intervened to modify the situation whereby individuals may be dismissed for taking part in industrial action. However, it did not create an individual right to take industrial action. In the 1970s, it was determined that selective dismissal of those taking industrial action was unfair. An employer must sack all. A complaint may be made to an industrial tribunal only about selective dismissal.

Two amendments have been made to this situation. The first amendment, in 1982, enables an employer to re-engage, three months after their termination, some but not necessarily all employees who have been dismissed. In 1990, selective dismissal was permitted of those who participated in industrial action not supported by their union.

Pay deductions

The third area where the law has had an impact on individual employees has been in relation to pay deductions. Case law during the 1980s clarified various issues. Where there is strike action and the employer is not dismissing the strikers then it is accepted that they will not be paid for the duration of this action. The situation in relation to other forms of industrial action has been more problematical. The courts have differentiated between 'accepted partial performance' of the contract and 'rejected partial performance'. The decision to accept or reject is with the employer.

With *accepted partial performance*, the employer accepts that some, but not all, of the contracted work is carried out. The difficult issue has been to calculate appropriate remuneration for part-performance of the contract. Limited case law suggests a degree of rough justice.

With *rejected partial performance*, specific guidance has been given in a Court of Appeal case. The key points are:

- Employees are not entitled to pick and choose what work they do under their contracts of employment.

- An employee could not refuse to comply with his contract and demand pay under the contract.

- An employer could not give an employee instructions and refuse to pay him if he had told the employee that he was not required to attend for work, as a result of partial performance, and that if he did, it would be voluntary.

- The character and volume of work was also a consideration. Even if it is small when assessed in terms of time, it might be of some considerable importance.

Employers, clearly, have legal remedies available to them to respond to industrial action. Both statute and case law have tilted the balance of power in favour of the employer since the 1980s. It is on rare occasions – for example, at News International in 1986, in cross-Channel ferry companies in 1988 and at Timex in 1993 – that the full force of the law is used against both individuals and union organizations. Employers have to balance short-term victories in industrial disputes with the maintenance of working relationships and the improvement of industrial relations.

SUMMARY AND CONCLUSION

The context of employment relations is being significantly affected by a number of legislative initiatives. These are prompted by political policies originating in either Britain or the European Union. At the centre of these policies is the exercise of power both by employers and by unions.

Trade unions, as the traditional vehicle for expressing the collective interests, have been subjected to various curbs on their power: in claiming bargaining rights; in representing employees; and in calling for and organizing industrial action. New forms of collective representation are developing alongside trade unionism. Some have been introduced voluntarily, at the instigation of employers and some are set up under new statutory consultation rights. The effectiveness of such emerging organizations is as yet untested. Given the recognition of collective interests in employment that occurs in EU social policy, employers will increasingly be called upon to accommodate such collectivism in their employee-relations policies.

CHAPTER 12

Conclusion

INTRODUCTION

By its very nature, the subject matter of this textbook is very wide-ranging. Nevertheless, as an examination of the context in which organizations operate, it has identified a number of themes and trends which may be common to various contextual influences. One purpose of this concluding chapter, then, is to bring together certain of these key themes. An attempt will also be made to identify some likely future developments that will have an impact on organizations.

Before considering these themes, it is important to reaffirm the characteristics of the organizational environment that have featured throughout the text.

- *Choice and determinism* – the extent to which employers, employees and governments have choice or are subject to constraints.
- *Change and stability* – the extent to which this environment is in flux or is characterized by inertia.
- *Objectivity and subjectivity* – the extent to which decisions and choices are made by objective criteria or may reflect personal opinions and prejudice.
- *Power relationships* – the nature of power relationships between employers, employees and governments.
- *Reciprocal relationships* – the extent to which action in one area, e.g. social attitudes, has an impact on another, e.g. legislation, which in turn has a reciprocal effect. For example, equal opportunities law modifies social attitudes and then creates demands for further legislative change.
- *Integration* – the degree to which economic, technological, social, political, and legislative factors are interrelated.

BROAD THEMES

It is always invidious to rank contemporary themes in order of importance. Each person's preferences will inevitably reflect his or her own values and ideological views. Consequently, those set out here reflect the authors' own experiences and ideological perspectives. The reader is, of course, free to disagree and determine his or her own preferences!

The broad sets of themes considered here are those deriving from the economy and those within society. There are two principal reasons for this selection. The economy provides the motor behind many other contextual developments in the organizational environment, i.e. social, political, legal and technological factors. Within society, values, attitudes, expectations and practices change – so affecting economic activity, attitudes to technological change and the environment, the political system and the legislative framework.

ECONOMIC THEMES

The principal economic themes are considered under the following headings: objectives; management of the economy; and the global context.

Objectives

At the level of the macro-economy, one central unresolved issue is the extent to which the pursuit of economic objectives should be modified by concerns for certain social values. These social values might relate, for example, to the effects of technological change, threats to the environment and the conduct of employee relations. Such tension has been evident in, for instance, the policy differences between British Conservative governments and the European Union over the character and extent of social policy and its potential cost to employers and the suggested damage to job creation.

This clash of objectives is also replicated at the level of any company or employing organization. The question to be answered is 'How far should cost-effectiveness, productivity, efficiency and flexibilities be limited by, for example, policies designed to provide "decent" pay levels and job security?' Employees bring expectations of fair treatment and social justice into the employment relationship, and so employers are forced to respond to this question. They may do this explicitly, by adopting standards of good human resource practice or negotiating collective agreements with trade unions. Alternatively, management's response may be implicit in the practices (good or bad) that they adopt.

Associated with the issue of economic objectives is a further debate about the distribution of wealth. This debate occurs both at the level of the employing organization and in the macro-economy. The central purpose of industrialized economies is wealth creation. Inevitably, however, questions arise about the distribution of this wealth and about the extent to which employees, as well as the owners of capital equipment, are considered as contributors to wealth creation. Furthermore, a supplementary question arises about the extent to which government should use some of this privately generated wealth for social purposes, such as schools, hospitals, houses, roads, defence, etc.

The issue of distribution of wealth is, consequently, highly political. It is concerned with the articulation and implementation of conflicting economic and social goals. The protagonists reflect often markedly different perspectives and values. One aspect of this debate centres on the notions of equality and inequality of treatment and also the concept of fairness. For example, in the early 1990s, at one level the public were critical about the disparate treatment of, on the one hand, very highly paid chief executives of recently privatized corporations and, on the other hand, the large number of employees whose security of income was being jeopardized by cost-cutting measures.

At the level of the national economy, the debate on distribution understandably concerns not just pay but much wider issues like the scale of social security benefits, the levels of taxation and the availability of 'goods', such as education, health care and living accommodation. Associated with this is the issue concerning the extent to which government can promote further wealth creation through economic and social policy measures.

Government, then, has to generate its income through taxation and borrowing. It has to determine the amounts to be raised. It has to allocate resources to these social provisions. It has to decide the criteria for allocation. In formulating policy in these interlocking areas, government has to manage the achievement of social policy standards, economic objectives and the consequences of its taxation policy. Various fundamental questions, which balance economic and social considerations, have become the focus of political debate in recent years.

- To what extent should there be inequalities in the provision of basic goods, such as education, health care and living accommodation?
- To what extent should private as opposed to public provision of these basic goods be encouraged?
- To what extent should there be universal as opposed to selective provision of social security benefits?
- To what extent should individuals supplement or replace state provision of benefits with private provision, e.g. pensions, medical insurance?
- In raising revenue, what are appropriate levels of government borrowing, and what levels of personal and corporate taxation create disincentives for taxpayers?

Such questions are endemic in economic management in liberal democracies. There are no definitive answers. However, there are alternative answers. Those suggested will, of course, vary according to the governing party's political purposes and the interests it represents.

The management of the economy

In order to achieve its economic objectives, government may choose from a selection of instruments for economic management. In *mixed* economies of liberal democracies – that is, those that have both a private and a public sector – there is a choice available to government. It can determine whether the balance of economic management tends towards a pure free market economy or towards one based on a degree of planning. The tendency to be located at one or other end of this spectrum depends upon the ideological perspective of the government.

A government's decision on specific economic policy objectives and particular instruments can have a substantial impact within that society. For example, new laws may be enacted to facilitate economic changes, e.g. the introduction or removal of minimum wage legislation. Changes in social behaviour may be promoted, e.g. the degree to which part-time work and flexible working practices are encouraged. Certain standards of good practice might be positively encouraged or not, e.g. equal treatment.

In addition to its promotion of a particular model of the economy, a government is likely to determine other related ancillary characteristics. The first is its choice of approach – whether this is to be characterized either by control mechanisms or by the encouragement of participation of the different interests in society. The second factor, which is closely associated with this first point, is the approach to any regulation – whether voluntary self-regulation is encouraged or whether an infrastructure for legal regulation will be enacted.

The global context

Just as companies are not free agents, able to manipulate policies across a range of areas, neither are governments of individual nation states. They are subject to wider contextual influences, which can constrain their economic freedom of action. At present, there are two significant discernible themes.

The international economy

The international economy has a number of facets. The economies of individual nation states are increasingly locked into a world economy and simultaneously these countries may be a member of a trading bloc – e.g. the North American Free Trade Area or, in a more developed form, the European Union.

Within this international economy, the exercise of power relations is important across a number of fronts: between member states within the trading blocs; between countries and trading blocs, on the one hand, and multinational companies on the other; and between trading blocs themselves.

Such internationalization can have a number of possible consequences:

- a more vigorous pursuit of cost-effective international competition;
- footloose multinational companies jeopardizing national or local economies by relocation;
- the development of laws, in the European Union, and codes of practice, under both the International Labour Organisation and the World Trade Organisation, to limit and regulate workforce exploitation and to establish protective rights;
- concern within individual countries about their sovereignty and freedom to act in their own perceived interests.

Environmentalism

The crisis of global warming, the social and economic dislocation through deforestation, and the impact of microelectronic technology have, for example, heightened the recognition of global interdependence. Public concern and campaigning have resulted in some attempts to control and regulate the adverse effects of these developments. Such attempts are, of course, clearly affected by the power relations and vested interests that exist within and between individual countries and multinational companies.

SOCIAL THEMES

This second broad set of themes derives from the interaction of people in society at large – for example, as citizens, employees, parents, women, men, and members of specific organizations.

Five such themes have infused discussion in the text:

1 Equal treatment and fairness

This establishes, albeit unsatisfactorily, certain principles to guide social behaviour both in employment and in social relations generally. Both fairness and equal treatment have been inextricably associated with anti-discrimination policies. The principle that certain categories of people should not suffer detriments and stereotyping and should not be excluded from various forms of social participation has been established. Protective legislation has been enacted in certain key areas, e.g. sex and race discrimination, but significant exceptions still apply in respect of age and sexual orientation.

2 Feminization

The shift in public consciousness about women's role in society combined with legislative action has provided the impetus for growing and widespread feminization. This is one of the most significant characteristics of contemporary society.

3 The management of diversity

As a result of combined demographic and social developments many, but certainly not all, European Union countries are both multiracial and also give recognition to the changing role of women. In the employment sphere, this has lead to the concept of the management of diversity. Indeed, as a concept, it is arguably much wider and deserves to infuse broader social policies.

It can be conceived as an issue of citizenship. For example, do different ethnic groups have full citizenship rights or are they, as in some countries, merely *guest workers*? It can be conceived as an issue of employment status. For example, how far are the skills, abilities and experiences of different groups – for example, the elderly and the disabled – used in employment? Finally, it can be conceived as a commercial issue. To what extent can businesses in marketing and selling target these differentiated groups of consumers?

4 Participation and enfranchisement

This concerns the basis of people's involvement in both civil society and employment.

Much of the language and rhetoric of liberal democracy is about citizenship and rights to participate in democratic decision making. Two important trends concern the quality of participation in democratic societies and the disenfranchisement of certain social groups.

The quality of participation by individual citizens can be poor. It is contended that the political processes that exist between elections to influence both legislators and the executive are, effectively, weak. Furthermore, cynicism about the political process and a lack of confidence in politicians as a group is frequently reported in some European countries (including Britain and France). There is, then, the danger of the atomization of political participation – individuals voting once every four or five years in general elections and engaging in no other active involvement.

The question of disenfranchisement of certain social groups has been remarked upon in several European countries. Sometimes, exclusion is a deliberate choice; sometimes it arises through force of economic circumstances; and sometimes it is a result of civic status. In Britain, the introduction of the 'Poll Tax' in 1990 resulted in over a million people not registering to vote, presumably to help evade liability. In Britain and France, there are sizable groups of homeless people who because they have no residence find participation in employment and political society difficult. In Germany, there are foreign guest workers, often resident in hostels, who are active in the economy but cannot participate in the civic society. This may be a differentiated group, but this aggregate phenomenon of *the underclass* or, in France, *les exclus* is an important political and social issue.

Some argue further that the political and industrial arenas should not be differentiated – that democratic participation should be extended to include the workplace. In Britain, particularly, this view is still contentious. It is less so in other European countries. In Britain, there is no consensus on the principle of participation at the workplace. If it is exists, it is subject to employer agreement and the enforcement of limited statutory rights.

5 The individual and collective dimensions of social activity

An associated theme is the basis upon which participation takes place: individual activity or collective action. Collectivism is seen as more acceptable in the wider political process; after all political parties and pressure groups are collective entities. In employment relations, however, these two bases of participation are frequently juxtaposed; and collectivism is seen by some as unacceptable. However, the reality of the employment relationship is that both individual and collective participation and representation are appropriate, depending upon the issue in question. Too great a shift to individualism would markedly increase the vulnerability of individual working people.

FUTURE TRENDS

It is difficult and perhaps foolhardy to predict the future. Nevertheless, those interested in economic, social and political affairs need to be sensitive to probable future trends. However, sometimes the probable does not occur and the surprising happens. All of the major political developments listed here have in varying ways had profound effects upon businesses, particularly with the collapse of product markets and the growth of new ones. This, in turn, can affect employment opportunities and even the economic stability of specific countries.

In 1986, who would have thought that within ten years ...

- the Soviet Union would have ceased to exist and the Cold War would end?
- East and West Germany would have united?
- Communist China would be developing into a major world economy exporting a wide range of goods?
- Apartheid would have been abolished and Nelson Mandela would have been elected President of South Africa?
- Yugoslavia would have fragmented, leading to the first war on European soil since 1945.

With warnings in mind, then, there are some future trends that seem likely within the medium term (the next five years or so):

Political and economic
- There will be widening of the European Union to include more eastern European states.
- There will be continuing and probably unresolved debate about 'deepening' the European Union through greater integration.
- A single European currency may, possibly, not be achieved by 1999.
- Nation states – particularly in Europe – will be subject to twin pressures: the possible loss of further sovereignty to supranational bodies like the European Union; and internal pressures for decentralization within the member state to regional governments.
- There will be changes to the electoral system in the United Kingdom and the possibility of constitutional changes relating to the House of Lords, and the status of Scotland, Wales and Northern Ireland within the UK.
- Economic competition from China and the Pacific rim countries will intensify.
- The balance of provision between private and public transport will be reappraised in favour of the latter.

Social
- There will be continued but slower improvement in equal opportunities for women as the more intractable obstacles are dealt with – for example, child care provision, training and development and equal pay.
- The ageing populations in European countries will provoke debates about social welfare costs.
- There will be increased potential for individualization and atomization both socially and as work is relocated to home as a result of technical change.
- There will be countervailing tendencies for collective action politically, through pressure groups and campaigns and at work through employee participation.
- There will be action to enfranchise groups disadvantaged on grounds of age and sexuality.
- Social fragmentation will occur between the more prosperous members of society and the emerging underclass.

- The level of crime and fear of crime will continue to grow and further security and surveillance techniques will be developed.
- The concept of *community* will be redefined with the growth of, for example, *network communities*.
- The concept of *life-long learning* will be developed.

Technology

- There will be wider diffusion of IT competence throughout the population.
- Technologies will continue to converge, e.g. one instrument to provide TV, PC, audio system and telecommunications link.
- The sphere of bio-technology will grow in importance.

Exercise 12.1

1 *From the perspective of your own organization, what do you see as the principal trends and changes that will have an impact upon it during the next ten years?*

2 *What impact do you think that these changes will have on the conduct of human resource management?*

APPENDIX

Answers to exercises

The exercises in the text have various purposes. Some are to encourage you to investigate and review practice within your own organization. Some ask you to think about your opinions on particular matters. A third group of exercises is designed to test knowledge. Suggested answers to many of the exercises are provided in this Appendix. Answers to the remaining exercises will vary according to the views of the reader and the nature of the organization chosen by the reader.

CHAPTER 1

Exercise 1.1
The external pressures facing Hodsons

Listed below are a few of the many external pressures currently confronting Hodsons. This is not intended to be an exhaustive list and you may have suggested a number of other specific or general issues which could also be included.

1 The economic recession of the late 1980s and early 1990s, together with increases in interest rates, led to a collapse in the housing and commercial property markets with knock-on effects on the level of construction activity and the size of the building industry.

2 Changing consumer tastes and growing interest in 'Do-It-Yourself' (DIY) home improvements have altered the types of goods and services that customers demand from builders and domestic suppliers.

3 Increased competition from large DIY centres based in out-of-town sites has drawn customers away from high street based building suppliers. These new centres are often owned by large retailers who have substantial marketing and advertising budgets – e.g. Homebase and Texas Homecare (Sainsbury's), B&Q (Kingfisher) and Do It All (WH Smith). The size of these centres means that products can be ordered direct from

source with a consequent reduction in the need for wholesalers and large warehousing facilities.

4 DIY centres tend to stock a more extensive range of basic building supplies and also sell highly profitable home furnishings, garden equipment and other recreational goods.

5 The growing use of Electronic Point of Sale (EPOS) equipment by retail companies allows customers to pay for their purchases using Credit and Debit cards as well as cheques and cash. It also enables staff to monitor sales and stock to ensure that the right goods are available at the right time at the right location. By forecasting sales on the basis of this information these companies can order in bulk from suppliers and thereby gain significant discounts.

6 Concern about green issues in general and fears about the effects of deforestation on global warming specifically have influenced the demand for timber and wood products.

7 The relaxation of the controls on retail trading hours, including the legalization of Sunday trading, and increased consumer demand for late-night shopping has led to longer shop opening hours.

8 Changes in the staffing of retail organizations – such as the increased use of staff on part-time, temporary and other non-standard forms of employment and the increased participation of women in the workforce – have altered the mix of staff in most retail stores.

Exercise 1.2
Representing the external environment

Examples of the results of different forms of environmental scanning activity undertaken on the Hodsons case study material are shown below. In the interests of space these examples are limited to a PEST analysts and to Metaphors/images. The answer to Exercise 1.1 provides an example of the list-based approach.

Categories

Political

Improved access to UK markets
for competitors from overseas activity,
especially the companies from
EU countries

Relaxation of regulations
on opening hours

Concerns that out-of-town shopping
centres promote car use and lead
to a decline in high-street shopping

Economic

Recession

Decline in building

Competition from
Do-It-Yourself centres

Social

Growing interest in Do-It-Yourself

Concern about damage to the
environment

Greater interest in out-of-town
shopping centres

Technological

Electronic stock
monitoring and sales technology

Just-in-time systems

Increased use of debit
and credit card sales.

Metaphors and images

Hodsons could be seen metaphorically as an iceberg. On the surface it appears that the company is melting away as sales decline, and it is dragged into less hospitable waters by a combination of recessionary currents, increased competition and John Hodson's view of the future of the company. However, these surface difficulties conceal a number of deeper problems which lie hidden below the surface, but which will ultimately determine the future direction of the company. These problems include the high level of skill and expertise among the workforce and their reluctance to downgrade the level of service and advice they provide to customers.

Exercise 1.3
Choosing an appropriate response to declining sales at Hodsons

Some of the possible responses Hodsons could consider adopting in response to the current recession include: doing nothing, selling up, consolidating, changing the markets that it serves, altering its product range, agreeing a joint venture/merger, or lobbying central government in order to get changes in the laws governing the industry.

Decisions reflecting the appropriateness, feasibility and suitability of these different solutions will reflect differences of individual opinion.

CHAPTER 2

Exercise 2.1
Reading the financial pages

(a) The most expensive shares: Sainsbury at 466p.

(b) The widest fluctuations in share price in the preceding year: Argyll with a total change in price of $114\frac{1}{2}$.

(c) The greatest number of issued shares: ASDA with 25 316 million shares.

(d) The appearance of high shareholder confidence in its future performance: ASDA with a P/E ratio of 17.2.

Exercise 2.2
Public or private?

Although it is tempting to think that all organizations are either publicly or privately owned, in practice the distinctions are not always easy to make. A number of organizations combine a mixture of publicly and privately owned assets. For example, the government has retained some shares in several recently privatized organizations. Similarly, a number of private organizations receive substantial grants, funding and support from either central or local government.

LIBRARY
BISHOP BURTON COLLEGE
BEVERLEY HU17 8QG

Table A.1 Flexington University: public or private?

	Ownership	Control	Objectives
Stanmead Technical College	Voluntary organization	Mechanical Institute	Meet local demand for education and training
	Local authority	Local politicians	Meet local demand for education and training
Stanmead Institute of Technology	Local authority	Local politicians	Meet need for undergraduate technical education and training
Flexington Polytechnic	Local authority	Local politicians and CNAA	Meet need for undergraduate education and training
Flexington University	Public corporation	University governors	Meet need for under-graduate education and training
Flexington University Enterprises Ltd	Private limited company	Board of directors	Commercially exploit enterprises, patents, limited copyrights and other materials

Exercise 2.3
Changes in the public sector

The following list summarizes how some of the changes in the public sector over the last 15 years have affected the staff and students at Flexington University. There is also a speculative list of possible future changes.

Examples of changes which might be introduced include the following:

- *Privatization* of universities through sale of their assets to the private sector.

- *Liberalization* of sector through sale of degree-awarding franchises.

- *Marketization* through introduction of student voucher system so that fees are paid by the student.

- *Managerialism* through appointment of business managers to oversee university operations.

Privatization	None to date
Deregulation	Relaxation of the rules governing the award of degrees. Controls devolved to institutions with the scrapping of the CNAA
Liberalization	Establishment of Buckingham University
Marketization	Universities and polytechnics encouraged to compete for students
Financial prudence	Strict limits on the level of student funding
Managerialism	Students' Charter, appraisals and performance-related pay
Commercialism	University encouraged to attract overseas students and to sell research and consultancy services as well as university merchandise

Exercise 2.5
Identifying the stakeholders

Figure A.1 shows the range of groups that constitute the environment in which Flexington University operates.

Fig A.1

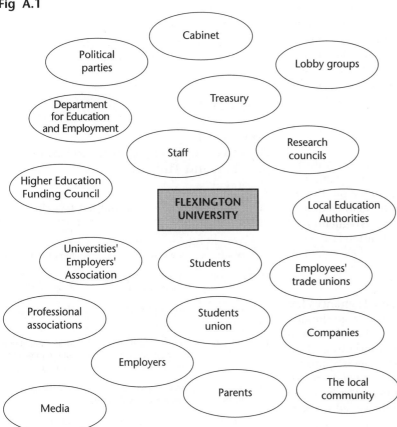

CHAPTER 3

Exercise 3.2
Market environments

- *Monopolistic.* A good example of monopolistic competition is provided by the player-transfer market within the international football league. Here skilled players with an international reputation are able to play several football clubs off against each other in order to ensure that they get the highest transfer payments and salaries from their future employers.

- *Oligopolistic.* The 'Net Book Agreement' was a formal arrangement between publishers and booksellers which regulated the retail prices of new books. Formally disbanded in 1995, this cartel arrangement received official support because it was suggested that maintaining artificially high prices for new books enabled publishers to invest in new authors and also ensured the continued existence of small bookshops.

- *Monopsonistic.* The purchase of armaments by governments. Here many companies will compete for a contract.
- *Near perfect competition.* As mentioned in the text, there are few examples of pure perfect competition; however, a number of markets come close to this ideal. One example of near perfect competition in the housing and second-hand car markets. Despite considerable government regulation stipulating what can and cannot be sold, there are considerable similarities in the quality of goods on offer for a specific price within any particular geographical region.

Exercise 3.3
Industry structure

Answers to the first part of this question will vary according to the market position of the organization chosen. In the second part of the question, Porter's model can be applied to the public sector, although there is likely to be more extensive regulation of competition, buyers and potential customers.

Exercise 3.4
Generic strategies

The owners and managers of Fine Fragrances Ltd have, consciously or unconsciously, traditionally adopted a generic strategy of differentiation focus when developing and marketing their range of soaps. Whether this strategy is appropriate in the longer term is a matter of judgement. The reader may believe that it would be better to either expand into previously untapped markets using the existing product line (differentiation), or to reduce the price of these soaps/launch another line which will enable them to compete on cost (cost leadership). Differentiation is probably more viable in the short to medium term than cost leadership.

Exercise 3.5
Product and market development

Among the initiatives which could be considered for the future market or product development of the soaps range currently offered by Fine Fragrances Ltd are the following:

- Consolidate and rationalize the organization's operations or withdraw totally by selling the business to another interested party.

- Adapt the existing product range or launch new soaps targeted at one or more of the following groups: men, younger women, environmentally aware consumers or the sports and leisure market.
- Launch a range of cosmetics or bathroom accessories (e.g. towels and face cloths) to complement the existing toiletries.
- Establish a presence in an unrelated market with greater growth potential.

CHAPTER 4

Exercise 4.1
The effects of labour market trends on Grimbles and Timpanies

Table A.2 Effects of labour market trends

	Grimbles	Timpanies
Feminization	More female staff	More female staff
Unemployment	A larger pool of potential recruits.	A larger pool of potential recruits
Occupational change	Not applicable	Not applicable
Sectoral change	More competition for staff from other service industries	More competition staff from service industries
Hours of employment	More part-time and temporary employment	No change
The 'demographic time bomb'	Targeted recruitment of older workers	No change

Exercise 4.2
UK labour market statistics

It is important to note that labour market statistics are presented in a variety of forms. In addition to adjustments for seasonal variation (*see* discussion in the text), there are also differences in terms of the units of analysis. For example, unemployment statistics are available for the following areas:

- United Kingdom (England, Scotland, Wales and Northern Ireland, excluding the Isle of Man and Channel Islands);

- Great Britain (United Kingdom excluding Northern Ireland);
- Nationally (i.e. England, Wales, Scotland or Northern Ireland);
- Regionally (i.e. South-West, South-East and North-West, etc.).

It is also possible to obtain labour market statistics for smaller areas. A common approach here is to use local authority districts and 'travel to work areas' (TTWAs) which relate to major cities, towns or other centres of high employment.

It is therefore important to ensure that you are collecting statistics for the appropriate geographical area.

Another potential source of confusion arises from the tendency for statistics to be revised some time after their initial publication. As a consequence, unemployment statistics are often published in a preliminary form (denoted by a *p* next to the appropriate figures). When new information becomes available this figure may be revised (denoted by an *r* next to the appropriate figures).

Exercise 4.3
Labour market segmentation and segregation

Table A.3 Labour market segmentation and segregation

	Grimbles	Timpanies
Horizontal	Personnel, women's fashion, perfumery, toiletries departments staffed by women	No information
Vertical	Men retain an above average proportion of management positions	No information
National	No information	Senior positions and design facilities based in Italy

Exercise 4.4
Analysing employers' approaches

See Table A.4.

Table A.4 Analysing employers' approaches

	Grimbles	Timpanies
Poacher	None mentioned in case	Recruitment of store staff
Gamekeeper	Traditional approach to recruitment of all – this approach is now reserved primarily for graduate management trainees	None mentioned in in the case
Contractor	Beginning to explore possibilities of contracting out floor space to other retail companies, like Timpanies. Also uses recruitment agencies and management consultancies	Contracts out production to firms in the Far East as well as franchising sales operations in the UK
Flexible	Sales staff increasingly treated as a numerically flexible group	Sales staff increasingly treated as a numerically flexible group

CHAPTER 5

Exercise 5.1
Market economies

Figures A.2(a) and (b) show the demand and supply function diagrams.

Fig A.2 (a)

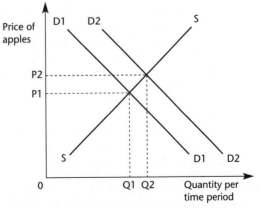

An increase in demand as denoted by the movement from D1 to D2 leads to an increase in both the price (P1 to P2) and the quantity demanded (Q1 to Q2).

Fig A.2 (b)

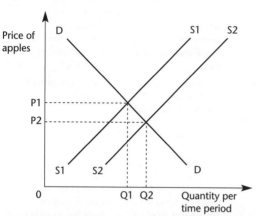

An increase in supply as denoted by the movement from S1 to S2 leads to an decrease in both the price (P1 to P2) and an increase in the quantity demanded (Q1 to Q2).

Exercise 5.2
A single European currency?

Advocates of a single European currency suggest the following benefits. For business, European Monetary Union (EMU) would eliminate the cost of foreign exchange transactions and hedging on currency movements. At current exchange rates and prices this is estimated to exceed $30 billion per year. It would also make trade and investment between member states more attractive as the returns from these activities would be less susceptible to currency movements. For individual European citizens, it would remove the cost of similar transactions when travelling on business or holiday trips. Meanwhile, it would protect the governments of individual member states from the effects of speculation by money market traders. And in the longer term, it might also promote more stable economic growth as governments are prevented from devaluing and have to submit themselves to the tough monetary policies characteristic of Germany – the largest and most economically powerful member state of the European Union.

Opponents of EMU suggest that the movement of decision making on monetary policy from national governments and central banks to a new European Central Bank represents an unacceptable reduction in national sovereignty. In short, they are concerned that this change will prevent their national politicians from taking short-term steps to correct local economic difficulties. There is also a fear that in the longer term European Union institutions will further reduce national sovereignty by taking a bigger role in determining fiscal policy. It is argued that without this central control or co-ordination of taxation and public spending, there is danger that economic problems in one country could have spill-over effects on others. To prevent this from happening, European Union institutions will therefore be forced to tax richer countries in order to promote investment and benefit spending in poorer regions. Over time there is a fear that this will lead to political union – the creation of a 'European Super State' – and an increase in the distance between individual citizens and the politicians who make decisions on their behalf.

CHAPTER 6

Exercise 6.1
Multi-media technology

The likely consequences of multi-media technology for the leisure industry and people's working lives and social pastimes could be:

- *Industry.* The widespread adoption of multimedia technology might lead to an increased number of mergers or joint ventures between companies which were previously involved in only one or two of the following areas: software programming, film making, telecommunications, record and video production. With a standard and universally available means of distributing these materials there would be substantial economies of scale for any company which could exploit the links between these previously diverse business areas. In addition, there are likely to be a range of new industries and businesses created directly or indirectly by the convergence of these technologies. These new direct businesses will include the organizations which provide the hardware and software to run these services. Meanwhile established and newer businesses may grow up to provide home shopping, banking and other services via this medium.

- *Working lives.* There is a possibility that improvements in the technology linking computers, televisions and telecommunications equipment will make tele-working and other forms of home-working more viable and available to employees. This movement of work away from large office blocks to people's homes may lead to a gradual de-urbanization of major cities and towns as people no longer need to commute to work or the shops.

- *Leisure habits.* The narrowing of geographical distances between people through the use of information and communications technologies may lead to a further atomization of society as individuals and families choose to spend their leisure hours in front of the box. Alternatively, the de-urbanization accompanying teleworking may lead to a rebirth of village life and smaller communities across the country. Finally, the possibility of contacts between people across the globe may lead to the formation of a network-based virtual society rather than physically localized communities. In this version of the future we will meet our friends on the screen more often than in the pub.

CHAPTER 7

Exercise 7.1
The consequences of demographic changes

The changes in the structure of population and the composition of families could have the following consequences for the personnel policies of an organization:

1 *Elderly population.* An increase in the number of pensioners will place further strains on government funds to cover the costs of benefits to the elderly. As a consequence the level of pension provision by the State may be expected to decline over time as a consequence of either (a) cutting benefits, (b) removing any linkages to the rate of inflation, (c) encouraging private pension provision, (d) introducing flexible retirement ages and inducements to encourage work after the statutory retirement age. Organizations could respond to these changes by improving its provision of pensions for employees. This could be done directly by establishing a company pension scheme or, alternatively and more realistically, by negotiating preferential rates with the provider of an occupational pension scheme.

Increases in the number of older people in the UK could provide organizations with a valuable pool of potential recruits. They could demonstrate their willingness to employ these people by developing policies and practices to prevent age discrimination.

2 *Declining birth rate.* Reductions in the number of young people available for employment and increases in the number of middle-aged employees could cause problems for many companies. If these organizations currently rely on attracting school leavers as recruits, the decline in the number of young people could lead to greater competition for potential employees. In addition, increases in the number of middle-aged people in 10 to 20 years may lead to increased frustration among junior and middle managers as they see their promotion and progression prospects decline. To overcome these difficulties companies could avoid the shortfall in school leavers by targeting other pools of potential recruits. They might also wish to consider establishing career paths or systems of job rotation for long-service employees to ensure that they feel valued even if traditional promotion opportunities are not available.

3 *Households and the family.* Family-friendly policies could help single parents, as well as couples, balance the demands of the workplace with those of caring for children, elderly relatives and the sick. Among the range of alternatives available to employers include: child care facilities, nursery vouchers, career breaks, flexi-time, job-sharing, maternity/paternity and carer leave as well as part-time, term-time and teleworking or homeworking.

4 *Migration.* The immigration policies of many countries which accept migrants from the UK favour the well qualified and highly skilled. In the long term the UK may suffer economically as a consequence of this 'brain drain'. Continued immigration from the countries of the Asian and African Commonwealth, as well as the higher birth rates of UK citizens from ethnic minorities, highlight the need for effective equal opportunities policies to protect and promote the career advancement of ethnic minority employees.

Exercise 7.2
Top executive pay

Explanations of the increases in executive pay during the 1980s usually rely on one or more of the following three explanations:

- Executive pay is linked to corporate performance. High levels of pay are needed to motivate board members to improve business operations.

- Pay levels must be competitive with the rates offered by other companies at home and overseas.

- Board members are employed on short-term contracts and have a higher degree of job insecurity than other employees.

These claims have come under increasing attack in recent years. Studies in the USA and UK have demonstrated no discernable link between executive pay levels and corporate performance as measured by share price, earnings per share, sales or corporate profitability (O'Reilly *et al*, 1988; Delacroix and Saudagaran, 1991; and Gregg *et al*, 1993). Other studies have demonstrated little difference between board level pay in the UK and the reward for comparable positions in France and Germany, although the pay of senior executives in the UK lags behind that of their counterparts in the USA (Hay, 1992). A survey by the American magazine *Fortune* of chief executive officers' pay at 200 of the largest US companies found median salaries of $1.2 million and average total reward packages of $2.4 million (Tully, 1992). Nevertheless, interviews by the staff of the popular documentary series *Panorama* with the heads of a number of American headhunting companies found little if any demand for UK-based executives. Whether high rates of pay are matched by higher turnover levels among top level employees has yet to be tested.

Exercise 7.3
A statutory minimum wage

Some of the arguments typically used to argue for or against a statutory national minimum wage are listed in Table A.5.

Table A.5 The statutory minimum wage debate

Arguments for	Arguments against
The employment relationship is by its nature unequal and therefore governments should protect employees who have low levels of market power	Governments should not interfere in the 'free market' negotiation of contracts between employers and workers
People should have a basic right to a fair day's wage for a fair day's work	A minimum wage is an inefficient means of reducing poverty. The majority of low wage earners live in high earning households
It would help groups who are discriminated against, e.g. women, ethnic minorities and the disabled	This is because most low wage earners are women engaged in part-time or other flexible forms of employment who live with men who earn more
The State should not foot the bill for employers who cannot, or are unprepared, to pay fair wages	A minimum wage is difficult if not impossible to enforce
A majority of European Union member states and the USA have minimum wage regulation of some form	The minimum wage rates in the USA and Southern Europe are much lower than those proposed by the TUC and Labour Party
The government should promote the formation of a high skill, high productivity, high wage economy, not a low skill, low wage society	Minimum wage regulation would remove worker motivation to train and improve their labour market position
Employers whose organizations cannot pay fair wages should not exist	The minimum wage would create unemployment. Estimates of the level of this unemployment vary between 150,000 and 1.5 million according to the assumptions made by researchers

Table A.5 (continued)

Arguments for	Arguments against
The absence of minimum wage regulation could lead to a spiralling down of wages with no consequent improvements in the level of employment	
A minimum wage could be financed by a cut in profits and dividends, not employment	A minimum wage would reduce employer freedom to use flexible forms of employment
Increased pay differentials, not a minimum wage create unemployment	A minimum wage would undermine pay differentials for more highly skilled and experienced staff
A minimum wage would prevent 'social dumping' within the European Union. Firms would no longer move to the UK just because it has low wages and poor conditions of employment	Firms should be allowed to compete on the basis of pay. We live in a global economy where employers have to compete with low wage economies in South East Asia etc.
The UK already has minimum income regulation in the form of social security benefits. A minimum wage would reduce the poverty trap i.e the gap between state benefits and the lowest paid jobs	People do not take jobs purely because of the money. If workers wish to accept low wages the government should not stop them
Low wage earners spend more of their income and this would mean more employment for people in firms which produce the goods and services demanded by these workers	A minimum wage would create pay and price inflation
A minimum wage would improve conditions in the non-unionized sector, i.e. sweatshop industries	A minimum wage would enlarge the size of the 'Black Economy' as poor employers sought to avoid regulation

Exercise 7.4

The Institute of Employment Studies has referred to the consequences of this expansion of educational qualifications as the *graduatization of employment*. According to their research an increasing number of jobs at lower levels within organizations are being reserved for graduates. For example, Harrods recently announced that in future sales assistants within their stores would need to be of graduate calibre. These changes appear to demonstrate that in the future either graduates will have to lower their career expectations or, alternatively, increased attention will need to be devoted to creating knowledge-intensive, high-skill jobs that can make use of the education these individuals have received.

In terms of the employment policies of a specific organization, the following list provides an outline of some possible alternatives.

1 *Abandon the graduate scheme and encourage graduate recruitment to all posts. This should improve the stock of knowledge and skills amongst all sections of the workforce, but it may lead to higher staff turnover as graduates feel that their career expectations are not being fulfilled.*

2 *Adopt a more selective graduate recruitment policy and target institutions known to produce high-calibre candidates.*

3 *Adopt a policy of encouraging existing staff to enrol part-time for graduate level studies. This would encourage staff to remain working for the company, while they complete their studies.*

4 *Abandon using degree qualifications as a selection criteria and concentrate instead on identifying other measures which give an indication of success within the organization in general or within specific job categories.*

Exercise 8.2
Political systems

The scatter diagram in Fig A.3 shows the location on Fig 8.1 of the numbers representing the list of political systems.

Fig A.3

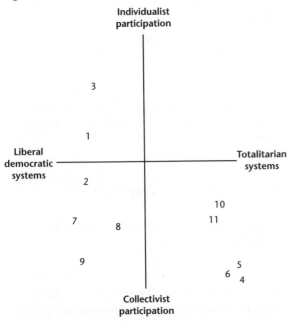

Issues specific to Selena

- As a pregnant worker with less than two years' service she is entitled to 14 weeks' maternity leave starting in May.

- She cannot be dismissed on the grounds of pregnancy or for a reason associated with pregnancy. These would be an *automatically unfair* reason for dismissal. There is no service qualification to make an application to an industrial tribunal.

- What is the real reason for her dismissal? It is said to be 'misconduct'. This might be a fair reason if it is the real reason.

- Is it reasonable for the employer to dismiss her for this reason in the circumstances of the case, having regard to the size and admininstrative resources of the employer?

- Was the dismissal handled fairly and in accordance with the guidance in the ACAS Code of Practice? She was not given a proper hearing and an opportunity to put her side of the case.

- She received no notice to terminate her employment. She might be entitled to claim *wrongful dismissal*. Suggestions that other discrimination law is infringed in respect of race and trade union membership.

CHAPTER 10

Exercise 10.1
Individual employment rights

The individual rights issues that arise in the Seymour Aerial and Cable Installations case study are:

General issues

- No 'Section 1 statements' setting out information on contractual terms.

- No formal procedures, e.g. discipline and equal opportunities.

- Unilateral changes in employment conditions by the employer are unacceptable.

- Health and safety standards in respect of VDUs are not being complied with, e.g. who are 'users', proper workstation, time spent at VDU, eye tests.

CHAPTER 11

Exercise 11.5
Collective representation rights

Employer/employee

- Disclosure of information about contracts, health and safety.

- Consultation about contractual changes, redundancy, transfers of undertakings and health and safety.

- Protection from dismissal or victimization because of union membership or non-membership.

Employer/trade union

- Disclosure of information for collective bargaining if union independent and recognized.

Employee/trade union

- Employee right to join or not to join union.

- Employee right not to be unreasonably excluded or expelled from a union.

- Employee right to participate in union activities and to vote in executive elections.

- Employee right to vote in industrial action secret ballot.

- Representation in redundancies, transfers of undertakings and health and safety, if union independent and recognized.

- Employee right not to be unjustifiably disciplined by union for non-participation in industrial action.

Exercise 11.6
The legal framework of industrial action

The following factors are important when considering the legal requirements in the Granny's Pride Bakery Case Study:

- Within the corporate group, there are various employers. The transport drivers work for Granny's Pride Deliveries Ltd which is not the same employer as the production workers.

- There are statutory consultation requirements in relation to redundancies.

- There are specific legal requirements about who can call workers out on strike. Likewise, within union rulebooks the authority will be with the national executive committee. Such authority will not rest with a local shop stewards' committee.

- Approval for industrial action must be through an individual secret ballot in order to attract immunity from legal proceedings for the organizers of the industrial action. This is regulated by a code of practice on balloting. A show of hands in a mass meeting does not constitute approval.

- Industrial action can be called 'in contemplation or furtherance of a trade dispute'. This trade dispute must be about specific employment-related matters between workers and their own employer. Secondary or sympathetic industrial action is unlawful. What is the production workers' trade dispute about? What is the transport drivers' trade dispute about?

- Picketing must be by employees at their own place of work and must involve peaceful persuasion and peaceful communication of information. There must be no intimidation or violence.

- A trade union is liable for the actions of its members in industrial action. If these are unlawful, then, the union may be subject to legal proceedings by the employer. An injunction and damages may be sought.

- A trade union may 'repudiate' members who do not call off unlawful action. Consequently, it escapes liability. The shop stewards' committee would probably then be liable.

- An employer can refuse to pay wages if no work is carried out because of a strike. In the circumstances of the case, an employer can determine when production and full working are to start again after the industrial action.

GLOSSARY

Backward integration when an organization buys a stake in, or control over, one or more of its suppliers.

Balance of Payments a measure of the shortfall or surplus between exports and imports of visible and invisible goods and services as well as capital funds.

Business or economic cycle a measure of the period of time between successive phases of economic growth and recession.

Civilian labour force a statistical measure of the number of people either in employment or actively seeking paid work.

Common law a term used to describe judge-made law, that is, laws which arise from precedents established in judicial decisions at the end of court hearings.

Contingency theory an approach to the analysis of organizations and their environments which attempts to specify influences (contingencies) which affect or constrain human decision making and action.

Corporatism a term used to describe political systems in which the state encourages participation by trade unions and employers' associations in national government. These bodies are consulted directly or indirectly by government ministers and in turn provide advice on general economic, employment and social policy issues.

Cyclical unemployment a term used to refer to fluctuations in the number of unemployed which arise as a consequence of the business cycle.

Demand function a measure of the relationship between the price of a good and the quantity demanded by consumers.

Deregulation a relaxation of statutory and other legal controls on the operation of organizations.

Determinism a belief that human choice and action is constrained or determined by external influences.

Economic growth increases in the productive capacity and wealth of a country or similar unit of economic activity. This is usually measured by changes in the Gross Domestic Product (GDP), Gross National Product (GNP) or National Income.

Economic and Monetary Union (EMU) the goal of the European Union, designed to create a single currency and European Central Bank.

Elasticity of demand or supply the degree to which the quantity of goods demanded or supplied is sensitive to changes in their price.

Employees in employment a measure of the number of the people who are actually in paid employment.

Exchange rate a comparative measure of the relative value of two currencies. For example, the dollar/sterling exchange rate specifies the rate at which dollars may be converted to sterling and vice versa.

Exchange rate mechanism (ERM) the official title of the European Union's managed exchange rate system. This system seeks to promote stability in the value of member state currencies in international money markets.

Externalities a term used by economists to refer to the social, environmental and other costs associated with production, which are not directly covered in the price of any resultant good or service.

Fatalism a belief that what will happen is bound to happen and that there is nothing humans can do to prevent it.

Feminization used to refer to an increase in the representation of women or women's issues. This term is commonly used to describe increases in the number of women in the labour force over the last 50 or more years.

Financial short-termism a description of business policies which place an emphasis on the achievement of high profit and share performance objectives over a one- to three-year period.

Flexibility a term used to refer to a variety of forms of employment practice including numerical flexibility (varying the number of people employed); functional flexibility (expanding the range of tasks performed by individual employees); financial flexibility (adjusting pay and conditions to reflect local conditions, business or employee performance); temporal flexibility (allowing variety in the period of time employees spend at work); and geographical flexibility (moving staff within an organization).

Footsie a colloquial phrase used to refer to the *Financial Times* Stock Exchange 100 Index. This index provides a measure of changes in the price of shares traded on the London Stock Exchange.

Fordism a system of production and distribution characterized by the manufacture of standardized goods by semiskilled and some skilled workers for a mass market of similar customers who have been persuaded to buy by big advertising campaigns.

Forward integration when an organization buys a stake in, or control over, the buyers of its goods or services.

Free rider an individual who seeks the benefits of a public good while avoiding the costs associated with its provision.

Horizontal integration when an organization buys a stake in, or control over, rivals in the same industry.

Inflation an increase in the price of any raw materials, labour, land or finished goods and services.

International division of labour the splitting of work between employees in different countries. This term is used most frequently to describe the concentration of well-paid and high-skilled jobs in developed western countries and low-paid and low-skilled jobs in developing countries.

Japanization the influence of the management practices used by Japanese multinational enterprises on the policies and practices of their subsidiary operations in overseas countries.

Keynesianism an economic philosophy based on the belief that government intervention is needed to avoid the failings of free market systems and to ensure the most productive deployment of a nation's scarce resources.

Labour market a term used by economists to describe the interaction between employers and those employees who are either in work or are actively looking for work. A further distinction separates the behaviour of these individuals within firms (the internal labour market) and between firms (the external labour market).

Liberalization a relaxation of laws and regulations which previously prevented private sector organizations from providing certain public services.

MAUT Multiple Attribute Utility Testing, a procedure for systematically evaluating the options available to an organization when responding to a particular pressure or problem.

MNE a multinational enterprise referring to organizations which directly employ staff in two or more countries.

Monetarism an economic philosophy based on the belief that the appropriate role for governments in modern economies is the maintenance of sound money and the removal of barriers to the operation of free markets.

Nationalization the process of taking a private sector company or organization into public sector ownership.

Opportunity cost refers to the cost of things that can not be done if a particular course of action is chosen.

Participation rate a measure of the percentage of the population in a particular category, i.e. women, ethnic minorities or all potential employees, who are actually in paid employment.

PEST an acronym used to describe analyses which consider the political, economic, social and technological pressures confronting an organization.

Pluralism a belief that societies in general, and organizations in particular, consist of individuals and groups who have different and often conflicting objectives and interests.

Positive action a term used to describe steps taken to encourage the recruitment and progression of various disadvantaged groups including women and ethnic minorities. This approach may involve targeted job advertisements and training programmes, but it should not be confused with positive discrimination or quota schemes in which a particular number of jobs or opportunities are reserved for applicants from disadvantaged backgrounds.

Post-Fordism a system of production and distribution which relies upon the manufacture of specialized products by skilled workers for small markets of customers with particular demands who are persuaded to buy by targeted marketing.

Privatization transferring the ownership of an organization from the public to the private sector.

Product life cycle a model of product sales which suggests that, like animals, the sales are born, grow, mature, decline and die.

Public good a good which is most effectively and efficiently provided if everyone is compelled to share in the costs of its provision.

Recession a period of declining economic fortune characterized by a contraction of productive capacity and wealth which lasts for more than six months.

Seasonal adjustment a term used to refer to the smoothing out of seasonal variations from annual collections of statistics.

Seasonal unemployment a term used to describe annual fluctuations in the level of unemployment which arise as a consequence of seasonal variations in the number of available jobs and employees.

Segmentation a term used to describe divisions within the workforce which arise because of status differences and discrimination between groups of workers, e.g. differences of gender, ethnic origin and disability. Sociologists typically refer to three types of segmentation: horizontal segmentation between different occupational and industrial categories, e.g. teachers, secretaries and lorry drivers; vertical segmentation between different hierarchical levels in an organization, e.g. sales assistants, departmental managers and directors in retail stores; and international segmentation between countries.

Segregation another term used to refer to vertical, horizontal and international segmentation.

Stagflation a combination of high levels of inflation and unemployment.

Stakeholders groups inside and outside an organization with an interest in its objectives and an influence over its operations.

Statute law a term used to describe laws made by the Houses of Parliament.

Structural unemployment a measure of the number of long term unemployed who are unable to find work because they lack relevant skills or alternatively because an insufficient number of appropriate jobs are available.

Supply function a measure of the relationship between the price of a good and the quantity supplied by producers.

SWOT an acronym used to describe analyses of the Strengths, Weaknesses, Opportunities and Threats confronting an organization.

Systems theory an approach which uses techniques developed in biological and engineering sciences. This approach attempts to specify the nature and form of interactions between internal interrelated elements of an organization and aspects of its external environment.

Unitarism a belief that societies in general, and organizations in particular, consist of individuals and groups who share or should share the same objectives and interests.

Voluntarism a term used to describe societies in which the State leaves employers and employees free to determine the nature of the employment relationship either directly through management–employee contact or indirectly through the medium of trade unions and employers' associations.

REFERENCES

Anderman, S (1986) 'Unfair Dismissals and Redundancy' in Lewis, R (ed) *Labour Law in Britain*, Oxford: Blackwell.

Ansoff, I (1968) *Corporate Strategy*, London, Penguin.

Atkinson, J (1984) 'Manpower strategies for flexible organizations', *Personnel Management*, Aug.

Atkinson, J (1989) 'Four stages of adjustment to demographic downturn', *Personnel Management*, Aug, pp 20–4.

Auerbach, S (1990) *Legislating for Conflict*, Oxford: Clarendon Press.

Bassett, P (1986) *Strike Free*, London: Macmillan.

Batstone, E and Gourlay, S (1986) *Unions, Unemployment and Innovation*, Oxford: Blackwell.

Ben-Shlomo, Y, Sheiham, A and Marmot, M (1991) 'Smoking and health' in *British Social Attitudes Survey*, Aldershot: Dartmouth.

Berle, A and Means, G (1932) *The Modern Corporation and Private Property*, New York: Macmillan.

Bohm, D (1980) *Wholeness and the Implicate Order*, London: Ark Books.

Boyden, T and Paddison, L (1986) Banking on Equal Opportunities, *Personnel Management Journal*, Sept.

Braverman, H (1974) *Labor and Monopoly Capital: The Degradation of Work in the Twentieth Century*, New York: Monthly Review Press.

Brown, R (1988) 'The Employment Relationship in Sociological Theory' in Gallie, D (ed) *Employment in Britain*, Oxford: Blackwell.

Brown, W (1994) *Bargaining for Full Employment*, Employment Policy Institute Economic Report, Employment Policy Institute.

Buchanan, D A and Boddy, D A (1983) *Organizations in the Computer Age: Technological Imperatives and Strategic Choice*, Aldershot: Gower Publishing.

Buchanan, D and McCalman, J (1989) 'Confidence, visibility and pressure: the effects of computer-aided hotel management' *New Technology, Work and Employment*, 3(1), pp 38–46.

Burns, T and Stalker, G (1961) *The Management of Innovation*, London: Tavistock Publications.

Child, J (1972) 'Organization structure, environment and performance: the role of strategic choice', *Sociology*, 6(1), pp 1–22.

Clark, G de N (1970) *Remedies for Unfair Dismissal: proposals for legislation* (PEP Broadsheet 518) Policy Studies Institutes.

Collin, A (1994) 'Human Resource Management in Context' in Beardwell, I and Holden, L *Human Resource Management: A Contemporary Perspective*, London: Pitman Publishing.

Commission on Social Justice (1994) *Report: Social Justice – strategies for national renewal*, London: Vintage.

Crompton, R (1993) *Class and Stratification: An Introduction to Current Debates*, Cambridge: Polity Press.

Cyert, R M and March, J G (1963) *A Behaviourial Theory of the Firm*, New York: Wiley.

Daniel, W W (1987) *Workplace Industrial Relations and Technical Change*, Policy Studies Institute.

Delacroix, J and Saudagaran, S (1991) 'Munificent Compensations as Disincentives: The Case of American CEOs', *Human Relations*, 44(7), pp 665–78.

Dickens, L, Jones, M, Weekes, B and Hart M (1985) *Dismissed*, Oxford: Blackwell.

Dore, R (1976) *The Diploma Disease: Education, Qualification and Development*, London: George Allen and Unwin.

Dunleavy, J (1993) 'The Political Parties' in Dunleavy, P, Gamble, A, Holliday, I and Peele, G (eds) *Developments in British Politics*, London: Macmillan.

Ellison, R (1994) 'British Labour Force Projections 1994–2006', *Employment Gazette*, April.

Equal Opportunities Commission (1991) *Equality Management: women's employment in the National Health Service*, Equal Opportunities Commission.

Etzioni, A (1988) *The Moral Dimension: Toward a New Economics*, London: Collier Macmillan.

Ewing, K (1990) *A Bill of Rights for Britain?*, Institute of Employment Rights.

Ewing, K D (1994) *Britain and the ILO* (2nd edn), Institute of Employment Rights.

Flanders, A (1968) 'Collective Bargaining in Theoretical Analysis', *British Journal of Industrial Relations*, Vol. 6, No 1.

Fox, A (1974) *Beyond Contract: Work, Power and Trust Relations*, London: Faber & Faber.

Freeman, C, Clark, J and Soete, L (1982) *Unemployment and Technical Innovation*, London: Francis Pinter.

Freeman, C (1987) 'The Case for Technological Determinism' in Finnegan, R, Salaman, G and Thompson, K (eds) (1987) *Information Technology: Social Issues. A Reader*, Sevenoaks, Hodder and Stoughton/the Open University.

Frobel, F, Hienrichs, J and Kreye, O (1980) *The New Industrial Division of Labour: Structural Unemployment in Industrialised Countries and Industrialisation in Developing Countries*, Cambridge: Cambridge University Press.

Galbraith, J K (1967) *The New Industrial State*, London: Hamish Hamilton.

Gill, C (1985) *Work, Unemployment and New Technology*, Cambridge: Polity Press.

Gleick, J (1987) *Chaos*, New York: Viking Press.

Greenlagh, L (1991) 'Organizational Coping Strategies' in Hartley, J, Jacobson, D, Klandermans, B, and van Vuuren, T (eds) *Job Insecurity: Coping with Jobs at Risk*, London: Sage.

Gregg, P, Machins, S and Szymanski, S (1993) 'The Disappearing Relationship Between Directors' Pay and Corporate Performance', *British Journal of Industrial Relations*, 31(1), pp 1–9.

Greiner, L (1972) 'Evolution and Revolution as Organizations Grow', *Harvard Business Review*, July–August.

Griffith, J (1985) *The Politics of the Judiciary*, London: Fontana.

Hall, M, Carley, M, Marginson P and Sisson, K (1995) *European Works Councils*, London: Eclipse Group.

Halsey, A H (1995) *Change in British Society*, London, Opus.

Hampden-Turner, C and Fons Trompenaars, C (1993) *The Seven Cultures of Capitalism*, London: Piaktus.

Handy, C (1989) *The Age of Unreason* (1st edn) London: Century Business Books.

Handy, C (1991) *The Age of Unreason* (2nd edn) London: Century Business Books.

Handy, C (1994) *The Empty Raincoat: Making Sense of the Future*, London: Hutchinson.

Hannan, M T and Freeman, J (1988) *Organizational Ecology*, Boston, Ma: Harvard University Press.

Hansard Society, The (1990) *Women on Top*, London: HMSO.

Hay (1992) *Hay Compensation Report*, July, London: Hay Management Consultants.

HMSO (1991) *Social Trends 1991*, No 21, London: HMSO/ Office for National Statistics.

HMSO (1992) 'The 1992 Share Register Survey' in *Economic Trends*, No 446, August, pp 90–8.

HMSO (1995a) *Annual Abstract of Statistics*, London: HMSO/ Office for National Statistics.

HMSO (1995b) *Social Trends 1994*, No 24, London: HMSO/ Office for National Statistics.

HMSO (1995c) *United Kingdom National Accounts: The Blue Book*, London: HMSO/Office for National Statistics.

Hofstede, G (1980) *Culture's Consequences*, London: Sage.

Huczynski, A and Buchanan, D (1991) *Organizational Behaviour: An Introductory Text*, Hemel Hempstead: Prentice-Hall.

Hunt, J W and Downing, S (1991) 'Mergers acquisitions and Human Resource Management', International Journal of Human Resource Management, Vol 1, No 2, Spring.

Hutton, W (1995) *The State We're In*, London: Jonathan Cape.

IDS (1993) *Smoking Policies*, Income Data Services, Study No 537, September.

IER (1993) *Review of the Economy and Employment*, Occupational Assessment, Institute for Employment Research, Warwick University.

Johnson, G and Scholes, K (1993) *Exploring Corporate Strategy: Text and Cases*, Hemel Hempstead: Prentice-Hall.

Kahn-Freund, O (1954) in Flanders, A and Clegg, H (eds) *The System of Industrial Relations in Great Britain*, Oxford: Blackwell.

Kahn-Freund, O (1983) in Davis and Freedland (eds) *Labour and the Law* (3rd edn) London: Stevens.

Kandola, R, Fullerton, J and Ahmed, Y (1995) 'Managing Diversity: succeeding where equal opportunities has failed', *Equal Opportunities Review*, 59.

Kanter, R M (1985) *The Change Masters: Corporate Entrepreneurs at Work*, New York: Counterpoint.

Kanter, R M (1989) *When Giants Learn to Dance: Mastering the Challenges of Strategy, Management and Careers in 1990s*, London: Unwin Paperbacks.

Katz, D and Kahn, R (1966) *The Social Psychology of Organizations*, New York: Wiley.

Kay, J (1993) *The Foundations of Corporate Success*, Oxford: Oxford University Press.

Kennedy, M (1992) 'The economy as a whole' in Artis, M J (ed) (1992) *Prest and Coppock's The UK Economy: A Manual of Applied Economics* (13th edn), London: Weidenfeld and Nicolson.

Lash, S and Urry, J (1987) *The End of Organised Capitalism*, Cambridge: Polity Press.

Lawrence, P R and Lorsch, J W (1967) *Organization and Environment*, Boston, Ma: Harvard University Press.

Leavitt, H J (1975) 'Marketing Myopia', *Harvard Business Review*, September–October.

Leonard, A (1987) *Judging Inequality*, London: The Cobden Trust.

Lewis, R and Clark, J (1993) *Employment Rights, Industrial Tribunals and Arbitration: the case for alternative dispute resolution*, Institute of Employment Rights.

Lindbloom, C (1959) 'The Science of Muddling Through,' *Public Administration Review*, 19, pp 79–88.

Lovelock, J (1979) *Gaia: A New Look at Life on Earth*, Oxford: Oxford University Press.

McCarthy, Lord (1989) 'The Case for Labour Courts', *Industrial Relations Journal*, 20.

McLoughlin, I and Clark, J (1994) *Technological Change at Work*, Milton Keynes: Open University Press.

Marr, A (1995) *Ruling Britannia: The Failure and Future of British Democracy*, pp 40–42, London: Michael Joseph.

Miles, R E and Snow, C C (1978) *Organizational Strategy, Structure and Process*, Maidenhead: McGraw-Hill.

Millward, N, Stevens, M, Smart, D and Howes, W R (1992) *Workplace Industrial Relations in Transition*, Aldershot: Dartmouth.

Morgan, G (1986) *Images of Organization*, London: Sage.

Morgan, G (1993) *Imaginisation: The Art of Creative Management*, London: Sage.

Murray, C (1990) *The Emerging British Underclass*, London: Institute of Economic Affairs.

NACAB (1993) *Job Insecurity: CAB Evidence on Employment Problems in the Recession*, London: The National Association of Citizens' Advice Bureaux.

Napier, B (1986) 'The Contract of Employment' in *Labour Law in Britain*, Oxford: Blackwell.

OECD (1994) *Main Economic Indicators*, Paris: OECD.

Omerod, P (1994) *The Death of Economics*, London: Faber and Faber.

O'Reilly, C, Main, B and Crystal, B (1988) 'CEO compensation as tournament and social comparison: a tale of two theories', *Administrative Science Quarterly*, 33, pp 257–74.

Packard, V (1957) *The Hidden Persuaders*, Harlow, Longman.

Peters, T (1989) *Thriving on Chaos: Handbook for a Management Revolution*, London: Guild Publishing.

Pettigrew, A and Whipp, R (1991) *Managing Strategy for Competitive Success*, Oxford: Blackwell.

Pfeffer, J (1992) *Managing With Power: Politics and Influence in Organizations*, Boston, Ma: Harvard Business School Press.

Piore, M and Sabel, C (1982) *The Second Industrial Divide – Possibilities for Prosperity*, London: Basic Books.

Pollert, A (1988) 'The flexible firm: fixation or fact?', *Work, Employment and Society*, 2(3) September.

Pond, C (1989) 'The Wealth of Two Nations', in McDowell, L, Sarre, P and Hamnett, C (eds) *Divided Nation: Social and Cultural Change in Britain*, London: Hodder and Stoughton/Open University.

Porter, M E. (1980) *Competitive Strategy*, New York: Free Press.

Porter, M E. (1985) *Competitive Advantage: Creating and Sustaining Superior Performance*, New York: Free Press.

Reich, R (1991) *The Work of Nations: Preparing Ourselves for 21st Century Capitalism*, Hemel Hempstead, Simon & Schuster.

Robbins, D (1986) *Wanted Railman*, London: HMSO.

SEN (1995) *Labour Market and Skill Trends 1994/95*, Nottingham: Skills and Enterprise Network.

Saunders, P (1990) *Social Class and Stratification*, London: Routledge.

Sawyer, M, (1992) 'Industry' in Artis, J. (ed) *Prest and Coppock's The UK Economy* (13th edn), London: Weidenfeld and Nicolson.

Schein, E H (1984) 'Coming to a new awareness of organizational culture', *Sloan Management Review*, winter, pp 3–16.

Schuler R S and Jackson, S E (1987) 'Linking competitive strategies with Human Resource Management practices', *Academy of Management Executive*, Vol 1, No 3, pp 209–13.

Schumpeter, J A (1987) *Capitalism, Socialism and Democracy*, London: Unwin Paperbacks.

Scott, J (1985) *Corporations, Classes and Capitalism*, London: Hutchinson.

Sewell, G and Wilkinson, B (1993) 'Human Resource Management in "Surveillance" Companies' in Clark, J (ed) (1993) *Human Resource Management and Technical Change*, London: Sage.

Silverman, D (1970) *The Theory of Organizations*, Aldershot: Gower.

Simon, H (1976) *Administrative Behaviour: A Study of Decision-Making in Administrative Organization.* (3rd edn), New York: Free Press.

Storey, J and Sisson, K (1993) *Managing Human Resources and Industrial Relations*, Milton Keynes: Open University Press

Szyszczak, E (1995) 'Future Directions in European Union Social Policy Law', *Industrial Law Journal*, 24(1).

Taylor, R (1994) *The Future of the Trade Unions*, London, Andre Deutsch.

Tully, S (1992) 'What CEOs Really Make', *Fortune*, 125(12), pp 94–9.

United Nations (1995) *Human Development Report*, Oxford: Oxford University Press.

Von Bertalanffy, L (1967) 'General Systems Theory' in Demerath, N and Peterson, R (eds) *System, Change and Conflict*, New York, Free Press.

WEF (1995) *The World Competitiveness Report*, Geneva: World Economic Forum.

Walton, R and Susman, G (1987) 'People policies for the new machines', *Harvard Business Review*, 2, March–April, pp 98–106.

Wedderburn, Lord (1986) *The Worker and the Law* (3rd edn), London: Penguin.

Wedderburn, Lord (1989) 'Freedom of association and Philosophies of Labour Law', *Industrial Law Journal*.

Wedderburn, Lord (1991) *Employment Rights in Britain and Europe*, London: Lawrence and Wishart.

Willey, B (1986) *Union Recognition and Representation in Engineering*, London: Engineering Employers' Federation.

Winner, L (1977) *Autonomous Technology: Technics-Out-of-Control as a Theme in Political Thought*, Cambridge, Massachussetts, MIT Press.

Winstanley, D (1992) in Winstanley, D and Woodall, J (eds) *Cases in Personnel Management*, London: Institute of Personnel Management.

Woodward, J (ed) (1970) *Industrial Organisation, Behaviour and Control*, Oxford: Oxford University Press.

Wright, E O (1985) *Classes*, Cambridge: Cambridge University Press.

Zuboff, S (1988) *In the Age of the Smart Machine: The Future of Work and Power*, Oxford: Heinemann Professional Publishing.

INDEX